Programming
Microsoft Azure
Service Fabric

Haishi Bai

KT-437-762

PUBLISHED BY
Microsoft Press
A division of Microsoft Corporation
One Microsoft Way
Redmond, Washington 98052-6399

Copyright © 2016 by Haishi Bai

All rights reserved. No part of the contents of this book may be reproduced or transmitted in any form or by any means without the written permission of the publisher.

Library of Congress Control Number: 2015953291
ISBN: 978-1-5093-0188-1

Printed and bound in the United States of America.

1   16

Microsoft Press books are available through booksellers and distributors worldwide. If you need support related to this book, email Microsoft Press Support at mspinput@microsoft.com. Please tell us what you think of this book at http://aka.ms/tellpress.

This book is provided "as-is" and expresses the author's views and opinions. The views, opinions and information expressed in this book, including URL and other Internet website references, may change without notice.

Some examples depicted herein are provided for illustration only and are fictitious. No real association or connection is intended or should be inferred.

Microsoft and the trademarks listed at http://www.microsoft.com on the "Trademarks" webpage are trademarks of the Microsoft group of companies. All other marks are property of their respective owners.

Acquisitions Editor: Karen Szall
Developmental Editor: Karen Szall
Editorial Production: Cohesion
Technical Reviewer: John McCabe; Technical Review services provided by Content Master, a member of CM Group, Ltd.
Copyeditor: Ann Weaver
Indexer: Lucie Haskins
Cover: Twist Creative • Seattle

Contents at a glance

Table of contents

What do you think of this book? We want to hear from you!

Microsoft is interested in hearing your feedback so we can continually improve our books and learning resources for you. To participate in a brief online survey, please visit:

microsoft.com/learning/booksurvey

v

PART II   SERVICE LIFECYCLE MANAGEMENT

Chapter 10   Diagnostics and monitoring   203

Chapter 11   Testing   227

Chapter 15 Multitenancy and hosting   325

Chapter 16 Multiplayer gaming   345

PART IV   ADVANCED TOPICS

Chapter 17 Advanced service hosting   371

PART V   APPENDICES

What do you think of this book? We want to hear from you!

Microsoft is interested in hearing your feedback so we can continually improve our books and learning resources for you. To participate in a brief online survey, please visit:

microsoft.com/learning/booksurvey

Introduction

Azure Service Fabric is Microsoft's new platform as a service (PaaS) offering for developers to build and host available and scalable distributed systems. Microsoft has used Service Fabric internally for years to support some of Microsoft's cloud-scale applications and Azure services such as Skype for Business, Cortana, Microsoft Intune, Azure SQL Database, and Azure DocumentDB. The same platform is now available to you to write your own highly available and highly scalable services.

Programming Microsoft Azure Service Fabric is designed to get you started and productive with Azure Service Fabric quickly. The book covers fundamentals, practical architectures, and design patterns for various scenarios such as the Internet of Things (IoT), big data, and distributed computing. For fundamentals, the book provides detailed step-by-step walkthroughs that guide you through typical DevOps tasks. For design patterns, the book focuses on explaining the design philosophy and best practices with companion samples to get you started and moving in the right direction.

Instead of teaching you how to use Azure Service Fabric in isolation, the book encourages developers to make smart architecture choices by incorporating existing Azure services. When appropriate, the book briefly covers other Azure services that are relevant to particular scenarios.

Who should read this book

This book is intended to help new or experienced Azure developers get started with Azure Service Fabric. This book is also useful for architects and technical leads to use Azure Service Fabric and related Azure services in their application architecture.

Most of the book was written while the service was still in preview. So, this book is most suitable for readers who want to keep on the edge of Azure development. As one of the earliest Service Fabric books on the market, this book provides some early insights into a new service that is still under active development. Although the precise operational steps and programming APIs might change, the design patterns presented in this book should remain relevant into the foreseeable future.

Assumptions

This book expects that you are proficient in .NET, especially C# development. This book covers a broad range of topics and scenarios, especially in later chapters. Prior understanding of DevOps, application lifecycle management (ALM), IoT, big data, and big compute will help you understand these chapters.

Although no prior Azure knowledge is required, experience with the Azure software development kit (SDK), Azure management portal, Azure PowerShell, Azure command-line interface (CLI), and other Azure services definitely will be helpful.

This book might not be for you if...

This book might not be for you if you are a beginner in programming. This book assumes you have previous experience in C# development and ASP.NET development. Although this book covers topics in service operations, its primary audience is developers and architects, not IT pros.

Organization of this book

This book is divided into four sections, each of which focuses on a different aspect of Azure Service Fabric. Part I, "Fundamentals," provides complete coverage of designing and developing Service Fabric applications using stateless services, stateful services, and Reliable Actors. Part II, "Service lifecycle management," focuses on the operations side and introduces how to manage Service Fabric clusters and how to manage, test, and diagnose Service Fabric applications. Part III, "Patterns and scenarios," introduces practical design patterns and best practices in implementing typical application scenarios including scalable web applications, IoT, big data, multitenant applications, and gaming. Finally, Part IV, "Advanced topics," covers two advanced topics: advanced service hosting and modeling complex systems using Service Fabric.

Finding your best starting point in this book

This book is an introduction to Service Fabric. It's recommended that you read the chapters in the first two parts sequentially. Then, you can pick the topics that interest you Part III and Part IV.

If you are	Follow these steps
New to Service Fabric	Read through Part I and Part II in order.
Interested in applying Service Fabric in IoT scenarios	Focus on Chapter 13 and Chapter 14.
Interested in building scalable web applications	Focus on Chapters 12, 14, and 15. You may also want to skim through other chapters in Part III to discover some patterns that may be applicable to your scenarios.
Interested in gaming	Focus on Chapter 16. Also read Chapter 14, especially the section about the Web Socket communication stack, which provides satisfactory performance in many web-based multiplayer gaming scenarios.
Interested in operating a Service Fabric cluster	Chapters 8, 9, 10, and 11 introduce related tools and services. You may also want to browse through Chapters 5, 6, and 7 to understand application lifecycle management topics.
Interested in the Actor programming model	Focus on Chapter 4. Also browse through chapters in Part III because these chapters cover a number of Actor-based design patterns.
Interested in Service Fabric container integration	Focus on Chapter 17. Appendix C also gives you great background information on container integrations.
Interested in modeling complex systems with Service Fabric	Focus on Chapter 18.

Some of the book's chapters include hands-on samples that let you try out the concepts just learned. No matter which sections you choose to focus on, be sure to download and install the sample applications on your system.

System requirements

You will need the following hardware and software to run the sample code in this book:

- Windows 7, Windows 8/Windows 8.1, Windows Server 2012 R2, or Windows 10.

- Visual Studio 2015.

- Latest Service Fabric runtime, SDK, and tools for Visual Studio 2015 (install via Web PI).

- Latest version of Azure SDK (2.8 or above, install via Web PI).

- Latest version of Azure PowerShell (1.0 or above, install via Web PI).

- Latest version of Azure CLI.

- 4 GB (64-bit) RAM.

- 30 GB of available hard disk space.

- An active Microsoft Azure subscription. You can get a free trial from *www.azure.com*.

- Internet connection to use Azure and to download software or chapter examples.

Depending on your Windows configuration, you might require Local Administrator rights to install or configure Visual Studio 2015 and related SDKs and tools.

Downloads: Code samples

Most of the chapters in this book include sample code that lets you interactively try out new material learned in the main text. All sample projects can be found on the book's download webpage:

http://aka.ms/asf/downloads

Using the code samples

The book's webpage contains all samples in this book, organized in correspond-ing chapter folders. It also contains two additional folders: ComplexSystems and AdditionalSamples. The AdditionalSamples folder contains additional sample scenarios. The ComplexSystems folder contains frameworks and sample scenarios of complex systems.

- **Chapter 1**   This folder contains samples from Chapter 1.

  HelloWordApplication: The hello world application.

- **Chapter 2**   This folder contains samples from Chapter 2.

  CalculatorApplication: The calculator application used in the communicate stack samples.

- **Chapter 3**   This folder contains samples from Chapter 3.

  SimpleStoreApplication: The simple store application.

  SimpleStoreApplication-NamedPartitions: The simple store application using named partitions.

- **Chapter 4** This folder contains samples from Chapter 4.

  ActorTicTacToeApplication: The tic-tac-toe game using Actors.

- **Chapter 5** This folder contains samples from Chapter 5.

  ConsoleRedirectTestApplication: The sample application used in package format samples.

- **Chapter 13** This folder contains samples from Chapter 13.

  SensorAggregationApplication-Pull: The IoT scenario that aggregates sensor states using pull mode.

  SensorAggregationApplication-Push: The IoT scenario that aggregates sensor states using push mode.

  IoTE2E End-to-end: The IoT sample scenario.

- **Chapter 14** This folder contains samples from Chapter 14.

  *NumberConverterA*pp: The number converter service.

  *ECommerceApplicatio*n: The sample e-commerce application.

- **Chapter 15** This folder contains samples from Chapter 15.

  MetadataDrivenApplication: The sample metadata-driven application (shows actor polymorphism).

  ThrottlingActorApplication: The sample application shows the Throttling Actor pattern.

- **Chapter 16** This folder contains samples from Chapter 16. Both scenarios are under development. Please see release announcements in the repository for releasable versions.

  MessyChess: The Messy Chess sample (under development).

  AIQuest: The A.I. Quest sample (under development).

- **Chapter 17** This folder contains samples from Chapter 17.

  *GuestApplicatio*n: A simple guest application sample with a watchdog.

- **Chapter 18** This folder contains samples from Chapter 18.

  TermiteModel: A simulation of termites moving and collecting wood chips.

ActorSwarmApplication: A simulation of people moving closer to neighbors with similar attributes. This sample shows a preliminary implementation of an actor swarm.

AdditionalSamples: This folder contains additional sample scenarios (see README.md under the folder).

ComplexSystems: This folder contains frameworks and samples for modeling complex systems.

To complete an exercise, access the appropriate chapter folder in the root folder and open the project file. If your system is configured to display file extensions, C# project files use .csproj as the file extension.

Acknowledgments

I'd like to thank my wonderful editor Karen Szall who has guided me through every single step along the way to get this book published. I'd also like to thank John McCabe for his insightful reviews. Especially, I'd like to thank Boris Scholl who, regardless of his busy schedule to get the service released on time, has helped me tremendously reviewing the book and providing me insights into container integrations.

I'd also like to thank the amazing team behind Service Fabric. I've personally worked with many of the team members including Mark Fussell, Matthew Snider, Vaclav Turecek, and Sean McKenna. The creativity and dedication of the team has inspired me while writing this book. I also gained a lot of knowledge from the Microsoft internal community, including the *www.azure.com* author group and the Yammer group.

Last but not least, I'd like to thank my wife Jing and my daughter Sabrina who have tolerated my late hours and busy weekends in the past six months. I couldn't do this without your support.

Free ebooks from Microsoft Press

From technical overviews to in-depth information on special topics, the free ebooks from Microsoft Press cover a wide range of topics. These ebooks are available in PDF, EPUB, and Mobi for Kindle formats, ready for you to download at:

http://aka.ms/mspressfree

Check back often to see what is new!

Quick access to online references

Throughout this book are addresses to webpages that the author has recommended you visit for more information. Some of these addresses (also known as URLs) can be painstaking to type into a web browser, so we've compiled all of them into a single list that readers of the print edition can refer to while they read.

The list is included in the companion content, which you can download here:

http://aka.ms/asf/downloads.

The URLs are organized by chapter and heading. Every time you come across a URL in the book, find the hyperlink in the list to go directly to the webpage.

Errata, updates, & book support

We've made every effort to ensure the accuracy of this book and its companion content. You can access updates to this book—in the form of a list of submitted errata and their related corrections—at:

http://aka.ms/asf/errata

If you discover an error that is not already listed, please submit it to us at the same page.

If you need additional support, email Microsoft Press Book Support at *mspinput@microsoft.com.*

Please note that product support for Microsoft software and hardware is not offered through the previous addresses. For help with Microsoft software or hardware, go to *http://support.microsoft.com.*

We want to hear from you

At Microsoft Press, your satisfaction is our top priority, and your feedback our most valuable asset. Please tell us what you think of this book at:

http://aka.ms/tellpress

We know you're busy, so we've kept it short with just a few questions. Your answers go directly to the editors at Microsoft Press. (No personal information will be requested.) Thanks in advance for your input!

Stay in touch

Let's keep the conversation going! We're on Twitter: *http://twitter.com/MicrosoftPress*

Fundamentals

CHAPTER 1

Hello, Service Fabric!

This book is about Microsoft Azure Service Fabric, a distributed systems platform that makes it easy to build large-scale, highly available, low-latency, and easily manageable services. Service Fabric brings you the same technology that empowers cloud-scale applications such as Cortana, Skype for Business, and SQL databases so that you can easily design, implement, scale, and manage your own services leveraging the power of next-generation distributed computing.

Before you embark on the journey with Service Fabric, let's reflect on what makes a great platform as a service (PaaS) and why you need a new PaaS to build the next generation of cloud-based services.

A modern PaaS

A PaaS is designed with agility, scalability, availability, and performance in mind. Microsoft Azure Service Fabric is a PaaS that is built from the ground up to support large-scale, highly available cloud applications.

Designed for agility

The software industry is all about agility. Developers have the privilege to work in a virtual world without physical constraints to drag us down. Innovations can happen at a speed that is unimaginable to other fields. And as a group, we've been in a relentless pursuit for speed: from software frameworks to automation tools, from incremental development to Heroku's 12-factor methodology (Wiggins 2012), from minimum viable product (MVP) to continuous delivery. Agility is the primary goal so that developers can innovate and improve continuously.

Microservices

The essence of Microservices is to decompose complex applications into independent services. Each service is a self-contained, complete functional unit that can be evolved or even reconstructed without necessarily impacting other services.

All software can be abstracted as components and communication routes between them. Monolithic applications are hard to maintain or revise. An overly decomposed system, in contrast, is hard to understand and often comes with unnecessary overhead due to the complex interaction paths across different components. To a great extent, the art of a software architect is to strike a balance between the number of components and the number of communication paths.

A PaaS designed for Microservices encourages separation of concerns, emphasizes loose coupling, and facilitates flexible inter-component communication. While allowing other architectural choices, Service Fabric is designed for and recommends Microservices. A Service Fabric application is made up of a number of services. Each service can be revised, scaled, and managed as an independent component, and you still can manage the entire application as a complete logical unit. The Service Fabric application design is discussed in Chapter 2, "Stateless services," Chapter 3, "Stateful services," and Chapter 4, "Actor pattern." We'll review several application patterns and scenarios in Part III.

> **Note** Architecture choices
>
> Microservices is strongly recommended but not mandatory. You can choose to use other architectures such as n-tiered architecture, data-centric architecture, and single-tiered web applications or APIs.

Simplicity

A PaaS platform is not just about scheduling resources and hosting applications. It needs to provide practical support to developers to complete the tasks at hand without jumping through hoops.

At a basic level, a PaaS platform helps developers deal with cross-cutting concerns such as logging, monitoring, and transaction processing. Taking it a step further, a PaaS platform provides advanced nonfunctional features such as service discovery, failover, replication, and load balancing. All these nonfunctional requirements are essential to a scalable and available system. And providing built-in constructs to satisfy these requirements leads to a significant productivity boost. Because PaaS takes care of all these troubles, developers can focus on building up core business logic. To achieve this, these nonfunctional features should be available without getting in the way. As you progress through this chapter and book, you'll see how Service Fabric enables you to focus on business logic and to incorporate these features whenever you need them.

Can you go a step further? What if a PaaS platform provides easy programming models that help you tackle complex problems? And what if the PaaS platform also provides guidance and patterns for typical scenarios? We'll come back to this in the discussion of different service types in Chapter 2, Chapter 3, and Chapter 4.

Comprehensive application lifetime management

Continuous improvement is at the core of the agile software movement and the Lean movement in various industries. The faster you can iterate through revision cycles, the quicker you can innovate, reduce waste, and create additional value. A mature PaaS platform has to offer comprehensive application lifecycle management (ALM) functionalities to keep the innovation engine running without friction.

Because more companies are adopting continuous delivery, software is being released at a faster pace than in the past. Some companies claim they do hundreds of deployments on a daily basis. This calls for automated testing, continuous integration, rapid deployments, robust version management, and fast rollbacks. Only when a PaaS platform provides all these features can developers and independent software vendors (ISVs) realize such continuous delivery scenarios.

A comprehensive ALM strategy is critical to DevOps. If you look carefully, you'll see that a lot of so-called friction between development and operations is rooted in discrepancies among different environments. PaaS platforms such as Service Fabric allow applications to be placed in self-contained packages that can be deployed consistently to different environments—such as development, test, QA, and production.

Part II of this book is dedicated to ALM.

Designed for QoS

A successful cloud service is based on a healthy partnership between the service developer and the cloud platform. The service developer brings business know-how and innovation, and the cloud platform brings Quality of Service (QoS) opportunities such as scalability, availability, and reliability.

Scalability

Through innovation, you can do unprecedented things. However, the increasing complexity of problems constantly challenges developers to improve methodologies to maintain momentum. A PaaS platform should be designed with scalability in mind so that applications can be scaled out naturally without much effort from the developers.

> ### Increasing complexity and scale
>
> Increasing complexity can be demonstrated easily with some examples. According to the "NASA Study on Flight Software Complexity" (NASA Office of Chief Engineer, 2009), flight software complexity has been increasing exponentially with a growth rate of a factor of 10 approximately every 10 years. *Apollo 8* had about 8,500 lines of code in 1968. In contrast, the International Space Station (ISS) was launched with 1.5 million lines of code in 1989.
>
> Besides software complexity, the sheer volume of data presents a new set of problems. According to Twitter statistics (Company Facts at *https://about.twitter.com/company*), Twitter is handling 500 million tweets every day. Data ingress, transformation, storage, and analysis at such a scale is an unprecedented challenge. Modern services also need to deal with the potential for rapid growth. Over the past five years or so, Azure Storage has grown into a service that needs to handle 777 trillion transactions per day (Charles Babcock, "Microsoft Azure: More Mature Cloud Platform," InformationWeek, Sept 30, 2015, *http://aka.ms/asf/maturecloud*).

On a cloud platform, *scaling up*, which means increasing the processing power of a single host, is a less preferable approach. Typically, virtual machines are offered with preconfigured sizes. To scale up, you'll need to migrate your workload to a virtual machine with a bigger size. This is a long and disruptive process because services need to be brought down, migrated, and relaunched on the new machine, causing service interruptions. Furthermore, because there are finite choices of machine sizes, scaling options run out quickly. Although Azure provides a large catalog of virtual machine sizes, including some of the largest virtual machines in the cloud, large-scale workloads still can exceed the processing power of a single machine.

In contrast, *scaling out* dynamically adjusts system capacity by adding more service instances to share the workload. This kind of scaling is not disruptive because it doesn't need to shut down existing services. And theoretically, there's no limit to how much you can scale because you can add as many instances as you need.

When scaling out, there are two fundamental ways to distribute workloads. One way is to distribute the workloads evenly across all available instances. The other way is to partition the workloads among service instances. Service Fabric supports both options, which we'll discuss in detail in Chapter 7, "Scalability and performance."

Availability

Availability commonly is achieved by redundancy—when a service fails, a backup service takes over to maintain business continuity. Although the idea sounds simple, difficulties can be found in the details. For example, when a service fails, what happens to its state that it has been maintaining locally? How do you ensure that the replacement service can restore the state and pick up wherever it left off? In a different case, when you apply updates, how do you perform a zero-downtime upgrade? And how do you safely roll back to previous versions if the new version turns out to be broken? The solution to these questions involves many parts such as health monitoring, fault detection, failover, version management, and state replication. Only a carefully designed PaaS can orchestrate these features into a complete and intuitive availability solution. Reliability and availability is the topic of Chapter 6, "Availability and reliability."

Reliability

Reliability is compromised by system faults. However, in a large-scale, distributed system, monitoring, tracing, and diagnosing problems often are challenging. If a PaaS doesn't have a robust health subsystem that can monitor, report, and react to possible system-level and application-level problems, detecting and fixing system defects becomes incredibly difficult.

We'll examine what Service Fabric has to offer in terms of reliability in Chapter 6.

Separation of workload and infrastructure

The cloud era brings new opportunities and new challenges. One advantage of cloud infrastructure as a service (IaaS) is that it shields you from the complexity of physical or virtualized hardware management—and that's only the starting point. To enjoy the benefits of the cloud fully, you need PaaS to help you forget about infrastructure altogether. After all, for a program to run, all you need are some compute and storage resources such as CPU, memory, and disk space. Do you really need to control which host is providing these resources? Does it really matter if your program stays on the same host throughout its lifetime? Should it make a difference if the program is running on a local server or in the cloud? A modern PaaS such as Service Fabric provides a clear separation of workload and infrastructure. It automatically manages the pool of resources, and it finds and assigns resources required by your applications as needed.

Placement constraints

Sometimes, you do care how components in your application are laid out on a PaaS cluster. For example, if your cluster comprises multiple node types with different capacities, you might want to put certain components on specific nodes. In this case, your application can dictate where PaaS places different components by defining placement constraints. In addition, if you want to minimize the latency between two components that frequently interact with each other, you can suggest that PaaS keep them in close proximity. In some other cases, you might want to distribute the components far apart so that a failing host won't bring down all the components. We'll discuss placement constraints later in this book.

Such clear separation of concerns brings several significant benefits. First, it enables workloads to be transferred from host to host as needed. When a host fails, the workloads on the failing host can be migrated quickly to another healthy host, providing fast failovers. Second, it allows higher compute density because independent workloads can be packed into the same host without interfering with one another. Third, as launching and destroying application instances usually is much faster than booting up and shutting down machines, system capacity can be scaled dynamically to adapt to workload changes. Fourth, such separation also allows applications to be architected, developed, and operated without platform lock-in. You can run the same application on-premises or in the cloud, as long as these environments provide the same mechanism to schedule CPU, memory, and disk resources.

Service Fabric concepts

In this section, you first briefly review the architecture of Service Fabric. Then, you learn about some of the key concepts of Service Fabric in preparation for service development.

Architecture

An overview of Service Fabric architecture is shown in Figure 1-1. As you can see, Service Fabric is a comprehensive PaaS with quite a few subsystems in play. The discussion here gives you a high-level overview of these subsystems. We'll go into details of each of the subsystems throughout this book, so don't worry if you are not familiar with some of the terms.

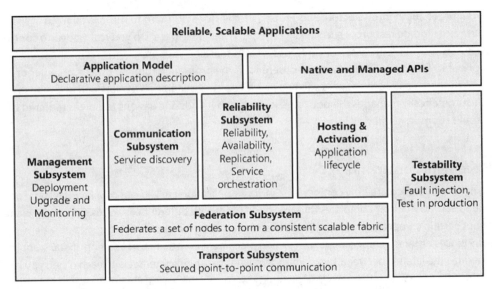

FIGURE 1-1 Service Fabric architecture

The subsystems shown in Figure 1-1 are as follows:

- **Transport subsystem**   The transport subsystem is a Service Fabric internal subsystem that provides secured point-to-point communication channels within a Service Fabric cluster and between a Service Fabric cluster and clients.

- **Federation subsystem**   The federation subsystem provides failure detection, leader election, and consistent routing, which form the foundation of a unified cluster. We'll examine these terms in upcoming chapters.

- **Reliable subsystem**   The reliable subsystem manages state replication, failovers, and load balancing, which a highly available and reliable system needs.

- **Management subsystem**   The management subsystem provides full application lifetime management, including services such as managing application binaries; deploying, updating and deprovisioning applications; and monitoring application health.

- **Hosting subsystem**   The hosting subsystem is responsible for managing application life cycles on a cluster node.

- **Communication subsystem**   The primary task of the communication subsystem is service discovery. With complete separation of workloads and infrastructure, service instances may migrate from host to host. The communication subsystem provides a naming service for clients to discover and connect to service instances.

- **Testability subsystem**   The idea of test in production was popularized by the Netflix Chaos Monkey (and later the Netflix Simian Army). The testability subsystem can simulate various failure scenarios to help developers shake out design and implementation flaws in the system.

Nodes and clusters

To understand Service Fabric clusters, you need to know about two concepts: node and cluster.

- **Node** Technically, a node is just a Service Fabric runtime process. In a typical Service Fabric deployment, there's one node per machine. So you can understand a node as a machine (physical or virtual). A Service Fabric cluster allows heterogeneous node types with different capacities and configurations.

- **Cluster** A cluster is a set of nodes that are connected to form a highly available and reliable environment for running applications and services. A Service Fabric cluster can have thousands of nodes.

Figure 1-2 is a simple illustration of a Service Fabric cluster. Notice that all nodes are equal peers; there are no master nodes or subordinate nodes. Also notice that although in the diagram the nodes are arranged in a ring, all the nodes can communicate directly with each other via the transport subsystem.

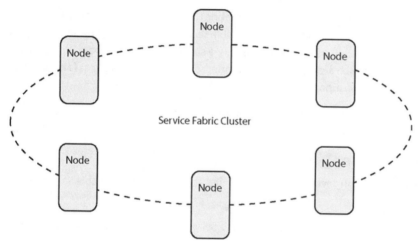

FIGURE 1-2 A Service Fabric cluster

> **Note** Node and containers
>
> In addition to physical machines and virtual machines, nodes can reside in Windows-based Docker containers, which are part of Windows Server 2016. Containerization is described in more detail in Chapter 17, "Advanced service hosting."

A Service Fabric cluster provides an abstraction layer between your workloads and the underlying infrastructure. Because you can run Service Fabric clusters on both physical machines and virtual machines, either on-premises or in the cloud, you can run your Service Fabric applications without modifications in a variety of environments such as on-premises datacenters and Microsoft Azure.

Applications and services

A Service Fabric *application* is a collection of services. A *service* is a complete functional unit that delivers certain functionalities.

You author a Service Fabric application by defining the Application Type and associated Service Types. When the application is deployed to a Service Fabric cluster, these types are instantiated into application instances and service instances, respectively.

An application defines an isolation unit in Service Fabric. You can deploy and manage multiple applications independently on the same cluster. Service Fabric keeps their code, configuration, and data isolated from one another. You can deploy multiple versions of an application on the same cluster.

Partitions and replicas

A service can have one or more partitions. Service Fabric uses partitions as the scaling mechanism to distribute workloads to different service instances.

A partition can have one or more replicas. Service Fabric uses replicas as the availability mechanism. A partition has one primary replica and may have multiple secondary replicas. The states of replicas are synchronized automatically. When a primary replica fails, a secondary replica automatically is promoted to primary to keep service availability. And the number of secondary replicas is brought back to desired level to keep enough redundancy.

We'll introduce partitions and replicas in more detail in Chapter 2, Chapter 3, and Chapter 7.

Programming modes

Service Fabric provides two high-level frameworks to build applications: the Reliable Service APIs and the Reliable Actor APIs.

- The *Reliable Service APIs* provide direct access to Service Fabric constructs such as reliable collections and communication stacks.

- The *Reliable Actor APIs* provide a high-level abstraction layer so that you can model your applications as a number of interacting actors.

With Reliable Service APIs, you can add either stateless services or stateful services to a Service Fabric application. The key difference between the two service types is whether service state is saved locally on the hosting node.

Stateless vs. stateful

Some services don't need to maintain any states across requests. Let's say there's a calculator service that provides both an Add operation and a Subtract operation. For each of the service calls, the service takes in two operands and generates a result. The service doesn't need to maintain any contextual information between calls because every call can be carried out based solely on given parameters. The service behavior is not affected by any contextual information; that is, adding 5 and 3 always yields 8, and subtracting 6 from 9 always yields 3.

The majority of services, in contrast, need to keep some sort of states. A typical example of such a service is a shopping cart service. As a user adds items to the cart, the state of the cart needs to be maintained across different requests so that the user doesn't lose what she has put in the cart.

Services that don't need to maintain states or don't save states locally are called *stateless* services. Services that keep local states are called *stateful* services. The only distinction between a stateful service and a stateless service is whether the state is saved locally. Continuing with the previous shopping cart example, the service can be implemented as a stateless service that saves shopping cart states in external data storage or as a stateful service that saves shopping cart states locally on the node.

> **Note** "Has state" and "stateful"
>
> Most services have states. However, this doesn't mean they are stateful. The only difference between stateful services and stateless services is where states are stored.

A stateful service can cause some problems. When a service is scaled out, multiple instances share the total workload. For a stateless service, requests can be distributed among the instances because it doesn't matter which instance handles the specific request. For a stateful service, because each service instance records its own state locally, a user session needs to be routed to the same instance to ensure a consistent experience for the user. Another problem with a stateful service is reliability. When a service instance goes down, it takes all its state with it, which causes service interruptions for all the users who are being served by the instance.

To solve these problems, a stateful service can be transformed into a stateless service by externalizing the state. However, this means every service call will incur additional calls to an external data source, increasing system latency. Fortunately, Service Fabric provides a way to escape this dilemma, which we'll discuss in Chapter 3.

Getting started

To get started with Service Fabric development, you need two things:

- A development environment
- A Service Fabric cluster

In this section, first you'll set up a local development, which includes a local multinode cluster that allows you to deploy and test your applications. Then, you'll provision a managed Service Fabric cluster on Microsoft Azure. This book primarily focuses on developments using C# in Visual Studio 2015. However, we'll briefly cover developments using other languages such as Node.js.

Setting up a development environment

To set up a development environment, you'll need Visual Studio 2015 and Service Fabric SDK. You can install Service Fabric SDK via Microsoft Web Platform Installer (Web PI, *https://www.microsoft.com /web/downloads/platform.aspx*). Just follow the installation wizard and accept all default options to complete the installation. This book uses the Preview 2.0.135 version.

In addition, install the following tools:

- Latest version of Microsoft Azure SDK for .NET (using Web PI, this book uses 2.8.1)

- Latest version of Microsoft Azure PowerShell (using Web PI, this book uses 1.0)

Service Fabric SDK provides a local multinode Service Fabric cluster to which you can deploy and test your applications.

Provisioning a Service Fabric cluster on Azure

Although you can use the local cluster provided by Service Fabric SDK for local development and tests, you'll want a hosted cluster on Azure for your production deployments.

> **Note** Microsoft Azure subscription
>
> To use Microsoft Azure, you need a Microsoft Azure subscription. If you don't have one, you can apply for a free one-month trial at *https://azure.microsoft.com/pricing/free-trial/*.

You can follow these steps to create a new Service Fabric cluster.

> ### Microsoft Azure management portal terms
>
> As you click links in the portal, the display areas that expand to the right are called *blades*. You also may see the following terms used in talks and articles:
>
> - **Hub** A hub gathers and displays information from multiple data sources. For instance, all notifications from different services are displayed in a centralized notification hub, which can be brought up by the Bell icon on the top command bar.
>
> - **Dashboard** The home page after you log in is called a dashboard, where you can pin various types of resources for quick access.
>
> - **Tile** Each item you pin on the dashboard is represented by a tile.
>
> - **Journey** As you go through a workflow, your navigation steps are recorded as a journey. You can see the history of your journey at the top of the page, and you can click any of the steps to track back or to jump ahead. Journeys are recorded automatically, and you can access previous journeys by clicking the down arrow icon beside the Microsoft Azure label, as shown in the following figure.

To provision a Service Fabric cluster, complete the following steps:

1. Sign in to Microsoft Azure management portal (*https://portal.azure.com*).

2. Click the New icon in the upper-left corner of the home page. Then, click Marketplace, as shown in Figure 1-3.

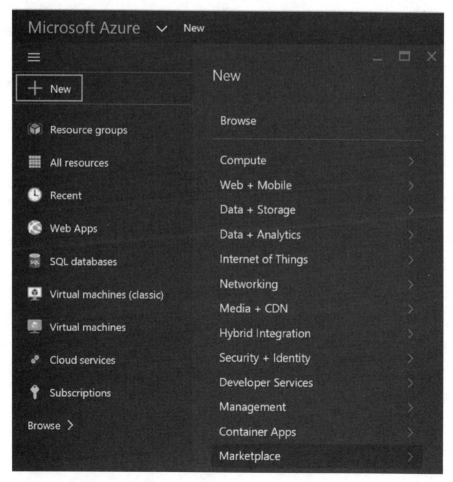

FIGURE 1-3 Create a new resource on Microsoft Azure

3. Under the Everything category, type **service fabric** in the Search box and press Enter. You'll see a Service Fabric Cluster entry, as shown in Figure 1-4. Click the entry to create a new Service Fabric cluster.

FIGURE 1-4 Service Fabric in Marketplace

4. On the Service Fabric Cluster blade, click the Create button to continue, as shown in Figure 1-5.

FIGURE 1-5 Service Fabric template blade

5. On the Basics blade, enter a Cluster Name. Enter the user credentials for VM. Select the Azure Subscription you want to use, and type a name for the new Resource Group. Then, pick an Azure Location where you want the cluster to be hosted, and click OK to continue, as shown in Figure 1-6.

FIGURE 1-6 Service Fabric Cluster creation blade

Note Azure resource groups

A *resource group* is a collection of resources on Azure. On Azure, every resource, such as a virtual machine or a virtual network, belongs to a resource group. A resource group defines a management boundary and a security boundary. You can provision and deprovision all resources in a resource group as a logical unit. And you can apply group-level Role-Based Access Control (RBAC) policies, which are inherited by all members in the group.

6. Click Node Type and create a new node type configuration. (You'll find more information about types of nodes later in this book.) In the Node Type Configuration blade, enter a name for the node type and pick a virtual machine size. Type **80** for the Custom Endpoints value, and then click OK , as shown in Figure 1-7.

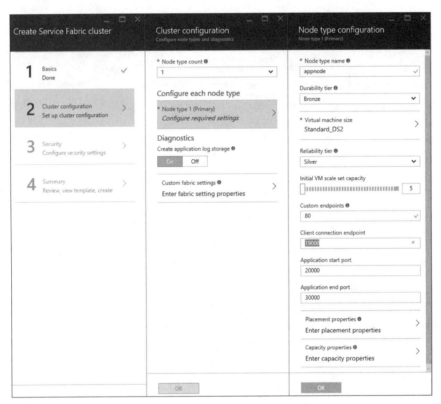

FIGURE 1-7 Service Fabric Cluster settings blade

7. Change the Security mode to Unsecure, and follow the creation wizard to complete provisioning the cluster.

8. The provisioning process takes a few minutes. Once that is done, you'll have a new tile on your dashboard to access the cluster. Figure 1-8 shows the cluster blade, on which you can find the cluster public address (in the format of <cluster name>.<region>.cloudapp.azure.com) and the port number (the default is 19000). You'll need this information to connect to the cluster later.

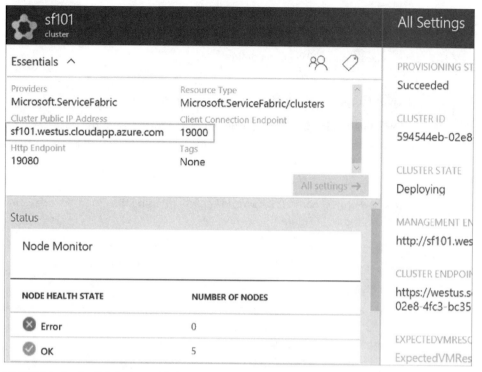

FIGURE 1-8 Service Fabric cluster blade

Hello, World

This is the moment you've been waiting for—a chance to implement the beloved "Hello, World" in a new way.

> ### A tribute to Hello, World
>
> The following code was my first "Hello, World" program, which was written in BASIC about 27 years ago:
>
> ```
> 10 PRINT "Hello, World"
> 20 END
> ```
>
> What's yours? I'm glad to see that such simplicity and elegance is being carried over throughout the years collectively by the community to get developers started with new languages and platforms. Of course, because Service Fabric is designed to tackle complex problems, you need to inherit some established frameworks and structures from the platform. However, as you'll see in a moment, the "Hello, World" program still calls for only a couple lines of changes.

Now you are ready to create your first Service Fabric application. This application contains a stateless service that generates a time stamped "Hello World" string every five seconds.

1. Launch Visual Studio 2015 as an administrator.

> **Note** Launching Visual Studio as an administrator
>
> You need to launch Visual Studio as an administrator in this case because you are going to test the application with a local test cluster, which needs administrative rights to be launched.

2. Create a new project named HelloWorldApplication using the Cloud\Service Fabric Application template, as shown in Figure 1-9.

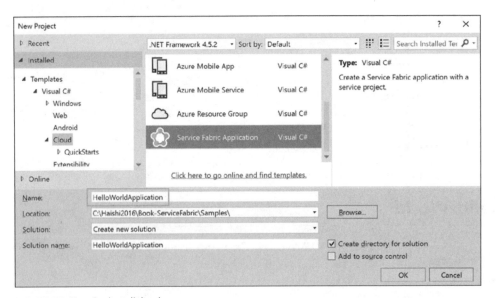

FIGURE 1-9 New Project dialog box

3. In the New Service Fabric Service dialog box, select the Stateless Service template, enter **HelloWorldService** as the Service Project Name, and then click OK to create the Hello World service, as shown in Figure 1-10.

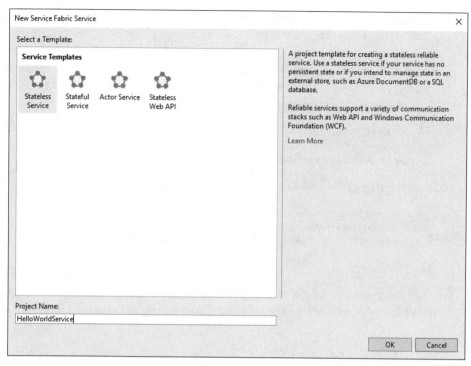

FIGURE 1-10 New Service Fabric Service dialog box

Now, in the solution you have two projects: A HelloWorldApplication project for the Service Fabric application and a HelloWorldService project for the stateless service. You'll go through the rest of the solutions in a moment. For now, focus on the *HelloWorldService* class in the service project:

```
internal sealed class HelloWorldService : StatelessService
{
    public HelloWorldService(StatelessServiceContext context)
        : base(context)
    { }
    protected override IEnumerable<ServiceInstanceListener>
CreateServiceInstanceListeners()
    {
        return new ServiceInstanceListener[0];
    }
    protected override async Task RunAsync(CancellationToken cancellationToken)
    {
        long iterations = 0;
        while (true)
        {
            cancellationToken.ThrowIfCancellationRequested();
            ServiceEventSource.Current.ServiceMessage(this, "Working-{0}", ++iterations);
            await Task.Delay(TimeSpan.FromSeconds(1), cancellationToken);
        }
    }
}
```

4. To implement a stateless service, your service class needs to inherit from the *StatelessService* base class. Service Fabric doesn't mandate a communication protocol. Instead, you can plug in different communication stacks by providing an ICommunicationListener implementation. You'll see a number of communication stack implementations throughout this book. For this example, you'll skip the communication stack, which means your service is a background service that doesn't take any client requests.

5. Modify the *RunAsync* method to implement your service logic.

```
protected override async Task RunAsync(CancellationToken cancellationToken)
{
  while (!cancellationToken.IsCancellationRequested)
  {
ServiceEventSource.Current.ServiceMessage(this, "Hello World at " +
DateTime.Now.ToLongTimeString());
    await Task.Delay(TimeSpan.FromSeconds(5), cancellationToken);
  }
}
```

As you can see in this code snippet, to implement a background service, all you need to do is override the *RunAsync* method and construct your processing loop.

Note Cancellation token

In the .NET asynchronous programming pattern, the CancellationToken structure is used to propagate notification that operations should be canceled. Because a cancellation token can be passed to multiple threads, thread pool work items, and Task objects, it can be used to coordinate cancellation across these boundaries.

When the token's IsCancellationRequested property is set to True, the owning object has requested cancellation of associated tasks. You should stop processing when receiving the notification. If you are calling downstream tasks in your code, you should pass the cancellation token along so that the downstream tasks can be cancelled, like the Task.Delay call in the previous code sample.

6. Service Fabric SDK automatically generates an Event Tracing for Windows (ETW) event source implementation for you to generate trace events. Examine the generated *ServiceEventSource* class if you are interested.

Note Use ETW for tracing and logging

It's recommended to use ETW for tracing and logging because ETW is fast and has minimum impact on your code performance. Furthermore, because Service Fabric also uses ETW for internal tracing, you can view your application logs interleaved with Service Fabric traces, making it easier to understand the relationships between your applications and Service Fabric. Last but not least, because ETW tracing works both in local environment and in the cloud, you can use the same tracing mechanism across different environments.

7. Now, you can press F5 to run the application. Visual Studio will launch a test cluster, deploy the application, and start the services. Once the service is launched, you can see the "Hello World" output in the Diagnostic Events window, as shown in Figure 1-11.

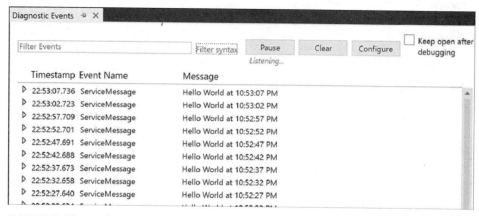

FIGURE 1-11 Diagnostic Events window

Note Bring up the Diagnostic Events view

If you don't see the Diagnostic Events view, you can bring it up by using the View\ Other Windows\Diagnostic Event Viewer menu.

8. Click Stop Debugging on the Visual Studio toolbar or press Shift+F5 to stop the debugging session. If you bring back the Diagnostic Event view, you can see the "Hello World" strings are still coming in. This is because the Stop Debugging button only stops your debugging session; it doesn't stop the service.

Congratulations! You've implemented, deployed, and tested your first Service Fabric application. Next, you'll take a peek into the local cluster.

Managing your local cluster

There are multiple ways to manage your local cluster. You can use Visual Studio Server Explorer, Cloud Explorer, Service Fabric Local Cluster Manager, or PowerShell. You'll walk through all the options in this section.

Visual Studio Server Explorer

You can bring up Server Explorer from the Visual Studio View\Server Explorer menu. Under the Azure node, you'll see a Service Fabric Cluster (Local) node, along with other Azure resource types if you have Azure SDK installed. Figure 1-12 shows that on my cluster I have five nodes, and I have a single Hello World application deployed. You should note that applications and cluster nodes are presented separately, showing the clear separation between workloads and cluster resources that was introduced earlier in this chapter.

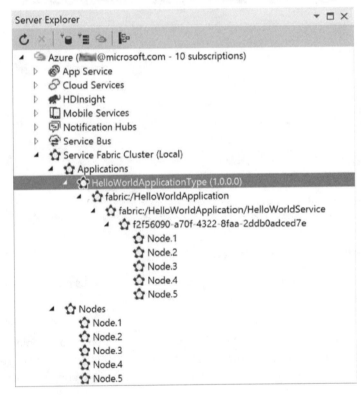

FIGURE 1-12 Server Explorer

The Nodes view in Figure 1-12 seems straightforward—it shows a cluster that consists of five nodes. The application view, however, needs some explanation. What do those levels of nodes mean? Don't worry, you'll go through each of them next.

Application Type node

At the top level, there is an Application Type node that represents an application type, which in this case is HelloWorldApplicationType. When you write your application code in Visual Studio, you define an application type. When the application is deployed, you get an application instance on the cluster. This relationship is similar to the relationship between a class and an object in Object Oriented Programming (OOP).

Application Instance node

Below the Application Type node is the Application Instance node, which is identified by the application's name (fabric:/HelloWorldApplication in this case). By default, an application is named after the corresponding application type name. But you can change to any other name in the format of fabric:/<string>; for example, fabric:/MyApplication.

Service Type node

Under the Application Instance node, you have Service Type nodes. Each node represents a registered service type, such as the HelloServiceType in this example. Each service in a Service Fabric application is named as fabric:<application name>/<service name>. This name also is the address of the service. Service Fabric built-in naming service resolves this name to the actual service instance address at run time.

Partition node

A partition is identified by a GUID, suggesting it's not something that a client would use to address a partition directly. Instead, the Service Fabric naming service will figure out the correct partition to which a service request should be sent.

Replica node

Figure 1-12 shows that by default, Service Fabric maintains multiple replicas for a partition for high availability. In this case, the Hello World service has a single partition with five replicas.

> **Note** Replica and service instance
>
> A replica is a service instance. The term *service instance* often is used in logical descriptions of deployment topologies, and the term *replica* often is used when explicit replica behaviors or concepts are being discussed.

Visual Studio Cloud Explorer

Microsoft Azure SDK comes with a Visual Studio extension named Cloud Explorer, which you can access by the View\Cloud Explorer menu. Cloud Explorer is similar to Server Explorer in terms of Service Fabric cluster management functionalities, as shown in Figure 1-13.

FIGURE 1-13 Cloud Explorer

Service Fabric Explorer

Neither Server Explorer nor Cloud Explorer is designed as a full-fledged management tool. They are designed for you to navigate and view your cloud resources and server resources easily and with limited management functionality.

Service Fabric SDK provides a powerful tool named Service Fabric Explorer. To bring up the management UI, you can use any browser and navigate to *http://localhost:19080/Explorer.*

The left panel of the Service Fabric Explorer looks much like Server Explorer or Cloud Explorer. However, the tool also has a details panel to the right providing very detailed information on the currently selected item, as shown in Figure 1-14.

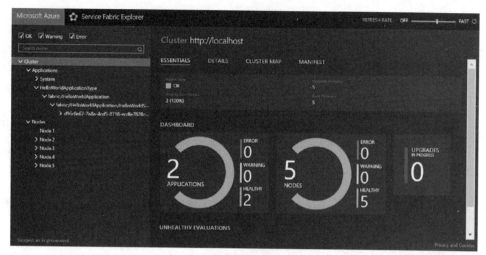

FIGURE 1-14 Local Cluster Manager

The management tool is loaded with features. You'll use this tool frequently throughout this book for different scenarios. For now, perform a little exercise to familiarize yourself with the tool. In this exercise, you'll delete the Hello World application from the cluster.

1. In the Service Fabric Explorer, select the fabric:/HelloWorldApplicationnode in the left pane. Then, in the right pane, click the Actions button and then click the Delete Application menu, as shown in Figure 1-15.

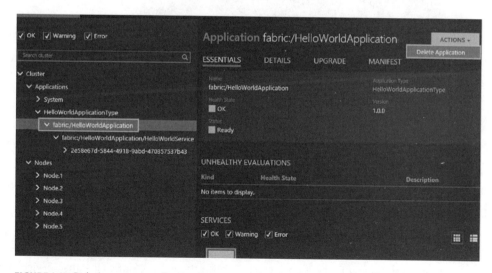

FIGURE 1-15 Deleting a new application instance

2. In the Confirm Application Deletion dialog box, shown in Figure 1-16, click the Delete Application button to continue.

FIGURE 1-16 Confirm Application Deletion dialog box

3. The UI refreshes itself every few seconds. Once the UI is refreshed, you can see the application instance has been removed, as shown in Figure 1-17.

FIGURE 1-17 Two application instances

Note Resetting the cluster

Service Fabric SDK installs a Service Fabric icon on your taskbar, which provides a couple of shortcut menus for some cluster-level operations. This comes in handy when you want to reset everything and make a fresh start. To reset the cluster, right-click the Service Fabric icon on the taskbar and select the Reset Cluster menu.

Windows PowerShell

Windows PowerShell is a powerful automation and configuration management framework. Service Fabric SDK installs a number of PowerShell cmdlets for you to manage your applications and clusters using command lines or automation scripts.

If you look under the Scripts folder of the HelloWorldApplication, you can find a Deploy-FabricApplication.ps1, which in turn calls a number of prebuilt scripts under your Service Fabric SDK folder (C:\ Program Files\Microsoft SDKs\Service Fabric\Tools\Scripts by default) to deploy, upgrade, and remove your applications.

To get started, open a new Windows PowerShell window and use the Connect-ServiceFabricCluster cmdlet to connect to the local cluster, as shown in Figure 1-18.

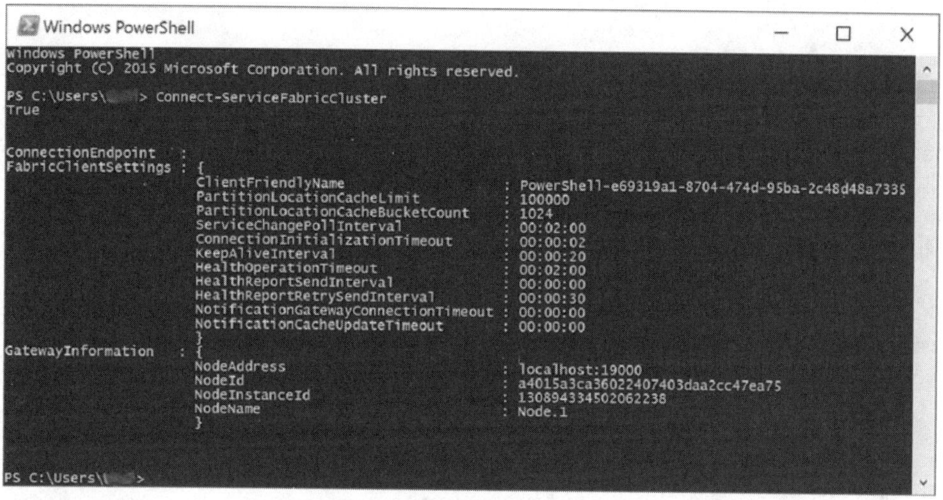

FIGURE 1-18 Connect-ServiceFabricCluster cmdlet

Next, try a few commands. You'll be introduced to more cmdlets as you go through the chapters.

- List application instances.

  To list application instances on the cluster, type the following cmdlet:

  ```
  Get-ServiceFabricApplication
  ```

  The above cmdlet generates the following output on my environment (before the application instance is removed. To restore the instance, press F5 in Visual Studio to redeploy application):

  ```
  ApplicationName        : fabric:/HelloWorldApplication
  ApplicationTypeName    : HelloWorldApplicationType
  ApplicationTypeVersion : 1.0.0.0

          ApplicationStatus      : Ready
          HealthState            : Ok
          ApplicationParameters  : { "HelloWorldService_InstanceCount" = "-1" }
  ```

- List cluster node names and statuses.

    To list all the nodes and their current statuses, use the following cmdlet:

    ```
    Get-ServiceFabricNode | Format-Table NodeName, NodeStatus
    ```

    A healthy cluster would look like this:

    ```
    NodeName NodeStatus
    -------- ----------
    Node.1        Up
    Node.2        Up
    Node.3        Up
    Node.4        Up
    Node.5        Up
    ```

Additional information

At the time of this writing, Service Fabric is still in preview. It's likely that service APIs, tooling experiences, and management UIs will change over time. However, key concepts covered in Part I and Part II of this book and the patterns and applicable scenarios in Part III and Part IV of this book should remain valid in future releases.

For up-to-date Service Fabric documentations, please visit *https://azure.microsoft.com /documentation/services/service-fabric/*.

CHAPTER 2

Stateless services

The service you implemented in Chapter 1, "Hello, Service Fabric!," was a background service that does processing by itself. It doesn't respond to any user requests. Although the background service is useful, most services need to take in user requests. In this chapter, you'll learn several ways to handle user requests by using a stateless service. First, you'll learn how to add an ASP.NET 5 Web Service to your application. Then, you'll learn how to implement a few common communication stacks for your services to take client requests via different protocols.

Implement ASP.NET 5 applications

It's common for a cloud-based application to have a web front end. So, Service Fabric provides a built-in ASP.NET Web API template that helps you easily add a web API to your Service Fabric application. In this section, you create a new application with an ASP.NET 5 Web API. Then, you deploy it to both your local cluster and your cluster on Azure.

Creating an ASP.NET 5 Web API is fairly easy. Just pick the ASP.NET 5 Web API template when you add a service, and you'll get a functional Web API site that is ready to be deployed. The following walk-through shows you the steps of creating an ASP.NET 5 Web API in your Service Fabric application.

1. Create a new Service Fabric application.

2. In the Create A Service dialog box, pick the ASP.NET 5 Web API template and click OK to continue, as shown in Figure 2-1.

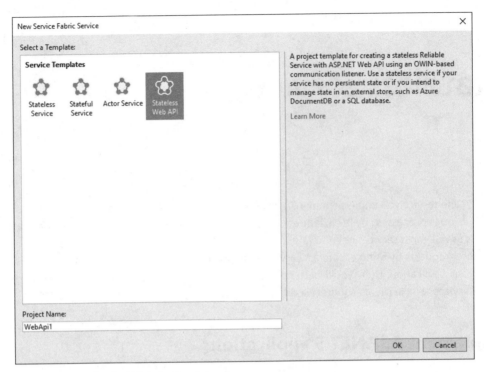

FIGURE 2-1 New Service Fabric Service dialog box

3. Once the application is created, publish the application to your local cluster. By default, the service is configured to have a singleton partition with a single instance listening to an automatically assigned port. If you open the application view in Service Fabric Explorer, you can see where the instance is located and which port it's listening on. As shown in Figure 2-2, the service instance in this case is running on Node.2, and it's listening to address *Http://+:34001*.

FIGURE 2-2 The ASP.NET Web Service on the cluster

4. Open a browser and navigate to *http://localhost:34001* (the port on your system likely is different), and you'll see the running web API with a sample request sent to the values controller, as shown in Figure 2-3.

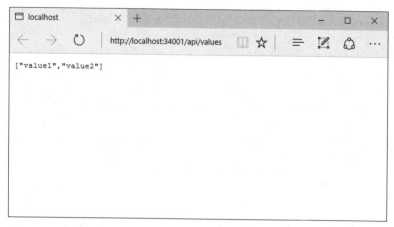

FIGURE 2-3 localhost

5. Now, modify the *ApplicationManifest.xml* file under your Service Fabric application project to change the *InstanceCount* attribute of the *StatelessService* element to -1, which means to deploy an instance on every available node (you'll take a closer look at the file in a moment):

```
<Service Name="Web1Service">
    <StatelessService ServiceTypeName="Web1Type" InstanceCount="-1">
      <SingletonPartition />
    </StatelessService>
</Service>
```

6. Save the change and deploy the application again.

Once the application is deployed, you can see there is one instance running on each of the nodes as shown in Figure 2-4. Each instance is listening to a unique, automatically assigned port.

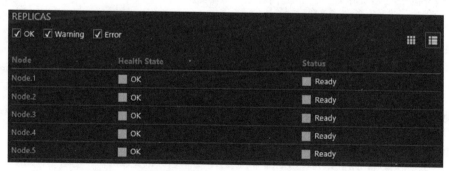

FIGURE 2-4 List of service instances (replicas)

Scalability and availability of a stateless service

Multiple instances of the service listening to different ports introduce a new problem. Certainly, you can connect to each of the instances by the specific replica addresses. And you can use a client program that queries for proper instances to connect to. However, when a user uses a web browser to connect to the service, she doesn't (and shouldn't) have the knowledge of individual instance addresses, and the browser doesn't have the capability to perform instance address lookups. Ideally, she should be able to connect to a well-known port (such as 80) and be redirected to any of the working instances. Load balancing in this case is a solution for both availability and scalability.

Availability

Because a browser doesn't know how to use the naming service to locate a healthy instance to connect to, you'll have to move that logic to the service side. This can be done either by a gateway that implements the instance discovery logic or by a load balancer that routes user traffic to healthy nodes. Here, I'll focus on load balancer because this is what Azure provides out-of-box. Commonly, a load balancer uses probes to determine the health state of attached instances and distributes traffic only to healthy nodes, as shown in Figure 2-5.

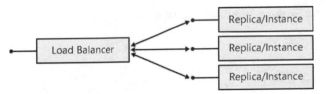

FIGURE 2-5 A basic load balancer configuration

In Chapter 5, "Service deployments and upgrades," you'll learn about details of setting up a load balancer in front of your service instances on Microsoft Azure.

Scalability

Using a load balancer also provides service scalability because the load balancer automatically distributes traffic across healthy instances.

For certain scenarios, you also can partition stateless services to segment your customers—for instance, when you want to send different types of workloads to different node types. However, such partitioning is more about segmenting customer traffic than about scaling the application. The ups and downs of partitioning a stateless service are discussed in Chapter 5.

Another level of scaling is to deploy multiple instances of an application. For example, you can deploy an application instance per customer and scale out or scale up the service instances in an application instance based on the workload of the particular customer. This scaling mechanism also will be discussed in Chapter 5.

Implement communication stacks

Hosting ASP.NET 5 Web Services is not the only way to respond to user requests. As mentioned in Chapter 1, Service Fabric allows you to implement custom communication stacks for different communication protocols. The way to define the communication mechanism is to provide an implementation of an *ICommunicationListener* interface.

Next, you'll implement a simple calculator service that provides two operations: add and subtract. You'll implement three different communication stacks for the service as you progress through this chapter.

Default communication stack

Service Fabric provides an out-of-box communication stack based on RPC Proxy. The first version of your calculator service will use this default communication stack.

The first version

1. Launch Visual Studio 2015. Create a new Service Fabric application named CalculatorApplication with a stateless service named *CalculatorService*.

2. Define a *ICalculatorService* service contract in the CalculatorService project. Note the service interface needs to inherit from an *IService* interface under the *Microsoft.ServiceFabric.Services. Remoting* namespace as follows:

    ```
    public interface ICalculatorService: IService
    {
        Task<int> Add(int a, int b);
        Task<int> Subtract(int a, int b);
    }
    ```

3. Modify the *CalculatorService* to implement the service contract, as shown in the following code snippet. There are a couple of places worth noticing in the following code. First, if your service doesn't need a long-running back-end process, you can remove the *RunAsync* method. Second, to use the default remoting communication stack, you just need to create a new *ServiceRemotingListener* instance.

    ```
    internal sealed class CalculatorService : StatelessService, ICalculatorService
    {
        public Task<int> Add(int a, int b)
        {
            return Task.FromResult<int>(a + b);
        }
        public Task<int> Subtract(int a, int b)
        {
            return Task.FromResult<int>(a - b);
        }
        protected override IEnumerable<ServiceInstanceListener>
    CreateServiceInstanceListeners()
        {
    ```

```
        return new[]
        {
            new ServiceInstanceListener(initParams =>
                new ServiceRemotingListener<ICalculatorService>(initParams, this))
        };
    }
}
```

Comparing with RunAsync in Azure Cloud Service

If you are familiar with Azure Cloud Service, you may remember that Azure Cloud Service requires the *RunAsync* method to stay running. If the *RunAsync* method fails or exits, the role instance is considered dead and Cloud Service will try to restart the role instance for you. This is not the case for Service Fabric. In Service Fabric, it's fine to complete the task in your *RunAsync* or, as in this case, to ignore the *RunAsync* implementation altogether. You can continue to accept and handle client requests through the communication listener.

4. Rebuild the solution. Then, right-click the CalculatorApplication project and select the Publish menu. In the Publish Service Application dialog box, select the local target profile, as shown in Figure 2-6. Then, click the Publish button to publish the application to your local cluster.

FIGURE 2-6 Publish Service Fabric Application dialog box

5. Add a new console application named *CalculatorClient* to the solution.

6. Right-click the CalculatorClient project and select the Manage NuGet Packages menu. In NuGet Package Manager, select the Include Prelease check box and search for Microsoft.ServiceFabric. Services. Then, click Install to install the package, as shown in Figure 2-7.

FIGURE 2-7 NuGet Package Manager

7. Add a link to the *ICalculatorService.cs* file under the CalculatorService project. This brings the service contract definition to the client. In a proper implementation, you probably want the contract defined in a shared assembly. This example takes a shortcut by directly referring the file.

Note Adding a file link

To add a link to another source file, right-click a project and select the Add\Existing Items menu item. Then, browse to the file and select it. Instead of clicking the Add button directly, click the small triangle beside the Add button to pull down a menu and then select Add As Link to add a link to the original file (instead of copying it over). All updates to the original file are reflected in the linked file.

8. Right-click the CalculatorClient project. Select the Properties menu item. Switch to the Build tab and update Platform target from the default Any CPU to x64.

9. Open the *Program.cs* file. Add the follonamespace imports:

```
using CalculatorService;
using Microsoft.ServiceFabric.Services.Remoting.Client;
```

10. Modify the *Main* method as shown in the following code snippet.

```
static void Main(string[] args)
{
var calculatorClient = ServiceProxy.Create<ICalculatorService>
(new Uri("fabric:/CalculatorApplication/CalculatorService"));
    var result = calculatorClient.Add(1, 2).Result;
    Console.WriteLine(result);
    Console.ReadKey();
}
```

11. Now that the client is ready, you can try it. Right-click the CalculatorClient project and select the Debug\Start New Instance menu item. After some delay and possibly some security warnings that you can discard, you'll see that the correct result, which is 3 in this case, is returned.

That wasn't particularly exciting, but there is something interesting. When the client connects to the service, it's using a URI with address "fabric:/CalculatorApplication/CalculatorService", which doesn't look like a familiar HTTP or TCP service address. This address will be translated into the service listener endpoint by the Service Fabric naming service. Figure 2-8 shows how the local cluster looks now (the table layout is edited slightly to remove some columns for clarity). The figure shows that there are several system services running, including a *ClusterManagerService*, a *FailoverManagerService*, and a *NamingService*. The figure also shows that under your singleton service partition run five replicas, each listening to a unique net.tcp address.

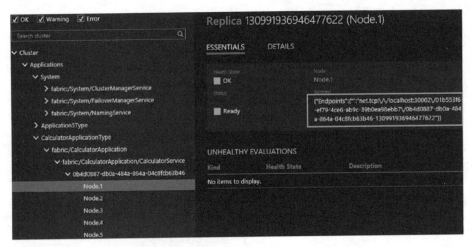

FIGURE 2-8 Service replicas with unique addresses

Service Fabric application model

Before you make more modifications to the calculator service, examine the Service Fabric application model to understand more about the structure of a Service Fabric application.

You know that a Service Fabric application is composed of services. A Service Fabric service consists of three parts: code, configuration, and data.

- **Code** The executable binaries of the service. These binaries are packaged into a code package.

- **Configuration** Settings that can be loaded at run time. These settings are declared by a *Settings.xml* file in the service project, and they are packaged into a configuration package.

- **Data** Data contains arbitrary static data to be used by the service. Data is packaged in a data package.

Figure 2-9 depicts the Service Fabric application model.

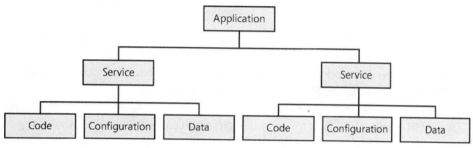

FIGURE 2-9 Service Fabric application model

The Service Fabric application model is described declaratively by an application manifest and a number of service manifests, one for each of the included services. The *application manifest* describes the application structure, and the *service manifest* describes code, configuration, and data in a service. The application manifest and service manifests have associated version numbers, which are used to identify versions of application type and service type, respectively.

Service manifest You can find a service's manifest under the project's PackageRoot folder. The manifest is an XML file with the following key elements:

- **ServiceTypes** Defines the supported service types in the service's code packages. For example, your calculator service manifest declares that it supports a single *CalculatorServiceType* service type.

```
<ServiceTypes>
        <StatelessServiceType ServiceTypeName="CalculatorServiceType" />
</ServiceTypes>
```

- **CodePackage** Describes a code package that contains the executable binaries. A service manifest can contain multiple code packages. When a service type is instantiated by Service Fabric, all code packages in the manifest will be activated, and their entry points are invoked. Calling the entry point creates a new service process, and the process is expected to register its supported service types upon start. For example, look at the *CodePackage* element of your calculator service:

```
<CodePackage Name="Code" Version="1.0.0.0">
    <EntryPoint>
            <ExeHost>
                    <Program>CalculatorService.exe</Program>
            </ExeHost>
    </EntryPoint>
</CodePackage>
```

In this case, the entry point is defined as an executable named *CalculatorService.exe*. Your calculator service code is no more than a console application with reference to Service Fabric libraries. When you examine the *Main* method of the service project, you can see the program registers the supported service types with the Service Fabric runtime as expected:

```
    using (FabricRuntime fabricRuntime = FabricRuntime.Create())
    {
        fabricRuntime.RegisterServiceType("CalculatorServiceType",
                        typeof(CalculatorService));
        ...
    }
```

- **ConfigPackage**   A service manifest can contain a number of *ConfigPackage* elements, each of which is identified by the *Name* attribute. Under the service project's PackageRoot folder, there should be a corresponding folder with the same name for each of the *ConfigPackage* elements. Under each folder is a *Settings.xml* file, which contains key-value pair settings that can be loaded at run time.

- **DataPackage**   A service manifest can contain a number of *DataPackage* elements. Each *DataPackage* element corresponds to a folder under the PackageRoot folder. Each folder holds a number of arbitrary static data files that can be used by the service.

Application manifest   The application manifest describes the overall structure of an application. Specifically, it describes what services are in the application and how these services should be laid out on a Service Fabric cluster. You'll learn about advanced elements and attributes in this document later in this book. For now, look at just a few of them:

- **ServiceManifestImport**   This element defines references to service manifests composing the application.

- **DefaultServices**   Default services are instantiated automatically when the application is instantiated. The default services are not special services. They behave exactly as other services except for the auto instantiation.

The second version

Now, modify the service to return the replica id along with the calculation result so that you can know which service instance handled the request. To do this, you'll modify the service contract to return strings instead of integers.

1. Modify the *ICalculatorService* interface to change method return types from *Task<int>* to *Task<string>*.

   ```
   public interface ICalculatorService: Iservice


   {
       Task<string> Add(int a, int b);
       Task<string> Subtract(int a, int b);
   }
   ```

2. Modify the calculation method implementations in the *CalculatorService* class. The following code snippet demonstrates how you can use the *ServiceInitializationParameters* attribute of *StatelessService* to access the current instance (replica) id.

   ```
   public Task<string> Add(int a, int b)
   ```

```
    {
        return Task.FromResult<string>(string.Format("Instance {0} returns: {1}",
            this.ServiceInitializationParameters.InstanceId,
            a + b));
    }
    public Task<string> Subtract(int a, int b)
    {
        return Task.FromResult<string>(string.Format("Instance {0} returns: {1}",
            this.ServiceInitializationParameters.InstanceId,
            a - b));
    }
```

3. Because you've modified the service contract, it makes sense to declare this modified service version 2. To do this, you'll modify both the service manifest and the application manifest. Modify the *ServiceManifest.xml* file under the PackageRoot folder of the CalculatorService project. Change the *Version* attribute on both the *ServiceManifest* element and the *CodePackage* element to "2.0.0.0". This change updates both the code package version and the service version to "2.0.0.0".

4. Edit the *ApplicationManifest.xml* under the CalculatorApplication project and change the *ApplicationTypeVersion* attribute on the *ApplicationManifest* element and the *ServiceManifestVersion* attribute on the *ServiceManifestRef* element to "2.0.0.0". This change updates the service reference to refer to the new version of the service and updates the application itself to version "2.0.0.0".

5. Rebuild and deploy the application to your local cluster.

6. Now, update the client to call the service repeatedly in a loop:

```
while (true)
{
        var calculatorClient = ServiceProxy.Create<ICalculatorService>(new
                Uri("fabric:/CalculatorApplication/CalculatorService"));
        var result = calculatorClient.Add(1, 2).Result;
        Console.WriteLine(result);
        Thread.Sleep(3000);
}
```

7. Launch the client. The client will connect to a random instance and keep receiving results. Figure 2-10 shows that in this case, the client is connected to an instance with id 130897044575029205.

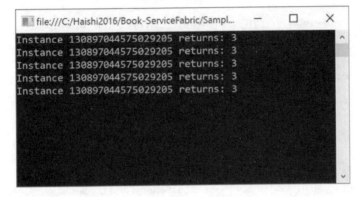

FIGURE 2-10 Multiple calculator service clients

On Service Fabric Explorer, open the service partition to see all its replicas (refer to Figure 2-8). By cross-referencing the instance ids displayed on client screens, identify the hosting node. Select the node in the left pane. Click on the Actions button in the right pane and then select the Deactivate (restart) menu item. This simulates that the node has crashed. Figure 2-11 shows that Node.3 is selected for shutdown, which is the host of the replica 130897044575029205 (replica ids on your environment will be different).

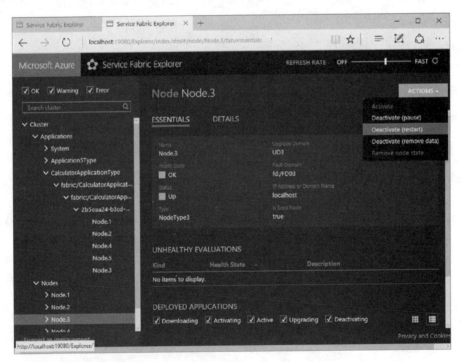

FIGURE 2-11 Shutting down a node

8. Once the node is shut down, the client is disconnected from the original service instance and automatically is reconnected to another healthy instance. Figure 2-12 shows that the client in

this example has reconnected to another replica with id 130897044575029205, as indicated by the arrow. This is the failover mechanism here. Although the originally connected service instance is down, the client experiences no interruptions and automatically is reconnected to a healthy instance.

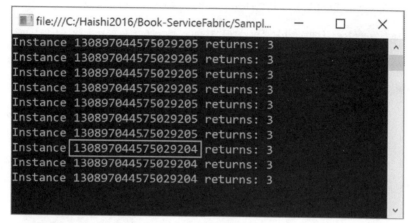

FIGURE 2-12 Service failover

Resetting the cluster

In my experience, shutting down nodes sometimes causes the local cluster to become unstable. You may have to reset the cluster to restore the cluster to a healthy state and try again if you encounter some unexpected errors.

WCF communication stack

Next, you'll examine another communication stack implementation provided by Service Fabric—the WCF communication stack. In this exercise, you modify your calculator service to serve WCF clients.

Note WCF troubleshooting

This exercise isn't intended to teach WCF, so there aren't many WCF-specific details provided here. If you are familiar with WCF, the following code shouldn't be a surprise to you. If you encounter some problems and feel rusty with WCF, remember the ABCs of WCF: Address, Binding, and Contract. Most WCF problems are caused by mismatches in these three parts. You can find more information about WCF at *https://msdn.microsoft.com/library /ms731082(v=vs.110).aspx*.

The third version

1. Modify the *CalculatorService* class to replace the default communication stack with the WCF communication stack. The *EndpointResourceName* points to the corresponding endpoint configuration in your service manifest file. The *CreateListenBinding* is a private method to create a binding for the endpoint, which you'll implement next.

```
protected override IEnumerable<ServiceInstanceListener> CreateServiceInstanceListeners()
{
    return new[]
    {
    new ServiceInstanceListener(initParams =>
        new WcfCommunicationListener(initParams, typeof (ICalculatorService), this)

        {

            EndpointResourceName = "ServiceEndpoint",
            Binding = this.CreateListenBinding()
        })
    };
}
```

2. Implement the *CreateListenBinding* method. The following implementation uses hard-coded values. In a production implementation, you may want to put these values in your service configuration.

```
private NetTcpBinding CreateListenBinding()
    {
        NetTcpBinding binding = new NetTcpBinding(SecurityMode.None)
        {
                SendTimeout = TimeSpan.MaxValue,
                ReceiveTimeout = TimeSpan.MaxValue,
                OpenTimeout = TimeSpan.FromSeconds(5),
                CloseTimeout = TimeSpan.FromSeconds(5),
                MaxConnections = int.MaxValue,
                MaxReceivedMessageSize = 1024 * 1024
                };
            binding.MaxBufferSize = (int)binding.MaxReceivedMessageSize;
            binding.MaxBufferPoolSize
    = Environment.ProcessorCount * binding.MaxReceivedMessageSize;

        return binding;
    }
```

3. Modify *ICalculatorService* to remove the *IService* base interface.

4. Modify the service manifest and the application manifest to upgrade version numbers to "3.0.0". Rebuild and deploy the application.

5. Add a new *Client* class to the CalculatorClient project.

```
public class Client : ServicePartitionClient<WcfCommunicationClient<ICalculatorService>>,
ICalculatorService
{
```

```
        public Client(WcfCommunicationClientFactory<ICalculatorService> clientFactory,
            Uri serviceName)
                : base(clientFactory, serviceName)
        {
        }
        public Task<string> Add(int a, int b)
        {
            return this.InvokeWithRetryAsync(client => client.Channel.Add(a, b));
        }
        public Task<string> Subtract(int a, int b)
        {
            return this.InvokeWithRetryAsync(client => client.Channel.Subtract(a, b));
        }
    }
```

6. Modify the *Main* method of the client program:

```
Uri ServiceName = new Uri("fabric:/CalculatorApplication/CalculatorService");
ServicePartitionResolver serviceResolver = new ServicePartitionResolver(() =>

        new FabricClient());
NetTcpBinding binding = CreateClientConnectionBinding();
Client calcClient = new Client(new WcfCommunicationClientFactory<ICalculatorService>
        (serviceResolver, binding, null), ServiceName);
Console.WriteLine(calcClient.Add(3, 5).Result);
Console.ReadKey();
```

7. Implement the *CreateClientConnectionBinding* method to create a matching binding for the client:

```
private static NetTcpBinding CreateClientConnectionBinding()
{
    NetTcpBinding binding = new NetTcpBinding(SecurityMode.None)
    {
        SendTimeout = TimeSpan.MaxValue,
        ReceiveTimeout = TimeSpan.MaxValue,
        OpenTimeout = TimeSpan.FromSeconds(5),
        CloseTimeout = TimeSpan.FromSeconds(5),
        MaxReceivedMessageSize = 1024 * 1024
    };
    binding.MaxBufferSize = (int)binding.MaxReceivedMessageSize;
    binding.MaxBufferPoolSize = Environment.ProcessorCount * binding.
MaxReceivedMessageSize;
    return binding;
}
```

8. Build and launch the client. You should see the successful service output.

Custom communication stack

For the last exercise of this section, you'll build a custom communication stack using ASP.NET Web API with OWIN self-hosting. In case you're not familiar with some of the terms that are mentioned, the following is a little detour to introduce these concepts. Once you are ready, you'll implement a new version of the calculator service that provides calculator methods via Web API.

OWIN, ASP.NET Web API, and Project Katana

Traditionally, ASP.NET has been tightly coupled with IIS. Then came OWIN (OWIN 2015), or Open Web Interface for .NET, which decouples ASP.NET applications and web servers. This opens up the opportunity for you to host ASP.NET applications on any host implementations that affiliate to the OWIN specification or to host ASP.NET applications in your own process, hence the term *self-host*. Figure 2-13 shows a high-level overview of OWIN architecture: The Host is the hosting process. The Server accepts client requests and serves up responses. The requests are passed through a customizable stack of Middleware before they reach the Application built on top of various Frameworks.

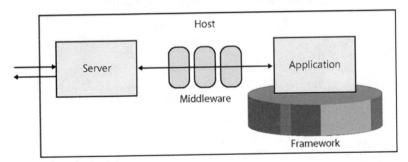

FIGURE 2-13 OWIN architecture

Project Katana is the Microsoft implementation of OWIN components. In this sample, you'll use Katana's OWIN self-host implementation as the host and OWIN HttpListener (based on the .NET Framework HttpListener) as the server.

ICommunicationListener with OWIN self-host

As mentioned earlier, to implement a communication stack, all you need to do is provide an implementation of *ICommunicationListener*:

```
public interface ICommunicationListener
{
    void Abort();
    Task CloseAsync(CancellationToken cancellationToken);
    Task<string> OpenAsync(CancellationToken cancellationToken);
}
```

You should initialize and start up the stack in the *OpenAsync* method and shut down the stack in both the *Abort* method and the *CloseAsync* method.

- **OpenAsync** Set up the address that the server will be listening on and start taking requests.

- **CloseAsync** Stop taking new requests, finish pending requests, and stop.

- **Abort** Cancel and stop immediately.

How does *ICommunicationListener* work with OWIN self-host and ASP.NET Web API? In this example, the communication listener will launch an OWIN server, which in turn will initialize the ASP.NET Web API via the *IAppBuilder* interface, as shown in Figure 2-14.

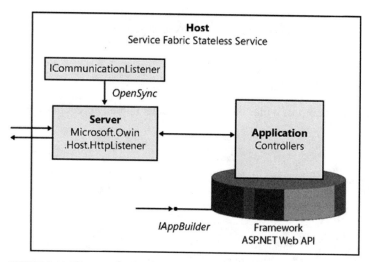

FIGURE 2-14 *ICommunicationListener* and OWIN self-host

> **Note** Sample origin
>
> This following sample is inspired by Vaclav Turecek's sample code on azure.microsoft.com: *https://azure.microsoft.com/documentation/articles/service-fabric-reliable-services -communication-webapi/.*

The fourth version

1. Create a new WebCalculatorApplication Service Fabric application with a stateless service named WebCalculatorService.

2. In the WebCalculatorService project, add a reference to the Microsoft.AspNet.WebApi. OwinSelfHost NuGet package.

3. Next, you build up the ASP.NET API. There is nothing special here; you just build up common ASP.NET API structures and classes you see in ASP.NET API projects. First, create the following folders under the WebCalculatorService project:

   - App_Start

   - Controllers

4. Add a basic Web API configuration class under the App_Start directory named *FormatterConfig.cs*:

```
namespace WebCalculatorService

{
    using System.Net.Http.Formatting;
    public static class FormatterConfig
```

```
        {
            public static void ConfigureFormatters(MediaTypeFormatterCollection formatters)
            {
            }
        }
    }
```

5. Add a basic route configuration class under the App_Start folder named *RouteConfig.cs*:

```
namespace WebCalculatorService
{
    using System.Web.Http;
    public static class RouteConfig
    {
        public static void RegisterRoutes(HttpRouteCollection routes)
        {
            routes.MapHttpRoute(
                    name: "CalculatorApi",
                    routeTemplate: "api/{action}",
                    defaults: new { controller = "Default" }
                );
        }
    }
}
```

6. Under the Controllers folder, add a new *DefaultController* that provides the calculator methods:

```
namespace WebCalculatorService.Controllers
{
    using System.Collections.Generic;
    using System.Web.Http;
    public class DefaultController : ApiController
    {
        [HttpGet]
        public int Add(int a, int b)
        {
            return a + b;
        }
        [HttpGet]
        public int Subtract(int a, int b)
        {
            return a - b;
        }
    }
}
```

7. Define a *IOwinAppBuilder* interface:

```
namespace WebCalculatorService
{
    using Owin;
    public interface IowinAppBuilder
    {
        void Configuration(IAppBuilder appBuilder);
    }
}
```

8. Finally, define a *Startup* class that registers routing and other configurations. This is where the ASP.NET Web API framework is plugged into the host.

```
namespace WebCalculatorService
{
    using Owin;
    using System.Web.Http;
    public class Startup : IowinAppBuilder
    {
        public void Configuration(IAppBuilder appBuilder)
        {
            HttpConfiguration config = new HttpConfiguration();

            FormatterConfig.ConfigureFormatters(config.Formatters);
            RouteConfig.RegisterRoutes(config.Routes);

            appBuilder.UseWebApi(config);
        }
    }
}
```

9. Before you implement the communication stack, modify the service manifest to configure the service endpoint:

```
<Resources>
  <Endpoints>
    <Endpoint Name="ServiceEndpoint" Protocol="http" Port="80" Type="Input"/>
  </Endpoints>
</Resources>
```

10. When the service is initiated, Service Fabric will allocate requested ports and set up proper ACL for the service address. If you don't specify a port here, Service Fabric automatically will pick a port from the application reserved port range. When a port is specified, Service Fabric will try to honor the request; however, sometimes the request can't be fulfilled because of port conflicts. So, if your service doesn't need to listen to fixed ports, you should avoid setting a specific port number here.

11. However, in cases when you do need to listen to specific port (such as port 80 for web servers), you should be aware that other applications deployed on the cluster may have taken the requested ports. To alleviate the situation, Service Fabric guarantees no more than one instance of any stateless service on a single node. So, it's relatively safe to have fixed ports defined in your stateless services. However, there's still a caveat: when you are using the local cluster, there still could be conflicts when you run multiple replicas of the same stateless service that has fixed ports. What you can do is run a single instance locally and scale out only on the cloud. Later in this chapter, you'll see how you can set up different configurations for different environments.

12. Now it's time to add your *ICommunicationListener* implementation. Add a new *OwinCommunicationListener* class to the service project:

```
namespace WebCalculatorService
{
```

```
using Microsoft.ServiceFabric.Services;
using System;
using System.Threading.Tasks;
using System.Fabric;
using System.Threading;
public class OwinCommunicationListener : IcommunicationListener
{
    public void Abort()
    {
    }
    public Task CloseAsync(CancellationToken cancellationToken)
    {
    }
    public Task<string> OpenAsync(CancellationToken cancellationToken)
    {
    }
}
}
```

13. Define some local variables and a new constructor:

```
private readonly IOwinAppBuilder startup;
private IDisposable serverHandle;
private string listeningAddress;

public OwinCommunicationListener(IOwinAppBuilder startup)
{
    this.startup = startup;
}
```

14. Now, move on to the *OpenSync* method. First, you read the endpoint settings through the *ServiceInitializationParameters* parameter, and then you construct an HTTP URL based on the port. Then, The *OpenSync* method starts the web server and returns the address that the server listens on. Service Fabric registers the returned address with its naming service so that a client can query for the address by service name. This is necessary because a service instance may get moved for load balancing or fail over, hence the listening address could change. However, a client always can use the stable service name to look up the correct address to talk to.

```
public Task<string> OpenAsync(CancellationToken cancellationToken)
{

    EndpointResourceDescription serviceEndpoint = serviceInitializationParameters
        .CodePackageActivationContext.GetEndpoint("ServiceEndpoint");
    int port = serviceEndpoint.Port;
    this.listeningAddress = String.Format("http://+:{0}/", port);

    this.serverHandle = WebApp.Start(this.listeningAddress,
        appBuilder => this.startup.Configuration(appBuilder));
    string resultAddress = this.listeningAddress.Replace("+",
        FabricRuntime.GetNodeContext().IPAddressOrFQDN);
    ServiceEventSource.Current.Message("Listening on {0}", resultAddress);
    return Task.FromResult(resultAddress);

}
```

15. Finally, implement the *CloseAsync* method and the *Abort* method.

```
public Task CloseAsync(CancellationToken cancellationToken)
{
    this.StopWebServer();
    return Task.FromResult(true);
}
public void Abort()
{
    this.StopWebServer();
}
private void StopWebServer()
{
    if (this.serverHandle != null)
    {
        try
        {
            this.serverHandle.Dispose();
        }
        catch (ObjectDisposedException)
        {
            // no-op
        }
    }
}
```

16. Now, your custom communication stack is ready. All that is left to do is to return a new instance in the *WebCalculatorService* class:

```
protected override IEnumerable<ServiceInstanceListener> CreateServiceInstanceListeners()
{
    return new[]
    {
        new ServiceInstanceListener(initParams => new OwinCommunicationListener("webapp",
new Startup(), initParams))
    };
}
```

Before you deploy this new application, take a brief look at application manifest parameters. Service Fabric application manifests support parameters, for which you can supply different values at deployment time. By default, Service Fabric Visual Studio tooling generates an instance count parameter for each of the included services. In this case, there's a *WebCalculatorService_InstanceCount* parameter that controls the instance count of the calculator service. You can see how the parameter is defined and referenced in the following manifest snippet.

```
<ApplicationManifest …>
    <Parameters>
        <Parameter Name="WebCalculatorService_InstanceCount" DefaultValue="1" />
    </Parameters>
    …
    <DefaultServices>
        <Service Name="WebCalculatorService">
            <StatelessService ServiceTypeName="WebCalculatorServiceType"
InstanceCount="[WebCalculatorService_InstanceCount]">
```

```
        <SingletonPartition />
      </StatelessService>
    </Service>
  </DefaultServices>
</ApplicationManifest>
```

When you publish a Service Fabric application from Visual Studio, you can pick one of the publish profiles (under the PublishProfiles folder), with each profile associated with a different parameter file (under the ApplicationParameters folder). If no parameter files are provided or no matching parameters are found in the parameter file, the default values in the application manifest will be used.

For your service, you can set the parameter in the Cloud.xml file to -1, which means to deploy an instance on every available node, andset the parameter in the Local.xml file to 1, which means you only want one instance when testing locally.

Then, when you publish the application, you can pick the desired profile and parameter file to use, as shown in Figure 2-15.

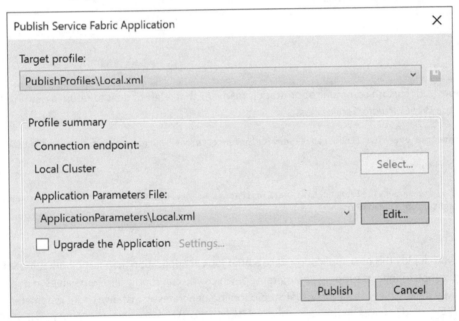

FIGURE 2-15 Publish Service Fabric Application dialog box

Once the application is deployed, you can use a browser to test the methods:

```
http://localhost:80/webapp/api/add?a=1&b=2
http://localhost:80/webapp/api/subtract?a=8&b=3
```

Additional information

We used several technologies besides Service Fabric in this book. To get more information on WCF, please see *https://msdn.microsoft.com/library/ms731082(v=vs.110).aspx*. To get more information on ASP.NET, please see *http://www.asp.net/*. For more information on OWIN, please see *http://owin .org/*.

In January 2016, Microsoft has announced that ASP.NET 5 is going to be replaced by ASP.NET Core 1.0, which is based on the new .NET Core 1.0. ASP.NET Core 1.0 is an entirely new web application stack based on a new .NET core framework. The original ASP.NET stream will continue under ASP.NET 4.6. At the time of this writing, the transition is in process.

CHAPTER 3

Stateful services

As discussed in Chapter 1, "Hello, Service Fabric!," many services have states by nature. However efficient and reliable, state management is a challenge. In this chapter, you'll first review the challenges of state management in a distributed system. Then, you'll learn how Service Fabric solves this problem. And once you understand the theory, you'll move to a number of exercises that walk you through the steps of creating stateful services.

Service Fabric state management

In a distributed environment, especially in a large-scale distributed environment, any messages could get lost, any nodes could fail, and any communication channels could stall at any time. The CAP theorem states that it's impossible to achieve consistency, availability, and partition tolerance at the same time. However, this doesn't mean a system can't achieve a satisfactory level of both consistency and availability. Service Fabric state management uses a combination of strategies to strike a balance between consistency and availability.

Architecture of stateful services

A stateful service uses reliable data structures provided by Service Fabric to store states. These data structures are persisted and replicated automatically by Service Fabric. Figure 3-1 shows the architecture of a stateful Service Fabric service. Similar to a stateless service, a stateful service can take requests from clients via the *ICommunicationListener* interface. When it needs to persist state, it can use one of the reliable collections such as reliable dictionaries and reliable queues, which are persisted by a component called Reliable State Manager. The states are replicated by a Transactional Replicator to secondary replicas for reliability and availability.

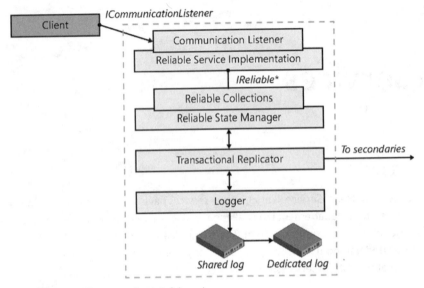

FIGURE 3-1 Architecture of a stateful service

Reliable collections

At the time of this writing, Service Fabric provides two reliable collections: reliable dictionaries and reliable queues. Each of the reliable collections is a state provider. And the state provider exposes an interface that allows you to interact with it as if you are using a local data structure. For instance, *IReliableDictionary* provides an interface that allows you to work with the state provider as if you were using a dictionary.

Service Fabric uses a pluggable architecture that allows additional state providers to be implemented over time.

Reliable State Manager

Reliable State Manager manages lifetimes of state providers. Although your service can access reliable collections as if they were local data structures, it can't directly instantiate a new reliable collection instance. Because the data structure is supposed to be replicated to multiple nodes, structure instances have to be created in a coordinated manner so they are available across multiple nodes.

All stateful services implement from a *StatefulService* or a *StatefulServiceBase* class, which provides an *IReliableStateManager* interface for you to access the state manager. You then can use the state manager to get a reference to a reliable collection, which is identified by a string name. For example, to get a reference to a reliable dictionary named *myDictionary*, use the following code:

```
var myDictionary = await this.StateManager.GetOrAddAsync
<IReliableDictionary<string, long>>("myDictionary");
```

Reliable State Manager also provides transaction supports. All operations in a transaction are atomic, which means all changes are either committed or cancelled together, regardless of the number of operations and data structures involved. The following code snippet shows an example of incrementing a keyed value in a reliable dictionary within a transaction.

```
using (var tx = this.StateManager.CreateTransaction())
{
    var result = await myDictionary.TryGetValueAsync(tx, "Counter-1");
    await myDictionary.AddOrUpdateAsync(tx, "Counter-1", 0, (k, v) => ++v);
    await tx.CommitAsync();
}
```

Transactional Replicator

Transactional Replicator is responsible for replicating reliable collections to secondaries. It also calls a logger to persist states to local disks.

Logger

All service state changes are persisted to local disks by using append-only log files. This allows states to survive process or node crashes. Service Fabric will be able to restore the complete service state by playing back these logs. By default, there are two levels of logs: shared logs and dedicated logs. Shared logs are saved under a node-level working directory for saving transactional data. Dedicated logs are replica-level logs saved under the service working directory. The state information first is saved to the shared log and then is lazily transferred to dedicated logs in the background.

You can configure the logger to optimize performance and throughput under different environments. For instance, if solid-state drives (SSDs) are used, you can configure the logger to skip the shared log and directly write to the dedicated logs because there are no head movement penalties.

Reliable State Manager also takes periodic snapshots of entire service states. This allows change logs to be trimmed to save disk space. During recovery, reliable collections will restore the last known checkpoint, and then the Reliable State Manager will play back all the state change logs since the checkpoint to restore the state fully.

Consistency

Service Fabric state management provides strong consistency guarantees out of box. State changes are handled in transactions, which are considered committed only when all the transactions have been applied to a quorum of replicas, including the primary.

All data writes go through the primary replica. And Service Fabric guarantees that at any time there can be only one primary replica of a partition. Data changes are replicated to secondary replicas. When the primary replica fails, a secondary replica is elected as the new primary. Data can be read from either the primary replica or secondary replicas.

If a service prefers weaker consistency for certain scenarios, it can respond to client requests before the update transaction is committed fully.

The Simple Store application

Now you are ready to write some stateful services! Throughout the rest of this chapter, you'll work on a Simple Store application that allows users to purchase some merchandise. You'll first implement a shopping cart service using Service Fabric stateful service. Then, you'll explore a couple of different partitioning schemes.

Before we continue, however, I need to clarify that the one-cart-per-partition partitioning scheme isn't necessarily a good way to implement shopping carts, especially when you have very sparsely populated partitions. We'll see a better design in Chapter 12, "Web applications." Meanwhile, let's continue with the example for its simplicity.

The shopping cart service

First, you'll work on the shopping cart service. In the following exercise, you'll use a WCF communication stack and a WCF client.

1. Create a new Service Fabric application named SimpleStoreApplication with a stateful service named ShoppingCartService.

2. Add a new class library named Common into the solution. You'll define data models and service contracts in this library. Add a reference to System.ServiceModel.

3. Modify the properties of the Common project to change the target framework to .NET Framework 4.5.1, and the target platform to x64.

4. Add a new class named *ShoppingCartItem* into the Common library. This class defines a structure that describes a line item in a shopping cart:

```
public struct ShoppingCartItem
{
    public string ProductName { get; set; }
    public double UnitPrice { get; set; }
    public int Amount { get; set; }
    public double LineTotal
    {
        get
        {
            return Amount * UnitPrice;
        }
    }
}
```

5. Define the service contract. The contract has only a few methods: an *Add* method to add an item to the shopping cart, a *Delete* method to remove an item from the shopping cart, and a *GetItems* method that lists all items in the cart:

```
[ServiceContract]
public interface IShoppingCartService
{
    [OperationContract]
    Task AddItem(ShoppingCartItem item);
    [OperationContract]
    Task DeleteItem(string productName);
    [OperationContract]
    Task<List<ShoppingCartItem>> GetItems();
}
```

6. Return to the *ShoppingCartService* and add references to the Common project.

7. Add a private method to define the WCF binding just as you did in the WCF communication stack sample:

```
private NetTcpBinding CreateListenBinding()
{
    NetTcpBinding binding = new NetTcpBinding(SecurityMode.None)
    {
        SendTimeout = TimeSpan.MaxValue,
        ReceiveTimeout = TimeSpan.MaxValue,
        OpenTimeout = TimeSpan.FromSeconds(5),
        CloseTimeout = TimeSpan.FromSeconds(5),
        MaxConnections = int.MaxValue,
        MaxReceivedMessageSize = 1024 * 1024
    };
    binding.MaxBufferSize = (int)binding.MaxReceivedMessageSize;
    binding.MaxBufferPoolSize = Environment.ProcessorCount * binding.
MaxReceivedMessageSize;
    return binding;
}
```

8. Similarly, implement the WCF communication stack as before:

```
protected override IEnumerable<ServiceReplicaListener> CreateServiceReplicaListeners()
{
    return new[]
    {
        new ServiceReplicaListener(initParams =>
            new WcfCommunicationListener(initParams, typeof (IShoppingCartService), this)
            {
                EndpointResourceName = "ServiceEndpoint",
                Binding = this.CreateListenBinding()
            })
    };
}
```

9. Now, implement the *IShoppingCartService*, starting with the *AddItem* method:

```
public async Task AddItem(ShoppingCartItem item)
{
    var cart = await this.StateManager.GetOrAddAsync<IReliableDictionary<string,
ShoppingCartItem>>("myCart");
    using (var tx = this.StateManager.CreateTransaction())
    {
        await cart.AddOrUpdateAsync(tx, item.ProductName, item, (k, v) => item);
        await tx.CommitAsync();
    }
}
```

The first line of the method shows how to create a new instance of a reliable collection. Because reliable data collections are data structures shared by multiple service instances across different processes and even different machines, you somehow need to notify Service Fabric that a new instance of such a collection is being created and can be shared across the instances. The *StateManager* provided by the *StatefulServiceBase* class is designed for this. This example uses the *StateManager* to locate or create a reliable dictionary identified by a string name.

The *StateManager* also provides transaction management capabilities. As shown in this example, you can create a transaction with one or more operations on one or more reliable data collections, and Service Fabric guarantees these operations are atomic. All operations are committed by the *CommitAsync* call, or they are rolled back upon exceptions or by an explicit *Abort* call.

10. The *DeleteItem* method follows the same pattern:

```
public async Task DeleteItem(string productName)
{
    var cart = await this.StateManager.GetOrAddAsync<IReliableDictionary<string,
ShoppingCartItem>>("myCart");
    using (var tx = this.StateManager.CreateTransaction())
    {
        var existing = await cart.TryGetValueAsync(tx, productName);
        if (existing.HasValue)
            await cart.TryRemoveAsync(tx, productName);
        await tx.CommitAsync();
    }
}
```

11. The *GetItems* method enumerates the collection and returns the list of items in the shopping cart. Although there are no update operations in this method, a transaction is used so that you can isolate the enumeration from transactions that may get committed during the iteration process. Essentially, the method returns a snapshot of the shopping cart at the beginning of the transaction.

```
public async Task<List<ShoppingCartItem>> GetItems()
{
    var cart = await this.StateManager.GetOrAddAsync<IReliableDictionary<string,
ShoppingCartItem>>("myCart");
```

```
using (var tx = this.StateManager.CreateTransaction())
{
    var ret = from t in cart
                  select t.Value;
    return ret.ToList();
}
}
```

12. Publish the application to your local cluster.

The Simple Store client

Now, you'll move to the client. You'll create a simple WCF-based client that is similar to the earlier WCF client example.

1. Add a new console application named SimpleStoreClient to the solutions.

2. Add a reference to NuGet package *Microsoft.ServiceFabric.Services*.

3. Change the console application's platform target from Any CPU to x64. Also, change the project's target framework to .NET Framework 4.5.1.

4. Add a reference to the Common project.

5. Add a new *Client* class:

```
public class Client:
ServicePartitionClient<WcfCommunicationClient<IShoppingCartService>>,
IShoppingCartService
{
    public Client(WcfCommunicationClientFactory<IShoppingCartService> clientFactory, Uri
serviceName)
            : base(clientFactory, serviceName, 1)
    {
    }

    public Task AddItem(ShoppingCartItem item)
    {
        return this.InvokeWithRetryAsync(client => client.Channel.AddItem(item));
    }

    public Task DeleteItem(string productName)
    {
        return this.InvokeWithRetryAsync(client => client.Channel.
DeleteItem(productName));
    }

    public Task<List<ShoppingCartItem>> GetItems()
    {
        return this.InvokeWithRetryAsync(client => client.Channel.GetItems());
    }
}
```

This code is similar to the earlier WCF client example. One thing worth noticing is that the class constructor calls a different overload of the base class constructor with an additional partition id parameter, which is hard-coded to 1 for now. We'll discuss partitioning after this sample.

6. Modify the *Program* class to add a *CreateClientConnectionBinding* binding just like you did in the earlier example:

```
private static NetTcpBinding CreateClientConnectionBinding()
{
    NetTcpBinding binding = new NetTcpBinding(SecurityMode.None)
    {
        SendTimeout = TimeSpan.MaxValue,
        ReceiveTimeout = TimeSpan.MaxValue,
        OpenTimeout = TimeSpan.FromSeconds(5),
        CloseTimeout = TimeSpan.FromSeconds(5),
        MaxReceivedMessageSize = 1024 * 1024
    };
    binding.MaxBufferSize = (int)binding.MaxReceivedMessageSize;
    binding.MaxBufferPoolSize = Environment.ProcessorCount * binding.MaxReceivedMessageSize;

    return binding;
}
```

7. Modify the *Main* method to add an item to the shopping cart and then read back the cart content:

```
static void Main(string[] args)
{
    Uri ServiceName = new Uri("fabric:/SimpleStoreApplication/ShoppingCartService");
    ServicePartitionResolver serviceResolver = new ServicePartitionResolver(() => new FabricClient());
    NetTcpBinding binding = CreateClientConnectionBinding();
    Client shoppingClient = new Client(new
WcfCommunicationClientFactory<IShoppingCartService>(serviceResolver, binding, null),
            ServiceName);
    shoppingClient.AddItem(new ShoppingCartItem
    {
        ProductName = "XBOX ONE",
        UnitPrice = 329.0,
        Amount = 2
    }).Wait();
    var list = shoppingClient.GetItems().Result;
    foreach(var item in list)
    {
        Console.WriteLine(string.Format("{0}: {1:C2} X {2} = {3:C2}",
            item.ProductName,
            item.UnitPrice,
            item.Amount,
            item.LineTotal));
    }
    Console.ReadKey();
}
```

8. Launch the client, and you should see the following output:

```
XBOX ONE: $329.00 X 2 = $658.00
```

Service partition

As introduced in Chapter 1, a Service Fabric service can be split into multiple partitions for scaling. In the earlier stateless service examples, you used singleton partitions, which are defined in the application manifests:

```
<StatelessService ServiceTypeName="…">
  <SingletonPartition />
</StatelessService>
```

Service Fabric supports two other partition schemes: uniformed 64-bit integer partition (UniformInt64Partition) and named partitions (NamedPartition).

UniformInt64Partition

UniformInt64Partition uniformly distributes a continuous key range to the number of partitions you specify. The following application manifest specifies that you'd like to distribute the key range (defined by *LowKey* and *HighKey*) to 10 partitions (defined by *PartitionCount*).

```
<StatefulService ServiceTypeName="ShoppingCartServiceType" TargetReplicaSetSize="3"
MinReplicaSetSize="3">
  <UniformInt64Partition PartitionCount="10" LowKey="1" HighKey="100" />
</StatefulService>
```

Then, a client can resolve to a particular partition by providing a key in the key range: keys 1 to 10 resolve to the first partition, keys 11 to 20 resolve to the second partition, and so on.

If you open the application manifest of the Simple Store application, you can see by default the partition scheme puts a large key range (Int64.MaxValue – Int64.MinValue) into a single partition. (I've replaced parameter references with numbers for clarity.)

```
<StatefulService ServiceTypeName="ShoppingCartServiceType" TargetReplicaSetSize="3"
MinReplicaSetSize="3">
  <UniformInt64Partition PartitionCount="1" LowKey="-9223372036854775808"
HighKey="9223372036854775807" />
</StatefulService>
```

Recall that in the example above, your *Client* class always passes in 1 as the partition id when it calls the base constructor:

```
public Client(WcfCommunicationClientFactory<IShoppingCartService> clientFactory, Uri
serviceName)
        : base(clientFactory, serviceName, 1)
{
}
```

It wouldn't have mattered if you passed in any 64-bit integer values because all the keys would end up in the same single partition. However, if you increase the partition count, the clients can be distributed among the partitions by different partition keys. If the client doesn't care which partition it talks to, it can generate a random number within the key range, and it will have a uniform chance to be routed to any of the partitions. In reality, a client will use some sort of hashing algorithm to achieve different distributions of keys.

As an exercise, modify your application to use a simple partition scheme that grants one partition to each of the customers.

1. Modify the application manifest of your simple service to have 10 partitions with partition keys ranging from 0 to 9. In other words, your service is designed to support 10 customers in this case. Each customer is identified by a customer id from 0 to 9, and each customer will have his own partition. Having a large number of partitions might not always be desirable, especially when the partition range is sparsely populated (because of a low customer number). However, because you can't change the number of partitions or the type of partitioning scheme for a running service, you need to define enough partitions so that you can scale out the service when needed. For example, if you have 1,000 partitions and your cluster has 10 nodes, each node will get 100 partitions. If the workload turns out to be too much a burden for each of the nodes, you can scale the cluster to have 100 nodes, which brings down the partition number on each node to 10. However, if you begin with only 10 partitions, increasing cluster size doesn't help you because the additional nodes can't be leveraged.

```
<Service Name="ShoppingCartService">
    <StatefulService ServiceTypeName="ShoppingCartServiceType" TargetReplicaSetSize="3"
MinReplicaSetSize="2">
        <UniformInt64Partition PartitionCount="10" LowKey="0" HighKey="9" />
    </StatefulService>
</Service>
```

> ### Local environment constrains
>
> Don't define too many partitions when you use your local environment. With default logging configurations, this can put too much burden on your disks. If you deployed a large number of partitions by mistake, you will need to reset you cluster to restore your machine to a working state. Refer to Chapter 9, "Managing Service Fabric with management portal," and Chapter 10, "Diagnostics and monitoring," for more details on diagnostics and cluster management using PowerShell.

2. In the SimpleStoreClient project, modify the client constructor to take in and use a customer id (from 0 to 9) as the partition key.

```
public Client(WcfCommunicationClientFactory<IShoppingCartService> clientFactory, Uri
serviceName, long customerId)
        : base(clientFactory, serviceName, customerId)
```

```
{
}
```

3. In the same project, add a new static method to the *Program* class:

```
private static void PrintPartition(Client client)
{
    ResolvedServicePartition partition;
    if (client.TryGetLastResolvedServicePartition(out partition))
    {
        Console.WriteLine("Partition ID: " + partition.Info.Id);
    }
}
```

This method retrieves the information of the last resolved partition. You'll use this method to display resolved partition ids to examine the partitions the client talks to.

4. Modify the *Main* method to call the service with different customer ids:

```
for (int i = 0; i < 10; i++)
{
Client shoppingClient = new Client(new WcfCommunicationClientFactory<IShoppingCartServi
ce>
(serviceResolver, binding, null),
            ServiceName, i);
    shoppingClient.AddItem(new ShoppingCartItem
    {
        ProductName = "XBOX ONE (" + i.ToString() + ")",
        UnitPrice = 329.0,
        Amount = 2
    }).Wait();
    shoppingClient.AddItem(new ShoppingCartItem
    {
        ProductName = "Halo 5 (" + i.ToString() + ")",
        UnitPrice = 59.99,
        Amount = 1
    }).Wait();
    PrintPartition(shoppingClient);
    var list = shoppingClient.GetItems().Result;
    foreach (var item in list)
    {
        Console.WriteLine(string.Format("{0}: {1:C2} X {2} = {3:C2}",
            item.ProductName,
            item.UnitPrice,
            item.Amount,
            item.LineTotal));
    }
}
```

5. The preceding code generates the following output (partially shown) in Figure 3-2. You can see each customer is routed to her own partition based on her customer id.

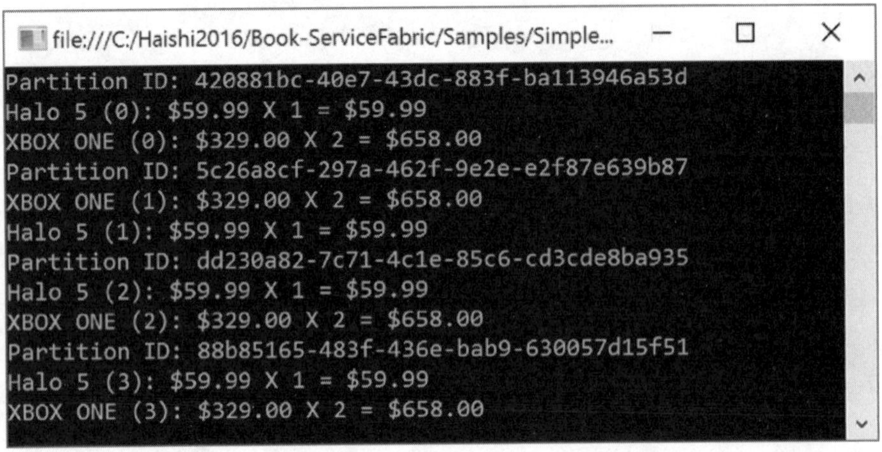

FIGURE 3-2 Output of modified Simple Store client

In Chapter 12, you'll see a different shopping cart design using the Actor pattern.

NamedPartition

You also can define partitions explicitly by using named partitions. In some scenarios, the number of partitions is known in advance and remains static over time. For example, a service partitioned by the individual states in the United States will have stable partitions over time.

As an exercise, modify your service to use named partitions.

1. Modify the application manifest to define three customer partitions. In a real-life scenario, you'd never want to define customer partitions explicitly for each of the customers. This exercise is intended only to familiarize you with the named partition syntax.

```
<Service Name="ShoppingCartService">
    <StatefulService ServiceTypeName="ShoppingCartServiceType" TargetReplicaSetSize="3"
                    MinReplicaSetSize="2">
      <NamedPartition>
          <Partition Name="Customer 1" />
          <Partition Name="Customer 2" />
          <Partition Name="Customer 3" />
      </NamedPartition>
    </StatefulService>
</Service>
```

2. In the SimpleStoreClient project, modify the client constructor to use a different overload that takes a string partition key:

```
public Client(WcfCommunicationClientFactory<IShoppingCartService> clientFactory,
                    Uri serviceName, string customerId)
      : base(clientFactory, serviceName, customerId)
{
}
```

3. In the *Program* class, modify the loop to test Customer 1, 2, and 3. Note how a string partition name is used in this case.

```
for (int i = 1; i <= 3; i++)
{
    Client shoppingClient = new Client(new WcfCommunicationClientFactory<IShoppingCartSe
rvice>
        (serviceResolver, binding, null),
        ServiceName, "Customer " + i);
...
```

4. Deploy the service and run the test client. You should see output similar to what you've seen previously.

Partitions and replicas

Now that you have seen partitions in action, take a closer look at partitions and replicas.

Replica roles

At any given time, a service replica can be in one of the following roles (or states): Primary, Active Secondary, Idle Secondary, or None. Logically, there's also an Unknown state, which is a temporary null state when the replica is being created. A replica never transits back to the Unknown state once initiated.

Replicas of a partition form a replica set. All replicas in the set assume one of the following roles:

- **Primary**   The main replica through which all writes go. Each replica set has at most one primary at a time. A write operation needs to be acknowledged by a quorum of the replicas in the set before it's considered done. For interested readers who want to understand the underlying Paxos algorithm, refer to The "Part-Time Parliament" paper.[1]

- **Active Secondary**   Participates in the write quorum for a replica set. There can be multiple secondaries in a replica set. When a write is applied, active secondaries participating in the write quorum need to take and update the state from the primary and acknowledge the write operation.

- **Idle Secondary**   Receives all state updates from the primary and is ready to become an active secondary. An idle secondary doesn't participate in the write quorum.

- **None**   Represents a replica that is being decommissioned from a replica set. A none replica doesn't hold any state.

Figure 3-3 illustrates how a replica transits among different roles (states).

---

[1] Lamport, Leslie. "The Part-Time Parliament." *ACM Transactions on Computer Systems* 16, 2 (1998): 133-169

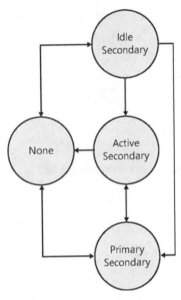

FIGURE 3-3 Replica state transitions

To examine the replica states, you can use the Service Fabric Explorer. In the tree view, expanding a partition reveals its replicas and their roles, as shown in Figure 3-4.

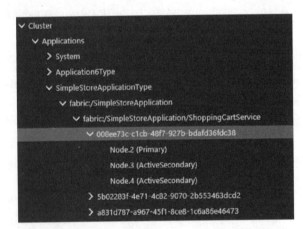

FIGURE 3-4 Partitions and replicas

If you click each of the replicas, you'll see that only the primary replica is bound to a listening address, indicating all reads and writes are going through the primary replica, as shown in Figure 3-5.

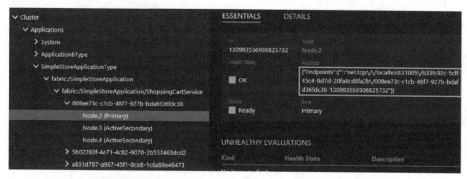

FIGURE 3-5 Essentials of a primary replica

Scaling

Replicas can be moved among nodes when needed. This feature allows Service Fabric to provide failovers and scaling by relocating replicas. When a node fails, Service Fabric can move the replicas to a healthy node to keep service continuity. When more nodes become available on the cluster, Service Fabric can redistribute the replicas among all available nodes to share the workload.

To illustrate the scaling process, assume we have four partitions with three replicas each. These replicas are distributed across three nodes, as shown in Figure 3-6.

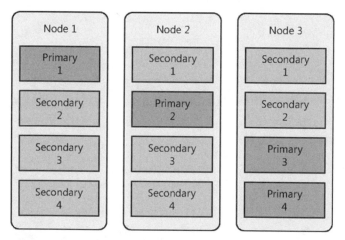

FIGURE 3-6 Replica distribution on a three-node cluster

Assume another node is added to the cluster. Service Fabric keeps getting load information from all nodes on the cluster. When it detects an additional node is available to take on more workload, it will try to relocate replicas to even out workload on all the nodes. (Chapter 6, "Availability and reliability," and Chapter 7, "Scalability and performance," provide more detail about this mechanism.) Figure 3-7 illustrates the result of such redistribution. In this case, a Node 4 is added to the cluster, and a couple of replicas have been moved to the new Node 4 to even out the workload on the nodes.

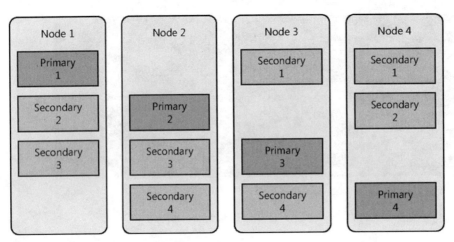

FIGURE 3-7 Replica distribution on a four-node cluster

Additional information

If you are interested in Paxos, in addition to the referenced book you can read the "Paxos Made Simple" paper from Leslie Lamport here: *http://research.microsoft.com/en-us/um/people/lamport/pubs/paxos -simple.pdf.*

CHAPTER 4

Actor pattern

As we've learned from object-oriented programming (OOP) in the past 65 years or so, many problems can be modeled as interacting objects that assume some sort of behavior and hold some sort of states. The Actor model[1] further specified that many problems can be modeled as independent agents that interact with each other by messaging.

The Actor pattern (also known as the Actor architecture or the Actor model) provides a powerful tool to abstract complex distributed systems in which a large number of individual agents work together without necessarily needing any central governance. Agents are self-sufficient to make local decisions based on the messages they receive and their own states, making them adaptable to a variety of heterogeneous environments. Because agents can be evolved, migrated, replaced, or destroyed without breaking other agents, such systems often demonstrate impressive robustness, adaptiveness, and concurrency.

The easiest way to visualize the Actor pattern at work is to look at human society. Each human (agent) is an independent entity. We all hold our own attributes, and we make decisions based on our knowledge (state and behavior) and in reaction to the surrounding stipulates (messages). We communicate with (send messages to) each other. And collectively we form a vibrant, dynamic society.

Similarly, if a system can be described by a number of independent, interactive actors, it can be modeled using the Actor pattern. For example, in a multiplayer game, each player can be considered as an actor; in an e-commerce system, each shopping cart can be considered as an actor; in an Internet of Things (IoT) scenario, a sensor can be considered as an actor. A player, a shopping cart, and a sensor don't seem to have anything in common, yet because they all have states, they all demonstrate some behaviors, and they all represent independent entities, they can be abstracted as actors.

Modeling complex systems

In human society, there are no central entities that dictate our actions. There are governments and laws, but no one tells you your course of the action, move by move, during a day. Instead, we formulate our behaviors ourselves based on our learnings and observations. And what's more fascinating is that although we make decisions locally, some social phenomena emerge

---

[1] Hewitt, Carl, Peter Bishop, and Richard Steiger. "A Universal Modular ACTOR Formalism for Artificial Intelligence ," IJCAI. (1973): 235-245.

without centralized coordination. Modeling complex systems[2] such as our society is the topic of Chapter 18, "Modeling Complex Systems." It's important to realize that a cloud-scale Actor pattern framework like Azure Service Fabric is a revolutionary addition to the toolset.

Service Fabric Reliable Actors

Service Fabric Reliable Actors API provides an asynchronous, single-threaded programming model using actors. This programming model enables you to implement actors as if you were writing a singleton, single-threaded implementation. Service Fabric will take care of the rest—life cycles, failovers, scales, upgrades, and so on.

Actors

An actor is an independent single-threaded component that encapsulates certain states and behaviors. You can understand an actor type as a class in OOP. Out of each actor type you can create any number of actor instances, which is analog to instantiating a class in OOP. Each actor instance is identified by a unique actor id, which is used for clients or other actors to address the actor.

An actor can have state. An actor with state is called a stateful actor, and an actor without state is called a stateless actor. The state is managed by an actor state provider, which can save the state in memory, on disk, or in external storage.

When using Service Fabric, to implement an actor means to derive from a *StatelessActor* base class (for stateless actors) or *StatefulActor<T>* base class (for stateful actors) and implement your own actor behavior interface, which inherits from an empty *IActor* interface. We'll see examples of both later in this chapter.

Actor lifetime

Actors are virtual, which means logically they always exist. You don't need to create or destroy an actor. When you need to talk to an actor, you just use the actor proxy to send a message to it, Service Fabric will activate the actor if it hasn't been activated or if it has been deactivated. After an actor hasn't been used for a while, Service Fabric automatically will deactivate the actor to reduce resource consumption.

Service Fabric invokes several different callbacks upon certain events. When an actor is activated (which means the corresponding .NET object is loaded into memory), an *OnActiveAsync()* method will be called. And when an actor is deactivated (which means the actor is being garbage collected), an *OnDeactiveAsync()* method will be called.

---

[2] Boccara, Nino, *Modeling Complex Systems, Second Edition*. New York: Springer, 2010

Actor states

A stateful actor inherits from the *StatefulActor<T>* generic class, where *T* is the state type. The state type is a serializable data contract (Service Fabric Actor pattern uses System.Runtime.Serialization. DataContractSerializer for state data serialization). A stateful actor should initialize its state in the *OnActiveAsync()* method. For example:

```
public override Task OnActivateAsync()
{
    if (this.State == null)
    {
        this.State = new Actor1State() { Count = 0 };
    }
}
```

Note that you don't need to place locks on the State property because Service Fabric guarantees only one method on an actor is called at any given time. See the "Concurrency" section below for more details.

Updating the state is done by simple assignments. For example:

```
this.State.Count = count;
```

Again, because only one method is called at a time and actor state is local to an actor instance, there's no need for locks and transactions.

Actor communications

Actors communicate with each other by sending messages. To simplify the programming model, Service Fabric provides an actor proxy, which allows you to send messages to actors as if you were invoking methods defined by these actors. You can use the proxy for both client-to-actor communications and actor-to-actor communications. For example:

```
var proxy = ActorProxy.Create<IActor1>(ActorId.NewId(), "fabric:/Application29");
proxy.SetCountAsync(10).Wait();
```

An actor instance might get migrated. For instance, when a node fails, actor instances on the node will be migrated to a healthy node. The actor proxy hides the physical actor locations and allows clients to address an actor by its id. The proxy also has built-in retry logic to handle transient errors so your client code doesn't need to handle the complexity. However, this means a message may get sent to an actor multiple times when the actor fails to acknowledge reception of earlier copies.

Concurrency

Actors provide a turn-based concurrency mode in which an actor-level lock is used to allow a single method call on an actor at any time. This concurrency mode allows developers to write actor code as a single-threaded component. This concurrency is reinforced for all actor method calls from clients and other actors and for timer callbacks and reminder callbacks, which I'll cover in a moment. When a method is executing, new requests will wait asynchronously for the lock until they can acquire the actor-level lock.

The actor-level lock is released only when the running method returns and the returned Task completes. However, there's nothing to stop you from using additional threads and asynchronous methods in your code. In such cases, the turn-based concurrency is not reinforced.

If a method doesn't modify the state, you can mark the method with a *ReadOnly* property. When a method is marked as read-only, the state update logic is skipped, providing faster performance. However, a read-only method still is under the governance of the turn-based concurrency.

Actors allow reentry by default. So, if Actor A calls a method of Actor B, which in turn calls another method of Actor A, the call is allowed because it is a single logical call chain context. Timer callbacks and reminder callbacks always start a new call context. So, in the previous case, as Actor A is calling Actor B, if a Timer callback arrives, it will need to wait for the actor-level lock because it is in a different call context.

If you want to disable reentrancy on an actor, you can annotate the actor with a *Reeentrant* attribute:

```
[Reentrant(ReentrancyMode.Disallowed)]
public class Actor1 : Actor<Actor1State>, IActor1
...
```

Note that actors are concurrent by nature. The turn-based concurrency only applies to a single actor instance. Multiple actor instances can run in parallel in the same host.

An actor-based tic-tac-toe game

Now, let's use the Actor pattern to build a simple two-player tic-tac-toe game.

Actor models

What are the actors in this system? Even for such a simple application, there could be multiple ways to define the actor models. One straightforward way to design the actors is to use a player actor type and a game actor type. The player actor represents a player, and the game actor represents a game session, with the game board as its state.

For any online games, an important design consideration is eliminating ways to cheat. For a tic-tac-toe game, it's important to make sure that two players are indeed taking turns to make moves. To ensure this, the game actor will hold an attribute that indicates which player has the next turn. Even if a player tries to cheat by making multiple moves, the requests won't be handled unless the player holds the current turn.

For simplicity, I'll use a single Console application as the test client. However, in the client I'll use two separate threads to simulate two players trying to make plays at the same time—in other words, they both are trying to cheat. The system ensures the game progresses in an orderly fashion.

Create the application

First, create all the skeleton classes. Then, implement the actors in the system.

1. Create a new Service Fabric Application named *ActorTicTacToeApplication* with a Stateless Actor Service named *Player*.

2. Once the application is created, right-click the *ActorTicTacToeApplication* project and select the New Fabric Service menu.

3. Add another Stateful Actor Service named *Game*.

4. Add a new console application named *TestClient* to the solution. Change the target framework to .NET Framework 4.5.1 and platform target to x64.

5. In the *TestClient* project, add a reference to the *Game.Interfaces* assembly and the *Player. Interfaces* assembly.

6. Add a reference to the Microsoft.ServiceFabric.Actors NuGet package.

Define actor interfaces

The Player actor is implemented as a stateless actor. It has a simple interface with only two methods: to join a game and to make a move. The Game actor has a more complex interface, which allows players to join and to make moves and returns board state and the winner.

1. Modify the *IPlayer* interface in the Player.Interfaces project:

    ```
    public interface IPlayer : IActor
    {
        Task<bool> JoinGameAsync(ActorId gameId, string playerName);
        Task<bool> MakeMoveAsync(ActorId gameId, int x, int y);
    }
    ```

2. Modify the *IGame* interface in the Game.Interfaces project:

    ```
    public interface IGame : IActor
    {
        Task<bool> JoinGameAsync(long playerId, string playerName);
        Task<int[]> GetGameBoardAsync();
        Task<string> GetWinnerAsync();
        Task<bool> MakeMoveAsync(long playerId, int x, int y);
    }
    ```

Implement the Game actor

In this part, we'll focus on the Game actor. We'll define the game state, and then we'll implement the *IGame* interface.

1. Modify the *ActorState* class in the Game project:

```
[DataContract]
public class ActorState

{
    [DataMember]
    public int[] Board;
    [DataMember]
    public string Winner;
    [DataMember]
    public List<Tuple<long,string>> Players;
    [DataMember]
    public int NextPlayerIndex;
    [DataMember]
    public int NumberOfMoves;
}
```

The game board (the Board property) is presented as a nine-member byte array. Each item in the array can be 0 (empty), -1 (player 1 piece), or 1 (player 2 piece). The Winner property holds the name of the game winner. When the game is in progress, the value is empty. When a player wins, this property is set to the name of the winner. If the game is a tie, it's set to "TIE." The Players property holds the list of players. The NextPlayerIndex indicates which player has the next turn. Finally, the NumberOfMoves tracks how many pieces have been put on the board. This helps us tell if the game board has been filled.

2. Modify the *OnActivateAsync()* method to initialize the state when the actor is activated:

```
public override Task OnActivateAsync()
{
    if (this.State == null)
    {
        this.State = new ActorState()
        {
            Board = new int[9],
            Winner = "",
            Players = new List<Tuple<long,string>>(),
            NextPlayerIndex = 0,
            NumberOfMoves = 0
        };
    }
    return Task.FromResult(true);
}
```

3. Implement the *JoinGameAsync()* method. The method allows only two players with unique names to join. Although there could be multiple clients trying to join the game at the same time, we don't need to place any locks on the players list because the turn-based concurrency mechanism ensures this method is invoked by only one caller at a time.

```
public Task<bool> JoinGameAsync(long playerId, string playerName)
{
    if (this.State.Players.Count >= 2
        || this.State.Players.FirstOrDefault(p => p.Item2 == playerName) != null)
        return Task.FromResult<bool>(false);
    this.State.Players.Add(new Tuple<long, string>(playerId, playerName));
    return Task.FromResult<bool>(true);
}
```

4. The state getter methods are easy to implement, as shown below. Note how both methods are annotated with the *ReadOnly* attribute:

```
[Readonly]
public Task<int[]> GetGameBoardAsync()
{
    return Task.FromResult<int[]>(this.State.Board);
}
[Readonly]
public Task<string> GetWinnerAsync()
{
    return Task.FromResult<string>(this.State.Winner);
}
```

5. The *MakeMoveAsync()* method is the core of the game engine. First, it checks if the move is valid, which means the move is made by the player who has the current turn, is placed on an empty place on the board, and is played before the game is over. Then, it updates the board and decides who the winner is. If the game continues, it flips the next player index to indicate who will have the next turn. Again, because of the turn-based concurrency control, we implement the logic without worrying about concurrency issues.

```
public Task<bool> MakeMoveAsync(long playerId, int x, int y)
{
    if (x < 0 || x > 2 || y < 0 || y > 2
        || this.State.Players.Count != 2
        || this.State.NumberOfMoves >= 9
        || this.State.Winner != "")
        return Task.FromResult<bool>(false);

    int index = this.State.Players.FindIndex(p => p.Item1 == playerId);
    if (index == this.State.NextPlayerIndex)
    {
        if (this.State.Board[y * 3 + x] == 0)
        {
            int piece = index * 2 - 1;
            this.State.Board[y * 3 + x] = piece;
            this.State.NumberOfMoves++;

            if (HasWon(piece * 3))
                this.State.Winner = this.State.Players[index].Item2 + " (" +
                                    (piece == -1 ? "X" : "O") + ")";
            else if (this.State.Winner == "" && this.State.NumberOfMoves >= 9)

                this.State.Winner = "TIE";
```

```
                    this.State.NextPlayerIndex = (this.State.NextPlayerIndex + 1) % 2;
                    return Task.FromResult<bool>(true);
                }
                else
                    return Task.FromResult<bool>(false);
            }
            else
                return Task.FromResult<bool>(false);
        }
```

6. The *HasWon()* method is a simple implementation with O(1) complexity to check if a line has been made across the board horizontally, vertically, or diagonally:

```
private bool HasWon(int sum)
{
    return this.State.Board[0] + this.State.Board[1] + this.State.Board[2] == sum
        || this.State.Board[3] + this.State.Board[4] + this.State.Board[5] == sum
        || this.State.Board[6] + this.State.Board[7] + this.State.Board[8] == sum
        || this.State.Board[0] + this.State.Board[3] + this.State.Board[6] == sum
        || this.State.Board[1] + this.State.Board[4] + this.State.Board[7] == sum
        || this.State.Board[2] + this.State.Board[5] + this.State.Board[8] == sum
        || this.State.Board[0] + this.State.Board[4] + this.State.Board[8] == sum
        || this.State.Board[2] + this.State.Board[4] + this.State.Board[6] == sum;
}
```

Implement the Player actor

The Player implementation is simple. The methods call the corresponding methods on the Game actor. The implementation shows that an actor uses the same actor proxy to communicate with other actors. Note that you need to add a reference to the *Game.Interfaces* assembly.

```
public Task<bool> JoinGameAsync(ActorId gameId, string playerName)
{
    var game = ActorProxy.Create<IGame>(gameId, "fabric:/ActorTicTacToeApplication");
    return game.JoinGameAsync(this.Id.GetLongId(), playerName);
}

public Task<bool> MakeMoveAsync(ActorId gameId, int x, int y)
{
    var game = ActorProxy.Create<IGame>(gameId, "fabric:/ActorTicTacToeApplication");
    return game.MakeMoveAsync(this.Id.GetLongId(), x, y);
}
```

Implement the test client

Now, let's move to the TestClient project. To demonstrate the turn-based concurrency, I'll launch two concurrent player actors. Neither player waits for turns. They just make random moves. However, the turn-based concurrency and our player turn logic ensure that they can play together nicely.

1. Implement the *Main()* method. The method starts three parallel tasks: two player tasks for both players to place their moves and a game task to refresh and display the game board.

```
public static void Main(string[] args)
{
    var player1 = ActorProxy.Create<IPlayer>(ActorId.NewId(),
        "fabric:/ActorTicTacToeApplication");
    var player2 = ActorProxy.Create<IPlayer>(ActorId.NewId(),
        "fabric:/ActorTicTacToeApplication");
    var gameId = ActorId.NewId();
    var game = ActorProxy.Create<IGame>(gameId, "fabric:/ActorTicTacToeApplication");
    var rand = new Random();

    var result1 = player1.JoinGameAsync(gameId, "Player 1");
    var result2 = player2.JoinGameAsync(gameId, "Player 2");

    if (!result1.Result || !result2.Result)
    {
        Console.WriteLine("Failed to join game.");
        return;
    }
    var player1Task = Task.Run(() =>{ MakeMove(player1, game, gameId);});
    var player2Task = Task.Run(() => { MakeMove(player2, game, gameId); });
    var gameTask = Task.Run(() =>
    {
        string winner = "";
        while (winner == "")
        {
            var board = game.GetGameBoardAsync().Result;
            PrintBoard(board);
            winner = game.GetWinnerAsync().Result;
            Task.Delay(1000).Wait();
        }

        Console.WriteLine("Winner is: " + winner);
    });

    gameTask.Wait();
    Console.Read();
}
```

2. The *MakeMove()* method is used for a player to make random moves. The player "thinks" for a random number of seconds between moves, and it keeps playing forever.

```
private static async void MakeMove(IPlayer player,IGame game, ActorId gameId)
{
    Random rand = new Random();
    while (true)
    {
        await player.MakeMoveAsync(gameId, rand.Next(0, 3), rand.Next(0, 3));
        await Task.Delay(rand.Next(500, 2000));
    }
}
```

3. Finally, the *PrintBoard()* method prints out the board:

```
private static void PrintBoard(int[] board)
{
    Console.Clear();
```

```
for (int i = 0; i < board.Length;i++)
{
    if (board[i] == -1)
        Console.Write(" X ");
    else if (board[i] == 1)
        Console.Write(" O ");
    else
        Console.Write(" . ");
    if ((i+1) % 3 == 0)
        Console.WriteLine();
}
}
```

Test it

Deploy the application and then launch the test client. If everything works, you should be able to observe a simulated game session, as shown in Figure 4-1.

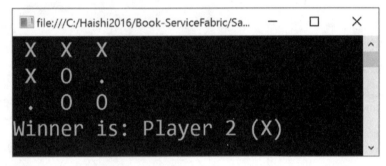

FIGURE 4-1 Simulated game session

Additional thoughts

There are several ways the game can be improved. The following are exercises for interested readers:

- **User interactions**   The preceding implementation isn't really a game, and you can't play the game yourself. It's easy to adapt the program into a real game. Just take user inputs instead of generating random moves automatically.

- **A smarter player**   The current player implementation just makes random moves. However, it's easy to write a player that makes smart moves. In fact, tic-tac-toe is one of the few board games for which you can enumerate all possible moves and come up with a player implementation that will never lose. Of course, that will annoy your customers because they can never defeat the game. So, once in a while, you might want the player to make a random move to give its opponent a chance.

- **Avoid invalid moves**   Currently, the players make random moves without checking the board. As the game progresses, the chances of making an invalid move increase as the board is filled.

This is why as you observe the game, the pace slows down toward the end. As an improvement, you can have the players check the board before making their next move to reduce invalid moves.

Timers, reminders, and events

An actor encapsulates behaviors and states. Some of these behaviors are reactive, and other behaviors are self-motivated. For example, an actor who represents a car might have several reactive behaviors that respond to driver inputs, such as turning, accelerating, and breaking. However, it keeps moving in the current direction at the current speed until it receives new commands from the driver. In this case, the actor needs to be able to update its own state at certain rate, which can be done by a timer or a reminder.

Actor timers

An Actor timer is a wrapper around a .NET timer that honors the turn-based concurrency. To use a timer, first declare an *IActorTimer* local variable:

```
IActorTimer mTimer;
```

Then, you can use the *RegisterTimer()* method on the base class to register a new timer. This usually is done in the *OnActiveAsync()* method:

```
public override Task OnActivateAsync()
{
    ...
    mTimer = RegisterTimer(Move, //callback function
        someObject, //callback state
        TimeSpan.FromSeconds(5), //delay before first callback
        TimeSpan.FromSeconds(1)); //callback interval
}
```

The callback method is a simple method that returns a Task:

```
private Task Move(Object state)
{
    ...
    return Task.FromResult(1);
}
```

You can unregister the timer by using the *UnRegisterTimer()* method. For example:

```
public override Task OnDeactivateAsync()
{
    if (mTimer != null)
        UnregisterTimer(mTimer);
    return base.OnDeactivateAsync();
}
```

Because the Actor timer follows the turn-based concurrency, there's only one callback called at a time. This means the timer is stopped while the callback is executing and is restarted when the callback has completed.

If an actor is a stateful actor, the Service Fabric runtime automatically saves the state when the timer callback completes. However, if the saving operation fails, the actor instance will be deactivated and a new instance will be activated. If your callback doesn't modify the state, you can mark the callback method as *ReadOnly* to skip the state-saving stage.

Another thing to notice is that if an actor doesn't get external function calls, it will be deactivated and garbage collected after a period of time. In other words, timer callbacks don't keep the actor alive. It's your code's responsibility to register the timer again when the actor is reactivated.

Actor reminders

Actor reminders provide another triggering mechanism to invoke callbacks at certain intervals. The main difference between Actor reminders and Actor timers is that the Actor reminder callbacks always are triggered under all circumstances until they are explicitly unregistered. Even if an actor has been deactivated, an Actor reminder callback will reactivate the actor.

Only stateful actors support reminders.

To register a reminder, use the *RegisterReminder()* method on the base class. For example, the following code snippet registers a reminder that triggers every 15 days to pay a bill of $1,700 (US).

```
string task = "Pay bill";
int amountInDollars = 1700;
Task<IActorReminder> reminder = RegisterReminder(
    task, //reminder name
    BitConverter.GetBytes(amountInDollars), //callback state
    TimeSpan.FromDays(3), //delay before the first callback
    TimeSpan.FromDays(15), //callback interval
    ActorReminderAttributes.None); //callback flag - if the method is ReadOnly.
```

An actor that uses reminders needs to implement an *IRemindable* interface, which defines a single *ReceiveReminderAsync()* method. For example, to handle the above reminder, implement the *ReceiveReminderAsync()* method as follows:

```
public Task ReceiveReminderAsync(string reminderName, byte[] context, TimeSpan dueTime, TimeSpan
period)
{
    if (reminderName.Equals("Pay bill"))
    {
        int amountToPay = BitConverter.ToInt32(context, 0);
        System.Console.WriteLine("Please pay your bill of ${0}!", amountToPay);
    }
    return Task.FromResult(true);
}
```

If your actor registers multiple reminders, the preceding method is called whenever any of the reminders is due. Your code is supposed to check the reminder name to decide which type of reminder messages are received.

If your reminder callback doesn't change the actor state, you can use the *ActorReminderAttributes. ReadOnly* attribute to mark the callback as read-only when you register the reminder. This differs from timers, for which the callback methods themselves are marked as read-only.

To unregister a reminder, first use the *GetReminder()* method on the base class to get a reference to the reminder registration, then use the *UnregisterReminder()* method to unregister the reminder:

```
IActorReminder reminder = GetReminder("Pay bill");
Task reminderUnregistration = UnregisterReminder(reminder);
```

Actor events

Service Fabric also allows actors to send best effort notifications back to clients by using events. This mechanism is designed for actor-client communications only and is not supposed to be used for actor-actor communications.

To use actor events, first you need to define an event interface that inherits from the *IActorEvents* interface. All methods on the interface have to return void, and all parameters have to be data contract serializable. For example, the following actor event interface defines an event that a new challenger has joined the game:

```
public interface IGameEvents : IActorEvents
{
    void NewChallengerHasArrived(string playerName);
}
```

The actor who publishes events needs to implement an *IActorEventPublisher<T>* interface. For example:

```
public interface IGameActor : IActor, IActorEventPublisher<IGameEvents>
{
    ...
}
```

On the client side, to handle an actor event, you need to declare an event handler:

```
class GameEventsHandler : IGameEvents
{
    public void NewChallengerHasArrived(string playerName)
    {
        Console.WriteLine(@"A New Challenger Has Arrived: {1}", playerName);
    }
}
```

Then, you can use the actor proxy to register the handler:

```
var proxy = ActorProxy.Create<IGameActor>(actorId, serviceUri);
proxy.SubscribeAsync(new GameEventsHandler()).Wait();
```

When an actor is failed over to a different node, the actor proxy is smart enough to resubscribe the events. The *SubscribeAsync()* method takes a second parameter, which is the timespan that controls the interval of resubscription attempts.

To unsubscribe an event, use the *UnsubscribeAsync()* method on the actor proxy.

Finally, to trigger an event, an actor needs to use the *GetEvent<T>()* method to get the event and then trigger events by calling methods on the event interface:

```
var evt = GetEvent<IGameEvents>();
evt.NewChallengerHasArrived(State.PlayerName);
```

Actor internals

Service Fabric Actors removes lots of details and provides a simple programming model for developers. However, it's worth digging into some of the details behind the scenes, which will help you understand what choices you have, what limitations you need to recognize, and what pitfalls you need to avoid.

Actor diagnostics and performance monitoring

EventSource events and performance counters are two ways to troubleshoot and monitor Service Fabric Actors.

EventSource keywords

The name of the EventSource for Service Fabric Actors is Microsoft-ServiceFabric-Actors, under which are a number of keywords with which all events are associated. You can use these keywords to filter events to focus on different problem areas. The keyword bits are defined in Table 4-1.

TABLE 4-1 Service Fabric EventSource keywords

Bit	Description
0x1	Events related to Fabric Actors runtime.
0x2	Events related to actor method calls.
0x4	Events related to actor state.
0x8	Events related to turn-based concurrency.

Actor method events   The events in Table 4-2 are related to actor method calls.

TABLE 4-2 Actor method events

Event Name	Event Id	Level	Keywords	Description
ActorMethodStart	7	Verbose	0x2	An actor method is about to be called.
ActorMethodStop	8	Verbose	0x2	An actor method has completed executing, which means the method has returned and the returned Task has been completed.
ActorMethodThrewException	9	Warning	0x3	An exception has been thrown by the actor method itself or by the returned Task.

Concurrent events The events in Table 4-3 are related to concurrency.

TABLE 4-3 Concurrency events

Event Name	Event Id	Level	Keywords	Description
ActorMethodCallsWaitingForLock	12	Verbose	0x8	This event is logged whenever a new turn in an actor starts. The number records how many method calls are pending to acquire the actor-level lock.

State management events The events in Table 4-4 are related to state management.

TABLE 4-4 State management events

Event Name	Event Id	Level	Keywords	Description
ActorSaveStateStart	10	Verbose	0x4	The actor runtime is about to save actor state.
ActorSaveStateStop	11	Verbose	0x4	The actor runtime has finished saving actor state.

Stateless actor events The events in Table 4-5 are related to stateless actors.

TABLE 4-5 Stateless actor events

Event Name	Event Id	Level	Keywords	Description
ServiceInstanceOpen	3	Informational	0x1	The service instance is open for new actor instances to be created on it.
ServiceInstanceClose	4	Informational	0x1	The service instance doesn't allow new actor instances to be created. Existing actor will be destroyed once the in-progress requests are completed.

Stateful actor replica events The events in Table 4-6 are related to stateful actor replicas.

TABLE 4-6 Stateful actor replica events

Event Name	Event Id	Level	Keywords	Description
ReplicaChangeRoleToPrimary	1	Informational	0x1	A replica became primary. Actors for the partition will be created inside this replica.
ReplicaChangeRoleFromPrimary	2	Informational	0x1	A replica no longer is primary. No new actor instances will be created in this replica. Existing actor instances will be destroyed once the in-progress requests are completed.

With Visual Studio, you can view EventSource events in the Diagnostic Events Viewer, as shown in Figure 4-2.

FIGURE 4-2 Diagnostic Events viewer

When the actors are hosted on Azure, these events also can be routed to Azure Application Insights, which will be covered in more detail in Chapter 10, "Diagnostics and monitoring."

Performance counters

Service Fabric Actors runtime defines a couple of performance counter categories for Service Fabric Actors, as listed in Table 4-7.

TABLE 4-7 Service Fabric Actors runtime performance counter categories

Category name	Description
Service Fabric Actor	Events related to Service Fabric Actors
Service Fabric Actor Method	Events specific to Service Fabric Actor methods

The following performance counters are defined.

Service Fabric Actor Method performance counters The performance counters listed in Table 4-8 are related to actor method invocations.

TABLE 4-8 Service Fabric Actor Method performance counters

Category name	Counter name	Description
Service Fabric Actor Method	Invocations/Sec	Number of actor method calls per second
Service Fabric Actor Method	Average milliseconds per invocation	Average method execution time in milliseconds
Service Fabric Actor Method	Exceptions thrown/Sec	Number of exceptions thrown per second

Service Fabric Actor performance counters   The performance counters listed in Table 4-9 are related to concurrency and state management.

TABLE 4-9   Service Fabric Actor concurrency performance counters

Category name	Counter name	Description
Service Fabric Actor	# of actor calls waiting for actor lock	The number of methods waiting for the actor-level lock that reinforces the turn-based concurrency
Service Fabric Actor	Average milliseconds per save state operation	Average time spent to save actor state, in milliseconds

The preceding performance counters follow a fixed naming convention to name performance counter instances. By understanding the naming convention, you can find performance counter instances for specific partitions more easily.

For the Service Fabric Actor category, the performance counter instance names use the following format:

Partition Id_Unique Id

The Partition Id is a GUID (formatted with a "D" specifier) that indicates the partition to which the actor instance belongs. The Unique Id is a 64-bit integer that identifies a specific performance counter instance. For example, in the id 079df741-2fe5-476e-94c1-338fe3ad573a_635831562007134558, 079df741-2fe5-476e-94c1-338fe3ad573a is the partition id, and 635831562007134558 is the unique performance counter instance id.

For the Service Fabric Actor Method category, the performance counter instance names use the following format:

Method Name_Method Id_Partition Id_Unique Id

The Partition Id and the Unique Id are the same as above. The Method Name is the actor method name, which might be reformatted to fit with performance count name constraints. The Method Id is a 32-integer id generated by the runtime. The following is an example of such an instance id:

```
igame.getgameboarddasync_2_25e0a146-b400-467a-9e9f-fac6b5330388_635831562006694245
```

State management performance

As an exercise, use Windows Performance Monitor to monitor the Average Milliseconds Per Save State Operation counter and try to influence that value by using different service configurations.

1. Launch Windows Performance Monitor, remove existing performance counters, and add the Average Milliseconds Per Save State Operation Counter. Because you are not sure which instance will be hit, add all instances, as shown in Figure 4-3.

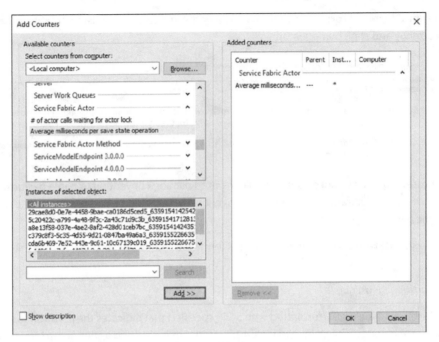

FIGURE 4-3 Adding counters to Performance Monitor

2. Launch the tic-tac-toe game and wait for the game session to complete. This will generate a graph similar to that shown in Figure 4-4. The graph shows that on my local cluster, the average time needed to save (and replicate) state is about 50 milliseconds.

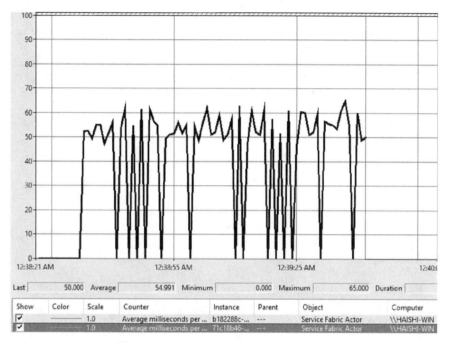

FIGURE 4-4 Average milliseconds per state operation

3. By default, Service Fabric Actor runtime persists states on local disk using a state provider. (I'll discuss state providers in the next section, "Actors and Reliable Services.") You also can use a volatile state provider that saves states in memory. Now, let's experiment to determine if changing the state provider will have significant impacts on performance.

4. In the tic-tac-toe application, modify the *Game* class in the Game project to annotate the class with the *VolatileActorStateProvider* attribute:

```
[VolatileActorStateProvider]
public class Game : Actor<GameState>, IGame
...
```

5. Redeploy the application and capture the performance graph again.

> **Note** Instinct tells me that using an in-memory state provider would have pro-vided performance improvements. However, on my machine, I don't observe any noticeable changes. My laptop uses SSD, so the disk itself is fast. But I think the majority of the overheads resides in replica coordination. Let's test this hypothesis now.

6. Modify the application manifest to change both the minimum replica size and the target replica size to 1. This essentially turns off replication:

```
<Parameter Name="GameActorService_MinReplicaSetSize" DefaultValue="1" />
<Parameter Name="GameActorService_TargetReplicaSetSize" DefaultValue="1" />
```

7. Redeploy the application and capture another performance graph. As shown in Figure 4-5, the saving state operation takes nearly no time without replication.

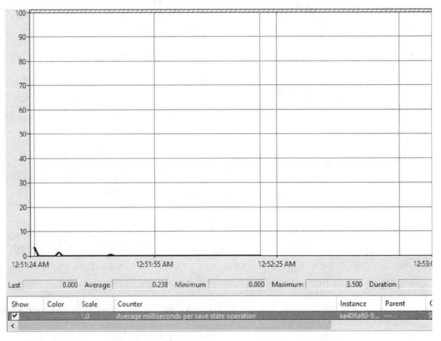

FIGURE 4-5 Average milliseconds per state operation without replication

The preceding exercise teaches (or reminds of) us two things. First, when it comes to performance tuning, measurement is a key step. Objective measurements help us establish performance baselines, test hypotheses we make, and verify the effectiveness of code changes. Without objective measurements, performance tuning is shooting in the dark.

Second, when tuning an application to achieve different characteristics, tradeoffs often need to be made. As an extreme example, reliability is sacrificed completely in exchange for performance in the preceding exercise. It will be unrealistic to try to achieve a perfect system with the highest level of Quality of Service (QoS) in all aspects. Instead, you'll need to make educated decisions (based on data, not on imagination) to find an optimum solution under the constraints of your system requirements.

A better way to deal with the 50-millisecond delay

In the preceding example, you took an extreme approach: you sacrificed reliability altogether in exchange for performance. There's a better way to bring down the response time without sacrificing the reliability, which is introduced in the next section about state providers. If you wonder what causes the 50-millisecond delay, be sure to check out the "Rethink the 50-millisecond delay" section later in this chapter.

Actors and Reliable Services

Service Fabric Actors is built on top of Service Fabric Reliable Services. Each actor type is a reliable service type. These actor services are packaged and deployed as Service Fabric applications.

Actor instances

Actor instances are created in the service instance processes. Figure 4-6 illustrates a possible distribution of actor instances for our tic-tac-toe application on a three-node cluster. The diagram shows four players (player A through player D) playing in two game sessions (game 1 and game 2).

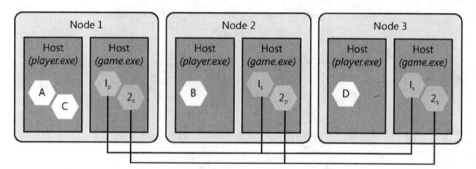

FIGURE 4-6 Actor instances on a three-node cluster

On each of the nodes are two service hosts, player.exe and game.exe. The host names are defined in corresponding service manifests:

```
<CodePackage Name="Code" Version="1.0.0.0">
  <EntryPoint>
    <ExeHost>
      <Program>Game.exe</Program>
    </ExeHost>
  </EntryPoint>
</CodePackage>
```

The player actor is a stateless actor, which allows only one instance per partition. In the above example, nine partitions are defined by default in the application manifest:

```
<Parameter Name="PlayerActorService_PartitionCount" DefaultValue="9" />
```

When a new actor instance is created, Service Fabric uses a hashing algorithm to decide which partition the instance goes into. As the application runs multiple times, more actor instances are accumulated in these partitions until the actor instances are garbage collected.

The game actor is a stateful actor. When a new game actor is initiated, a primary replica and a number of secondary replicas are created for reliability. Service Fabric tries to distribute primary replicas across the node so a single failing node won't take down many primary replicas.

Figure 4-7 is a screen shot of the Service Fabric Explorer tree view (with slight modifications to save space). As you can see in the picture, a primary replica of the game actor is placed on Node.1, and a secondary replica is placed on Node.2. Player actor instances (replicas) are scattered across cluster nodes.

FIGURE 4-7 Service Fabric Explorer tree view

Actor states

Actor states are saved in a reliable dictionary associated with the partition. At the time of this writing, each actor instance corresponds to a single key in the dictionary. This means that when you modify a property in your state, the whole state needs to be serialized and replicated across the replica quorum. Until a better solution exists, you may want to constrain what you put in actor states. Or, you may want to split your actor model so that each actor has less state to save. For example, you may want to separate player profile from the player actor so that as a player plays in a game session, their profiles don't need to be replicated and synced.

Actor state providers

Service Fabric uses a key-value store (KVS) state provider to manage actor states. A state provider manages both state persistence and state replication. The behavior of the state provider can be configured by the settings.xml file under the PackageRoot\Config folder of the corresponding actor project. This file generated by Visual Studio tooling is sufficient for common cases. However, you may want to browse through the following setting properties so that you understand what you can do to fine-tune your actor performance.

Replicator configuration

You can use a couple of configuration sections to control the behavior of the state replicator. Specifically, you can configure security and performance characteristics of the replica by using the following two sections.

Replicator security settings   Replicator security configuration allows you to specify different authentication schemes and protection levels to protect a service's replication traffic from other services running on the same cluster. By default, there's no authentication, as shown in the following example:

```
<Section Name="GameActorServiceReplicatorSecurityConfig">
  <Parameter Name="CredentialType" Value="None" />
</Section>
```

You can use other credential types including claims, Windows credential, and X509 certificates. The following is an example of using an X509 certificate as credential (with protection level set to "encrypt and sign"):

```
<Section Name="GameActorServiceReplicatorSecurityConfig">
    <Parameter Name="CredentialType" Value="X509" />
    <Parameter Name="FindType" Value="FindByThumbprint" />
    <Parameter Name="FindValue" Value="xx xx xx xx … xx" />
    <Parameter Name="StoreLocation" Value="LocalMachine" />
    <Parameter Name="StoreName" Value="My" />
    <Parameter Name="ProtectionLevel" Value="EncryptAndSign" />
    <Parameter Name="AllowedCommonNames" Value="principle1, principle2 " />
</Section>
```

> ## Configuration section names
>
> Service Fabric uses a specific naming rule to name the configuration sections. You should not modify these names generated by Visual Studio tooling. When you add a new configuration section, you should follow the same naming patterns to name your sections.

Replicator behavior settings   Table 4-10 summarizes some of the configuration settings you can use to influence the behaviors of the replicator.

TABLE 4-10 Replicator behavior settings

Name	Units	Default	Remarks
BatchAcknowledgementInterval	Seconds	0.05	Acknowledgements from replicators at secondaries can be batched together. This value controls the time window during which the acknowledgements are grouped into a single response.
ReplicatorEndpoint	N/A	N/A	The endpoint replicators use to communicate with each other to exchange data. This value should reference one of the endpoints defined in the service manifest.
RetryInterval	Seconds	5	How long a replica waits for acknowledgement before it considers the last transmission has failed and retransmits a message.
MaxReplicationMessageSize	Bytes	50MB	Maximum message size of replica data.
MaxPrimaryReplicationQueueSize	# of ops	1024	Maximum pending operations in the primary queue. An operation is released only when all acknowledgements from the replica quorum have been received. This value has to be bigger than 64 and has to be a power of 2.
MaxSecondaryReplicationQueueSize	# of ops	2048	Maximum operations in the secondary queue. An operation is released after the data has been persisted. This value has to be greater than 64 and has to be a power of 2.

Local store settings   Local store settings allow you to configure the local persistence store, as summarized in Table 4-11.

TABLE 4-11 Local store settings

Name	Unit	Default	Remarks
MaxAsyncCommitDelay	Milliseconds	200	Maximum batching window of local store commits
MaxVerPages	# of pages	8192	Maximum number of version pages in the local store database

Rethink the 50-millisecond delay

The *BatchAcknowledgementInterval* setting looks interesting. Its default value, 50 milliseconds, coincides with the state persistence delay we've observed in the earlier exercise. Is it the reason we saw the 50-millisecond delay? Let's test it.

1. Modify PackageRoot\Config\Settings.xml under the Game project. Set *BatchAcknowledgementInterval* to 0.01 (10 milliseconds):

```
<Section Name="GameActorServiceReplicatorConfig">
  <Parameter Name="ReplicatorEndpoint" Value="GameActorServiceReplicatorEndpoint" />
  <Parameter Name="BatchAcknowledgementInterval" Value="0.01" />
</Section>
```

2. Restore the replica settings in the application manifest to the default values:

```
<Parameter Name="GameActorService_MinReplicaSetSize" DefaultValue="2" />
<Parameter Name="GameActorService_TargetReplicaSetSize" DefaultValue="3" />
```

3. Build, deploy, and run through another game session. Indeed, the performance counter graph changes. Figure 4-8 shows that with this change, the average response time goes down to 10 milliseconds.

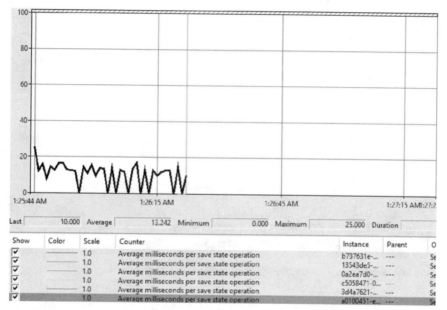

FIGURE 4-8 Average milliseconds per state operation with lower batch interval

4. Modify the setting to 0. Retest the application. As shown in Figure 4-9, the average response time has gone down to one millisecond as expected.

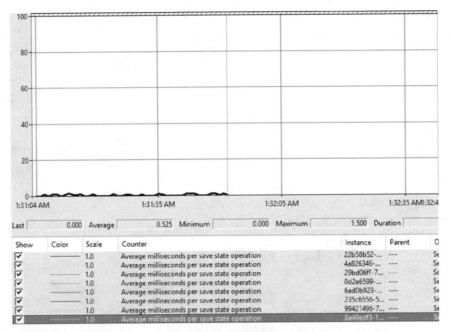

FIGURE 4-9 Average milliseconds per state operation with zero batch interval

The *BatchAcknowledgementInterval* setting allows you to balance throughput and latency. As shown in the preceding example, lowering this value can improve the response time. However, this improvement comes with a price. As the batching window narrows, acknowledgements need to be sent and processed more frequently, affecting the system throughput.

Additional information

This chapter uses Windows Performance Monitor. To learn more about the tool, please see *https://technet.microsoft.com/library/cc749249.aspx*.

CHAPTER 5

Service deployments and upgrades

This chapter focuses on the operations side and discusses how Service Fabric applications are deployed and upgraded. You'll first go through the application deployment process, covering how a Service Fabric application is packaged, staged, and deployed. Next, the discussion moves to how to perform zero-downtime upgrades of different service types, including Reliable Services and Reliable Actor services.

Service Fabric application deployment process

In earlier exercises, you have been using Visual Studio to deploy Service Fabric applications to a local cluster. The deployment process seems like a one-step operation. However, there are many steps happening behind the scenes. Figure 5-1 depicts an overview of the deployment process.

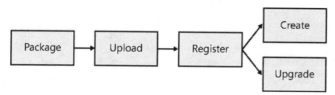

FIGURE 5-1 Service Fabric application deployment process

Package

Before a Service Fabric application can be deployed, the application manifest, service manifests, compiled code packages, data files, and configurations need to be packaged into a specific layout. Figure 5-2 shows a screen shot of running the tree command against the Hello World application in Chapter 1, "Hello, Service Fabric!".

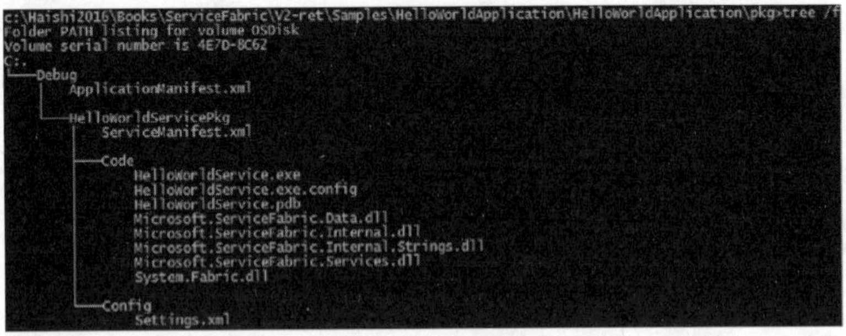

FIGURE 5-2 Service Fabric application folder structure

At the root of the folder is the application manifest (ApplicationManifest.xml). Then, for each service type there's a service package folder. The service package folder consists of the service manifest file (ServiceManifest.xml) at the root and three folders: a code folder, a configuration folder, and a data folder (not shown in Figure 5-2).

The code folder holds the code package, which consists of compiled code assemblies including the service host (HelloWorldService.exe in this case) and all dependent assemblies. The configuration folder holds the service configuration file, which can be updated independently from the code package. The data folder holds static data that you want to deploy with the service.

The names of these folders are defined in the service manifest. The following service manifest sample shows a code folder named Code, a configuration folder named MyConfig, and a data folder named TestData:

```
<CodePackage Name="Code" Version="1.0.0.0">
  <EntryPoint>
    <ExeHost>
      <Program>HelloWorldService.exe</Program>
    </ExeHost>
  </EntryPoint>
</CodePackage>
<ConfigPackage Name="MyConfig" Version="1.0.0.0" />
<DataPackage Name="TestData" Version="1.0.0.1" />
```

Code package

The code package contains the application's code. Service Fabric doesn't mandate a fixed folder structure under your application package root as long as you have a code folder and a configuration folder (with names of your choice as explained above). You can create additional folders and subfolders as you wish because Service Fabric will perform an XCOPY of the entire folder structure when it copies the application package.

As you've seen in earlier examples, a code package contains an entry point (EntryPoint), which points to an executable (ExeHost). When a service type is initialized, all entry points in the code package will be invoked. In addition to the entry point, you can specify a setup entry point, which is invoked before the entry point is called. You can use the setup entry point to execute a batch file, a

Windows PowerShell script, or a setup program to configure the node before the service entry point is called.

The following is an example of using the setup entry point. The example calls a scripts\test.cmd batch file before the service entry point is called.

```
<CodePackage Name="Code" Version="1.0.0">
  <SetupEntryPoint>
    <ExeHost>
      <Program>scripts\test.cmd</Program>
     <ConsoleRedirection FileRetentionCount="5" FileMaxSizeInKb="2048"/>
    </ExeHost>
  </SetupEntryPoint>
  <EntryPoint>
    <ExeHost>
      <Program>HelloWorldService.exe</Program>
    </ExeHost>
  </EntryPoint>
</CodePackage>
```

The test.cmd file should be put under a Code\scripts folder under the package root, where *Code* is the name of the code package. The above example also redirects stdout and stderr outputs to text files for diagnostics.

As an exercise, generate some outputs in the above test.cmd batch file and practice how to locate the redirected log files.

1. Create a new Service Fabric application named *ConsoleRedirectTestApplication* with a stateless service named *ConsoleRedirect*.

2. Under the PackageRoot folder of the ConsoleRedirect project, create a new folder named *Code*.

3. Under the Code folder, create a *scripts* folder.

4. Add a new test.cmd file to the scripts folder with the following content:

   ```
   @echo This is a test message
   ```

5. Add the following setup entry point under the *CodePackage* element of the ServiceManifest. xml file:

   ```
   <SetupEntryPoint>
     <ExeHost>
       <Program>scripts\test.cmd</Program>
       <ConsoleRedirection FileRetentionCount="5" FileMaxSizeInKb="2048"/>
     </ExeHost>
   </SetupEntryPoint>
   ```

6. Publish the application.

7. Open the Local Cluster Manager. Expand any node to locate its disk location, as shown in Figure 5-3. The service project template set instance count to -1, which means to create a service instance on every available node. So, it doesn't matter which node you select in this case.

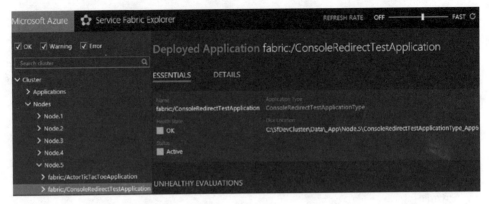

FIGURE 5-3 Application disk location

8. Under the folder, you can find a log subfolder, which contains a number of .out files and .err files. The .out files contain the redirected standard outputs, and the .err files contain the redirected error outputs. Open the latest .out file, and you'll see the echo message in the file.

In addition to *Program* and *ConsoleRedirection*, the *ExeHost* element supports the following elements:

- **Arguments**   The value of this element holds the arguments to be passed to the program.

- **WorkingFolder**   This value of this element can be either *CodeBase* or *CodePackage*. The *CodeBase* refers to the code folder under the application package, and the *CodePackage* refers to the application package root.

- **WorkingDirectory**   This value configures the current working directory so that the service code or the setup scripts can use relative paths.

Configuration package

You can define custom setting sections and parameters in the Settings.xml file under the configuration folder. The following configuration file defines a MyConfigSection section with a single MyParameter parameter underneath.

```xml
<?xml version="1.0" encoding="utf-8" ?>
<Settings xmlns:xsd="http://www.w3.org/2001/XMLSchema"
xmlns:xsi="http://www.w3.org/2001/XMLSchema-instance"
xmlns="http://schemas.microsoft.com/2011/01/fabric">
  <Section Name="MyConfigSection">
    <Parameter Name="MyParameter" Value="Value1" />
  </Section>
</Settings>
```

To read configurations in Reliable Services, use the *ServiceInitializationParameters. CodePackageActivationContext.GetConfigurationPackageObject()* method:

```
var configSection = this.ServiceInitializationParameters.CodePackageActivationContext
.GetConfigurationPackageObject("Config");
var text = configSection.Settings.Sections["MyConfigSection"].Parameters["MyParameter"].Value;
```

For Reliable Actors, you can use the *Host.ActivationContext.GetConfigurationPackageObject()* method following the same syntax as above.

Data package

To include static data in a service package, just add folders and files under the service project's PackageRoot folder and then define data packages in the service manifest file. As an exercise, modify the Hello World application to include some static data.

1. Under the *HelloWorldService* project, create a new folder named *TestData* under the PackageRoot folder.

2. Add a new text file named *Data.txt* under the TestData folder.

3. Modify the ServiceManifest.xml file to add a *DataPackage* element under the root *ServiceManifest* element:

   ```
   <DataPackage Name="TestData" Version="1.0.0.0" />
   ```

4. Modify the *RunAsync* method to read and log the file content:

   ```
   while (!cancellationToken.IsCancellationRequested)
   {
       var dataPackage = this.ServiceInitializationParameters.
           CodePackageActivationContext.GetDataPackageObject("TestData");
       var text = File.ReadAllText(Path.Combine(dataPackage.Path, "data.txt"));
       ServiceEventSource.Current.ServiceMessage(this, text);
       await Task.Delay(TimeSpan.FromSeconds(5), cancellationToken);
   }
   ```

5. Deploy and run the application again, and you should see the file content logged in the Diagnostic Event Viewer.

For Reliable Actors, you can access the data packages by using the *Host.ActivitationContext. GetDataPackageObject* method:

```
var gameData = Host.ActivationContext.GetDataPackageObject("GameData");
var moves = File.ReadAllLines(Path.Combine(gameData.Path, "moves.txt"));
```

Upload

An application package needs to be uploaded to an image store before it can be registered and deployed. For local clusters, the image store is a local file folder. For Azure-hosted clusters, by default the image store is a hosted image store service. The location of the image store is defined in the cluster manifest.

The following cluster manifest snippet shows the default location of a local cluster:

```
<Section Name="Management">
        <Parameter Name="ImageStoreConnectionString"
                   Value="file:C:\SfDevCluster\Data\ImageStoreShare" />
```

```
                <Parameter Name="ImageCachingEnabled" Value="false" />
                <Parameter Name="EnableDeploymentAtDataRoot" Value="true" />
        </Section>
```

The following cluster manifest snippet shows the default configuration of the image store service on
an Azure-hosted cluster:

```
        <Section Name="ImageStoreService">
                <Parameter Name="MinReplicaSetSize" Value="3" />
                <Parameter Name="PlacementConstraints" Value="NodeTypeName==App" />
                <Parameter Name="TargetReplicaSetSize" Value="5" />
        </Section>
        <Section Name="Management">
                <Parameter Name="ImageStoreConnectionString" Value="fabric:ImageStore" />
        </Section>
```

Register/provision

After an application package is uploaded to the image store, the package is verified to make sure
everything is in place. Then, the corresponding application type is registered with the system, and the
package content is prepared and made available for deployments.

Multiple versions of the same application type can be registered. Service Fabric allows you to
perform rolling updates on applications. Before a new version can be applied, the version needs to be
registered. Service Fabric also allows running different versions of the same application, or multiple
instances of the same application version, at the same time.

Create/replace/upgrade

Once an application type is registered, new application instances can be created. When you use Visual
Studio to deploy an application, the old application instances are removed, the application type is unregistered, and the new package is registered and instantiated. This allows you to keep developing and
testing the same version of the application.

However, in a production environment, usually you want to perform a rolling update to maintain
service continuity. With rolling updates, instances of the older versions gradually are taken down as instances of the newer version are brought online. The rolling update process is discussed in detail next.

Health model

Service Fabric provides a hierarchical health model that enables you to monitor individual components
separately and to observe health states at any aggregated level. The health model entities mirror the
Service Fabric entities, so it's straightforward to understand which health model entity is representing
which Service Fabric entity. Figure 5-4 depicts the health model entities and how their states are rolled
up along the health model hierarchy.

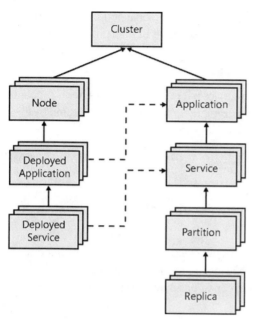

FIGURE 5-4 Service Fabric health model

Health entities

Each health entity defines health-related attributes associated with the entity. The health state of an entity is decided by its own attributes and the states of its children. The following health entities are defined in the Service Fabric health model:

- **Cluster**   The health of the entire cluster. It reports problems at the cluster level, such as multiple primaries being elected because of communication issues.

- **Node**   The health of a node. It reports problems such as the node running low on disk space, running out of memory, or losing connections. Such problems are likely to affect all service instances running on the node.

- **Application**   The health of an application instance.

- **Service**   The health of a service. This entity captures problems that affect the overall health of a service, such as misconfigurations.

- **Partition**   The health of the entire replica set. This entity captures problems such as the number of replicas falling below the target number or more severe problems such as a quorum loss, which means all replicas are lost before Service Fabric can build up new ones.

- **Replica**   The health of a stateful service replica or a stateless service instance. This is the smallest health entity that reports on replica-specific issues, such as a primary replica not being able to replicate states to secondaries or a stateless service instance having connectivity issues.

- **DeployedApplication** The health of an application running on a node. This entity reflects application problems that pertain to a particular node. Examples of such problems include failures in downloading an application package to a node and issues in setting up security principles for an application.

- **DeployedServicePackage** The health of a service package running on a node. Problems such as failing to start a code package or locating a configuration package are captured by this entity.

Health states

Service Fabric defines four health states: Ok, Warning, Error, and Unknown.

- **Ok** The health entity is in a healthy state. There are no issues detected on the entity or its associated descendants.

- **Warning** The health entity is having problems but still is functional. Some warning conditions are transient, which means the entity may restore to a healthy state at a later time without the user's intervention. However, the warning conditions may escalate and render the entity unhealthy.

- **Error** The entity is unhealthy and is not functioning correctly. Some actions need to be taken to fix the errors to restore the entity to a healthy state.

- **Unknown** The entity's health information doesn't exist in the system-level health store.

Health policy

When evaluating the health state of an entity, Service Fabric by default uses a strict health policy that considers an entity unhealthy if any of its children are unhealthy. You can set up a percentage threshold that the number of unhealthy children has to reach before the parent is considered unhealthy.

There are three types of policies: cluster health policy, application health policy, and service type health policy. Cluster health policies are defined in a cluster's manifest files. Application health policies and service health policies are defined in an application's manifest files. Service type health policies are embedded in application health policies.

The following XML snippet is a sample cluster health policy defined in a cluster manifest file:

```
<FabricSettings>
  <Section Name="HealthManager/ClusterHealthPolicy">
    <Parameter Name="ConsiderWarningAsError" Value="False" />
    <Parameter Name="MaxPercentUnhealthyApplications" Value="0" />
    <Parameter Name="MaxPercentUnhealthyNodes" Value="20" />
  </Section>
</FabricSettings>
```

The preceding policy doesn't tolerate any unhealthy applications, and it allows a maximum of 20 percent of the nodes to be unhealthy on a cluster. It treats warnings and errors separately instead of taking warnings as errors.

The following XML snippet is a sample application health policy with embedded service type health policies:

```xml
<Policies>
        <HealthPolicy ConsiderWarningAsError="true"
MaxPercentUnhealthyDeployedApplications="20">
            <DefaultServiceTypeHealthPolicy
                MaxPercentUnhealthyServices="0"
                MaxPercentUnhealthyPartitionsPerService="10"
                MaxPercentUnhealthyReplicasPerPartition="0"/>
            <ServiceTypeHealthPolicy ServiceTypeName="FrontEndServiceType"
                MaxPercentUnhealthyServices="0"
                MaxPercentUnhealthyPartitionsPerService="20"
                MaxPercentUnhealthyReplicasPerPartition="0"/>
            <ServiceTypeHealthPolicy ServiceTypeName="BackEndServiceType"
                MaxPercentUnhealthyServices="20"
                MaxPercentUnhealthyPartitionsPerService="0"
                MaxPercentUnhealthyReplicasPerPartition="0">
            </ServiceTypeHealthPolicy>
        </HealthPolicy>
    </Policies>
```

Most of the policy should be self-explanatory, but a few spots might need some explanation:

- You can specify different health policies for different service types.

- When an application is deployed to multiple nodes of a cluster, deploying the application on each node is counted as a separate deployment. *MaxPercentUnhealthyDeployedApplications* refers to the percentage of failed application deployments over the total number of deployments.

- These policies can be overwritten by upgrade parameters, which are covered in the section "Upgrade modes and upgrade parameters."

Health reporting and aggregation

Service Fabric provides built-in watchdogs that monitor and report on health events of health entities. In addition, you can use custom watchdogs that report on health events. Reports from both internal watchdogs and custom watchdogs are written to the health store. Then, these reports are used to evaluate health states of entities.

When implementing a watchdog, you should monitor the events pertaining to the monitored entity only because health state aggregation and propagation are decided by the health model hierarchy. The aggregated health state is decided by the worst health reports of the entity and its descendants. In other words, if any of an entity's descendants is in an Error state, the entity ends up in the Error state. If there are only warnings in an entity's descendants, the entity's state is either Error or Warning, depending on whether the *ConsiderWarningAsError* flag is set.

Custom health reporting is covered in Chapter 10, "Diagnostics and monitoring."

Rolling upgrade

As introduced earlier, a rolling upgrade gradually phases out the older version as it applies the newer version so that your service is not interrupted during the upgrade process. This process also is called zero-downtime upgrade. To understand the process, you first need to understand a couple of basic concepts such as fault domains and update domains.

Fault domains and update domains

A *fault domain* is a physical unit of failure. It represents a group of infrastructure resources that fail together. For example, a personal computer can be considered a fault domain because once it's unplugged, all its resources, including CPU, memory, and disk, will stop functioning. In a datacenter, a server rack sometimes can be considered a fault domain because when a rack fails, all servers on the rack will fail because they share the same power, cooling, or network infrastructure. When a service is deployed, service instances should be scattered across the fault domains so that a failing domain won't take out all service instances.

An *update domain* is a logical unit for updates. Service instances in the same update domain are allowed to be brought down at the same time. However, at any given time, only one update domain is being updated. When performing a rolling upgrade, service instances are brought down and upgraded per update domains. This process also is called an update domain walk.

The update domain walk allows service instances to be updated gradually in a controlled manner. However, this means that during upgrades, there will be multiple versions of the service running at the same time. This requires that the versions are compatible: the new version needs to be backward-compatible, and the old version needs to be forward-compatible. If compatibility is broken, a rolling upgrade isn't possible. In this case, the administrator needs to use a compatible intermediate version to perform two rolling upgrades: one from the older version to the intermediate version and another from the intermediate version to the new version. If a compatible intermediate version isn't available, service interruption isn't avoidable. Although some techniques such as virtual IP swap reduce the interruptions to a minimum, a brief interruption still can be observed.

It's necessary to clarify that although a zero-downtime upgrade ensures that at any given time there will be at least one service instance running, this doesn't mean a particular client won't be interrupted. For example, if a client needs to hold onto a long-time connection to a service instance, shutting down the instance will break the client. The client will need to create another connection, which will be routed to a new, healthy service instance to continue with work.

Another thing to notice is that the number of update domains affects the speed of upgrade. Because only one update domain is updated at a time, if you have many update domains, walking through all these update domains will take a long time. However, if you have many instances in a single update domain, bringing down the domain will have a great impact on overall system capacity, which may trigger hidden scalability and performance bugs due to the increased pressure on remaining service instances.

Service Fabric automatically distributes cluster nodes across fault domains and update domains. Figure 5-5 shows that by default, nodes on a five-node cluster are scattered into five fault domains and five update domains.

FIGURE 5-5 Fault domains and update domains in a local Service Fabric cluster

Upgrade process

Service application revision and upgrade takes the following steps:

1. Service code is modified as needed. Then, the service manifest is updated to use a new version number:

    ```
    <CodePackage Name="Code" Version="2.0.0">
    ```

2. Correspondingly, the application manifest is updated to reference the correct service manifest number. The application version also is updated because the application now contains a newer version of services:

    ```
    <ApplicationManifest ApplicationTypeName="Application30Type"
                         ApplicationTypeVersion="2.0.0"
                         xmlns=http://schemas.microsoft.com/2011/01/fabric
                         xmlns:xsd=http://www.w3.org/2001/XMLSchema
                         xmlns:xsi="http://www.w3.org/2001/XMLSchema-instance">
      <ServiceManifestImport>
        <ServiceManifestRef ServiceManifestName="Stateless1Pkg"
    ServiceManifestVersion="2.0.0" />
      </ServiceManifestImport>
      ...
    ```

3. The new application package is packaged, uploaded, and registered.

4. Rolling upgrade is kicked off. Service Fabric walks through update domains to bring up the service instances to the specified version.

You can kick off the upgrade process from Visual Studio or through Windows PowerShell (see Chapter 8, "Managing Service Fabric with Windows PowerShell"). To perform an upgrade from Visual Studio, just right-click the Service Fabric application project and select the Publish menu. Then, on the

Publish Service Fabric Application dialog, select the Upgrade The Application check box, as shown in Figure 5-6. Finally, click the Publish button.

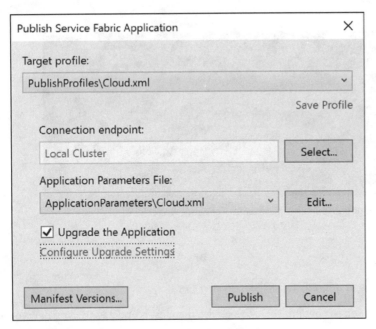

FIGURE 5-6 Publish Service Fabric Application dialog box

Optionally, before clicking the Publish button, you can click the Configure Upgrade Settings link to open the Edit Upgrade Settings dialog box, which allows you to modify a number of upgrade options, as shown in Figure 5-7. You'll go through these options in the next section, "Upgrade modes and upgrade parameters."

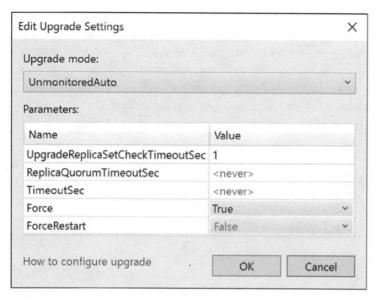

FIGURE 5-7 Upgrade settings

Upgrade modes and upgrade parameters

As more independent software vendors (ISVs) and enterprises are adopting short deployment cycles, upgrading an application is becoming one of the most common operations that need to be carried out frequently. As a generic platform as a service (PaaS), Service Fabric provides quite a few knobs that allow you to tailor your upgrade process to meet your application's needs.

During rolling upgrades, Service Fabric needs to know the health of service instances as it walks through update domains. It needs to know that the instances in an update domain have been restored to a working state before it can safely bring down another update domain. As introduced earlier, Service Fabric allows you to define health evaluation policies that dictate how service health should be evaluated and what actions to take when a certain event happens.

Upgrade modes

Service Fabric supports three upgrade modes: Monitored, UnmonitoredAuto, and Manual.

- **UnmonitoredAuto** This upgrade mode skips health checks. Because Service Fabric doesn't wait for service instances to become fully functional before moving to the next update domain, this mode provides the fastest performance. This mode is ideal during the active developing phase because it allows new bits to be pushed quickly to the testing environment for quicker dev-test iterations.

- **Monitored** This upgrade mode is what you'd commonly use in a production environment. Under this mode, Service Fabric verifies the health state of the service instances in an update domain before it moves to the next update domain.

■ **Manual** This upgrade mode requires you to update each update domain manually. An administrator will need to call the *MoveNextApplicationUpgradeDomainAsync()* method manually to traverse update domains or roll back to the previous version as needed. Manual mode can be useful in several situations. For example, when you deploy a new version that has potential compatibility issues, you might want to deploy to a smaller scope and run through necessary tests to make sure nothing is broken before you roll out to the entire cluster.

Upgrade parameters

Service Fabric supports a number of upgrade parameters that you can use to fine-tune the upgrade process. These parameters allow you to control how application health is determined and how to react to certain deployment states.

■ FailureAction

- Allowed values: Rollback, Manual

- Applicable mode: Monitored

- What should happen when an upgrade fails. When an update of an update domain fails, you can choose either to roll back to the previous version or to enter the manual upgrade mode so that you can check the failing domain manually.

■ HealthCheckWaitDurationSec

- Applicable mode: Monitored

- This parameter controls the interval Service Fabric should wait before it evaluates application health. Some services need some time to initialize before they become functional. Setting this value to an appropriate time span avoids possible false positives when service health is checked before the service is initiated fully. If the health check passes, Service Fabric continues with the next update domain. If the health check fails, Service Fabric keeps checking application health at this interval until HealthCheckRetryTimeoutSec (see below) is reached.

■ HealthCheckRetryTimeoutSec

- Applicable mode: Monitored

- This parameter controls the maximum duration of health checks. During this time period, Service Fabric keeps evaluating application health at the interval specified by the HealthCheckWaitDurationSec parameter.

■ HealthCheckStableDurationSec

- Applicable mode: Monitored

- This parameter adds an extra delay before the application health is evaluated again to make sure the application is in a stable health state before Service Fabric moves to the next update domain or completes the update process.

- UpgradeDomainTimeoutSec

  - Applicable mode: Monitored

  - This is the total time allowed to update an update domain. If an update domain fails to update within this time window, the upgrade is considered failed and the FailureAction is triggered. This parameter is set to infinite (<never>) by default.

- TimeoutSec

  - Applicable mode: Monitored

  - This is the total time allowed to complete the entire upgrade process.

- ConsiderWarningAsError

  - Applicable mode: Monitored

  - This controls if warning health events should be treated as errors.

- MaxPercentUnhealthyDeployedApplications

  - Applicable mode: Monitored

  - This is the maximum allowed percentage of failed application deployments over total number of application deployments. If needed, see the "Health policy" section earlier in this chapter for more details.

- DefaultServiceTypeHealthPolicy and ServiceTypeHealthPolicyMap

  - Applicable mode: Monitored

  - These specify service type health policies. See the "Health policy" section earlier in this chapter for more details.

- UpgradeReplicaSetCheckTimeout

  - Applicable modes: All

  - For a stateless service, if the target instance count is more than 1, Service Fabric waits for more than one instance to be available in a single update domain before progressing, until the specified timeout expires. When the timeout expires, Service Fabric proceeds with upgrades regardless of the number of service instances. If the target instance count is 1, Service Fabric doesn't wait.

  - For a stateful service, Service Fabric waits for the replica set in a single update domain to have a quorum. When the timeout expires, Service Fabric proceeds with the upgrade regardless of whether a quorum has been reached.

- ForceRestart

  - Applicable modes: All

- When only the configuration package or data package is updated, the service instance is not restarted unless the *ForceRestart* flag is set. Your service will be notified of configuration or data changes, and it's up to the service to apply these changes and restart if necessary.

Multiple environments

Throughout the lifetime of an application, the application needs to be deployed to different environments such as a dev, QA, staging, and production. Service Fabric allows you to define multiple deployment profiles and parameter files for different environments.

Application parameters and parameter files

Although a Service Fabric application can be deployed onto different environments without modification, sometimes you may want to use different application parameters for different environments. One example is the number of service instances. For a local cluster, you need to set the instance count to 1 to avoid multiple service instances trying to listen on the same port, but you probably want to set the instance count to more than 1 on a cloud cluster for availability and load balancing.

You can define application parameters in the application's manifest file; for example:

```
<Parameters>
  <Parameter Name="Stateless1_InstanceCount" DefaultValue="-1" />
</Parameters>
```

Then, you can supply different sets of parameter values by defining multiple parameter files, which are under the ApplicationParameters folder of the application project. For example, the following parameter file sets the service instance count parameter to 1 for the local cluster:

```
<?xml version="1.0" encoding="utf-8"?>
<Application xmlns:xsd="http://www.w3.org/2001/XMLSchema" xmlns:xsi="http://www.w3.org/2001/
XMLSchema-instance" Name="fabric:/Application33" xmlns="http://schemas.microsoft.com/2011/01/
fabric">
    <Parameters>
        <Parameter Name="Stateless1_InstanceCount" Value="1" />
    </Parameters>
</Application>
```

Application publish profiles

Application publish profiles allow different cluster connection information, application parameter files, and upgrade options to be specified. The following is a sample publish profile that uses a secured cluster connection using certificate authentication, selects an ..*ApplicationParameters\Cloud.xml* application parameter file, and specifies the Monitored upgrade mode with a number of parameters set.

```
<?xml version="1.0" encoding="utf-8"?>
<PublishProfile xmlns="http://schemas.microsoft.com/2015/05/fabrictools">
  <ClusterConnectionParameters ConnectionEndpoint="mycluster.westus.cloudapp.azure.com:19000"
```

```
              X509Credential="true"
              ServerCertThumbprint="0123456789012345678901234567890123456789"
              FindType="FindByThumbprint"
              FindValue="9876543210987654321098765432109876543210"
              StoreLocation="CurrentUser"
              StoreName="My" />
  <ApplicationParameterFile Path="..\ApplicationParameters\Cloud.xml" />
  <UpgradeDeployment Mode="Monitored">
    <Parameters FailureAction="Rollback"
                UpgradeReplicaSetCheckTimeoutSec="1"
                Force="True"
                MaxPercentUnhealthyDeployedApplications="20" />
  </UpgradeDeployment>
</PublishProfile>
```

Figure 5-6 (shown previously) shows that when you publish your application, you can pick from existing publish profiles and application parameter files. You can choose a different application parameter file than what's specified in the publish profile. And you can override any parameters by clicking the Edit button beside the Application Parameters File drop-down box.

Using implicit hosts

As a PaaS platform, Service Fabric provides the reliable services programming model and the reliable actors programming model. In addition, Service Fabric allows you to package existing applications such as a Node.js application or a Java application and deploy it onto a Service Fabric cluster.

Defining implicit hosts

Because these applications won't be taking advantage of Service Fabric state management features, they are treated as stateless services. However, they still can enjoy features such as high availability, high density, health monitoring, and lifetime management.

When you declare the service type in your service manifest file, you should use the *UseImplicitHost* flag to indicate that the service process won't be connected to Service Fabric runtime and won't register .NET service implementations with the runtime. Service Fabric will treat the service process as a simple process and monitor the service instance health by monitoring the process.

The following is an example service manifest that describes a Node.js-based application as a Service Fabric stateless service.

Example source

The following service fabric manifest and the following example are inspired by this article: *https://azure.microsoft.com/documentation/articles/service-fabric-deploy-existing-app.*

```
<?xml version="1.0" encoding="utf-8"?>
<ServiceManifest xmlns:xsd="http://www.w3.org/2001/XMLSchema" xmlns:xsi="http://www.
w3.org/2001/XMLSchema-instance" Name="NodeApp" Version="1.0.0.0" xmlns="http://schemas.
```

```
 microsoft.com/2011/01/fabric">
    <ServiceTypes>
        <StatelessServiceType ServiceTypeName="NodeApp" UseImplicitHost="true"/>
    </ServiceTypes>
    <CodePackage Name="code" Version="1.0.0.0">
        <SetupEntryPoint>
            <ExeHost>
                <Program>installNode.cmd</Program>
            </ExeHost>
        </SetupEntryPoint>
        <EntryPoint>
            <ExeHost>
                <Program>node.exe</Program>
                <Arguments>app.js</Arguments>
                <WorkingFolder>CodePackage</WorkingFolder>
            </ExeHost>
        </EntryPoint>
    </CodePackage>
    <Resources>
        <Endpoints>
            <Endpoint Name="NodeAppTypeEndpoint" Protocol="http" Port="8080" Type="Input" />
        </Endpoints>
    </Resources>
</ServiceManifest>
```

The preceding service manifest defines a NodeApp service type with a *SetupEntryPoint* that installs Node.js and an endpoint resource for the Node.js server to listen on. The package entry point in this case is Node.exe, and an app.js is passed to Node.exe as an argument.

RunAs policies

The *SetupEntryPoint* runs before any other endpoints. It runs under the default Service Fabric account, which usually is the Network account. However, installing software packages usually needs local administrator access. Service Fabric allows you to define RunAs policies that can put the service processes under different accounts from the default account. Moreover, you can define local user groups and user accounts in your application's manifest file and use these accounts to run your services.

For example, you can create a new user under the application manifest's *Principals* element:

```
<Principals>
    <Users>
        <User Name="SetupAdminUser">
            <MemberOf>
                <SystemGroup Name="Administrators" />
            </MemberOf>
        </User>
    </Users>
</Principals>
```

The preceding XML snippet defines a new *SetupAdminUser* account under the *Administrator* user group. You also can create user groups under the *Principals* element; for example:

```
<Groups>
   <Group Name="MyGroup">
     <Membership>
       <SystemGroup Name="Administrators"/>
     </Membership>
   </Group>
 </Groups>
```

Then, in the same manifest file, you can refer to these principals in RunAs policies that are applied to services, as shown in the following example:

```
<ServiceManifestImport>
     <ServiceManifestRef ServiceManifestName="MyServiceTypePkg"
                         ServiceManifestVersion="1.0.0" />
     <ConfigOverrides />
     <Policies>
        <RunAsPolicy CodePackageRef="Code" UserRef="SetupAdminUser" EntryPointType="Setup" />
     </Policies>
   </ServiceManifestImport>
```

The preceding XML snippet specifies that the *SetupEntryPoint* of the corresponding service code package should be invoked with the *SetupAdminUser* principle instead of with the default account. Similarly, you can assign RunAs policies to the service's main entry points, which have *EntryPointType* of Main.

When a service has multiple code packages, you can set up a default policy that gets applied to all code packages. To define a default policy, use the *DefaultRunAsPolicy* element:

```
<Policies>
  <DefaultRunAsPolicy UserRef="MyServiceAccount"/>
</Policies>
```

For services that use HTTP or HTTPS endpoints, additional definitions are needed when you use custom user accounts. First, you need to associate the desired user account explicitly to the endpoints so that access control lists (ACLs) on the endpoints can be updated correctly. For example, the following snippet defines that the service should run under a *WebUser* account. The account is associated with the *HttpEndPoint* by a *SecurityAccessPolicy* element so that the ACLs on the endpoint can be updated to allow the *WebUser* account to listen on the endpoint.

```
<Policies>
   <RunAsPolicy CodePackageRef="Code" UserRef="WebUser" />
   <SecurityAccessPolicy ResourceRef="HttpEndPoint" PrincipalRef="WebUser" />
</Policies>
```

For HTTP endpoints, you also need to bind desired certificates to them by using *EndpointBindingPolicy* elements, as shown below:

```
<Policies>
   <RunAsPolicy CodePackageRef="Code" UserRef="WebUser" />
```

```
<SecurityAccessPolicy ResourceRef="HttpsEndPoint" PrincipalRef="WebUser" />
    <EndpointBindingPolicy EndpointRef="HttpsEndPoint" CertificateRef="MyCert" />
</Policies>
```

Hosting a Node.js application

With the basic concepts covered, next you'll walk through the steps of deploying a Hello World Node.js application on Service Fabric as a stateless service.

1. Create a new *NodeJsHelloWorldApplication* Service Fabric application with a stateless service named *NodeApp*.

2. Remove the following files from the service project. You won't need any of these .NET implementations in this case:

    - NodeApp.cs

    - Program.cs

    - ServiceEventSource.cs

    - App.config

    - Packages.config

3. Create a new *Code* folder under the PackageRoot folder of the service project.

4. Add an installNode.cmd file under the Code folder with the following contents. The script installs the Chocolatey package manager and then uses Chocolatey to install Node.js. Finally, the script calls *npm install* to install required Node.js modules that you'll declare in a *package.json* file next.

    ```
    @powershell -NoProfile -ExecutionPolicy Bypass -Command "iex ((new-object net.
    webclient).DownloadString('https://chocolatey.org/install.ps1'))" && SET
    PATH=%PATH%;%ALLUSERSPROFILE%\chocolatey\bin
    cinst nodejs.install --force -y
    SET PATH=%PATH%;C:\Program Files\nodejs
    npm install
    ```

5. Add a *package.json* file, which describes a Node.js package with a dependency to the express module and the os module.

    ```
    {
    "name": "hello-world",
      "version": "1.0",
      "description": "A Node.js Hello World App",
      "author": "Haishi Bai<hbai@microsoft.com>",
      "dependencies": {
        "express": "*",
        "os": "*"
      }
    }
    ```

6. Add a *app.js* file, which is the Hello World Node.js application:

```
var express = require('express');
var app = express();
var os = require('os');
app.get('/', function (req, res) {
    res.send('Hello World from ' + os.hostname() + '!');
});
var server = app.listen(80);
```

7. Add a *launchApp.cmd* file, which will be the entry point of the service. The file contains only one line, which is to call node.exe with the command-line argument. The reason you need this extra wrapper instead of using node.exe directly is because node.exe is yet to be installed. During package validation, Service Fabric checks if the entry point program exists. If you use node.exe directly, the package validation will fail.

```
node %1
```

8. Modify the service manifest as shown below. In this manifest, the service type is set to use implicit host (UseImplicitHost="true"). And the setup entry point for the service is the *installNode.cmd* script. The main entry point is the *launchApp.cmd* script, with *app.js* passed in as the argument. Finally, the manifest defines a HTTP endpoint at port 80.

```xml
<?xml version="1.0" encoding="utf-8"?>
<ServiceManifest Name="NodeAppPkg"
                 Version="1.0.0"
                 xmlns=http://schemas.microsoft.com/2011/01/fabric
                 xmlns:xsd=http://www.w3.org/2001/XMLSchema
                 xmlns:xsi="http://www.w3.org/2001/XMLSchema-instance">
  <ServiceTypes>
    <StatelessServiceType ServiceTypeName="NodeAppType" UseImplicitHost="true" />
  </ServiceTypes>
  <CodePackage Name="Code" Version="1.0.0">
    <SetupEntryPoint>
      <ExeHost>
        <Program>installNode.cmd</Program>
        <WorkingFolder>CodeBase</WorkingFolder>
      </ExeHost>
    </SetupEntryPoint>
    <EntryPoint>
      <ExeHost>
        <Program>launchApp.cmd</Program>
        <Arguments>app.js</Arguments>
        <WorkingFolder>CodeBase</WorkingFolder>
      </ExeHost>
    </EntryPoint>
  </CodePackage>
  <ConfigPackage Name="Config" Version="1.0.0" />
  <Resources>
    <Endpoints>
      <Endpoint Name="ServiceEndpoint" Protocol="http" Port="80" />
    </Endpoints>
  </Resources>
</ServiceManifest>
```

9. Finally, modify the application manifest as follows. The manifest defines a *SetupAdmin* user account under the *Administrators* group and uses the account to invoke the services setup entry point.

```xml
<?xml version="1.0" encoding="utf-8"?>
<ApplicationManifest xmlns:xsd="http://www.w3.org/2001/XMLSchema" xmlns:xsi="http://www.
w3.org/2001/XMLSchema-instance" ApplicationTypeName="NodeJsHelloWorldApplicationType"
ApplicationTypeVersion="1.0.0" xmlns="http://schemas.microsoft.com/2011/01/fabric">
    <Parameters>
        <Parameter Name="NodeApp_InstanceCount" DefaultValue="-1" />
    </Parameters>
    <ServiceManifestImport>
        <ServiceManifestRef ServiceManifestName="NodeAppPkg" ServiceManifestVersion="1.0.0"
/>
        <ConfigOverrides />
        <Policies>
            <RunAsPolicy CodePackageRef="Code" UserRef="SetupAdmin" EntryPointType="Setup"
/>
        </Policies>
    </ServiceManifestImport>
    <DefaultServices>
        <Service Name="NodeApp">
            <StatelessService ServiceTypeName="NodeAppType" InstanceCount="[NodeApp_
InstanceCount]">
                <SingletonPartition />
            </StatelessService>
        </Service>
    </DefaultServices>
    <Principals>
        <Users>
            <User Name="SetupAdmin">
                <MemberOf>
                    <SystemGroup Name="Administrators" />
                </MemberOf>
            </User>
        </Users>
    </Principals>
</ApplicationManifest>
```

10. Deploy this application to your Service Fabric cluster. Then, you'll be able to access the Node.js site by accessing *http://[address of your Service Fabric cluster]*. How the requests are routed and handled in this case is explained in more detail in Chapter 9, "Managing Service Fabric with management portal."

Assumptions and known issues

The above walkthrough assumes that when you configured your Service Fabric cluster, you defined an application endpoint at port 80. Refer to the section "Load balancing rules" in Chapter 9 if you haven't done so. At the time of this writing, there seems to be a bug with the Node.js installer that disallows Node.js to be installed correctly in a script. To fix Node.js installation manually, you can remote connect to each of the nodes (see Chapter 8) and invoke the install script manually.

CHAPTER 6

Availability and reliability

One of the major benefits of hosting your services on cloud is that you can take advantage of the Quality of Service (QoS) opportunities provided by the cloud. In this chapter, I'll discuss what Service Fabric provides in terms of availability and reliability and how you can leverage these offerings in your application design, implementation, and operation.

Service availability and reliability

In my earlier cloud computing book, *Zen of Cloud* (CRC Press, 2015), I've tried to explain the concepts of availability and reliability in a strict scientific way that complies with how they are defined in computer science literature. Because these two concepts are related closely and sometimes can be confusing, I'll try to explain them from an end user's perspective, which I believe can bring additional insights and clarity to these concepts. The definitions below are not strictly accurate but are more practical and easier to understand.

A broken service

An end user might consider a service "broken" because of several problems. First, a service is broken if it can't be accessed. Second, a service is broken if it's not delivering the desired results. Third, a service is broken if it can't deliver results within an acceptable amount of time. Roughly speaking, the first problem relates to availability, the second problem relates to reliability, and the third problem relates to scalability.

A service can become inaccessible for various reasons, such as broken connections, service outages, client problems, and configuration mismatches. The primary concern of service providers is to reduce service outages. In other words, one of the main goals of service providers is to keep the service available for consumption.

A service being available doesn't mean the service is functioning correctly. Instead, the service might be in a faulty state that stops the service from generating correct results. In other words, an available service isn't necessarily a reliable service.

Users are getting less tolerant of slow services. If a service doesn't perform, it might be considered broken because users are impatient while waiting for results. Service performance characteristics often are tightly linked to scalability. A scalable service can maintain acceptable performance as its workload increases. I'll discuss scalability in Chapter 7, "Scalability and performance."

Improving availability

To keep a service available, you need to keep it running. Many things can bring down a service, including both hardware failures and software failures. Most intuitively, availability can be improved by introducing redundancy. Multiple instances of a service can be used so that when some instances fail, there are still some healthy instances to handle client requests. The service instances often are joined behind a load balancer that monitors the statuses of these instances and routes requests to healthy ones.

When some of the service instances fail, the service itself remains available. However, fewer running instances mean higher risk of service outage. So, to ensure service availability, it's important to be able to restore failed instances. Fortunately, in a virtualized datacenter, starting a new server instance is much faster and cheaper than allocating a physical server. This is precisely why cloud can provide high-availability offerings with much lower cost.

However, when some error conditions trigger software bugs, it doesn't matter if a new service instance can be brought online quickly because the new instance is likely to fail in the same way unless the error conditions are resolved. In this case, service availability heavily relies on maintainability, which refers to the ease of remedying a software defect and redeploying a service instance.

Improving reliability

To put it simply, a reliable service is less "buggy." The elusive nature of software allows software defects to manifest and hide, and to surface only at seemingly the most inconvenient moments. Over the past decades, various principles, techniques, tools, and services have been employed to help service developers shake out and fix bugs early. However, as the complexity of software increases, it has been an uphill battle, especially for distributed services.

Among these techniques and principals, several stand out. First and foremost is the principle of separation of concerns. Under this principle, complex software is composed of components with clear responsibilities. Service Fabric adopts *Microservices* architecture, which follows this principle. A Service Fabric application is made up of one or many distinct services that can be designed, implemented, tested, and hosted independently from one another.

Another important technique is the test-driven development process. The focus of this process is to ensure that software behaves as designed. The process captures detailed requirements as test cases, and it makes sure the implementations stay true to these requirements by repeatedly running through these test cases against every revision.

Monitoring and tracing are important to improving service reliability. Some of the most tenacious and destructive bugs reveal themselves only when the service is under stress. An effective monitoring and tracing system is critical for detecting and logging these bugs for rapid diagnostics.

Service Fabric services availability

Redundancy, load balancing, and failover are three pillars of service availability. Multiple service instances are joined behind a load balancer to provide a cluster of service instances that tolerate partial node failures. These service instances are distributed across fault domains and update domains to reduce the risk of total outages during failures and updates.

Service Fabric uses multiple service replicas to provide redundancy. When a replica fails, Service Fabric automatically creates a new replica to replace the broken one. Figure 6-1 shows the status of the single partition of a stateless service. The service has five running replicas, one on each of the cluster nodes.

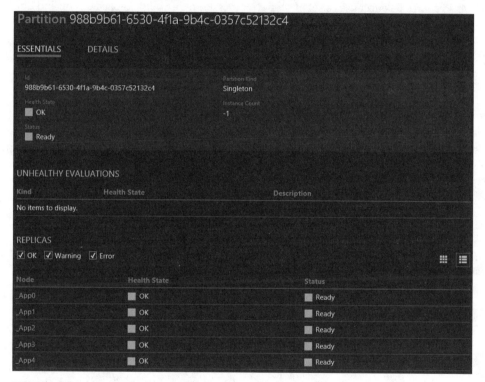

FIGURE 6-1 Partition view in Service Fabric Explorer

Service placements

When Service Fabric creates a new service replica, it picks a healthy node on the cluster based on several criteria, including current node loads, custom placement constraints, and service affinity requirements. This selection process is done through the collaboration of a Resource Balancer service and a Failover Manager service.

Resource Balancer and Failover Manager

On each of the Service Fabric cluster nodes runs an agent that collects and sends load reports to a centralized Resource Balancer service. The agent also sends failures and other node-level events to a Failover Manager service. When a replica fails, the agent sends an event to the Failover Manager, notifying it that a new service replica is to be created. The Failover Manager communicates with the Resource Balancer to ask for a placement recommendation. The Resource Balancer consults the load reports it has collected and returns a recommended node. Finally, the Failover Manager places a new service replica on the selected node.

Resource balancing metrics

By default, Resource Balancer uses a set of simple metrics: Primary Count, Replica Count, and Count:

- Primary Count: number of primary stateful replicas on a node

- Replica Count: number of stateful replicas on a node

- Count: number of service objects on a node

Figure 6-2 shows a possible distribution of service replicas across a five-node Service Fabric cluster. The average Primary Count, Replica Count, and Count are 0.6, 1.8, and 1.8, respectively. Correspondingly, the standard deviations of the three counts are 0.5, 0.4, and 0.4. To achieve balanced loads across the nodes, these standard deviations should be minimized. However, minimizing the standard deviations might not always be desirable—I'll come back to this later in the "Service defragmentation" section.

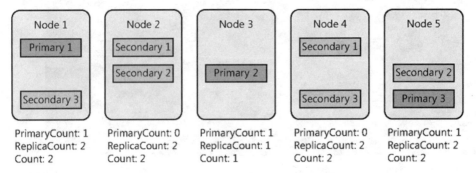

FIGURE 6-2 Replica distribution on a Service Fabric cluster

In some cases, resource balancing solely by replica counts may be insufficient. For example, for a memory-intensive service, you'll probably want to avoid placing multiple replicas on a same node to avoid out-of-memory errors. In this case, you can define and report on a memory-based metric so that the Resource Balancer can make smarter choices to make sure memory usages are evened out across cluster nodes.

Each of the custom metrics is identified by a string name. So, to make sure the Resource Balancer can correlate metrics from different services and applications correctly, you should use a consistent naming scheme across your Service Fabric applications.

A service can define multiple custom metrics such as memory usage, disk usage, and job queue length. Each custom metric can have an associated weight (High, Medium, or Low). Resource Balancer will make the best effort to make sure all custom metrics are distributed evenly. If such optimization isn't possible, Resource Balancer will try to satisfy metrics with higher weights first.

Last but not least, each custom metric can be assigned two default values, one for primary replicas and one for secondary replicas. Because the custom metrics are collected only during run time, the default values are necessary for Resource Balancer to make initial placement recommendations before these metrics are collected.

You can define custom metrics in several places. First, you can define these metrics in service manifest files, as shown in the following example. The manifest defines two metrics: *MemoryInMb* and *DiskInMb*. The *MemoryInMb* metric has high weight, and it has default value of 100 (MB) for primary replicas and 50 (MB) for secondary replicas.

```
...
<ServiceTypes>
  <StatefulServiceType ServiceTypeName="Stateful1Type" HasPersistedState="true">
    <LoadMetrics>
      <LoadMetric Name="MemoryInMb" Weight="High" PrimaryDefaultLoad="100"
SecondaryDefaultLoad="50"/>
      <LoadMetric Name="DiskInMb" Weight="Medium" PrimaryDefaultLoad="1000"
                  SecondaryDefaultLoad="500"/>
    </LoadMetrics>
  </StatefulServiceType>
</ServiceTypes>
...
```

Alternatively, you can define custom metrics in a *ServiceTemplates* element in your application manifest, as shown in the following example. The benefit of defining custom metrics in an application manifest is that you can make sure custom metric names are consistent across service types.

```
...
<ServiceTemplates>
  <StatefulService ServiceTypeName="Stateful1Type">
    <SingletonPartition />
    <LoadMetrics>
      <LoadMetric Name="MemoryInMb" PrimaryDefaultLoad="100"
SecondaryDefaultLoad="50" Weight="High" />
      <LoadMetric Name="DiskInMb" PrimaryDefaultLoad="1024"
SecondaryDefaultLoad="750" Weight="Medium" />
    </LoadMetrics>
  </StatefulService>
</ServiceTemplates>
...
```

You also can define custom metrics on the *DefaultServices* element in an application manifest, as shown in the following example:

```
<DefaultServices>
  <Service Name="Stateful1">
    <StatefulService ServiceTypeName="Stateful1Type"
```

```
TargetReplicaSetSize="3" MinReplicaSetSize="2">
        <UniformInt64Partition PartitionCount="10" LowKey="0" HighKey="9" />
        <LoadMetrics>
          <LoadMetric Name="MemoryInMb" PrimaryDefaultLoad="100"
SecondaryDefaultLoad="50" Weight="High" />
          <LoadMetric Name="DiskInMb" PrimaryDefaultLoad="1024"
SecondaryDefaultLoad="750" Weight="Medium" />
        </LoadMetrics>
      </StatefulService>
  </Service>
</DefaultServices>
```

To report custom metrics, you can use the *ReportLoad* method on the *ServicePartition* to send an array of *LoadMetric* instances, as shown in the following example:

```
this.ServicePartition.ReportLoad(new LoadMetric[]{new LoadMetric("MemoryInMb", 200)});
```

Batching load reports

The Service Fabric agent automatically batches and caches reported load metrics. So although the code repeatedly reports load metrics, only batched reports are sent.

You can observe the reported metrics on a partition's details view on Service Fabric Explorer. Figure 6-3 shows how the reported *MemoryInMb* metric appears in Service Fabric Explorer. Note that only the primary replica is sending metric reports because only the primary replica is handling requests.

FIGURE 6-3 Load metrics reports on Service Fabric Explorer

Placement constraints

You can override the Resource Balancer behavior by defining explicit placement constraints. Placement constraints are Boolean expressions that are evaluated against node properties. A node is a candidate for placement only if the expression returns *true*.

When you provision a Service Fabric cluster, you can associate a number of placement properties, which are just key-value pairs, to a node type. Figure 6-4 shows a series of blades on Azure management portal. The Service Fabric Cluster blade shows high-level information of the cluster. The Node Type Configurations blade shows a single node type is defined. The Node Type Properties blade shows configurations of the node type. Finally, the Placement Properties blade lists two placement properties, *MyBoolean* and *MyValue*. There's also an implied placement property, *NodeTypeName*, which reflects the name of the node type.

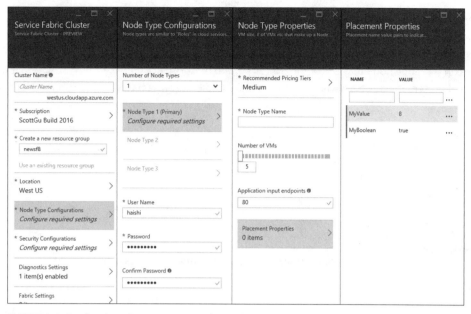

FIGURE 6-4 Configuring placement properties on Azure management portal

Placement properties are recorded in the cluster's manifest. The following manifest snippet shows how the above configuration screen translates into a service manifest:

```
<NodeType Name="App">
    <Endpoints>
      …
    </Endpoints>
    <PlacementProperties>
      <Property Name="myBoolean" Value="true" />
      <Property Name="myValue" Value="8" />
      <Property Name="NodeTypeName" Value="App" />
    </PlacementProperties>
</NodeType>
```

Then, in your service manifest file, you can specify placement constraints, as shown in the following example:

```
<ServiceTypes>
  <StatelessServiceType ServiceTypeName="Stateless1Type">
    <PlacementConstraints>(myBoolean == true &amp;&amp; myValue &gt;=4)</PlacementConstraints>
  </StatelessServiceType>
</ServiceTypes>
```

The following snippet is a simpler example that uses *NodeTypeName* as placement constraint:

```
<PlacementConstraints>(NodeTypeName == App)</PlacementConstraints>
```

Service affinity

Although Microservices architecture encourages independent service, there could be cases in which two services need to be collocated. For example, putting two services that need frequent data exchanges on the same node may boost the overall system performance. Service Fabric supports a special kind of placement constraint called *service affinity* to dictate two services be placed on the same node.

Service affinity is defined by a *ServiceCorrelation* element in an application's manifest. In the following snippet, The *Stateless1Type* service has an affinity with another service, *fabric:/otherApplication /parentService*.

```
<ServiceTemplates>
  <StatelessService ServiceTypeName="Stateless1Type" InstanceCount="5">
    <SingletonPartition></SingletonPartition>
    <ServiceCorrelations>
      <ServiceCorrelation Scheme="Affinity"
                          ServiceName="fabric:/otherApplication/parentService"/>
    </ServiceCorrelations>
  </StatelessService>
</ServiceTemplates>
```

Alternatively, service affinity can be defined under the *DefaultServices* element, as shown in the following example:

```
<DefaultServices>
  <Service Name="Stateless1">
    <StatelessService ServiceTypeName="Stateless1Type" InstanceCount="5">
      <SingletonPartition />
      <ServiceCorrelations>
        <ServiceCorrelation Scheme="Affinity"
                            ServiceName="fabric:/otherApplication/parentService"/>
      </ServiceCorrelations>
    </StatelessService>
  </Service>
</DefaultServices>
```

Service affinity limitations

Service affinity has limitations. The following list is from the official online documentation on azure.microsoft.com (*https://azure.microsoft.com/documentation/articles/service-fabric -resource-balancer-service-description/*):

- Cannot be used across stateless and stateful services.

- Cannot be used across stateless services with different instance counts; for example, both stateless services should have the same *InstanceCount* property when they are created.

- Cannot be used across stateful volatile or persistent services with different numbers of replicas; for example, both services must have the same specified Target and Min *ReplicaSetSizes* values.

- Cannot be used with partitioned services. Each service must have a FABRIC_PARTITION_SCHEME_SINGLETON partition scheme.

- Affinity relationships, like other properties of the service description, are set when the service is created and cannot be modified.

- Chains of services are not allowed. If multiple services must be brought into an affinity relationship, they must use a "star" model.

Service defragmentation

It makes sense to keep the standard deviations of placement metrics to a minimum to ensure loads on different nodes are balanced. However, on a busier cluster, this may lead to some negative consequences. Let's assume the cluster is fairly busy when a new resource-intensive service is to be placed on the cluster. In this case, Service Fabric may have to move existing replicas to make room for the new service replica. Moving replicas—especially stateful replicas with a large amount of data—is expensive. This slows down the speed to provision the new service replica.

It would be nice if Service Fabric could pack together the service replicas to leave enough space to accommodate other service replicas. This is what service defragmentation is about. With service defragmentation, service replicas are packed into as few nodes as possible while honoring all existing placement constraints. With Service Fabric, this is done through a mechanism called proactive metric packing. This mechanism allows you to identify placement metrics whose standard deviations are to be maximized instead of minimized.

The defragmentation process is triggered by balancing thresholds, which define the minimum allowed ratio between the most used and least used nodes per update or fault domain. If the ratio of any of the update or fault domains falls below the threshold, the defragmentation process begins.

To help you understand the concept, I'll go through an example. To simplify the scenario, I'll use one of the default placement constraints: Count, which represents the count of service replicas. Now, let's say I've defined the balancing threshold for this metric as 5. Then, the replica distribution in an update domain, as shown in Figure 6-5, is considered fragmented because the most used node is hosting eight replicas and the least used node is hosting two replicas. The ratio between the two is 4.

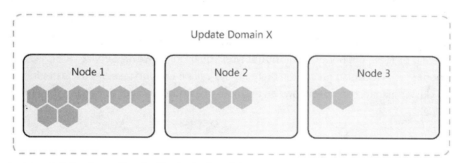

FIGURE 6-5 Service replica distribution before defragmentation

Because the ratio falls below the threshold, the defragmentation process begins, and service replicas are relocated so that the ratio is raised above the threshold. Figure 6-6 shows a possible outcome of the defragmentation process. In this case, one service replica has been moved from Node 3 to Node 1, bringing the ratio between the most used node (Node 1) and the least used node (Node 3) to 9, which is above the threshold. As you can see, Node 3 is nearly vacant after the process so that in the future, heavy service instances can be placed on it.

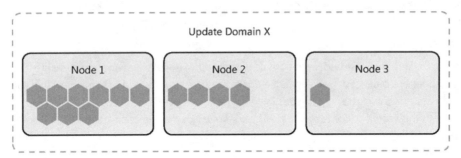

FIGURE 6-6 Service replica distribution after defragmentation

The following cluster manifest snippet shows how to identify defragmentation metrics and define load balancing thresholds. Note that when you identify defragmentation metrics, you need to assign a Boolean value to each of the placement metrics.

```
<FabricSettings>
  <Section Name="DefragmentationMetrics">
    <Parameter Name="MyBoolean" Value="true"/>
    <Parameter Name="MyValue" Value="false"/>
  </Section>
  <Section Name="MetricBalancingThresholds">
    <Parameter Name="MyValue" Value="5"/>
  </Section>
</FabricSettings>
```

If the load balancing threshold is not defined for a metric, the default threshold is 1, which means the defragmentation will be performed until there's at least one empty node per update domain or fault domain. If you don't want a metric to participate in the defragmentation process, set the threshold to 0.

In addition, you can allocate a node buffer to keep a percentage of nodes free for failovers. During the load balancing process, the nodes in this buffer won't be used. However, Service Fabric is allowed to use these nodes for failovers to guarantee there always will be enough reserves for faster failovers. The following cluster manifest snippet shows an example of a node buffer of 10 percent for a metric named *MyValue*:

```
<FabricSettings>
  <Section Name=" NodeBufferPercentage">
    <Parameter Name="MyValue" Value="0.1"/>
  </Section>
</FabricSettings>
```

Service failovers

Failovers may be triggered by either software errors or hardware errors. The multiple replicas of a stateless service serve as active backups for one another. When an instance fails, client requests are handled by other healthy replicas as Service Fabric tries to initiate a new service replica. For a stateful service, failing over means promoting one of the active secondaries as the primary. This promotion process usually is quick and negligible to clients.

It's fairly easy to experiment with service failovers with Service Fabric Explorer. The following example walks you through a quick failover test on a local Service Fabric cluster.

1. In Visual Studio 2015, create a new Service Fabric application with a single stateless service.

2. Publish the service on the local cluster using the local publish profile, which sets the instance count to 1.

3. Bring up the Diagnostic Event Viewer by using the View, Other Windows, Diagnostic Event Viewer menu. Observe diagnostic events in the view.

4. Open Service Fabric Explorer by navigating to *http://localhost:19080/* in a browser.

5. In the left pane, expand the application node and observe which node the single instance is deployed to. Then, expand the Nodes node and click the corresponding node.

6. In the right pane, click the Actions button and then select the Deactivate (restart) menu. This simulates a node crash. Because the node is hosting the only service instance, Service Fabric needs to bring up another instance on another healthy node to bring the service back online. If you observe closely, you can see a series of events captured in the Diagnostic Event Viewer, as shown in Figure 6-7. The bottom two entries are from the original service replica. The third entry from the bottom is the event entry for replica migration from *Node.1* to *Node.2*. The fourth entry from the bottom shows that a new service replica is being initiated while the service instance registers supported service types. The fifth entry shows the *RunAsync* method on the new service instance has been started. Finally, the last entry shows the new service replica is processing.

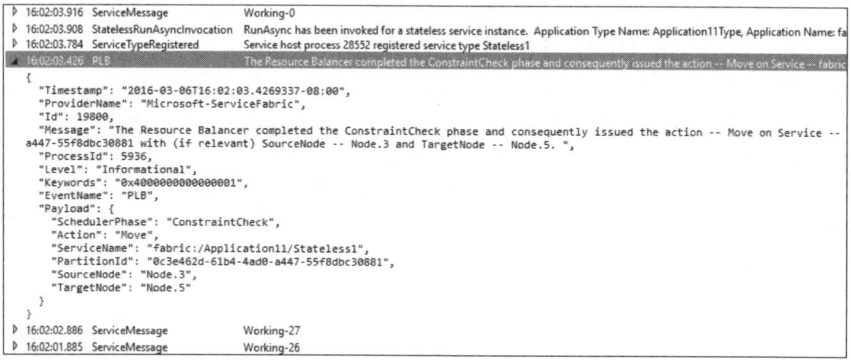

FIGURE 6-7 Diagnostic Event Viewer showing service replica migration

7. Go back to Service Fabric Explorer. In the left pane, expand the application node again and observe the service instance now running on a new node.

8. When you are done with the experiment, activate the deactivated node by using Service Fabric Explorer.

Routing and load balancing

Service Fabric provides a naming service that resolves service names into specific nodes. As you've seen in the previous section, a service replica may get relocated throughout its lifetime. The naming service allows clients to address services by stable service names, while individual requests are routed dynamically to appropriate nodes.

With default configuration, a Service Fabric cluster runs the naming service with three partitions to ensure the naming service is highly available. A client can connect to any of the three primary replicas to discover service addresses. Then, the client establishes a direct link to the discovered node, as you've seen in Chapter 1, "Hello, Service Fabric!"

A client such as a browser can't carry out this service discovery process. In this case, client requests are distributed to service replicas through a load balancer. The load balancer, like that provided by Azure, usually has no knowledge about Service Fabric. It just distributes traffic to all virtual machines that have been registered in its machine pool. This requires you to deploy an instance of your web-facing service onto each of the Service Fabric cluster nodes. I'll introduce how this is managed on Azure using Azure management portal in Chapter 9, "Managing Service Fabric with management portal."

> ### Gateway service
>
> At the time of writing, Service Fabric is introducing a new Gateway service that provides service discovery and load balancing for browser clients. It's not covered here because it's still unclear how this service would look eventually.

Advanced rolling upgrades

As introduced in Chapter 5, "Service deployments and upgrades," Service Fabric performs a rolling upgrade when upgrading an application. During this process, Service Fabric walks through update domains and makes sure an update domain has been upgraded and verified before moving to the next update domain. Rolling upgrades were covered in Chapter 5. Here, I'll cover a couple of advanced topics on rolling upgrades.

Configuration changes and data changes

A Service Fabric service is made up of code packages, configuration packages, and data packages. Each package is versioned separately. During rolling upgrades, only packages with newer version numbers are updated. This means that the service code only needs to be restarted when there are actual code changes.

Because changing configuration packages or data packages doesn't cause the service to restart, the service replica continuously runs during configuration or data changes. To pick up new configurations and data, your service code has to handle a couple of system events to load the updated contents.

Next, you'll walk through an example to see how to load new configurations dynamically.

1. Create a new Service Fabric application named *ConfigurationUpdate* with one stateless service named *Stateless1*.

2. Modify the *Settings.xml* file under the PackageRoot\Config folder of the service project to define an *IncrementStep* setting:

```
<Settings …>
  <Section Name="MyConfigSection">
    <Parameter Name="IncrementStep" Value="1" />
  </Section>
</Settings>
```

3. Define a local variable on the *Stateless1* class:

```
int incrementStep = 1;
```

4. At the beginning of the *RunAsync* method, add the following lines to read the configuration setting:

```
var configSection = this.ServiceInitializationParameters
            .CodePackageActivationContext.GetConfigurationPackageObject("Config");
var text = configSection.Settings.Sections["MyConfigSection"]
            .Parameters["IncrementStep"].Value;
incrementStep = int.Parse(text);
```

5. Modify the statement in the *while* loop to increment the iteration count by the configured increment:

```
ServiceEventSource.Current.ServiceMessage(this, "Working-{0}", iterations +=
incrementStep);
```

6. Publish the application. Observe diagnostic events in the Diagnostic Events Viewer.

7. Modify the *settings.xml* file to change the *IncrementStep* setting to *10*.

8. Modify the service manifest to change the version number on the *ConfigPackage* element and the version number on the *ServiceManifest* element to *2.0.0*.

9. Change the application manifest to update the *ServiceManifestVersion* to *2.0.0*:

```
<ServiceManifestImport>
    <ServiceManifestRef ServiceManifestName="Stateless1Pkg"
                        ServiceManifestVersion="2.0.0" />
    <ConfigOverrides />
</ServiceManifestImport>
```

10. Change the *ApplicationTypeVersion* on the root element to *2.0.0*.

11. Save all changes.

12. Right-click the application and select the Publish menu. In the Publish Service Fabric Application dialog box, make sure the Upgrade the Application check box is selected, as shown in Figure 6-8. This notifies Visual Studio tooling that you want to do a rolling upgrade instead of removing and redeploying the application.

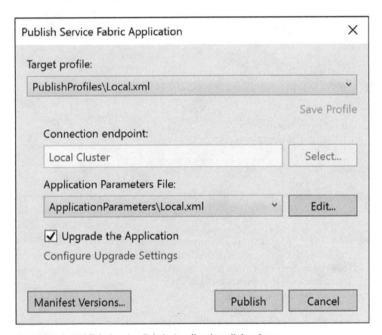

FIGURE 6-8 Publish Service Fabric Application dialog box

13. Click the Publish button to trigger the rolling upgrade.

14. Observe the diagnostic events. Figure 6-9 shows that the configuration update is applied (notice the increment step jump after 194) without restarting the process (notice the iteration counter, which is a local variable, is not reset).

```
▷  17:54:27.619  ServiceMessage Working-224
▷  17:54:26.617  ServiceMessage Working-214
▷  17:54:25.605  ServiceMessage Working-204
▷  17:54:24.604  ServiceMessage Working 194
▷  17:54:23.603  ServiceMessage Working-193
▷  17:54:22.602  ServiceMessage Working 192
   17:54:22.155  CM                Application upgrade domain completed: Application fabric:/Co
▷  17:54:21.588  ServiceMessage Working-191
▷  17:54:20.587  ServiceMessage Working 190
▷  17:54:19.586  ServiceMessage Working 189
```

FIGURE 6-9 Diagnostic events around configuration update

Upgrade with diff packages

A full Service Fabric application package contains everything needed to deploy a Service Fabric application. However, it would be wasteful to upload and deploy the entire package if only minor changes are made.

Service Fabric allows you to update an application with a diff package that contains only changed files, along with the complete service manifests and application manifest. The diff package doesn't have a special format. As long as the updated files are put under the same application package layout, you can use the diff package to update an application. Service Fabric automatically fills in omitted files from the image store.

Some continuous integration (CI) systems directly create application packages as part of the automated build process. Even if nothing has been changed, the newly built assemblies will have different checksums, which require revisions to all code packages. By using a diff package, you can provide only the files that have been updated.

Service Fabric services reliability

Reliability refers to the probability that an application functions as designed during any period of time. Designing and implementing reliable systems is a large topic that deserves its own book. The book just covers a number of techniques that help you with routine tasks. As introduced earlier, Service Fabric provides tools, services, and programming models for you to write reliable services and reliable actors. In addition, Service Fabric provides mechanisms that help you diagnose and test your services and back up and restore your service states.

A note on designing reliable services

All the tools introduced below help you improve your service reliability. They don't guarantee service reliability. You still need to follow good engineering principles and best practices to design, develop, and operate reliable services.

Architecturally, you should avoid things like single points of failure (SPoF), vague service responsibilities, overcomplicated object graphs, and tightly coupled dependencies. When writing code, you want to write clean and precise code, use test cases to capture requirements, avoid repeating yourself, and use injection to unit test components in isolation. Last but not least, operating a reliable service calls for automations to avoid human errors and to improve consistency across different environments and for data-driven insights and decisions.

Event Tracing for Windows

In Chapter 1, I introduced that Service Fabric recommends using Event Tracing for Windows (ETW) for tracing and logging. In earlier examples, you've been using Diagnostic Event Viewer to view tracing events.

When you create a new Service Fabric service, Visual Studio tooling automatically creates a *System.Diagnostics.Tracing.EventSource* subclass. You can use the template code as an example of generating custom ETW traces.

For each custom event you want to trace, you should define an instance method on the *EventSource* subclass. The following code snippet shows the autogenerated *ServiceTypeRegistered* event by Visual Studio tooling:

```
private const int ServiceTypeRegisteredEventId = 3;
[Event(ServiceTypeRegisteredEventId, Level = EventLevel.Informational,
Message = "Service host process {0} registered service type {1}",
Keywords = Keywords.ServiceInitialization)]
public void ServiceTypeRegistered(int hostProcessId, string serviceType)
{
WriteEvent(ServiceTypeRegisteredEventId, hostProcessId, serviceType);
}
```

The following code snippet shows how the event is used:

```
ServiceEventSource.Current.ServiceTypeRegistered(Process.GetCurrentProcess().Id,
    typeof(Stateless1).Name);
```

Visual Studio tooling provides a very smooth experience for local diagnostics. When an application is deployed to Azure, however, collecting and viewing ETW events takes more work.

Azure Diagnostics

Azure Diagnostics is an Azure extension that enables you to collect diagnostic and telemetry data from Azure virtual machines. It collects various types of telemetry from the machines, including IIS logs, IIS Failed Request logs, Azure diagnostic infrastructure logs, crash dumps, performance counters, Windows Event logs, custom error logs, .NET EventSource events, and manifest-based ETW events. Azure Diagnostics periodically transfers the telemetry data to an Azure storage account so that even if the virtual machine crashes, you can access the diagnostic data.

The best way to understand Azure Diagnostics is to see it in action. In the following walkthrough, I'll show you the steps to enable and use Azure Diagnostics on a new Service Fabric cluster. Enabling Azure Diagnostics on an existing cluster requires deeper understanding of how a Service Fabric cluster is constructed on Azure. Both topics are covered in Chapter 8, "Managing Service Fabric with Windows PowerShell."

1. In Azure management portal, create a new Service Fabric cluster. The steps are the same as those introduced in Chapter 1, except for Diagnostics Settings. As shown in Figure 6-10, you need to make sure Application Diagnostics is set to Enabled. Enabling Application Diagnostics enables three ETW event source providers: *Microsoft-ServiceFabric-Actors*, *Microsoft-ServiceFabric-Services*, and another event source for Service Fabric system events. The entries from the first provider are transferred to a *ServiceFabricReliableActorEventTable* Azure Storage table. The entries from the second provider are transferred to a *ServiceFabricReliableServiceEventTable* table. Finally, the entries from the third provider are transferred to a *ServiceFabricSystemEventTable* table.

FIGURE 6-10 Service Fabric cluster diagnostics settings

2. Create a new Service Fabric application with a stateless service. You need to make a couple of adjustments before you can deploy the application. First, modify the *ServiceEventSource* class to change the name of the *EventSource* attribute to *Microsoft-ServiceFabric-Services*. This is to match the name with what gets registered by the portal provisioning process. In Chapter 8, you learn how to customize this.

```
[EventSource(Name = "Microsoft-ServiceFabric-Services")]
```

3. To avoid generating too many events, modify the task delay in the service *RunAsync* loop to a longer interval than the default one-second interval. The following example changes the interval to 30 seconds:

```
await Task.Delay(TimeSpan.FromSeconds(30), cancelServiceInstance);
```

4. Once the cluster has been provisioned, deploy the new application to the cluster. Once the service is started, it will start generating tracing events.

5. Now is the tricky part: finding the Azure storage account to which the trace records are written. Chapter 8 introduces a more reliable method to find the account names and ways to customize these accounts. For now, use the Cloud Explorer that is installed as part of Azure SDK. In Visual Studio, select the View, Cloud Explorer menu.

6. Log in to your Azure subscription. You'll see a list of all resource types on Azure, as shown in Figure 6-11.

FIGURE 6-11 Cloud Explorer in Visual Studio

7. In the search box, type **sfdg** and press Enter. At the time of this writing, application tracing data is written to an autogenerated storage account with sfdg*[cluster name]* as the name prefix (*sf* stands for Service Fabric, and *dg* stands for diagnostics). Figure 6-12 shows the search result on my Azure subscription. Your storage account will have a different name. If you have multiple Service Fabric clusters, the search may return multiple storage accounts. Under the storage account are a number of storage tables. Double-click the *WADServiceFabricReliableServiceEventTable* table to browse its contents.

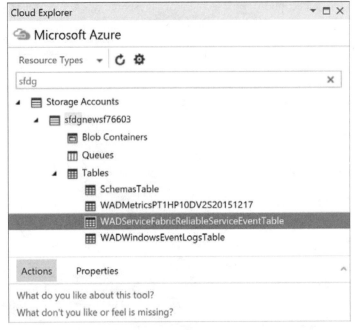

FIGURE 6-12 Storage tables in Cloud Explorer

8. Figure 6-13 shows some of the entries in my environment. Because I'm reusing the *Microsoft-ServiceFabric-Services* event resource name, events from the application are interleaved with system-generated trace entries.

FIGURE 6-13 Service Fabric tracing event table

Directly browsing tracing records in Azure storage accounts isn't convenient. In Chapter 10, "Diagnostics and monitoring," I'll show you how to browse the data using Microsoft Azure Operational Insights. I'll also show you how to collect other telemetry data such as CPU utilization in the same chapter.

Chaos tests

Most people learn about chaos tests from Netflix Chaos Monkey and, later, Simian Army tools. As one of the largest online media streaming companies, Netflix runs hundreds of services over a massive multiregion infrastructure to provide continuous entertainment to its millions of customers in the United States and around the world.

The Simian Army is formed by a number of variations of chaos monkeys, which generate random errors in the system to simulate unexpected errors such as machine crashes, network speed fluctuations, security penetrations, and even large-scale datacenter outages. The philosophy of the Simian Army is to encourage service developers to embrace errors.

Each cloud platform is built on top of enormous infrastructures that are comprised of millions of servers and switches. At any given moment, millions of pieces of hardware may fail for various reasons, and the failing ones could be exactly the ones on which you rely to deliver your services. In such cases, the platform provides you opportunities to fail over your services to other healthy hardware to maintain your service availability. However, you need to make sure your services are designed in such a way that they can take advantage of such offerings.

Chaos tests help you detect and fix problems in responding to infrastructure errors, which may occur at any time in any scope. Most developers are not used to dealing with such errors because traditionally, infrastructure errors require human interventions. In other words, they are operational problems, not dev problems. However, in a large-scale, cloud-based system such as Netflix, the system itself needs to be tolerant of and automatically recover from these errors. So, the value of chaos tests is to provide a new perspective from which developers can consider how to deal with infrastructural problems in an automated, efficient, predictable, and verifiable manner.

Service Fabric provides built-in support for chaos tests. These tests simulate possible errors that your service may encounter over months or even years in a few hours so that you can validate if your service is prepared for these errors, including the following:

- A node is restarted.
- A deployed code package is restarted.
- A primary/secondary replica or a stateless instance is removed.
- A primary/secondary replica is restarted.
- A primary/secondary replica is moved.

Service Fabric allows you to simulate all the above errors in a consistent, controlled manner. You can perform these tests in your dev environment or QA environment, or in a controlled segment of your production environment.

Testing in production

Testing in production is a proven technique to encourage developers to write error-resilient service code. However, testing in production has risks. First, testing in production has to be controllable. The last thing you want is to trigger real service outages or cause significant service quality degradations while running these tests. Second, these tests need to be monitored closely. As mentioned before, because these tests trigger code paths that many developers won't expect, some severe problems such as data corruptions may occur. Third, you need to be ready for recovering from errors that are not automatically recoverable (such as data corruptions). Later in this chapter, I'll discuss how to back up and restore service states in the "Service state backup and restore" section.

Perform a chaos test

You can perform chaos tests on Service Fabric clusters by using either C# code or Windows PowerShell cmdlets. I'll cover PowerShell cmdlets in Chapter 8. The following walkthrough shows you the steps to perform chaos tests using C#. The example shows you how to simulate a node restart.

 Note The following walkthrough is adapted from *https://azure.microsoft.com /documentation/articles/service-fabric-testability-scenarios/.*

1. Create a new Console application named *Testability*.

2. Add a reference to the *Microsoft.ServiceFabric.Testability NuGet* package. The package includes a *System.Fabric.Testability* assembly that provides chaos test APIs.

3. Change the solution target platform to x64.

4. Add a new static method to the *Program* class. To trigger a chaos test session, connect to a cluster using *FabricClient*, create a new *ChaosTestScenario* instance using appropriate parameters, and then invoke the *ExecuteAsync* method on the instance.

```
static async Task RunChaosTestScenarioAsync(string clusterConnection)
{
    TimeSpan maxClusterStabilizationTimeout = TimeSpan.FromSeconds(180);
    uint maxConcurrentFaults = 3;
    bool enableMoveReplicaFaults = true;

    FabricClient fabricClient = new FabricClient(clusterConnection);

    TimeSpan timeToRun = TimeSpan.FromMinutes(60);
    ChaosTestScenarioParameters scenarioParameters = new ChaosTestScenarioParameters(
        maxClusterStabilizationTimeout,
        maxConcurrentFaults,
        enableMoveReplicaFaults,
        timeToRun);

    ChaosTestScenario chaosScenario = new ChaosTestScenario(fabricClient,
scenarioParameters);

    try
    {
```

```
        await chaosScenario.ExecuteAsync(CancellationToken.None);
    }
    catch (AggregateException ae)
    {
        throw ae.InnerException;
    }
}
```

5. Modify the *Main* method. Errors detected during the test are captured as *FabricException* exception objects.

```
static int Main(string[] args)
{
    string clusterConnection = "localhost:19000";
    Console.WriteLine("Starting Chaos Test Scenario...");
    try
    {
        RunChaosTestScenarioAsync(clusterConnection).Wait();
    }
    catch (AggregateException ae)
    {
        Console.WriteLine("Chaos Test Scenario did not complete: ");
        foreach (Exception ex in ae.InnerExceptions)
        {
            if (ex is FabricException)
            {
                Console.WriteLine("HResult: {0} Message: {1}", ex.HResult, ex.Message);
            }
        }
        return -1;
    }
    Console.WriteLine("Chaos Test Scenario completed.");
    return 0;
}
```

6. Press Ctrl+F5 to launch the application. The test takes about an hour. And if everything checks out, you get no exceptions, as shown in Figure 6-14.

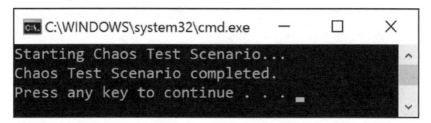

FIGURE 6-14 Chaos test with no errors

7. Now, let's make things more exciting. We'll intentionally create an application that does not handle failovers correctly and observe what happens. Create a new Service Fabric application named *BadApplication* with a stateful service named *BadStateful*.

8. Modify the service's *RunAsync* method. Declare two local variables. The *localValue* variable is used to save an in-memory state. The *key* variable identifies the key to the state value in a reliable dictionary.

    ```
    long localValue = 0;

    string key = "Counter-Unique";
    ```

9. Update all references to *Counter-1* to the *key* variable (two occurrences). Also, add the code to maintain the in-memory state (localValue++) and to check if the in-memory state is consistent with the reliable dictionary (the *if* statement in bold).

    ```
    var result = await myDictionary.TryGetValueAsync(tx, key);
    ...
    if (result.HasValue && localValue != result.Value)
                        throw new ApplicationException("State is inconsistent");
    await myDictionary.AddOrUpdateAsync(tx, key, 0, (k, v) => ++v);
    localValue++;
    ...
    ```

10. Deploy the application to your local cluster and observe the Diagnostics Event Viewer. The application will work as long as the key is a new key because the in-memory state is kept in sync with the reliable state. If the application is restarted, it will break because the in-memory state will be reset to 0 while the reliable state is not reset.

11. Launch the chaos test application again. As the test runs, chances are that the node hosting the primary replica will be restarted. When that happens, a secondary replica needs to be promoted and a new replica needs to be created. As the *RunAsnc* method kicks off on these replicas, things will break because the in-memory state is fresh while the reliable state remembers the previous value. You can observe this happening in the Diagnostics Event Viewer, as shown in Figure 6-15.

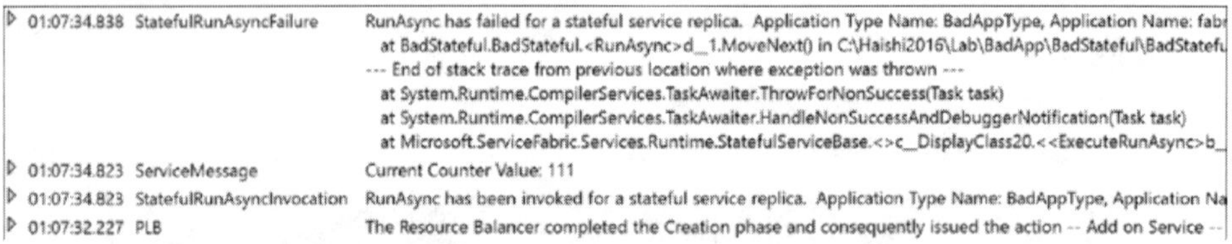

FIGURE 6-15 Diagnostics Event Viewer

12. Wait for the chaos test to complete. As shown in Figure 6-16, you'll see the complaint that the replica didn't get ready within the given timeout limit. The error doesn't disclose which chaos test action triggered the exception, and it doesn't include a time stamp. So, it will be tricky to correlate this exception with what you observe in the diagnostics events. I believe this will be improved in future versions.

FIGURE 6-16 Chaos test results with exceptions

Perform failover tests

You also can use chaos tests to perform failover tests against a specific service partition. Service Fabric provides a *PartitionSelector* helper class that helps you pick a random partition:

```
PartitionSelector randomPartitionSelector = PartitionSelector.RandomOf(serviceName);
```

Then, you can create a *FailoverTestScenarioParameters* instance, passing in the partition selector:

```
FailoverTestScenarioParameters scenarioParameters = new FailoverTestScenarioParameters(
    randomPartitionSelector,
    timeToRun,
    maxServiceStabilizationTimeout);
```

Finally, you can create a new *FailoverTestScenario* instance and then invoke its *ExecuteAsync* method:

```
FailoverTestScenario chaosScenario = new FailoverTestScenario(fabricClient, scenarioParameters);
```

The failover test simulates the following errors:

- The deployed Code Package that hosts the partition is restarted.

- A primary/secondary replica or stateless instance is removed.

- A primary/secondary replica is restarted.

- A primary/secondary replica is moved.

- A partition is restarted.

Graceful and ungraceful faults

Service Fabric testability features can simulate two types of faults: graceful and ungraceful. Ungraceful errors are crashes such as unexpected machine restarts and process crashes. There are no attempts to clean up the state properly before the application is started again for failover. Graceful errors, in contrast, are controlled replica interruptions because of load balancing, such as movements of replicas. States are supposed to be managed properly by Service Fabric in such cases.

Moreover, you can use *FabricClient* to trigger specific cluster events by using its *ClusterManager*, *ApplicationManager,* and *ServiceManager*. For example, you can use *ClusterManager* to restart a node, use *ApplicationManager* to restart a deployed code package, and use *ServiceManager* to remove a replica or move a primary replica. In your test code, you can mix these errors randomly with your actual service workloads to simulate failures while particular workloads are running.

You'll see a detailed example when I discuss testability further in Chapter 11, "Testing."

Service state backup and restore

Although Service Fabric provides reliable state management out-of-box, you may want to back up your service states manually to external storage for several reasons. First, you may want to back up the states in preparation for disastrous events such as permanent loss of the entire Service Fabric cluster. Second, you may want to back up the states in case human errors or application bugs cause data corruptions. Last but not least, in some cases you may want to capture and replay the state in an offline statement for diagnostic purposes or offline processing.

Once you have the service states backed up, Service Fabric provides you events to which you can hook up state restore logic to restore service states as needed.

Backup

To trigger a backup, your service needs to invoke the *IReliableStateManager.BackupAsync* method with a callback function. In Chapter 3, "Stateful services," I've introduced that the Reliable State Manager takes periodic snapshots, or checkpoints, to relieve pressure on the transactional logs. When your service invokes the *BackupAsync* method, the Reliable State Manager notifies all reliable objects to copy their latest checkpoint files to a local backup folder. Then, the Reliable State Manager collects and copies all log files to the backup folder as well. In this way, Service Fabric guarantees that all committed transactions before the *BackupAsync* method is invoked will be included in the backup. The transactions that are committed after the method call are not guaranteed to be included.

Once all files are collected to the local backup folder, your service's callback function will be invoked. It's up to this method to upload the files to external storage such as Azure Storage.

At any given time, there can be only one *BackupAsync* method in execution. Otherwise, a *FabricBackupInProgressException* exception is thrown. Because the method is invoked only on the primary replica, you just need to make sure you wait for the method to return before you make another backup attempt.

To trigger a backup, use the State Manager *BackupAsync* method:

```
await this.StateManager.BackupAsync(this.MyBackupCallbackAsync);
```

MyBackupCallbackAsync is the callback method that backs up filto external storage. The method takes a *BackupInfo* parameter, which carries information about where the local backup folder is (BackupInfo.Directory). The callback is expected to copy the entire folder to external storage and returns *true* to indicate the backup is successful.

```
private async Task<bool> MyBackupCallbackAsync (BackupInfo backupInfo)
{
    var backupId = Guid.NewGuid();

    await someUploadMethodAsync(backupInfo.Directory, backupId, CancellationToken.None);

    return true;
}
```

A backup operation may fail if a replica fails over during the backup. It's up to the service developer to restart the backup as necessary.

Restore

Typically, you may want to restore service state from an external backup when one of the following happens: a service partition loses its quorum, a service is removed or lost, or service state is corrupted because of application bugs. Service Fabric Reliable State Manager provides an *IReliableStateManager. RestoreAsync* method, which can be called only from the event handler of a system-defined *onDataLossEvent* event. When Service Fabric detects state loss in a partition, it triggers the *onDataLossEvent* event. In your custom event handler, you should download the backup data from the external storage and then invoke the *IReliableStateManager.RestoreAsync* method. The event handler should return *true* to indicate the restore operation is successful.

Whichever replica receives the *onDataLossEvent* first will be promoted to the primary replica. If the restore operation is successful, Service Fabric will rebuild other replicas based on the state of this new primary. All transactions committed to the primary during this process will be delayed to ensure consistency.

To hook up your custom *onDataLossEvent* event handler, you need to override the *CreateReliableStateManager* method of the *StatefulService* class, as shown in the following code snippet:

```
protected override IReliableStateManager CreateReliableStateManager()
{
    return new ReliableStateManager(new ReliableStateManagerConfiguration(
            onDataLossEvent: this.MyOnDataLossAsync));
}
```

The following code snippet shows a simplified implementation of the event handler:

```
protected override async Task<bool> MyOnDataLossAsync(CancellationToken cancellationToken)
{
    var localBackupFolder = await downloadExternalBackuptoLocalBackupfolder(cancellationToken);
    await this.StateManager.RestoreAsync(localBackupFolder);
    return true;
}
```

The *RestoreAsync* method has an overload that takes in a *RestorePolicy* parameter. If the parameter is set to Safe, Service Fabric checks if the state to be restored is ahead of the current state. Setting the parameter to *Force* will skip this check.

To restore service state completely (such as recovering from a destroyed or corrupted service), you can trigger the *onDataLossEvent* proactively by calling the *FabricClient.ServiceManager. InvokeDataLossAsync* method on all service partitions.

No matter how much support Service Fabric brings to the table, restoring previously archived states into a live system is a risky business. For example, transactions in flight may get lost; service availability may get interrupted because the primary's *RunAsync* method is held off until *onDataLossEvent* is handled; or the state change outside the regular service logic may trigger unexpected behaviors and bugs. So, you should use this feature with caution. You may want to create a parallel application instance and restore the backup state to the new instance to verify everything is in place before you restore states in a production environment.

CHAPTER 7

Scalability and performance

Scalability goes hand in hand with performance. A scalable system is a system that can maintain its performance characteristics as the load increases[1]. Cloud makes massive resource pools available to service developers. In theory, anyone can design and deploy global-scale services in the cloud without significant upfront investments. Service developers have this unprecedented opportunity to start small, to grow rapidly, and to become big. Scalability is the cornerstone of such systems. In this chapter, I'll discuss scalability and performance and introduce some key concepts, tools, and skills you need to master to design scalable Service Fabric applications.

Scalability concepts

Scaling a service in the cloud differs from scaling a service in a traditional datacenter. Before discussing specific techniques, review some of the key concepts of scaling in the cloud.

Vertical scaling vs. horizontal scaling

In traditional datacenters, increasing a service's capacity usually means upgrading the hardware where the service is hosted. For example, it's common for system administrators to add memory and disks to a file server or a relational database server to gain additional capacity. This kind of scaling is called *vertical scaling*. Vertical scaling has several inherent flaws. First, hardware upgrades often require shutting down the machine, causing service interruptions. Second, hardware upgrades aren't always possible. For example, the hosting machine may run out of memory slots. And it's usually fairly hard to add CPUs to an existing server. When such limitations are hit, vertical scaling can't continue without migrating the service to more capable servers.

Scaling in the cloud takes a different approach. Instead of upgrading the existing host, system capacity is increased by adding hosts to share the workload. This kind of scaling is called *horizontal scaling*. Horizontal scaling overcomes the limitations of vertical scaling. First, horizontal scaling doesn't require shutting down existing running service instances. New service instances can be added or removed dynamically so that the system can be adjusted without service interruptions. Second,

---

[1] Smith, Connie U., and Lloyd G. Williams. 2002. *Performance Solutions: A Practical Guide to Creating Responsive, Scalable Software.* New York: Pearson Education.

horizontal scaling isn't constrained by hardware limitations. Theoretically, a service can be scaled out to hundreds or even thousands of instances that collectively provide tremendous system capacity.

Vertical scaling does have one advantage over horizontal scaling when it comes to scaling legacy services. Vertical scaling often doesn't require significant code changes, so it can be carried out with much lower cost and risk. In contrast, a service has to be designed for horizontal scaling before it can be scaled out to multiple instances. Such modifications are expensive and not always possible, especially for legacy systems. This is precisely the reason why Microsoft Azure provides a variety of virtual machine sizes to accommodate applications with different resource needs.

Scaling stateless services vs. scaling stateful services

Scaling a stateless service in the cloud is relatively easy—just add service instances behind the load balancer to share the workload. Many platform as a service (PaaS) systems mandate services be stateless to be managed and scaled.

Scaling a stateful service is harder because the service state also needs to be scaled. This means the service state needs to be replicated and synced across service instances. Although platforms such as Service Fabric can provide efficient state management, state replication isn't free. When a service is scaled to hundreds of instances, state management becomes an unneglectable system overhead. To avoid this, Service Fabric scales stateful services by partitioning. With partitioning, system load is distributed to any number of partitions, and state replications happen within the scope of a single partition. This design reduces the amount of data to be replicated and limits the number of participating nodes so that even if the service is scaled to a massive scale, the state management overhead still is under control.

To sum up, for stateless services, both availability and scalability are achieved by using multiple service instances. For stateful services, availability is provided by service replicas, and scalability is provided by partitions.

Homogeneous instances vs. heterogeneous instances

All PaaS platforms include a resource scheduling system. The resource scheduling system is responsible for identifying a host in the cluster's resource pool that satisfies the requirement of a service instance. A simple scheduling system assumes all nodes on the cluster are homogeneous, which means any node on the cluster can be a valid candidate to fulfill a scheduling request.

A more sophisticated scheduling system can manage a mixture of node types. A scheduling request in this case can include additional criteria such as host operation system, hardware architecture, and other node-specific properties so that a service instance can be hosted on the most suitable node.

A homogeneous cluster is easier to manage, and it's more flexible in terms of making resource offers. As long as a node can satisfy the request, the node can be offered. A heterogeneous cluster is harder to manage because of the extra criteria matching. Moreover, a heterogeneous cluster makes implicit assumptions about the workload composition. If the assumptions are wrong, lots of scheduling requests can't be fulfilled, and many nodes will be unoccupied. So, a generic heterogeneous cluster that is targeted at hosting arbitrary applications won't work.

Service Fabric clusters are individual Azure resource groups on Azure. Because you can create as many Service Fabric clusters as needed, it's fine for you to create Service Fabric clusters with specific applications in mind. You can define a mixture of node types on the cluster and allocate different service instances to the most appropriate node types by using placement constraints. In addition, you can create different environments in a consistent manner by replicating the resource group. I'll go into more details on the relationship between Service Fabric clusters and Azure resource groups in Chapter 8, "Managing Service Fabric with Windows PowerShell."

Single-tenancy vs. multitenancy

A single-tenant system serves a specific customer. A multitenant system serves a number of different customers. A multitenant system can provide a common entry point for all customers or a separate entry point for each customer. When a common entry point is used, a tenant discovery process is needed to associate a logged-in user with a specific tenant.

A multitenant application can be scaled out naturally to support additional customers. Many multitenant applications also support self-service registrations so that a new customer can onboard herself. However, unless the application is designed with multitenancy in mind at the beginning, it's usually fairly hard to adapt a single-tenant application for multitenancy. Moreover, many customers feel more comfortable if the service provider offers strong isolation among tenants so that service processes and data are separated from those of other customers. In addition, some customers might want to stay with a particular application version instead of automatically being updated to later versions when the application updates.

If your Service Fabric applications are designed with multitenancy in mind, you can scale out using per-tenant partitions. Partitioning doesn't offer physical isolation among tenants or per-tenant versioning, however. In addition, because you can't dynamically repartition a running service, you need to come up with a partition scheme that will accommodate future customers. For example, an integer range from 0 to 999 can hold up to 1,000 customer tenants.

Another option is to scale your application at higher levels. You can deploy individual application instances for different customer tenants. And you can create different service deployments for different user segments. For example, you can logically partition customers who have registered in different years or have purchased different service levels to different service instances. Furthermore, you can use placement constraints to place customers with different subscription levels to different node types, such as putting gold-level subscribers to more powerful nodes.

One caveat of scaling at a higher level is that the clients need to be aware of how the users are segmented so that they can use the correct service addresses. You can employ some naming rules in service names for the clients to follow, or you can provide a lookup service so that clients can look up correct instances to which to connect.

Manual scaling vs. autoscaling

A system's capacity can be adjusted either manually or automatically based on system load. In reality, a combination of the methods often is used to adjust system capacity. Before a service goes into production, a service provider needs to go through a capacity planning phase to determine the size and the configuration of the cluster to support the expected initial workload and the expected growth. On top of the planned capacity, autoscaling can be used to adjust system capacity to handle workload variations such as unexpected spikes in traffic.

During the capacity planning phase, you need to consider how many resources, including RAM, CPU, and disk space, are needed to support your service instances. You also use this process to design a financial model for your service, such as how much you would charge your customers for the service and what the margin would look like. Service Fabric provides a sample Microsoft Excel workbook (*http://bit.ly/1ZCBtz0*) that you can use to jumpstart the planning process. Figure 7-1 shows a portion of the workbook. The sample data shows the system uses three object types: Inventory Item, User Profile, and Order. For each object type, the total size and the cost for hosting these objects are calculated based on expected number of objects, desired replica count, and standard Service Fabric pricing.

	A	B	C	D	E
1	Data Object Type		Inventory Item	User Profile	Order
2	Size of Object (KB)		4	2	1
3	Number of Objects		10,000	3,000,000	45,000,000
4	Total Size of Object (KB)		40,000	6,000,000	45,000,000
5					
6	Number of Desired Replicas		3	5	3
7	Total size of Replicas (KB)		120,000	30,000,000	135,000,000
8	Total size of data to store in the Cluster (GB)	157			
9					
10	Node Available RAM/Storage (GB)	6	(Put available RAM or disk size based on your perforr		
11	Node Cost/Month	$ 229.00	(Ex: Azure A3 pricing)		
12					
13					
14	Minimum Partitions Required		1	1	8
15	Number of Desired Partitions		1	6	8
16					
17	Minimum Number of Nodes	26			
18	Cost of Nodes/Month	$ 6,010			
19					
20	Number of Nodes (1 replica per node)	57			
21	Cost of Nodes/Month	$ 13,053			

FIGURE 7-1 Capacity planning workbook

Scaling a Service Fabric cluster

You can adjust a Service Fabric cluster manually, and you can set up autoscale rules to adjust a Service Fabric cluster based on system and application telemetry data.

Autoscaling support

At the time of this writing, autoscaling isn't supported out-of-box. However, when you read this book, it's expected that the autoscaling feature will have been provided. The discussion here focuses on the theory of how autoscaling should be done when the feature is released. It does not cover specific steps because the exact user experience is still to be developed at this time.

Manually scaling a Service Fabric cluster

You easily can scale out or scale in a Service Fabric cluster using Microsoft Azure management portal. To adjust the number of nodes on a cluster, you can log in to the portal, select the node type, and enter a new node count for the type, as shown in Figure 7-2.

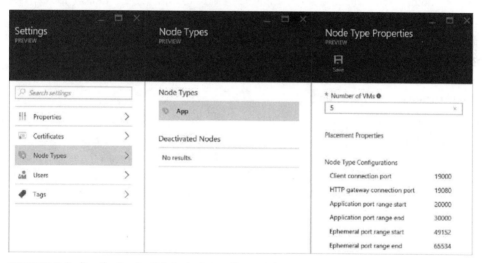

FIGURE 7-2 Scaling the Service Fabric cluster on the portal

When the number of nodes is increased, the Service Fabric load balancing mechanism kicks in to rearrange replicas to take advantage of the newly available resources. When the number of nodes is reduced, Service Fabric tries to pack replicas onto fewer nodes. However, due to placement constrains, some placement requests may be left unfilled, leading to service degradation or even service outages. Service Fabric requests that you keep at least five nodes for your primary node type.

Autoscaling a Service Fabric cluster

Autoscaling a Service Fabric cluster relies on two Microsoft Azure features: Azure Virtual Machine Scale Sets (Azure VM Scale Sets) and Azure Insights Autoscale. This section gives you a brief introduction to both features before introducing how the features collaboratively provide autoscaling support for Service Fabric.

Azure Resource Manager and Azure VM Scale Sets

Workloads like big compute and big data need to run on a large number of virtual machines. Azure VM Scale Sets are designed to support such large-scale service workloads. They enable you to deploy and manage a group of virtual machines as a single logical unit. Roughly speaking, scale sets provide a server cluster, which is an extra level of abstraction on top of virtual machines. When you deploy a workload, the deployment target is a single scale set (cluster) instead of tens or even hundreds of individual virtual machines.

Every entity you can provision on Azure is called a resource. For example, a virtual machine is a resource, a network card is a resource, and a load balancer is a resource. A VM scale set is another resource. Resources are managed by Azure Resource Manager.

You can put a number of related resources into a group, which is called a resource group. A resource group captures the entire infrastructure of an application so you can replicate the infrastructure consistently across multiple environments. For example, for a website with a SQL Database, you can create a resource group that consists of an Azure Web App and an Azure SQL Database. Then, you can take the resource group and deploy it to any environments where Azure Resource Manager is supported.

A resource group is described by a JSON-based document that is called an ARM template. The document captures all the attributes of the resources in the group so that it can be deployed consistently without human interpretation.

To define a VM scale set, you need to define a resource group with a VM scale set resource, along with other necessary infrastructural components such as virtual networks, public IP addresses, and load balancers. Azure Quickstart Template (*https://github.com/Azure/azure-quickstart-templates*) is an open source repository that hosts hundreds of ARM templates, among which are several VM Scale Set templates that you can use as a starting point for constructing your own ARM template.

Authoring an ARM template

Please refer to *https://azure.microsoft.com/documentation/articles/resource-group-authoring-templates/* for a quick tour of authoring an ARM template.

The following ARM template snippet shows a portion of a VM Scale Set definition. The definition specifies that the set should contain 500 *Standard_A2* virtual machines running the latest version of Ubuntu Server 15.04.

```
{
  "type": "Microsoft.Compute/virtualMachineScaleSets",
  "apiVersion": "2015-06-15",
  "name": "myScaleSet",
  "location": "West US",
  "sku": {
    "name": "Standard_A2",
    "tier": "Standard",
    "capacity": "500"
  },
```

```
        "properties": {
          "upgradePolicy": {
            "mode": "Manual"
          },
      "virtualMachineProfile": {
        "storageProfile": {
              ...
            "imageReference": {
              "publisher": "Canonical",
              "offer": "UbuntuServer",
              "sku": "15.04",
              "version": "latest"
            }
          },
          "osProfile": {
            "computerNamePrefix": "vm",
            "adminUsername": "haishi",
            "adminPassword": "[parameters('adminPassword')]"
          }
        }
      }
    }
}
```

Once the resource group is deployed, you can scale the scale set by modifying its *capacity* property.

Azure Insights Autoscale

Azure has two autoscaling APIs. Before I introduce these two APIs, I need to introduce the Azure API layer.

The Azure API layer, or Azure Service Management API, provides a unified programmable interface for all tooling and customization programmers. Microsoft's own tooling offerings such as Microsoft Azure management portal, Azure PowerShell, and Azure SDK are based on this API layer. The API also is exposed to the global community of developers to author their own tools, extensions, and customizations.

As Azure evolves, a new management API is designed. The new API, or Azure Resource Manager API, abstracts all Azure entities as resources. The API provides a pluggable framework where new resource types can be added by authoring new resource providers. The API also provides a declarative description of resources, which is the Azure Resource Manager template I've introduced previously in the "Azure Resource Manager and Azure VM Scale Sets" section.

It's expected that Azure Resource Manager API will become the new unified API in the future. However, during the transition phase, some of the Azure features are offered via the Azure Service Management API, which now is commonly referred to as the classic API.

Now I'm ready to talk about the two autoscaling APIs. The first autoscaling API is based on the classic API. It's designed to scale cloud services, virtual machines, websites, and mobile services automatically. The second autoscaling API is based on the Azure Resource Manager API as part of Azure Insights. The new API, in theory, is capable of scaling any scalable resources on Azure, including scale sets.

Both APIs work in a similar way. You define scaling rules that consist of metric triggers and scaling actions. A metric trigger defines the system metric to be monitored and the thresholds that trigger scaling actions. A scaling action defines how resource instances should be ramped up or ramped down in response to metric triggers.

The most intuitive metric trigger is based on CPU usage. High CPU usage indicates a busy system that can be relieved by adding servers to share the workload. Low CPU usage indicates an idle system whose allocated resources can be released to reduce hosting cost.

Service Fabric autoscaling

Service Fabric autoscaling is achieved by Azure Insights Autoscale scaling the VM scale set to where a Service Fabric cluster is deployed. The following ARM template snippet shows an Azure Insights auto-scale rule based on the CPU usage performance counter (\\Processor\\PercentProcessorTime). When the average usage percentage is above 50 percent for over five minutes, the scaling action is triggered to increase the scale set capacity by one node.

```
{
  "type": "Microsoft.Insights/autoscaleSettings",
  "apiVersion": "2015-04-01",
  "name": "autoscalewad",
  "location": "West US",
  "dependsOn": [
    "[concat('Microsoft.Compute/virtualMachineScaleSets/', 'myVMSS')]"
  ],
  "properties": {
    "name": "autoscalewad",
"targetResourceUri": "[concat('/subscriptions/',subscription().subscriptionId,
'/resourceGroups/',  resourceGroup().name,
'/providers/Microsoft.Compute/virtualMachineScaleSets/', 'myVMSS')]",
    "enabled": true,
    "profiles": [
      {
        "name": "Profile1",
        "capacity": {
          "minimum": "1",
          "maximum": "10",
          "default": "1"
        },
        "rules": [
          {
            "metricTrigger": {
              "metricName": "\\Processor\\PercentProcessorTime",
              "metricNamespace": "",
              "metricResourceUri": "[concat('/subscriptions/',subscription().subscriptionId,
'/resourceGroups/',  resourceGroup().name,
'/providers/Microsoft.Compute/virtualMachineScaleSets/', 'myVMSS')]",
              "timeGrain": "PT1M",
              "statistic": "Average",
              "timeWindow": "PT5M",
              "timeAggregation": "Average",
              "operator": "GreaterThan",
              "threshold": 50.0
```

```
        },
        "scaleAction": {
          "direction": "Increase",
          "type": "ChangeCount",
          "value": "1",
          "cooldown": "PT1M"
        }
      }
    ]
  }
 ]
 }
}
```

As mentioned earlier, the exact user experience of configuring and managing the autoscale settings of a Service Fabric cluster is under development. I assume the settings will be part of one of the cluster configuration blades on the management portal. Regardless, you always can modify the ARM template directly to update these settings if necessary.

Scaling with Content Delivery Network

The Azure Content Delivery Network service is an effective way to deliver static content to end users. The Content Delivery Network service caches and delivers content from its globally distributed edge nodes so that the content can be delivered to end users directly from a nearby edge node instead of from the original servers. A big fraction of Internet content is being delivered by the Content Delivery Network service today, including web pages, media files, and other downloadable content.

Content Delivery Network improves system performance by delivering content from edge nodes. It also improves system availability because content can be served from the edge nodes (before the cached content expires) even if the original servers have crashed. Content Delivery Network also is a mechanism to scale out a service. Lots of systems have many more reads than writes. When the read requests can be served directly by the Content Delivery Network edge nodes, the service hosts are freed up to take in more write requests.

Azure Content Delivery Network is the Azure service offering. It provides built-in support for delivering content from Azure storage accounts, Azure websites, and Cloud Services. Although it's not integrated with Service Fabric at this point, you can use its capability of caching content from custom origins and deliver static content from your web-facing services. For example, your service may have an image to be delivered as part of a web page. You can set up a custom origin pointing to the image URL, and the image will be made available via a corresponding Azure Content Delivery Network URL.

Figure 7-3 shows the management portal blade that adds an endpoint to an Azure Content Delivery Network profile. In this case, the origin type is set to Custom, and the origin URL is pointed at a /contents folder on *newsf7.westus.cloudapp.azure.com*. Once the folder is cached, the content can be accessed via *http(s)://sfcdn7.azureedge.net*.

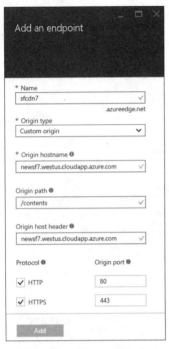

FIGURE 7-3 Adding an endpoint to an Azure Content Delivery Network profile

A detailed introduction to Azure Content Delivery Network is out of the scope of this book. Please consult the official documentation at *https://azure.microsoft.com/services/cdn/.*

Resolving bottlenecks

Bottlenecks are the biggest enemy of performance and scalability. A bottleneck constrains system throughput, decreases system performance, and in some cases jeopardizes system availability. A common phenomenon in software is that the response time linearly goes up as the system load increases until a threshold is hit. Then, the response time grows exponentially with the load, as shown in Figure 7-4.

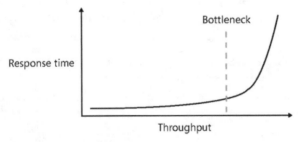

FIGURE 7-4 Relationship between throughput and response time

If a system is poorly designed, some centralized component easily can become the bottleneck, or even the single point of failure. However, even in a nicely designed system, bottlenecks likely will appear one way or another. And as the system evolves, the bottleneck of the system may change. In this section, I'll discuss several places where bottlenecks often manifest themselves and how to resolve these bottlenecks.

State bottlenecks

State persistence involves some sort of disk operations, which are much slower than in-memory operations. When a system needs to access states frequently, it's nearly unavoidable that the state persistence will become the bottleneck of the system. Especially when the state is stored in an external database or data service, the additional network latency or service throttling will slow the state operations further.

Service Fabric's reliable collections balance performance, consistency, and availability. States saved in reliable collections automatically are replicated for high availability. And all reads are from the local copy, ensuring the best performance and throughput. I've introduced how reliable collections are used in Chapter 3, "Stateful services." Now it's time to dig into more details and study how concurrent accesses of data are handled.

Isolation levels

Reliable collections support two isolation levels: repeatable read and snapshot. The repeatable read locks on the scanned keys to forbid other transactions from updating or deleting these records. However, newly inserted records from other transactions may be returned during the same transaction. The snapshot isolation level allows a transaction to take a snapshot of the state data at the beginning of the transaction. This isolation level uses optimistic concurrency. There are no locks placed on the read records, and other transactions are free to update the records during the transaction. The transaction commit fails only if there were committed conflicting updates for other concurrent transactions.

Depending on the type of read and the replica role, an isolation level is selected automatically. Table 7-1 shows how isolation levels are selected by Service Fabric for Reliable Dictionary.

TABLE 7-1 Isolation level choices for Reliable Dictionary

Operation	Primary replica	Secondary replica
Single entry read	Repeatable read	Snapshot
Enumeration & count	Snapshot	Snapshot

Table 7-2 shows how isolation levels are selected by Service Fabric for Reliable Queue:

TABLE 7-2 Isolation level choices for Reliable Queue

Operation	Primary replica	Secondary replica
Single entry read	Snapshot	Snapshot
Enumeration & count	Snapshot	Snapshot

As you can see from these two tables, the snapshot isolation level is selected for most cases. This provides optimum parallelism for read-heavy systems. The more restrictive repeatable read is used to ensure consistency during updates through the primary replica.

By default, repeatable read uses shared locks. Deadlocks may happen when two transactions try to read and update the same record. Service Fabric has a default timeout of four seconds to detect deadlocks. In this case, one or both transactions would time out. You can request to use update locks instead of shared locks to avoid such deadlocks.

Actor states

The Actor programming model provides a higher abstraction level for you to model your applications. However, as you push the application to a higher scale, you might want to dig a little deeper to understand how actor states are managed to avoid some pitfalls.

Actor state as a single entity The state of an actor is managed as a single entity. In fact, the state of an actor is just a single entry of a key-value store behind the scenes. This means when you read and update even one property on the actor state data structure, the entire structure needs to be deserialized, updated, serialized, and stored. So, as a best practice, you should constrain the amount of state that an actor holds. If you find an actor that needs to handle a large amount of state data, you might want to consider partitioning the actor into actors with smaller states or using reliable services instead.

Partitioned stateful actor services An actor service can be partitioned for scaling out. Actor instances are distributed into these partitions by a hashing algorithm based on actor ids. Because state replication is at the partition level, when you have many actors per partition and they all update states frequently, you may be triggering many state replications. Depending on the scale of your application, you may want to preallocate enough partitions so that you don't have an excessive number of actors per partition. Figure 7-5 shows a partitioned stateful actor service. As shown in the figure, the service has 10 partitions, and each partition has 1 primary replica and 2 secondary replicas. Actor instances are distributed into these 10 partitions, and states are replicated across the 3 replicas within each of the partitions.

State providers By default, actor states are provided by a state provider that uses a built-in distributed key-value store. The store persists actor states to disks on cluster nodes so that even if all replicas in a partition go down, the actor states can be restored from the disks when the nodes recover.

If you can rebuild actor states by other means (such as from external storage), you can use an in-memory state provider that provides faster performance. This state provider, which is called *VolatileActorStateProvider*, offers the same state replication and recovery as long as there are running replicas. The state is lost only when all replicas go down. To use the volatile actor state provider, just decorate your actor class with a *VolatileActorStateProvider* attribute (see Chapter 3).

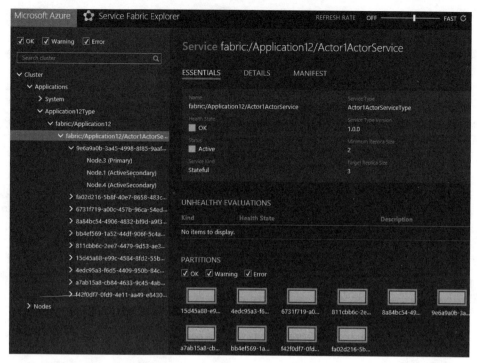

FIGURE 7-5 A partitioned stateful actor service

State serialization

Before service states can be replicated and persisted, they need to be serialized. Service Fabric Reliable State Manager provides built-in serializers for a number of types, including: bool, byte, char, decimal, double, float, guid, int, long, sbyte, short, string, uint, ulong, and ushort. For complex types, Reliable State Manager uses DataContractSerializer.

You may want to use a custom serializer for two reasons: performance and encryption. *DataContractSerializer* serializes objects to XML streams with member names. For example, the following class:

```
[DataContract(Name = "Customer", Namespace = "http://www.contoso.com")]
class Person
{
    [DataMember(IsRequired = true)]
    public string FirstName;
    [DataMember]
    public string LastName;
    [DataMember()]
    public int ID;
}
```

gets serialized into:

```
<Customer xmlns="http://www.contoso.com" xmlns:i="http://www.w3.org/2001/XMLSchema-
instance"><FirstName>Haishi</FirstName><ID>100</ID><LastName>Bai</LastName></Customer>
```

Because Reliable State Manager ensures that the correct serializer is used, instead of the generic *DataContractSerializer*, you can write a highly customized serializer to handle the specific type. For example, instead of the above XML representation, you can write a custom serializer that uses a CSV format like this:

```
Haishi,Bai,100
```

The second format is much less demanding in terms of network traffic and disk storage. To implement a custom serializer, you need to implement the *IStateSerializer<T>* interface. The following code snippet shows how to implement a custom serializer:

```
public class PersonSerializer : IStateSerializer<Person>
{
    public Person Read(BinaryReader binaryReader)
    {
        Person ret = new Person();
        ret.FirstName = binaryReader.ReadString();
        ret.LastName = binaryReader.ReadString();
        ret.ID = binaryReader.ReadInt32();
        return ret;
    }
    public Person Read(Person baseValue, BinaryReader binaryReader)
    {
        return ((IStateSerializer<Person>)this).Read(binaryReader);
    }
    public void Write(Person value, BinaryWriter binaryWriter)
    {
        binaryWriter.Write(value.FirstName);
        binaryWriter.Write(value.LastName);
        binaryWriter.Write(value.ID);
    }
    public void Write(Person baseValue, Person targetValue, BinaryWriter binaryWriter)
    {
        ((IStateSerializer<Person>)this).Write(targetValue, binaryWriter);
    }
}
```

To register the custom serializer, you first need to define a method that takes no parameters and returns a Task, as shown in the following example:

```
protected Task InitializeStateSerializers()
{
    this.StateManager.TryAddStateSerializer(new PersonSerializer());
    return Task.FromResult(false);
}
```

Experimental code

As of this writing, the *TryAddStateSerializer* method is marked as deprecated and subject to be changed or removed in furture SDK versions.

Finally, you need to override the *CreateReliableStateManager* method of your reliable service to invoke the above method when initializing the Reliable State Manager:

```
protected override IReliableStateManager CreateReliableStateManager()
{
    return new ReliableStateManager(
        new ReliableStateManagerConfiguration(
            onInitializeStateSerializersEvent: this.InitializeStateSerializers));
}
```

Communication bottlenecks

The essence of a distributed system design is the placement and interactions of components. Besides the performance of individual components, the performance of a distributed system largely is decided by the communication and synchronization patterns among the components.

The simplest communication pattern between two components is one component passing a message to another. In this section, I'll focus on several patterns that handle communications between two components. I'll disuss multicomponent communications in the next section.

Coupling

When examining the communications between two components, first determine if the two components are too "chatty," which means they exchange an excessive amount of data or interact with each other too frequently. For example, a service returns a list of customers. For each of the customers, it consults another service to get the customer's mailing address. This means if the service returns a list of 100 customers, it needs to call the other service 100 times before the list can be populated fully.

Chatty components give you strong hints that component boundaries may have been drawn incorrectly, which means the responsibility of a single component may have been split into multiple components because of overengineering or a single component is taking on too many responsibilities that other components should have taken on.

If there are justifiable reasons for the two components to remain separate, a coarse-grained data structure can be used to reduce the number of round trips. For example, instead of querying for customer addresses individually, the main service can pass the same query criteria to the address service to return a list of addresses.

For an Actor programming model, if customer addresses are held by individual customer actors, the problem becomes an aggregation problem, which I'll discuss later in this chapter in the "Aggregation" section.

Loose coupling

Under microservices architecture, services are independent entities that function and evolve at their own pace. This calls for a loosely coupled design in which components communicate with each other asynchronously and don't hold static references to each other.

Loosely coupled components often use some middleware for communication, such as a reliable queue. This layer of indirection brings several benefits. First, it matches up components with different performance characteristics. In a system, some components run faster, and some run slower. The middleware allows the faster components to queue up work items for slower components and remain responsive to user requests. Then, the slower components can process the work items at a slower pace and return results via callbacks or feedback messages. In some cases, the slower components may have opportunities to discard expired requests, delete duplicated requests, or group related requests to reduce the overall workload.

Second, the middle layer can help improve system availability in some cases. Assume there's a system with a front tier that takes user orders and a back tier that handles these orders. Even if the back tier fails, as long as the front tier remains responsive and queues up user orders, the system remains available to end users. When the back tier comes online later, it can get the requests from the reliable queue and handle the orders offline.

You can use the Service Fabric reliable queue as the middle tier. Or, you can choose an external reliable queue service such as Azure Service Bus Queue. The benefit of using an independent queueing service is to separate the communication middle tier from service components.

Batching

Batching is another effective way to reduce intercomponent communications. A number of requests can be grouped to reduce the number of messages going across component boundaries. Establishing a communication channel, especially a secured channel, comes with unavoidable overheads. Grouping the requests can reduce these overheads and improve the overall system throughput and performance.

Because a stateful service and a stateful actor can maintain local states, they easily can accumulate a certain amount of data before they send the data to downstream services. For example, an actor that represents a sensor can accumulate the last few readings from the sensor and only send out averages over certain time intervals.

Orchestration bottlenecks

As more components are involved in communications, things become complicated. One of the common patterns is aggregation, when a component needs to aggregate data from multiple components to fulfill a request. Another common pattern is coordination, when multiple components need to be coordinated to complete a workflow. In this section, I'll discuss both patterns and introduce some techniques to handle bottlenecks in each of the communication patterns.

Aggregation

For reliable services, aggregation is relatively straightforward: a number of stateless instances can report data concurrently to a stateful service to get their data aggregated. The stateful service can be scaled out by using multiple partitions. And multiple levels of aggregators can be used as necessary. For example, in an online voting system, a state-level service, which is partitioned by states, can be used to aggregate data at the state level. Another national/regional-level service can be used to aggregate data from the states.

It's tempting to follow the same pattern to aggregate actor states. However, because of the turn-based concurrency, when a large number of actors are trying to report states to the same actor, a bottleneck is formed. This is because the multiple invocations on the same actor are serialized, causing delays. If timeliness is important and the number of actors to be aggregated is large, you should avoid direct aggregations among actors.

Instead, you can use a stateful service as a point of aggregation. Then, the service can send aggregated data to higher-level actors. In this way, you can enjoy the simplicity of the Actor programming model but avoid the pitfall of turn-based concurrency.

Figure 7-6 shows a comparison of two architectures of the same online voting application. To the left, the county-level actors (marked with C) send data to state-level actors (marked with S), which in turn send data to nation/region-level actors (marked with N). This architecture is subject to the limitation of turn-based concurrency because a state-level actor accumulates data from county-level actors sequentially.

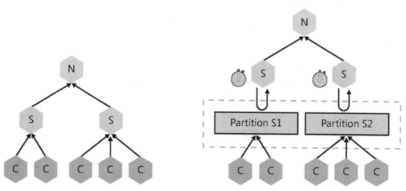

FIGURE 7-6 Two aggregation architectures

To the right, the county-level actors send data to an aggregation service that is partitioned by states. Behind the aggregation service is the group of state-level actors that refresh their states periodically from the aggregation service. The diagram shows that the nation/region-level aggregation is done by direct actor communications. An extra aggregation service can be inserted between the state-level actors and the nation/region-level actors if needed.

The architecture to the left would work for smaller-scale applications. Multiple levels of aggregations can eliminate some of the bottlenecks because of the turn-based concurrency. For example, if 1,000 actors are connected directly to a single aggregator, the aggregator needs to handle 1,000 calls sequentially. However, if an aggregation layer is added in the middle to have 1 intermediate aggregator handling 100 origin actors, the 10 intermediate aggregators each handle 100 sequential calls, and the results are rolled up to the final aggregator with another 10 sequential calls. This is close to a 10-time improvement in response time and throughput.

In Chapter 13, "Internet of Things," and Chapter 16, "Multiplayer gaming," we'll have more discussions on aggregation in the context of different practical scenarios.

Coordination

In a distributed system, a complex workflow may involve multiple services. A workflow may be initiated by a service, go through a number of services, and be completed by another service. The workflows are triggered by user requests or system-generated events such as scheduled events.

A master component can serve as a centralized control that governs execution of all workflows. However, this design may lead to a single point of failure or a bottleneck of the system because all workflow executions depend on a single component. Depending on specific applications scenarios, alternative designs can be used to avoid such centralized components.

Self-driven workflows Lots of workflows don't need close governance. They can be allowed to execute at their own pace as long as faulty workflows can be tracked. In this case, the steps in a workflow can self-organize by sending messages to one another. This design allows distinct workflow steps, which can be implemented as individual actors, to be orginzed to form flexible workflow structures such as branches and loops.

The primary challenge of self-driven workflows is tracking failed workflows. If an actor fails without sending any downstream messages, the workflow stops silently. To avoid this, some sort of bookkeeping is needed. This doesn't necessarily require a centralized bookkeeping service, however. A stateful actor that represents a workflow can be used for this purpose. The actor can set up a reminder that periodically checks for expected workflow state and sends notifications to a managing service to report a failed workflow.

Competing consumers Competing consumers is another pattern that coordinates work among multiple components. In this case, job creators add jobs to a reliable queueing service, and a number of job processors read from the job queue and projobs in parallel. Because these processors compete for jobs from the same queue, the pattern is called competing consumers.

This pattern has several benefits. First, the number of competing consumers can be adjusted dynamically based on system load. For example, as the size of the job queue increases, consumers can be added to drain the queue faster. Second, because a job is removed permanently from the queue only when it is completed, a failed job can be picked up by another consumer later. To achieve this, the reliable queueing service needs to support locks with expirations. When a consumer gets a job, it places a lock on the item so that other consumers won't get the same job. If the job is completed correctly, the consumer removes the job from the queue. If the consumer fails to process the job or crashes before it can remove the job, the job reappears on the queue once the lock expires for other consumers to pick it up. Azure's Service Bus Queue service provides such a locking mechanism. Third, because creators and consumers are loosely coupled, job creation and job processing can happen at different times, which enables scenarios such as batch processing and offline processing.

Figure 7-7 shows a diagram of the competing consumers pattern. A job creator (denoted by *C*) pushes jobs (J1 through Jn) to a job queue. And a number of processors (denoted by *P*) are competing to finish the jobs on the queue. In the following diagram, three of the jobs (J1, J2, and J3) are retrieved and locked by three individual processors for processing. Once a job is completed, it will be permanently removed. If it fails, it will reappear on the queue for another processor to pick it up.

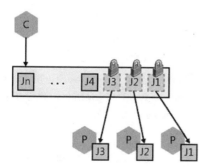

FIGURE 7-7 Competing consumers

The throughput of a system using competing consumers is decided by the throughput of the queuing system (times the number of consumers). To scale out, you can use multiple job queues. However, using multiple queues complicates job consumer management. The consumers need to be either partitioned to different queues or made aware of all the queues so they can pull jobs from all possible queues.

Distributed computing   Distributed computing has existed for a long time. Various specifications, tools, and systems have been built in the past decades to decompose complex problems into smaller chunks that can be solved on a cluster of computing nodes in parallel.

A lot of distributed computing problems involve handling large amounts of data. Programming models such as MapReduce and frameworks such as Hadoop have been introduced to handle such socalled big data problems. Service Fabric is not a big data platform out-of-box. However, it's feasible to implement a Hadoop-like system on a Service Fabric cluster or to run MapReduce workloads on Service Fabric. Detailed discussion on big data systems is out of the scope of this book.

A large part of a big data framework is to distribute data to different map functions. The map functions handle data locally, and the outputs are remapped for aggregations, which is the reduction phase. Both stateful services and reliable actors are capable of storing and handling local states. And instead of a centralized framework that takes care of data mapping, these services and actors can organize themselves by sending messages to one another.

Next, I'll introduce a scenario that runs a simple Monte Carlo simulation: estimating pi.

Sample source

The following example is based on the following Microsoft Azure documentation:
https://azure.microsoft.com/documentation/articles/service-fabric-reliable-actors
-pattern-distributed-computation/

First, I'd like to explain the simulation briefly: imagine you have a square target with an inscribed circle. When you shoot a bullet at the target, the probability of the bullet hitting the circle is the ratio of the area of the circle to the area of the square (assuming a bullet never misses the target and the hitting points are distributed evenly). If the square has unit-length sides, this probably becomes:

$$p = \frac{\pi\left(\frac{1}{2}\right)^2}{1} = \frac{\pi}{4}$$

So, whatever the probability is, we can estimate the value of pi by multiplying the value and 4. To estimate the probability, we'll just shoot lots of bullets at the target and count how many times the bullets hit the circle and the total number of bullets. The ratio between the two counts gives us a reasonable estimation of the probability, hence pi, if we repeat the test enough times.

This simulation can be composed with a number of Service Fabric actors. Figure 7-8 shows the system diagram, which is a simplified version of the Azure documentation. The diagram shows that a Processor (denoted with *P*) takes in simulation requests and invokes a poll of Task actors (denoted with *T*) to shoot at the target. Each Task actor shoots at the target a certain number of times, and the results are sent to Aggregators (denoted with *A*). Finally, a Finalizer (denoted with *F*) gets results from the Aggregators and calculates the final result.

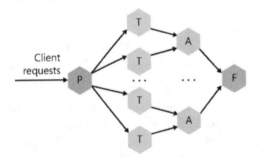

FIGURE 7-8 Monte Carlo simulation with Service Fabric actors

Among the actors, the Processor and the Task actors are stateless. The Processor serves as a simple service gateway, so it doesn't need to save any states. The Task actors run a number of simulations locally and directly send results to the Aggregators, so they don't need to have their own states, either. As a result, if a Task actor crashes, the group of simulation results is lost. However, because the impact on the final result won't be significant (when there are enough Task actors), this risk is acceptable.

PART II

Service lifecycle management

CHAPTER 8

Managing Service Fabric with Windows PowerShell

Windows PowerShell is a powerful tool for managing Windows-based systems and Azure services. In this chapter, I'll introduce how to use Windows PowerShell to perform various management tasks on Service Fabric clusters.

Creating a secured Service Fabric cluster

So far in this book, I've been using unsecured clusters. These clusters are open to the public without any authentications or protections. This means that anyone on the Internet not only can browse the cluster using the Service Fabric Explorer, but also can make any changes to the cluster. This obviously is a very bad idea. We'll fix it in this section.

Service Fabric supports certificate security and Windows security. You can set up both server authentication and client authentication by using certificates.

Protecting your cluster by using a certificate

You can assign an x509 certificate to your cluster to sign and encrypt data sent from the server. This provides integrity (the signature can be validated), privacy (the data is encrypted), and authenticity (the data indeed is originated from the server) of the data.

Using Azure PowerShell commands

In this chapter, you'll be using both Azure PowerShell commands and Service Fabric commands. Before you can use Azure PowerShell commands, you need to sign in to your Azure subscription. See Appendix B for instructions on signing in to Azure subscriptions.

The following steps walk you through the process of configuring a self-signed certificate to your cluster. Of course, for your production environments, you want to use a certificate issued by a trusted root certificate authority (CA).

1. Create a new self-signed certificate. Here, I chose to use Windows PowerShell, but you also can use tools such as openSSL. In the following commands, replace *[password]* with a password of your choice; replace *[cluster DNS]* with the DNS name of your Service Fabric cluster, for example *mycluster.westus.cloudapp.azure.com*; replace *[Path to pfx file]* with a path to the output *.pfx* file.

```
$password = ConvertTo-SecureString -String [password] -AsPlainText -Force

New-SelfSignedCertificate -CertStoreLocation Cert:\CurrentUser\My -DnsName [cluster DNS]
-Provider 'Microsoft Enhanced Cryptographic Provider v1.0' | Export-PfxCertificate -File
[Path to pfx file] -Password $password
```

2. Now you need to put the certificate file in a cloud-based certificate store so that it can be associated with the Service Fabric cluster. Azure provides a service called *Azure Key Vault* that is designed to manage your keys and passwords in the cloud. If you already have a key vault created, you can skip to step 3. Otherwise, use the following command to create a new key vault. You need to replace *[your vault name]* with a vault name of your choice. The vault name has to be globally unique. In addition, you need to replace *[resource group name]* with the name of your resource group. You can place the vault into the resource group where your Service Fabric cluster is hosted (see Chapter 9, "Managing Service Fabric with management portal," to learn how to find out the resource group to which a cluster belongs). Or, to create a new resource group, use the command *New-AzureRmResourceGroup –Name '[resource group name]' –Location '[location]'*. Finally, replace *[location]* with the Azure location where you want the vault to be created; for example, West US or East US. If you are adding the vault to an existing resource group, you should use the location where the resource group is located.

```
New-AzureRmKeyVault -VaultName '[your vault name]' -ResourceGroupName '[resource group
name]' -Location '[location]' -EnabledForDeployment
```

3. Once the command succeeds, you can find the vault URI in the command output, as shown in Figure 8-1.

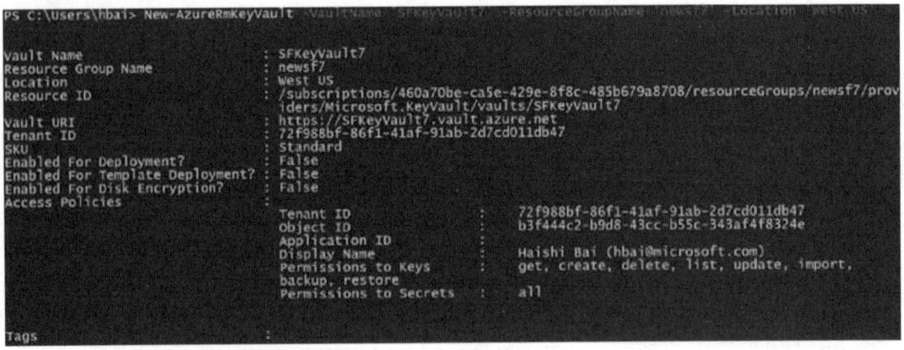

FIGURE 8-1 Key vault summary

4. If you forgot to set the *EnabledForDeployment* flag, or you want to allow the secrets in an existing vault to be used in Azure resource group deployments, use the following command:

```
Set-AzureRmKeyVaultAccessPolicy -VaultName '[vault name]' -EnabledForDeployment
```

5. To upload the .pfx file to the vault, use the following command. You need to replace *[your vault name]* with the name of your key vault and replace *[path to the .pfx file]* with the file path you used in step 1.

```
$key = Add-AzureKeyVaultKey -VaultName '[your vault name]' -Name '[key name]'
-KeyFilePath '[path to the .pfx file]' -KeyFilePassword $password
```

6. To verify if the key has been uploaded successfully, use the following command to display the key URI:

```
$key.key.kid
```

For example, the above command returns the following output in my environment:

```
https://sfkeyvault7.vault.azure.net/keys/SFKey/2642da0a4e6b4d38ab1a2d52e0edae8a
```

7. Now you need to create a secret based on the certificate. The process is a little involved: you need to create a secret using a JSON payload with the content of the .pfx file. This can be done by using the following commands. You need to replace *[path to the .pfx file]*, *[your vault name]*, *[your private key password]*, and *[key name]* as you did in previous steps.

```
$bytes = [System.IO.File]::ReadAllBytes('[path to the .pfx file]')
$base64 = [System.Convert]::ToBase64String($bytes)
$jsonBlob = @{
data = $base64
dataType = 'pfx'
password = [your private key password]
} | ConvertTo-Json
$contentBytes = [System.Text.Encoding]::UTF8.GetBytes($jsonBlob)
$content = [System.Convert]::Tobase64String($contentBytes)
$secretValue = ConvertTo-SecureString -String $content -AsPlainText -Force
Set-AzureKeyVaultSecret -VaultName '[your vault name]' -Name [key name] -SecretValue
$secretValue
```

8. The last command above returns a summary of the generated secret. You need to copy the *ID* attribute, which you'll need to create a secured cluster. Figure 8-2 shows a sample output in my environment.

FIGURE 8-2 Secret summary

9. When you create the cluster, you also need to provide the thumbprint of the certificate. You can use tools such as *certmgr* to get the thumbprint. Alternatively, you can use the following commands:

```
$cert = new-object System.Security.Cryptography.X509Certificates.X509Certificate2 '[path
to the .pfx file]', $password
$cert.Thumbprint
```

10. Now you can use the certificate to protect a Service Fabric cluster. You can use the steps in Chapter 1, "Hello, Service Fabric!," to create a new Service Fabric cluster, except for the step that configures security. Instead of selecting the Unsecured option, select the Secured option. For the Cluster protection level field, choose the default *EncryptAndSign* option, which means the data returned from the server will be encrypted and signed using the certificate.

11. In the Source Vault field, enter the Resource ID (see Figure 8-1) of the key vault. The ID has the format of /subscriptions/[subscription id]/resourceGroups/[resource group name]/providers/Microsoft.KeyVault/vaults/[vault name].

12. In the Certificate URL field, enter the secret ID in step 5.

13. In the Certificate Thumbprint field, enter the certificate thumbprint in step 6.

14. Once every field is entered, click the OK button to save the security settings. Then, click the Create button to provision the cluster, as shown in Figure 8-3.

FIGURE 8-3 Service Fabric cluster security configurations

15. In Chapter 1, I showed how to use Connect-ServiceFabricCluster to connect to a local, unsecured Service Fabric cluster. Because the cluster is not protected by a self-signed certificate, you

first need to import the certificate to the local "trusted people" store. This can be done using the following PowerShell command. The command requires elevated privilege, so you'll need to launch the PowerShell command prompt as an administrator.

```
Import-PfxCertificate -Exportable -CertStoreLocation Cert:\CurrentUser\TrustedPeople
-FilePath '[path to the .pfx file]' -Password $password
```

16. Once the cluster is provisioned, you can connect to the cluster using the following command line. You need to replace *[cluster name]* with your cluster name (see Figure 8-3). You also need to replace *[cert thumbprint]* with the certificate thumbprint in step 6.

```
Connect-ServiceFabricCluster [cluster name]:19000 -X509Credential -ServerCertThumbprint
[cert thumbprint] -FindType FindByThumbprint -FindValue [cert thumbprint] -StoreLocation
CurrentUser -StoreName TrustedPeople
```

Figure 8-4 shows a sample command and its outputs.

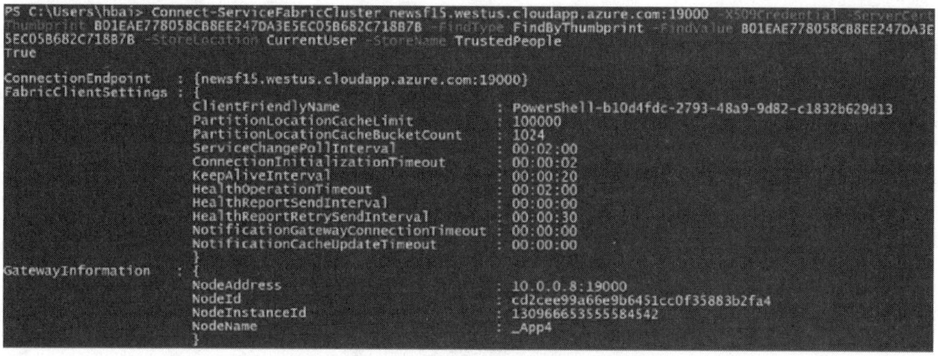

FIGURE 8-4 Connecting to a Service Fabric cluster by using a certificate

Once you associate a certificate with a Service Fabric cluster, the address of Service Fabric Explorer will use HTTPS protocol instead of HTTP. When you open the link in the browser, you'll get an untrusted certificate warning because the certificate is a self-signed certificate. If this annoys you, for testing for demo purposes you can import the certificate to the Trusted Root Certificate Authority of Local Computer store by using the following command (you need to run the command with administrative privileges):

```
Import-PfxCertificate -Exportable -CertStoreLocation Cert:\LocalMachine\Root -FilePath '[path to
the .pfx file]' -Password $password
```

Client authentication using a certificate

You also can enable client authentication using certificates. Service Fabric allows you to set up certificates for two client types: Admin client and Read Only client. The Admin client is allowed to perform all administrative operations, and the Read Only client can perform only read-only operations.

To specify a client authentication certificate, you can enter either the subject name or the certificate's thumbprint to the corresponding input boxes, as shown in Figure 8-3. When you use the subject name, you also need to enter the issuer thumbnail. You can enter multiple subjects or thumbnails as comma-separated lists.

Publishing applications from Visual Studio

Publishing applications from Visual Studio to a secured cluster follows the same process as publishing to an unsecured cluster, as long as the server certificate has been imported to the Cert:\CurrentUser\ My store or the Cert:\LocalMachine\My store. If you've followed the above tutorial to create the self-signed certificate, the certificate already has been placed into the Cert:\CurrentUser\My store. There are no additional actions needed in this case.

When you click the Publish button on the Publish Service Fabric Application dialog box (see Figure 6-8), VS tooling automatically modifies the corresponding publish profile to include the certificate information. The following is an example of a modified profile, with auto-generated attributes highlighted:

```
<?xml version="1.0" encoding="utf-8"?>
<PublishProfile xmlns="http://schemas.microsoft.com/2015/05/fabrictools">
  <ClusterConnectionParameters ConnectionEndpoint="newsf15.westus.cloudapp.azure.com:19000"
                              X509Credential="true"
                              ServerCertThumbprint="B01EAE778058CB8EE247DA3E5EC05B682C718B7B"
                              FindType="FindByThumbprint"
                              FindValue="B01EAE778058CB8EE247DA3E5EC05B682C718B7B"
                              StoreLocation="CurrentUser"
                              StoreName="My" />
  <ApplicationParameterFile Path="..\ApplicationParameters\Cloud.xml" />
</PublishProfile>
```

Cluster management commands

In the previous tutorial, you've seen an example of using the Connect-ServiceFabric command to connect to a Service Fabric cluster. This section introduces more cluster management commands.

Queries

First, let's review query commands that query information of different entities including cluster, nodes, applications, services, partitions, and replicas.

Cluster-level queries

The following commands allow you to query various aspects of a Service Fabric cluster.

- Get-ServiceFabricClusterConnection

  Get the connection information to a Service Fabric cluster. The output of this command is identical to what is presented in Figure 1-18 (unsecured) and Figure 8-4 (secured).

- Get-ServiceFabricClusterManifest

  This command returns the complete cluster manifest. You can load the output of the command to an XmlDocument and perform further queries using Xpath. The following code snippet is an example of getting the cluster credential type:

  ```
  $manifest = & Get-ServiceFabricClusterManifest

  $xml = new-object System.Xml.XmlDocument
  $xml.LoadXml($manifest)
  $ns = new-object System.Xml.XmlNamespaceManager($xml.NameTable)
  $ns.AddNamespace("sf", "http://schemas.microsoft.com/2011/01/fabric")
  $node = $xml.SelectSingleNode("//sf:Section[@Name='Security']/sf:Parameter[@
  Name='ClusterCredentialType']", $ns)
  $node.Value
  ```

  The preceding snippet should return X509 for a certificate-protected cluster.

- Get-ServiceFabricClusterHealth

  This command returns aggregated health states of the cluster, the nodes, and the deployed applications. I've introduced the Service Fabric health model in Chapter 5, "Service deployments and upgrades." Please review the "Health model" section if needed. Figure 8-5 is a sample output of the command when it's executed against a healthy cluster.

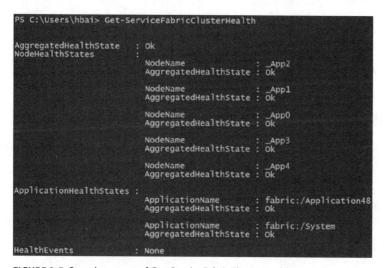

FIGURE 8-5 Sample output of Get-ServiceFabricClusterHealth

Figure 8-6 shows a (partial) sample output generated from a cluster with problems.

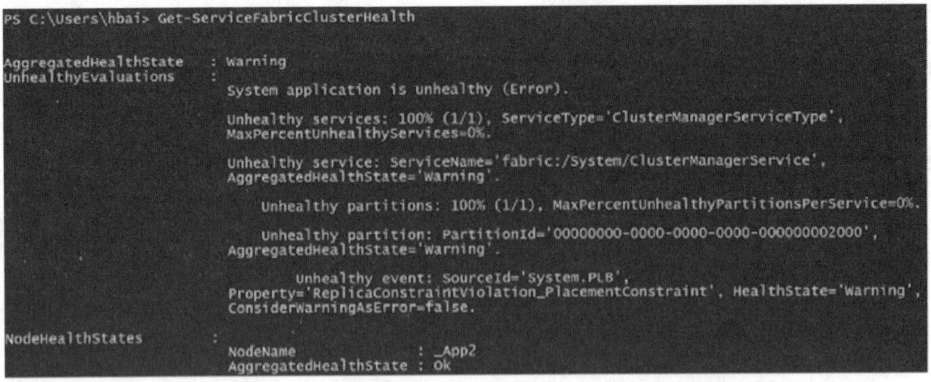

FIGURE 8-6 Sample output of Get-ServiceFabricClusterHealth against an unhealthy cluster

The preceding state was triggered by shutting down the node that was hosting the primary replica of the *fabric:/System/ClusterManagerService*. This problem should be resolved automatically by Service Fabric fairly quickly by selecting a different primary. So, if you saw the above message, chances are the message will go away when you repeat the queries seconds later.

In a large cluster with many nodes and many applications, this command may generate lots of outputs. Fortunately, you can filter the results easily by using a number of parameters. For example, the following code snippet returns only errors and warnings.

```
$filter = [System.Fabric.Health.HealthStateFilter]::Warning.value__ + [System.Fabric.
Health.HealthStateFilter]::Error.value__
Get-ServiceFabricClusterHealth -NodesHealthStateFilter $filter
-ApplicationsHealthStateFilter $filter
```

You also can query and filter health states by using health policies (see Chapter 5) and health policy maps, which allow you to map different health policies to different health entities. The following code snippet is a sample query that treats warnings in a *fabric:/CriticalApp* application as errors and filters results to display only errors. The last command also shows how to extract part of the output and format it as a list.

```
$appHealthPolicy = new-object System.Fabric.Health.ApplicationHealthPolicy
$appHealthPolicy.ConsiderWarningAsError = $true
$appHealthPolicyMap = New-Object System.Fabric.Health.ApplicationHealthPolicyMap
$appHealthPolicyMap.Add((New-Object System.Uri "fabric:/CriticalApp"), $appHealthPolicy)
$errorFilter = [System.Fabric.Health.HealthStateFilter]::Error.value__
(Get-ServiceFabricClusterHealth -NodesHealthStateFilter $filter
-ApplicationsHealthStateFilter $filter).ApplicationHealthStates | format-list
```

In my test environment, where the CritialApp has errors (or warnings, which are treated as errors in this case), the preceding snippet generates the following clean output:

```
ApplicationName        : fabric:/Application43
AggregatedHealthState: Error
```

- Get-ServiceFabricClusterLoadInformation

  This command returns load reports (see Chapter 6, "Availability and reliability") of a Service Fabric cluster. The following command lists all load metric names on the cluster.

  ```
  (Get-ServiceFabricClusterLoadInformation).LoadMetricInformation | format-list -Property
  Name
  ```

  In my environment, this returns the following name list:

  ```
  Name : Count
  Name : PrimaryCount
  Name : ReplicaCount
  Name : __ClusterManagerServicePrimaryCount__
  Name : __ClusterManagerServiceReplicaCount__
  Name : __FileStoreServicePrimaryCount__
  Name : __FileStoreServiceReplicaCount__
  Name : __NamingServicePrimaryCount__
  Name : __NamingServiceReplicaCount__
  ```

- Get-ServiceFabricClusterUpgrade

  This command returns the status of the current cluster upgrade process or the status of the last cluster upgrade operation. When the code or the configuration of the cluster is updated, a rolling upgrade is initiated on the cluster. You can use this command to monitor an ongoing cluster upgrade or to examine the status of the last cluster upgrade. Figure 8-7 shows a sample output of the command while a cluster upgrade is in progress. The output shows that the cluster configuration is being updated to version 2; the rolling upgrade is in progress; and the next upgrade domain to be updated is domain 4.

```
PS C:\Users\hbai> Get-ServiceFabricClusterUpgrade

TargetCodeVersion                          : 4.4.87.9494
TargetConfigVersion                        : 2
StartTimestampUtc                          : 1/8/2016 9:58:22 AM
UpgradeState                               : RollingForwardInProgress
UpgradeDuration                            : 00:06:01
CurrentUpgradeDomainDuration               : 00:00:00
NextUpgradeDomain                          : 4
UpgradeDomainsStatus                       : { "3" = "InProgress";
                                             "0" = "Completed";
                                             "1" = "Completed";
                                             "2" = "Completed";
                                             "4" = "Pending" }
UpgradeKind                                : Rolling
RollingUpgradeMode                         : Monitored
FailureAction                              : Rollback
ForceRestart                               : False
UpgradeReplicaSetCheckTimeout              : 00:10:00
HealthCheckWaitDuration                    : 00:00:30
HealthCheckStableDuration                  : 00:00:30
HealthCheckRetryTimeout                    : 00:05:00
UpgradeDomainTimeout                       : 00:15:00
UpgradeTimeout                             : 01:15:00
ConsiderWarningAsError                     : False
MaxPercentUnhealthyApplications            : 0
MaxPercentUnhealthyNodes                   : 0
ApplicationTypeHealthPolicyMap             : {}
EnableDeltaHealthEvaluation                : True
MaxPercentDeltaUnhealthyNodes              : 0
MaxPercentUpgradeDomainDeltaUnhealthyNodes : 0
```

FIGURE 8-7 Sample output of Get-ServiceFabricClusterUpgrade

In addition to these commands, you can use Get-ServiceFabricReigsteredClusterCodeVersion to query registered cluster code versions and Get-ServiceFabricRegisteredClusterConfigurationVersion to query registered configuration version.

Node-level queries

The following commands query node-level information.

- Get-ServiceFabricNode

  This command lists nodes in a Service Fabric cluster. For example, the following command lists node name, status, fault domain, and upgrade domain.

  ```
  Get-ServiceFabricNode | format-table -Property NodeName, FaultDomain, UpgradeDomain,
  NodeStatus
  ```

  This command generates the following output in my test environment:

  ```
  NodeName FaultDomain UpgradeDomain NodeStatus
  -------- ----------- ------------- ----------
  _App2    fd:/0       3             Up
  _App1    fd:/1       4             Up
  _App0    fd:/1       1             Up
  _App3    fd:/0       0             Up
  _App4    fd:/2       2             Up
  ```

- Get-ServiceFabricNodeConfiguration

  This command returns node configuration information. At the time of this writing, the command seems to always return information on the local cluster. This is expected to be fixed in future versions. The following sample command lists all parameters in fabric settings:

  ```
  (Get-ServiceFabricNodeConfiguration).FabricSettings.Parameter | format-table -Property
  Name, Value
  ```

- Get-ServiceFabricNodeHealth

  This command gets node health information, including health events. In the basic format, you invoke the command with a node name:

  ```
  Get-ServiceFabricNodeHealth -NodeName [node name]
  ```

  Figure 8-8 shows a sample output of the command. The output shows the node name, the aggregated health state, and health events associated with the node. Two health events are recorded. The first one reflects the node coming online; the second one reflects the state change when a secondary certificate is added.

```
PS C:\Users\hbai> Get-ServiceFabricNodeHealth -NodeName _App0

NodeName           : _App0
AggregatedHealthState : Ok
HealthEvents       :
                     SourceId           : System.FabricNode
                     Property           : Certificate_cluster
                     HealthState        : Ok
                     SequenceNumber     : 130967215046289549
                     SentAt             : 1/8/2016 10:11:44 AM
                     ReceivedAt         : 1/8/2016 10:11:55 AM
                     TTL                : Infinite
                     Description        : Certificate expiration: (2017-01-07 18:25:57.000,
                     B01EAE778058CB8EE247DA3E5EC05B682C718B7B)
                     RemoveWhenExpired  : False
                     IsExpired          : False
                     Transitions        : Warning->Ok = 1/7/2016 6:38:42 PM, LastError = 1/1/0001 12:00:00 AM

                     SourceId           : System.FM
                     Property           : State
                     HealthState        : Ok
                     SequenceNumber     : 1
                     SentAt             : 1/7/2016 6:37:13 PM
                     ReceivedAt         : 1/7/2016 6:39:24 PM
                     TTL                : Infinite
                     Description        : Fabric node is up.
                     RemoveWhenExpired  : False
                     IsExpired          : False
                     Transitions        : Warning->Ok = 1/7/2016 6:39:24 PM, LastError = 1/1/0001 12:00:00 AM
```

FIGURE 8-8 Sample output of Get-ServiceFabricNodeHealth

You can use the health event filter to filter out unwanted events. For example, the following snippet lists only error events:

```
$errorFilter = [System.Fabric.Health.HealthStateFilter]::Error.value__
Get-ServiceFabricNodeHealth -NodeName [node name] -EventsHealthStateFilter $errorFilter
```

■ Get-ServiceFabricNodeLoadInformation

This command retrieves detailed load metric information on a node. The following sample command lists load metrics on the node as a table:

```
(Get-ServiceFabricNodeLoadInformation [node name]).NodeLoadMetricInformationList |
format-table Name, NodeLoad, NodeCapacity, NodeRemainingCapacity
```

Application-level queries

The following set of commands allows you to query applications and application types.

■ Get-ServiceFabricApplicationType

This command lists all application types registered on the cluster or shows information about an application type that is specified by the *ApplicationTypeName* parameter.

■ Get-ServiceFabricApplication

This command lists all deployed applications or shows information about a deployed application that is specified by the *ApplicationName* parameter.

■ Get-ServiceFabricApplicationManifest

This command retrieves the application manifest of an application type. For example:

```
Get-ServiceFabricApplicationManifest -ApplicationTypeName SomeAppType
-ApplicationTypeVersion 1.0.0
```

- Get-ServiceFabricApplicationHealth

  This command reads health state and assessments of a deployed application. It provides aggregated health of the application and health states of its services and hosting nodes. It also returns health events and evaluations that lead to an unhealthy state.

  To use the command, you need to provide an application name in the format of a Service Fabric address, which is fabric:/[*application name*]. For example:

  ```
  Get-ServiceFabricApplicationHealth -ApplicationName fabric:/SomeApp
  ```

  Among the returned properties is *UnhealthyEvaluations*. When an application is in an unhealthy state, you can drill down this property to get evaluations at different levels including services, service, partitions, partition, and health event so that you can determine the origin of the problem. For example, the following code snippet drills down to the partitions level:

  ```
  $eval = Get-ServiceFabricApplicationHealth -ApplicationName fabric:/SomeApp
  $eval.UnhealthyEvaluations.UnHealthyEvaluations
  ```

  This snippet generates the output in Figure 8-9 in my test environment. You can keep appending *UnhealthyEvaluations* to drill down the levels until you reach the bottom level. You can check which level you are on by looking at the *Kind* property.

  FIGURE 8-9 Sample output of Get-ServiceFabricApplicationHealth

- Get-ServiceFabricApplicationUpgrade

  This command returns the state of an ongoing application upgrade or the state of the last upgrade.

  The following code snippet is an example of using a PowerShell loop to wait for a rolling upgrade to reach the RollingForwardCompleted state:

  ```
  $state=''; While ($state -ne "RollingForwardCompleted") {$state = (Get-
  ServiceFabricApplicationUpgrade -Applicationname fabric:/SomeApp).UpgradeState.
  ToString(); write-host $state; sleep 1}
  ```

Service-level queries

The following set of commands allows you to query applications and application types.

- Get-ServiceFabricServiceType

   This command lists all services defined on an application type or shows information about a service type that is specified by the *ServiceTypeName* parameter. The following sample command lists all services on a *MyAppType* application type.

   ```
   Get-ServiceFabricServiceType -ApplicationTypeName MyAppType -ApplicationTypeVersion 1.0.0
   ```

- Get-ServiceFabricService

   This command lists all services in a deployed application or shows information about a deployed service that is specified by the *ServiceName* parameter. The following sample lists all services under a *fabric:/MyApp* application. This command returns the basic information about a service, including the service name, service address, and service state. To get more detailed information on a running service, use Get-ServiceFabricServiceDescription.

   ```
   Get-ServiceFabricService -ApplicationName fabric:/MyApp
   ```

- Get-ServiceFabricServiceDescription

   This command gets the service description of a running service. Compared to Get-ServiceFabricService, this command returns more details such as partition information, load metrics, and number of replicas. The following command gets the service description of a *MyActorService* under a *MyApp* application.

   ```
   Get-ServiceFabricServiceDescription fabric:/MyApp/MyActorService
   ```

- Get-ServiceFabricServiceManifest

   This command gets the manifest of a service. It takes an application type name, an application type version, and a service manifest name. You should note that the service manifest name, not the service name, is defined in the application manifest for the corresponding service.

   ```
   Get-ServiceFabricServiceManifest -ApplicationTypeName MyAppType -ApplicationTypeVersion
   1.0.0 -ServiceManifestName [service manifest name]
   ```

- Get-ServiceFabricServiceHealth

   This command reads health state and assessments of a service. It provides aggregated health of the service and health states of its partitions. It also returns health events and evaluations that lead to an unhealthy state. This command works much like the Get-ServiceFabricApplicationHealth command. To invoke the command, you pass in the service address to the *ServiceName* parameter, for example:

   ```
   Get-ServiceFabricServiceHealth -ServiceName fabric:/MyApp/MyActorService
   ```

Partition-level queries

Because I've given quite a few examples of the query commands, I won't go into details of each partition-level query. Instead, these commands are summarized in Table 8-1.

TABLE 8-1 Partition-level queries

Command	Desription	Sample
Get-ServiceFabricPartition	Lists partitions of a service or gets information about a specific partition	Get-ServiceFabricPartition –ServiceName fabric:/MyApp /MyService
Get-ServiceFabricPartitionHealth	Gets health state of a partition, including aggregated states and states of replicas	Get-ServiceFabricPartitionHealth -PartitionId 1f5edeff-...
Get-ServiceFabricPartitionLoadInformation	Gets load information about a partition	Get-ServiceFabricPartitionLoadInformation -PartitionId 1f5edeff-...

Replica-level queries

Replica-level queries are summarized in Table 8-2.

TABLE 8-2 Replica-level queries

Command	Desription	Sample
Get-ServiceFabricReplica	Lists replicas of a stateful service or instances of a stateless service or gets information about a specific replica or instance	Get-ServiceFabricReplica -PartitionId 1f5edeff-... -ReplicaOrInstanceId 130...
Get-ServiceFabricReplicaHealth	Gets health state of a replica or service instance	Get-ServiceFabricReplicaHealth -PartitionId 1f5edeff-... -ReplicaOrInstanceId 130...
Get-ServiceFabricReplicaLoadInformation	Gets load information about a replica	Get-ServiceFabricReplicaLoadInformation -PartitionId 1f5edeff-... -ReplicaOrInstanceId 130...

Cross queries on cluster nodes

Service Fabric provides another set of queries that allow you to query deployed entities on a cluster node. These commands all take a *NodeName* parameter that specifies the node to be queried. For example, the following command queries that code packages in *MyApp* have been deployed to *Node0*.

```
Get-ServiceFabricDeployedApplication -NodeName Node0 -ApplicationName fabric:/MyApp
```

The preceding command generates the following output in my environment:

```
ApplicationName              : fabric:/MyApp
ApplicationTypeName          : MyAppType
DeployedApplicationStatus    : Active
WorkDirectory                : C:\ProgramData\Microsoft\SF\_App\MyAppType_App4\work
LogDirectory                 : C:\ProgramData\Microsoft\SF\_App\MyAppType_App4\log
TempDirectory                : C:\ProgramData\Microsoft\SF\_App\MyAppType_App4\temp
```

Cross queries on nodes often reveal useful information for diagnostics on a particular node. In the above example, you can get the working directory, log directory, and temporary directory of the application.

Cross queries are summarized in Table 8-3.

TABLE 8-3 Cross queries on cluster nodes

Command	Description	Sample
Get-ServiceFabricDeployedApplication	Gets deployed applications on a node	Get-ServiceFabricDeployedApplication -NodeName Node0 -ApplicationName fabric:/MyApp
Get-ServiceFabricDeployedApplicationHealth	Gets application health state on a node	Get-ServiceFabricDeployedApplicationHealth -NodeName Node0 -ApplicationName fabric:/MyApp
Get-ServiceFabricDeployedCodePackage	Gets deployed code packages of an application or a service on a node	Get-ServiceFabricDeployedCodePackage -NodeName Node0 -ApplicationName fabric:/MyApp [-ServiceManifestName Actor1Pkg]
Get-ServiceFabricDeployedReplica	Get deployed replicas of an application or a service on a node	Get-ServiceFabricDeployedReplica -NodeName Node0 -ApplicationName fabric:/MyApp -PartitionId 1f5edeff-... [-ServiceManifestName Actor1Pkg]
Get-ServiceFabricDeployedReplicaDetail	Gets details on a deployed replica on a node	Get-ServiceFabricDeployedReplicaDetail -NodeName Node0 -PartitionId 1f5edeff-... -ReplicaOrInstanceId 130..
Get-ServiceFabricDeployedServicePackage	Gets deployed service packages of an application or a service on a node	Get-ServiceFabricDeployedServicePackage -NodeName Node0 -ApplicationName fabric:/MyApp [-ServiceManifestName Actor1Pkg]
Get-ServiceFabricDeployedServicePackageHealth	Lists service health information for all services in an application or for a particular service on a node	Get-ServiceFabricDeployedServicePackageHealth -NodeName Node0 -ApplicationName fabric:/MyApp [-ServiceManifestName Actor1Pkg]
Get-ServiceFabricDeployedServiceType	Get registered service types in an application or a specific service type on a node	Get-ServiceFabricDeployedServiceType -NodeName Node0 -ApplicationName fabric:/MyApp [-ServiceTypeName MyServiceType]

Node operations

Service Fabric provides a number of PowerShell commands for manipulating cluster nodes for purposes such as debugging, testing, and adjusting cluster capacity. These commands need administrative privileges. So before you try the following commands, you need to make sure PowerShell is launched as an administrator.

- Disable-ServiceFabricNode

  This command informs Service Fabric that some administrative tasks will be performed on the node. Based on the expressed intention, Service Fabric makes sure the node is prepared for the upcoming administrative operations.

A key parameter of the command is *Intent*, which indicates why the node is being disabled. The parameter can be one of the following values:

- Pause: Informs Service Fabric that new replicas should not be placed on the node. However, existing replicas should be kept running. You can use this option to debug running replicas on a node.

- Restart: Informs Service Fabric that replicas on the node should be closed but the replicas should be kept on the node. You can use this option when a restart is required for installing a patch on the node.

- RemoveData: Informs Service Fabric that the data on the node will be lost and replicas running on the node should be migrated to other nodes. You can use this option when the hard drives on the node are to be wiped or the node is going to be removed from the cluster.

For example, the following command disables _App4 on a cluster with the intention of pausing the node.

```
Disable-ServiceFabricNode -NodeName _App4 -Intent Pause -Force
```

The node remains in "disabling" state until it's ready for intended operations. You can use the Get-ServiceFabricNode command to monitor whether the node has been disabled. Figure 8-10 shows a sample output of the Get-ServiceFabricNode command after the node has been disabled with an intention of Pause.

FIGURE 8-10 Sample output of Get-ServiceFabricNode after a node is disabled

- Enable-ServiceFabricNode

  Once the intended administrative operations have been completed, you can use this command to inform Service Fabric that the node is ready to be put back to normal use.

- Remove-ServiceFabricNodeState

  This command informs Service Fabric that the state on the node has been removed because of external processes or hardware failures. Once it has received the command, Service Fabric stops waiting for replicas on this node to come back online.

You should use this command only when you are sure the state has been removed and the replicas won't come back online later.

Additional cluster management commands

Service Fabric provides several other cluster management commands that are not covered above. You rarely should need to use the following commands. Many of these commands may have global impact on your clusters. Please consult Microsoft Azure documentation for details on these commands before using them.

These commands are summarized in Table 8-4. Some of the commands are related to updating a Service Fabric cluster, such as updating code package and configuration of a Service Fabric cluster. Although the commands are useful to automate updating a large number of clusters, I expect that some UI experiences will be provided to perform cluster upgrades instead of directly calling these commands. For example, when you upload a new certificate to a secured cluster, the operation will trigger a cluster configuration upgrade.

Information source

The following text is based on *https://msdn.microsoft.com/library/mt125965.aspx*. I haven't personally tested most of the commands in the following table. Please use with caution.

TABLE 8-4 Additional cluster management commands

Command	Description
New-ServiceFabricNodeConfiguration	Configures a single node to join a Service Fabric cluster.
Register-ServiceFabricClusterPackage	Registers a Service Fabric cluster package.
Remove-ServiceFabricClusterPackage	Removes a Service Fabric cluster package from the image store.
Remove-ServiceFabricNodeConfiguration	Removes information stored on an operating system instance related to a configured node.
Resume-ServiceFabricClusterUpgrade	Resumes an unmonitored Service Fabric cluster upgrade.
Send-ServiceFabricClusterHealthReport	Sends a health report on a Service Fabric cluster. This command allows you to make independent assessments on a cluster. The sent reports are available for other clients to query via the Get-ServiceFabricClusterHealth command.
Start-ServiceFabricClusterRollback	Starts rolling back a Service Fabric cluster upgrade.
Start-ServiceFabricClusterUpgrade	Upgrades a Service Fabric cluster.
Test-ServiceFabricClusterManifest	Validates a Service Fabric cluster manifest.
Unregister-ServiceFabricClusterPackage	Unregisters a Service Fabric cluster package.
Update-ServiceFabricClusterUpgrade	Modifies the upgrade description of an active cluster upgrade.
Update-ServiceFabricNodeConfiguration	Updates a Service Fabric cluster configuration.

Application management commands

In this section, I'll introduce PowerShell commands for deploying, upgrading, rolling back, and removing applications. To keep these commands in perspective, I'll use a sample application. The application has no actual functions. It's just used to illustrate how to perform various application management tasks.

Deploying an application

First, let's create and deploy a simple Service Fabric application. I've introduced the deployment process in Chapter 5. When you publish an application via Visual Studio, the tooling automates all the steps: package, upload, register, and create. In the following exercise, we'll execute each of the steps using PowerShell commands.

1. In Visual Studio 2015, create a new Service Fabric application named *DeploymentTest* with a single stateless service named *Stateless1*.

2. Right-click the application and select the Package menu. This will build and package the application under the project's pkg\Debug folder.

3. Use the following command to upload the package to the cluster's image store. In the following command, the *[path to the application package folder]* parameter should point to the package folder in step 2. The command uses *fabric:ImageStore* as the image store connection string. This string points to the default system image store provided by the *fabric:/System/ ImageStoreService* stateful service. You also can use an Azure Storage account as the image store, in which case the connection string has the format of: *xstore:DefaultEndpointsProtocol =https;AccountName=[StorageAccountName];AccountKey=[StorageAccountKey];Container=[ContainerName]*. The application package name can be a string of your choice. The command uses the string *TestDeployment\V1* to reflect both application name and version.

   ```
   Copy-ServiceFabricApplicationPackage -ApplicationPackagePath "[path to the application
   package folder]" -ImageStoreConnectionString "fabric:ImageStore"
   -ApplicationPackagePathInImageStore "TestDeployment\V1"
   ```

4. Once the application package is uploaded, you can use the following command to register the application type:

   ```
   Register-ServiceFabricApplicationType -ApplicationPathInImageStore "TestDeployment\V1"
   ```

5. To verify that the application type has been registered successfully, you can use Get-ServiceFabricApplicationType to list all registered application types on the cluster.

6. Now you can create application instances using the registered application type. The new application instance should have a unique name and be named with a *fabric:/* prefix.

   ```
   New-ServiceFabricApplication -ApplicationName fabric:/DeploymentTest DeploymentTestType
   1.0.0
   ```

7. To verify the application health state, you can use the following command:

```
(Get-ServiceFabricApplicationHealth -ApplicationName fabric:/DeploymentTest).
DeployedApplicationHealthStates
```

Upgrading an application

Next, we'll upgrade the application to a new version. The process of upgrading an application is similar to that of creating an application. The new package needs to be uploaded and registered. Then, a rolling upgrade can be launched.

1. Modify the ServiceManifest.xml file of the Stateless1 service. For this exercise, you'll update the Version attribute on the CodePackage element and the root ServiceManifest element from 1.0.0 to 2.0.0.

2. Update the *ApplicationManifest.xml* file to update the *Version* attribute on the root *ApplicationManifest* element and the *ServiceManifestVersion* attribute on the *ServiceManifestRef* element from 1.0.0 to 2.0.0:

```
<ApplicationManifest ApplicationTypeVersion="2.0.0" …>
    …
    <ServiceManifestImport>
        <ServiceManifestRef ServiceManifestName="Stateless1Pkg"
ServiceManifestVersion="2.0.0" />
        <ConfigOverrides />
    </ServiceManifestImport>
    …
```

3. Right-click the application and select the Package menu. This will build and package the new application version under the project's pkg\Debug folder.

4. Upload the new package. The command is the same as before except for the *ApplicationPackagePathInImageStroe* parameter, which is set to a different name to indicate a new version.

```
Copy-ServiceFabricApplicationPackage -ApplicationPackagePath "[path to the application
package folder]" -ImageStoreConnectionString "fabric:ImageStore"
-ApplicationPackagePathInImageStore "TestDeployment\V2"
```

5. Register the new application type version.

```
Register-ServiceFabricApplicationType -ApplicationPathInImageStore "TestDeployment\V2"
```

6. To verify that both versions have been registered, use the Get-ServiceFabricApplicationType command. The command should list both versions of the application, as shown below:

```
ApplicationTypeName     : DeploymentTestType
ApplicationTypeVersion : 1.0.0
DefaultParameters       : { "Stateless1_InstanceCount" = "-1" }

ApplicationTypeName     : DeploymentTestType
```

```
ApplicationTypeVersion : 2.0.0
DefaultParameters      : { "Stateless1_InstanceCount" = "-1" }
```

7. Start the application upgrade process by using the Start-ServiceFabricApplicationUpgrade command. See Chapter 5 for details on upgrade parameters and upgrade modes.

```
Start-ServiceFabricApplicationUpgrade -ApplicationName fabric:/DeploymentTest
-ApplicationTypeVersion 2.0.0 -HealthCheckStableDurationSec 60 -UpgradeDomainTimeoutSec
1200 -UpgradeTimeoutSec 3000 -FailureAction Rollback -Monitored
```

8. During the rolling upgrade process, you can use the Get-ServiceFabricApplicationUpgrade command to monitor the upgrade process:

```
Get-ServiceFabricApplicationUpgrade -ApplicationName fabric:/DeploymentTest
```

9. Once the upgrade is finished, you can use the Get-ServiceFabricApplication command to verify that the new version has been put in place, as shown in Figure 8-11.

FIGURE 8-11 Sample output of Get-ServiceFabricApplication

Rolling back an application

If the new version of the application turns out to be defective, you can roll it back to the previous version to restore the older services. This gives you time to fix the new version while keeping the existing service running.

First, when you invoke the Start-ServiceFabricApplicationUpgrade command, you can specify *Rollback* as the *FailureAction* so that when an upgrade fails the application automatically is rolled back to the previous version.

Second, while a rolling upgrade is in progress, you can use the command Start-ServiceFabricApplicationRollback to cancel the upgrade and roll back the application to the previous version. For example:

```
Start-ServiceFabricApplicationRollback -ApplicationName fabric:/DeploymentTest
```

Third, if an application needs to be rolled back after an upgrade has completed, you can use the command Start-ServiceFabricApplicationUpgrade to trigger a new application upgrade with the previous version as the target version. For example, the following Start-ServiceFabricApplicationUpgrade command rolls back the sample application to version 1.0.0:

```
Start-ServiceFabricApplicationUpgrade -ApplicationName fabric:/DeploymentTest
-ApplicationTypeVersion 1.0.0 -HealthCheckStableDurationSec 60 -UpgradeDomainTimeoutSec 1200
-UpgradeTimeoutSec 3000 -FailureAction Rollback -Monitored
```

Decommissioning an application

When an application no longer is needed, you can remove the application instances, unregister the application type, and remove the application package from the cluster to remove it completely from the system. The following exercise walks you through these steps.

1. Use the Remove-ServiceFabricApplication command to remove the application instance:

```
Remove-ServiceFabricApplication -ApplicationName fabric:/DeploymentTest -Force
```

2. Use the Unregister-ServiceFabricApplicationType command to unregister the application type. Note the command unregisters a specific application type version.

```
Unregister-ServiceFabricApplicationType -ApplicationTypeName DeploymentTestType
-ApplicationTypeVersion 2.0.0 -Force
```

3. Finally, use the Remove-ServiceFabricApplicationPackage command to remove the application package from the image store.

```
Remove-ServiceFabricApplicationPackage -ApplicationPackagePathInImageStore
"TestDeployment\V2" -ImageStoreConnectionString "fabric:ImageStore"
```

Additional information

In this chapter, you studied Service Fabric PowerShell commands (also known as cmdlets). You can use PowerShell to perform various cluster management tasks and application management tasks. For up-to-date documentation, consult MSDN at *https://msdn.microsoft.com/library/dn708514.aspx*.

Throughout the chapter, I showed samples that use different PowerShell features such as variables, conditions, and loops. However, because this book is not an introduction to PowerShell, detailed uses of these features are not explained. PowerShell is a powerful language that you can use to implement different automation scenarios. If you are not familiar with any of the syntax, a quick online search will bring immediate help.

Chacko Daniel has shared a PowerShell script that contains a number of helper functions for some cluster management tasks such as managing certificates and scaling the cluster. You can find the Git repo here: *https://github.com/ChackDan/Service-Fabric/tree/master/Scripts/ServiceFabricRPHelpers*. Among the functions is an *Invoke-ServiceFabricRPClusterScaleUpgrade* function that allows you to scale out (add nodes to) or to scale in (remove nodes from) a Service Fabric cluster. The function works with the clusters that are created using the Portal experience, and it directly modifies the underlying Azure resource group that supports the cluster. Because in future versions, Service Fabric clusters are likely to be supported by Azure VM Scale Sets instead of individual virtual machines, make sure to review the documentation and code and make sure the function still applies to your cluster before applying the function to your cluster.

I'll introduce the relationship between Azure resources and Service Fabric clusters in Chapter 9.

Managing Service Fabric with management portal

In earlier chapters I've covered the basics of creating a Service Fabric cluster with Microsoft Azure management portal. This chapter covers additional management tasks such as configuring security and configuring advanced settings.

Before I go into specifics, I'll take a closer look at how a Service Fabric cluster is constructed on Azure. This will help you understand how various Azure resources are organized to deliver a Service Fabric cluster and how a cluster can be customized and extended using standard Azure features.

Anatomy of a Service Fabric cluster

In Chapter 1, "Hello, Service Fabric!," and Chapter 7, "Scalability and performance," I've introduced that a Service Fabric cluster on Azure is an Azure resource group with a number of Azure resources. Figure 9-1 shows a screen shot of a Service Fabric cluster blade on the management portal. You can open its corresponding resource group by clicking the link at the upper-left corner of the blade.

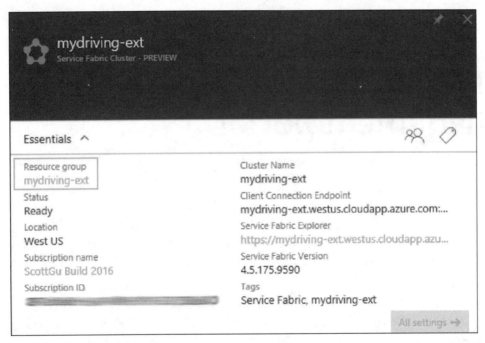

FIGURE 9-1 A Service Fabric cluster blade

Once you open the resource group, you can see the resource group is made up of a few different types of Azure resources, as shown in Figure 9-2.

NAME	TYPE	RESOURCE GROUP	LOCATION
ExtHost	Virtual machin...	mydriving-ext	West US
LB-mydriving-ext-0	Load balancer	mydriving-ext	West US
LBIP-mydriving-ext-0	Public IP addr...	mydriving-ext	West US
VNet-mydriving-ext	Virtual network	mydriving-ext	West US
mydriving-ext	Service Fabric...	mydriving-ext	West US
sflgmydrivingext3402	Storage account	mydriving-ext	West US
sfvmmydrivingext8199	Storage account	mydriving-ext	West US

FIGURE 9-2 Service Fabric cluster resources

Next, I'll go through each of the resources and analyze their roles in a Service Fabric cluster.

Availability set

When I presented rolling upgrade in Chapter 5, "Service deployments and upgrades," I introduced the concepts of fault domains and update domains. Both concepts are provided by an Azure resource type called availability set. An availability set defines a number of fault domains and update domains. And when multiple virtual machines are put into the same availability set, they automatically are distributed across these domains to ensure availability.

A virtual machine on Azure is maintained periodically to improve overall security, performance, and reliability. Most of these maintenance operations are transparent and don't affect the virtual machine. However, some operations may cause the virtual machine to reboot. When performing such planned updates, Azure updates one update domain at a time so that there are some virtual machines running within an availability set at any time.

Sometimes, a virtual machine fails because of hardware failures such as network problems and rack level problems. An availability set places virtual machines in different fault domains to reduce the probability of multiple machines failing at the same time.

The Service Fabric Explorer provides a nice presentation of fault domains and upgrade domains with the cluster map. Figure 9-3 shows how the five nodes in a Service Fabric cluster are distributed into three fault domains and five upgrade domains.

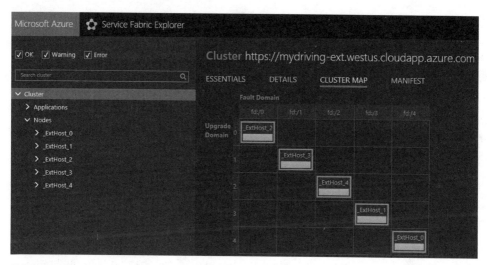

FIGURE 9-3 Cluster map on Service Fabric Explorer

If you have multiple node types defined on your Service Fabric cluster, an availability set is created for each of the node types.

Virtual machines and NICs

At the time of this writing, Service Fabric cluster nodes are individual Windows Server 2012 R2 virtual machines placed in the same availability set. As mentioned in Chapter 7, it's expected that in future versions, Service Fabric clusters will be based on Azure VM Scale Sets. Figure 9-2 shows a cluster based on Scale Set.

By default, five virtual machines are placed in a Scale Set forming the cluster. These are not special virtual machines. They are regular Azure virtual machine resources in the resource group. What makes them special is that they all have a Service Fabric extension installed on them.

Virtual machine extensions are software packages that you can acquire and install on new or existing virtual machines. Azure provides a variety of extensions that offer features such as configuration management and antivirus protection. The Service Fabric node runtime is added to these virtual machines as another extension, which is named *Microsoft.Azure.ServiceFabric.ServiceFabricNode*.

In Azure Resources Explorer (*https://resources.azure.com*), open a virtual machine under the Scale Set. You'll find the extension defined as a resource under the virtual machine, as shown in Figure 9-4.

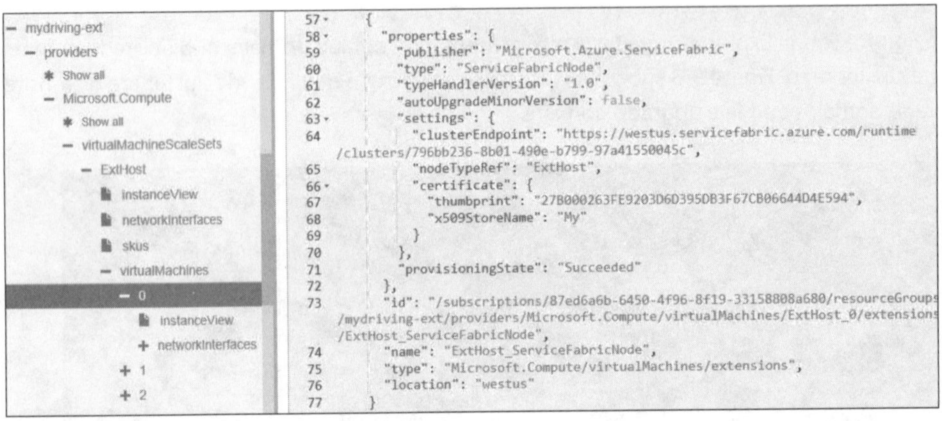

FIGURE 9-4 VM extensions

You can modify configurations on the virtual machines. For example, you can attach more data disks to the machines if necessary. You also can use remote desktop to connect to any of the virtual machines.

When you create a Service Fabric cluster, you can pick from a number of virtual machine sizes. Each machine size comes with different compute power, amount of memory, and disk throughput. Some virtual machines (such as D-series and DS-series machines) also come with local solid-state drives (SSDs) for faster local disk access. When the default state provider is used, Service Fabric stateful services save states to local drives. Using SSDs can improve the service performance by providing faster state access.

Cluster customizations

Remember that Service Fabric is a platform as a service (PaaS) offering. The modifications you make are ad hoc customizations that are not supported officially. So, before you make any modifications, you need to be sure that your modifications won't break the framework.

Throughout this chapter, I'll introduce a number of customizations that are relatively safe based on my tests. Unfortunately, I can't guarantee these customizations will not cause problems in current and future Service Fabric versions.

Each of the virtual machines is associated with a virtual network interface card (NIC). Each NIC is assigned a private IP address. A virtual machine is associated with a virtual network and a load balancer via the card.

Virtual network

All virtual machines on a Service Fabric cluster are placed on a virtual network. Based on my experiments, all machines are joined to the same subnet on the virtual network, even if multiple node types are used. At this point, it's unclear how multiple subnets will be used in future versions.

Figure 9-5 shows that the virtual network on my Service Fabric cluster consists of five virtual machines (that are associated via NICs). Because these virtual machines have only private IP addresses, they are not directly addressable outside the virtual network. Service Fabric clients access services on these machines via a load balancer, which I'll introduce next.

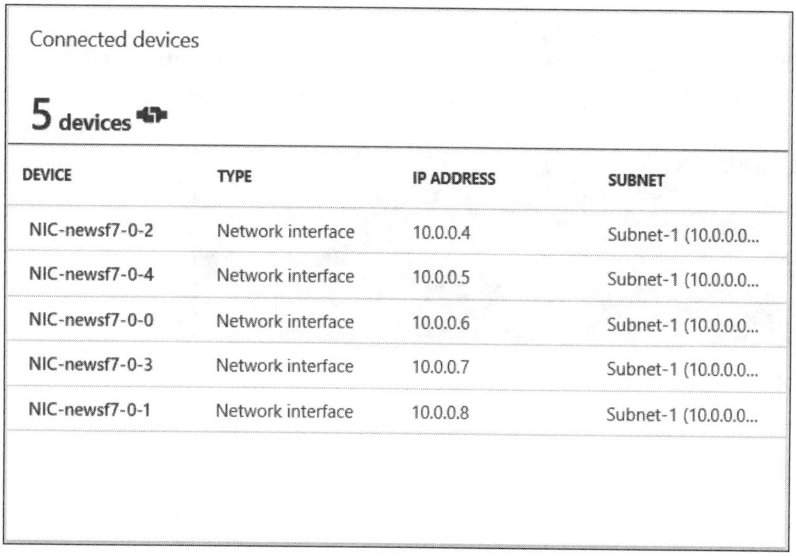

Connected devices			
5 devices			
DEVICE	TYPE	IP ADDRESS	SUBNET
NIC-newsf7-0-2	Network interface	10.0.0.4	Subnet-1 (10.0.0.0...
NIC-newsf7-0-4	Network interface	10.0.0.5	Subnet-1 (10.0.0.0...
NIC-newsf7-0-0	Network interface	10.0.0.6	Subnet-1 (10.0.0.0...
NIC-newsf7-0-3	Network interface	10.0.0.7	Subnet-1 (10.0.0.0...
NIC-newsf7-0-1	Network interface	10.0.0.8	Subnet-1 (10.0.0.0...

FIGURE 9-5 VMs on a virtual network

Load balancer

As stated above, virtual machines on a Service Fabric cluster have only private IP addresses. Management traffic and service traffic need to be routed via a load balancer.

All virtual machines on the cluster are added to the load balancer's backend pool, which means all these machines are equal candidates for traffic destinations. Network traffic is routed to these machines via two types of load balancing rules: NAT rules and load balancing rules. NAT rules are used to connect clients to specific machine instances. Load balancing rules distribute network traffic to all participating virtual machines in the pool in a round-robin fashion.

A load balancer has an associated public IP address with a DNS name in the format of *<cluster name>.<cluster location>*.cloudapp.azure.com. For example, my cluster "mydriving-ext" in Azure West US datacenter is named mydriving-ext.westus.cloudapp.azure.com. The public IP is another resource on the same resource group. In Figure 9-2, the entry LBIP-mydriving-ext-0 represents the public IP.

If you have multiple node types defined on the cluster, a load balancer is created for each of the node types.

NAT rules

By default, a number of NAT rules are defined to allow remote desktop connections from remote desktop clients to individual virtual machines. When a remote desktop client tries to make a connection, it uses the public IP address or the DNS name associated with the load balancer and a port to select a specific virtual machine instance.

Figure 9-6 lists the NAT rules on my sample load balancer. Each of the NAT rules is pointed at the same public IP (masked) that is associated with the load balancer. And each rule is targeted at a different virtual machine in the backend pool (App0 through App4). In addition, each rule corresponds to a unique port (33000 through 33004). A remote client uses this port to select a specific virtual machine.

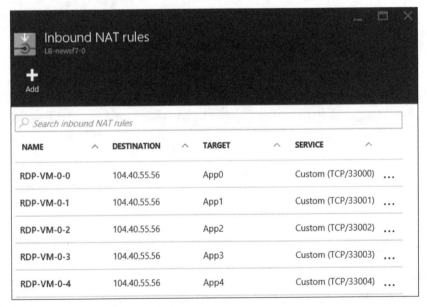

FIGURE 9-6 NAT rules on a load balancer

Load balancing rules

Load balancing rules are used to route traffic to both system services and user applications. By default, two TCP-based rules on port 19000 and port 19080 are defined for management clients to connect to the system cluster manager service (fabric:/System/ClusterManagerService). Port 19000 is used for the

Windows PowerShell client and management API calls. Port 19080 is used for browsers to access the Service Fabric Explorer.

The client requests are routed to a system naming service (fabric:/System/NamingService) to discover the address of the service to be called, and then they are routed to the correct service. The naming service needs to be highly available and scalable. By default, the naming service is created with multiple partitions, each of which has multiple replicas. All partitions are equivalent, so it doesn't matter to which partitions the load balancer routes the traffic.

When you create a new Service Fabric cluster, the management portal allows you to enter additional application endpoints as a comma-separated port list (see Figure 1-6). For each specified port, a new load balancing rule is added with a direct mapping from the load balancer port to the instance port. Figure 9-7 shows that on one of my sample clusters, I've defined three input endpoints (80, 90, and 100) while creating the cluster. A load balancing rule is added for each entered port.

Load balancing rules
LB-sfnew8-1

NAME	PROTOCOL/PORT	BACKEND POOL	PROBE	
AppPortLBRule1	TCP/80	LoadBalancerBEAddressPool	AppPortProbe1	...
AppPortLBRule2	TCP/90	LoadBalancerBEAddressPool	AppPortProbe2	...
AppPortLBRule3	TCP/100	LoadBalancerBEAddressPool	AppPortProbe3	...
LBHttpRule	TCP/19080	LoadBalancerBEAddressPool	FabricHttpGatewayProbe	...
LBRule	TCP/19000	LoadBalancerBEAddressPool	FabricGatewayProbe	...

FIGURE 9-7 Load balancing rules

Each load balancing rule has a corresponding probe, which periodically checks the specified address on each virtual machine to verify the machine is still responsive as expected. If a machine fails to acknowledge probe requests several times, the machine is considered unhealthy and is taken off the load balancer.

By default, the auto-generated probes are based on TCP protocol. You can modify these probes on the management portal. For instance, to change a probe to use HTTP protocol to query a specific page, follow these steps:

1. Click the load balancer in the resource group's resource list.

2. On the Load Balancer blade, click the All Settings link.

3. On the Settings blade, click the Probes link.

4. On the Probes blade, click the probe you want to modify.

5. Make necessary updates and save the changes. Figure 9-8 shows that a probe is being updated to use HTTP protocol to poll a */probeaddr* page every five seconds. If the page fails to respond

to two consecutive requests, the corresponding node is considered unhealthy and is taken off the load balancer. The figure also shows the navigation path from the Settings blade to the Probes blade and then to the probe properties blade.

FIGURE 9-8 Update probe properties

Customization tip

In a typical scenario in which a web-based stateless service is hosted, you probably would want to define an endpoint at port 80 and update the default probe to use HTTP protocol to poll against a page of your choice. If you forgot to define the input endpoint when the cluster was created, you can add a load balancing rule directly to the load balancer using the management portal UI to allow the web traffic to be routed.

Storage accounts

Each Service Fabric cluster is supported by a number of Azure storage accounts. There's a storage account (prefixed with "sfvm") that holds the virtual hard drives (VHDs) for participating virtual machines. There's also a storage account for logs (prefixed with "sflg") and another storage account for diagnostic data (prefixed with "sfdg"). In Chapter 6, "Availability and reliability," I've shown how to browse the data in the diagnostic data account. In Chapter 10, "Diagnostics and monitoring," I'll introduce other ways to use this data.

An Azure VM Scale Set often is backed up by a number of storage accounts to avoid storage account throttling when a large number of VHDs are needed to support the virtual machine instances in the set. In future versions in which VM Scale Sets are used, you likely will see more storage accounts in your resource group.

Advanced Service Fabric cluster configuration

Once you understand how a Service Fabric cluster is constructed, you can leverage Azure features such as Role-Based Access Control (RBAC) and Network Security Groups (NSGs) to set up additional protections on your clusters. Note that the following configurations are customizations that are not provided by the Service Fabric portal experience by default. It's not guaranteed that all of the custom settings will be kept if you use the default portal experience to update the cluster later.

Role-Based Access Control

Role-Based Access Control (RBAC) allows you to assign fine-grained access controls on Azure resources. You can assign different user roles to subscriptions, resource groups, and resources to grant different access rights to designated users or user groups.

By default, Azure defines four roles: Owner, Contributor, Reader, and User Access Administrator. The Owner role is allowed to perform all management tasks. The Contributor role can manage everything except resource access rights. The Reader role is the least privileged. It's allowed to view everything, but it's not allowed to change anything. Finally, the User Access Administrator role can manage only resource access rights.

RBAC rules are inherited along the resource hierarchy unless they are redefined at a lower level. By using the Azure management portal, you can assign any users or user groups on your Azure Active Directory with proper RBAC rules so that only designated users and groups can make modifications to your Service Fabric clusters.

To change RBAC settings for a Service Fabric cluster, do the following:

1. Click the Users icon on the Cluster blade.

2. To add a user to a role, click the Add icon on the Users blade, as shown in Figure 9-9.

FIGURE 9-9 Update Service Fabric cluster RBAC

3. Pick a role and select a user to add the user to the role, as shown in Figure 9-10. You can do this operation at subscription level, at resource group level, or at resource level on any of the resources.

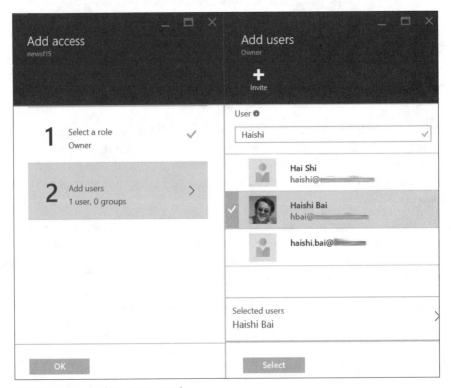

FIGURE 9-10 Assigning a user to a role

Network Security Groups

Network Security Groups (NSGs) control inbound and outbound traffic of a subnet, a virtual machine, or a specific network interface card (NIC).

When multiple virtual machines are put on the same virtual network, by default they can communicate with one another through any ports. If for any reason you want to constrain communications among the machines, you can define NSGs to segment the network or to isolate virtual machines from one another.

For example, you can use NSGs to forbid machines belonging to different node types from speaking with each other. This could be useful when you use node types to isolate deployments for different customers and want to provide stronger isolations among these customers.

You can define two types of NSGs: allow rules and deny rules. Allow rules explicitly define allowed ports, protocols, and IP ranges, implying everything else is disabled. Deny rules explicitly define denied ports, protocols, and IP ranges, implying everything else is allowed. You can define multiple rules for both inbound traffic and outbound traffic. Each rule is associated with a priority number, and rules are applied in order of priority.

A more detailed introduction of NSGs is out of the scope of this book. The following walkthrough demonstrates the basic steps for disallowing any nodes on the cluster to make outbound connections via port 80.

1. Sign in to Microsoft Azure management portal.

2. Click the New link in the upper-left corner. Then, in the search text box on the New blade, type **network security group** and press Enter to search for the resource type.

3. In the search result list, which is displayed on the Everything blade, click the Network Security Group entry.

4. On the Network Security Group blade, leave Select A Deployment Model as the default resource manager option and then click the Create button.

5. On the Create Network Security Group blade, enter a name for the NSG. Pick the subscription and the resource group you want to use. You should put the NSG into the resource group where the Service Fabric cluster is located.

6. Click the Create button to create the NSG, as shown in Figure 9-11.

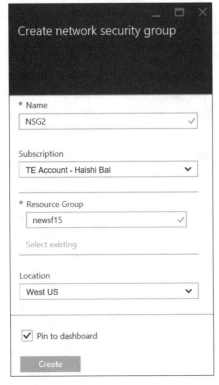

FIGURE 9-11 Creating an NSG

7. Open the Resource Group that contains the Service Fabric cluster. Click the security group entry to open its settings, as shown in Figure 9-12:

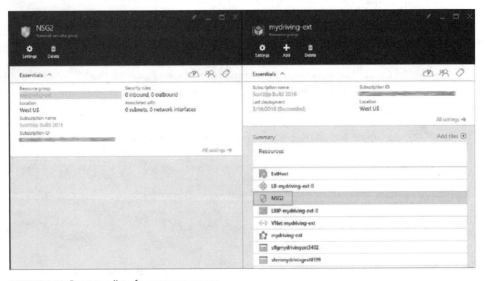

FIGURE 9-12 Resource list of a resource group

8. On the Settings blade of the NSG, click the Outbound Security Rules link. Then, on the Outbound Security Rules blade, click the Add icon.

9. On the Add Outbound Security Rule blade, configure the following values:

- Name: a descriptive name for the rule.

- Priority: a number between 100 and 4,096 that indicates the rule priority.

- Destination: destination address type. You can choose Any for any destination, CIDR block for a specific address space, and Tag for addresses identified by predefined tags.

- Destination tag: When the Destination is set to Tag, you can choose from the predefined tags: Internet represents any Internet addresses; VirtualNetwork represents all addresses on the virtual network; AzureLoadBalancer represents Azure Load Balancer health probe origin addresses.

- Source and Source tag: source addresses.

- Protocol: Any, TCP, or UDP.

- Source port range: source port range to which the rule is applied.

- Action: deny or allow access.

Figure 9-13 shows how to define a rule to stop outbound TCP traffic via port 80.

FIGURE 9-13 Outbound security rule

10. Click the OK button to define the rule.

11. Return to the Settings blade of the NSG. Click the Subnets blade.

12. On the Subnet Association blade, click the Associate button.

13. Pick the virtual network and the subnet to which you want to apply the NSG and then click the OK button to complete the association.

Additional information

Service Fabric clusters are backed by Azure resource groups. It's important to understand how Azure resources are organized into a Service Fabric cluster. Knowing the underlying structure enables you to carry out advanced customizations and optimizations. The knowledge also paves the way for advanced discussions in later chapters. However, Service Fabric is a PaaS offering, which is supposed to take care of all the underlying infrastructure management tasks. When you work directly at the resource group level, you need to be aware that your customizations are not officially supported.

CHAPTER 10

Diagnostics and monitoring

C hapter 6, "Availability and reliability," introduced the basic steps of using Event Tracing for Windows (ETW) and Azure Diagnostics to collect diagnostic data from your Service Fabric clusters. This chapter introduces how Service Fabric Diagnostics is enabled and configured. Then, it introduces how to use Azure Operational Management Suite (OMS) to gain insights into the collected data. Next, it introduces a couple of options that help you configure continuous monitoring on your clusters. Finally, you are introduced to some Azure features that enable additional diagnostics scenarios.

Diagnostics

Debugging a single process application is relatively easy because you can attach a debugger to step through the code and see exactly what's happening. Debugging a distributed system, in contrast, is rather hard. A common approach is to generate logs with enough details and hints for correlations to capture how the system runs. When errors are observed, the collected log files are correlated and analyzed to identify root causes of problems.

Generating and collecting logs produce overheads that may impact system performance. Storing logs leads to additional cost, and analyzing a large amount of log data requires efficient data management and sophisticated query capabilities. In Chapter 6, I introduced how Service Fabric uses Event Tracing for Windows (ETW) for efficient telemetry reporting and uses Azure Diagnostics for log collection and storage. In this chapter, we'll continue with the log data flow and learn how to prepare your environment for analyzing the log data.

Configuring Service Fabric Diagnostics

In Chapter 6, I introduced how to enable Azure Diagnostics when creating a new Service Fabric cluster. At the time of this writing, Service Fabric doesn't provide a UI for you to turn diagnostics on or off on an existing Service Fabric cluster. However, you can enable or disable diagnostics manually by changing VM settings on each of the cluster nodes.

Modify resource groups using Azure Resource template

You can perform the following steps to enable diagnostics on each of the Service Fabric cluster nodes. However, there are means to automate the process such as using Azure PowerShell or command line interface (CLI). Or, you can update VM extensions by constructing an Azure Resource template and then applying it to the existing resource group. By default, Azure Resource templates are deployed in incremental mode, which means only new and updated resources will be changed. This allows you to update resource settings safely without touching unchanged resources. You'll see an example in the next section.

Enabling Diagnostics on an existing cluster

The following walkthrough shows you steps to enable Azure Diagnostics manually on an existing Service Fabric cluster node.

1. On Microsoft Azure management portal, navigate to the resource group that supports the Service Fabric cluster. Browse its resources and click any of the virtual machine resources.

2. On the virtual machine's Summary blade, click the All Settings link.

3. On the Settings blade, click the Diagnostics link.

4. On the Diagnostics blade, click the On option at the top., you can select a storage account for saving the diagnostics data, as shown in Figure 10-1. You should avoid using the storage account where the VM VHDs are served to avoid service throttling affecting system performance.

5. Select the telemetry data you want to collect. You can collect from a number of data sources, including IIS logs, Windows event logs, .NET metrics, and custom logs. Structured or semi-structured data will be written to table storage, and unstructured logs such as crash dumps will be written to blob storage.

FIGURE 10-1 VM Diagnostics settings

6. Click the Save button.

   When Azure Diagnostics is enabled, a *Microsoft.Azure.Diagnostics.IaaSDiagnostics* VM exten-sion is provisioned on the VM. You can view installed extensions by clicking the Extensions link on the VM's Settings blade.

7. Repeat the above steps for all the nodes.

Defining custom event source

In the example in Chapter 6, you changed the *EventSource* attribute to "Microsoft-ServiceFabric-Services" to match the name that gets registered by the portal provisioning process. To use your own event source names, you need to update the Azure Diagnostics extension on the virtual machines.

Neither Service Fabric nor the extension provides a UI to update event source settings. To update the extension, you'll need to apply an Azure Resource Manager template with the new settings on top of the existing resource group.

The follow code snippet shows how the diagnostics configuration looks when you enable diagnostics during cluster provision. The extension has two event source providers defined: Microsoft-ServiceFabric-Actors provider that writes to a *ServiceFabricReliableActorEventTable* and

Microsoft-ServiceFabric-Services provider that writes to a *ServiceFabricReliableServiceEventTable*. Both tables belong to a *sfdgnewsf188899* storage account.

```json
{
    "properties": {
    "publisher": "Microsoft.Azure.Diagnostics",
    "type": "IaaSDiagnostics",
    ...
    "settings": {
        "WadCfg": {
        "DiagnosticMonitorConfiguration": {
            "overallQuotaInMB": "50000",
            "EtwProviders": {
            "EtwEventSourceProviderConfiguration": [
                {
                "provider": "Microsoft-ServiceFabric-Actors",
                "scheduledTransferKeywordFilter": "1",
                "scheduledTransferPeriod": "PT5M",
                "DefaultEvents": {
                    "eventDestination": "ServiceFabricReliableActorEventTable"
                }
                },
                {
                "provider": "Microsoft-ServiceFabric-Services",
                "scheduledTransferPeriod": "PT5M",
                "DefaultEvents": {
                    "eventDestination": "ServiceFabricReliableServiceEventTable"
                }
                }
            ],
        ...
        "StorageAccount": "sfdgnewsf188899"
    ...
```

You can use Azure Resource Explorer at *https://resources.azure.com* to examine the JSON representation of Azure resources. The tool gives you detailed views of Azure resources so you can examine all configuration details in simple text views. And if you need help in Azure Resource Manager template (ARM template) syntax, you can use the tool as a reference.

Figure 10-2 shows a sample screen shot of Azure Resource Explorer. To the left is a tree representation of resources. The *newsf18* node is the resource group that supports the Service Fabric cluster. The node is expanded to the individual virtual machine level, and the JSON representation of the resource is displayed in the right panel.

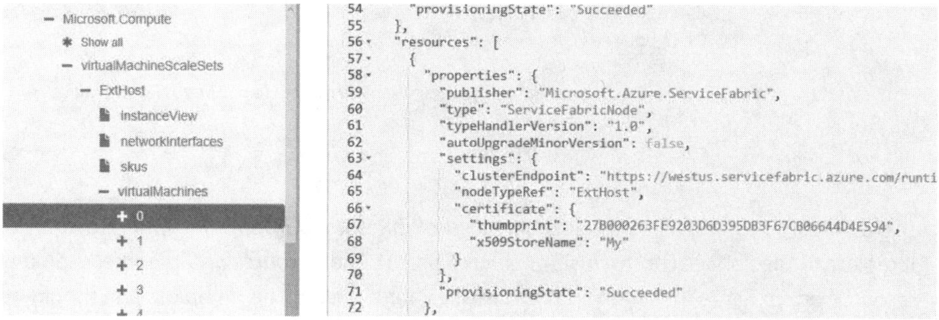

FIGURE 10-2 Azure Resource Explorer

To update the extension settings, you need to construct a new ARM template with desired settings and then use Azure Resource Manager to deploy the template onto the existing resource group. The following walkthrough shows you the steps to define a custom event source provider using an ARM template.

1. Create an UpdateWad.json file with the following content. Then, copy the Azure Diagnostic resource JSON from Azure Resource Explorer into the file, replacing *[Copy JSON snippet from Azure Resource Explorer here]*.

```
{
    "$schema": "http://schema.management.azure.com/schemas/2015-01-01/deploymentTemplate.json#",
    "contentVersion": "1.0.0.0",
    "resources": [
        [Copy JSON snippet from Azure Resource Explorer here]
    ]
}
```

2. Add the following attributes to the resource JSON. You should replace *[vm name]* with the virtual machine name to which this template is going to be applied.

```
"name": "[concat('[vm name]','/Microsoft.Insights.VMDiagnosticsSettings')]",
"location": "[resourceGroup().location]",
```

3. Update the *EtwEventSourceProviderConfiguration* element to include new custom event providers. You should keep the existing providers unchanged. The code in bold below defines a new *"My-Event-Source"* provider:

```
EtwEventSourceProviderConfiguration": [
                {
                    "provider": "Microsoft-ServiceFabric-Actors",
                    ...
                },
                {
                    "provider": "Microsoft-ServiceFabric-Services",
                    ...
                },
                {
                    "provider": "My-Event-Source",
```

```
                    "scheduledTransferKeywordFilter": "1",
                    "scheduledTransferPeriod": "PT5M",
                    "DefaultEvents": {
                      "eventDestination": "ServiceFabricReliableActorEventTable"
                    }
                  },
                ],
```

4. Use the Azure PowerShell command *New-AzureRmResourceGroupDeployment* to apply the template to the Service Fabric cluster resource group. The *[resource group name]* should be the resource group name that supports the Service Fabric cluster. The *[template file]* should be the file you created above.

```
New-AzureRmResourceGroupDeployment -ResourceGroupName [resource group name] -TemplateFile
[template file]
```

The preceding walkthrough uses a simple template that doesn't take any parameters and is applicable only to a single hard-coded virtual machine. You can make improvements using ARM syntax such as parameters and loops to generalize the template and make it applicable to a group of virtual machines. Authoring ARM templates is out of the scope of this book.

Using Elasticsearch and Kibana

Elasticsearch (*https://www.elastic.co/guide/index.html*) is an open-source full-text search and analytics engine for storing, searching, and analyzing big volumes of data in near real-time. You report log data to Elasticsearch via its REST API, and data is indexed and made available for analysis quickly. You can host a highly available Elasticsearch deployment on Azure and send Service Fabric logs to it for immediate analysis. Kibana (*https://www.elastic.co/products/kibana*) is an open-source analytics and visualization platform. It provides data discovery and visualization over data indexed by Elasticsearch.

To report logs to Elasticsearch, you can use either in-process code or an external agent. You'll learn about both methods in the following sections.

Provisioning an Elasticsearch cluster on Azure

You can provision an Elasticsearch cluster on Azure by deploying a predefined ARM template or by using Azure Marketplace. To use the ARM template approach, you can choose from the following templates:

- The Elasticsearch template on the Azure quickstart template open-source repository:
  https://github.com/Azure/azure-quickstart-templates/tree/master/elasticsearch

- Microsoft Azure Diagnostics with ELK from the Microsoft Patterns & Practices team:
  https://github.com/mspnp/semantic-logging/trefe/elk/

The following are the steps for using the Azure Marketplace experience.

1. Sign in to Microsoft Azure management portal.

2. Click the New link on the upper-left corner of the dashboard.

3. On the New blade, type **elasticsearch** in the search box and press Enter to search for entries.

4. On the search result blade, click the Elasticsearch and Kibana entry.

5. On the Elasticsearch and Kibana blade, click the Create button to launch the Provisioning wizard.

6. Follow the wizard to configure your cluster. Use the following parameters:

   - Basic settings

     - **User name:** The user name for accessing virtual machines on the cluster.

     - **Authentication type:** Password. You also can use a SSH key if preferred.

     - **Password:** Password for the above user.

     - **Subscription:** The Azure subscription to use.

     - **Resource group:** The resource group that will hold the Elasticsearch cluster. You can choose the resource group that hosts your Service Fabric cluster or put the Elasticsearch cluster in a new resource group.

     - **Location:** Where the Elasticsearch cluster should be provisioned. You should choose the region where your Service Fabric cluster is to avoid cross-region network delays.

   - Cluster settings

     - **Elasticsearch version:** Leave the option at the default v2.0.0.0 version.

     - **Cluster name:** Enter a name for your Elasticsearch cluster.

   - Nodes configuration

     - Leave all options at default values. An Elasticsearch cluster can have a number of master nodes, a number of data nodes, and optionally a number of client nodes. To reduce the number of virtual machines on the cluster, you can set the Data Nodes Are Master Eligible option to Yes. This allows a data node to be elected as the master node. Once this option is selected, dedicated master nodes no longer are provisioned. Client nodes are smart load balancers. By default, there are no client nodes provisioned.

   - Shield users

     - Shield (*https://www.elastic.co/products/shield*) is an Elasticsearch plug-in that provides authentication and Role-Based Access Control (RBAC) on an Elasticsearch cluster. On this screen, you can set up passwords for three users: es_admin, es_read, and es_kibana. The *es_admin* user is the cluster administrator; the *es_read* user is a read-only user that isn't granted any write access; and *es_kibana* is the administrator for the Kibana UI.

   - Extended Access

     - **Install Kibana:** Yes

- **Use a jump box:** No

- **Load balancer type:** External

7. After reviewing the cluster summary and purchase agreement, click the Create button on the last step of the wizard to provision the cluster.

8. After the resource group has been provisioned, open the Resource Group blade. Browse to its resources list and then click the *publicIp* resource, as shown in Figure 10-3:

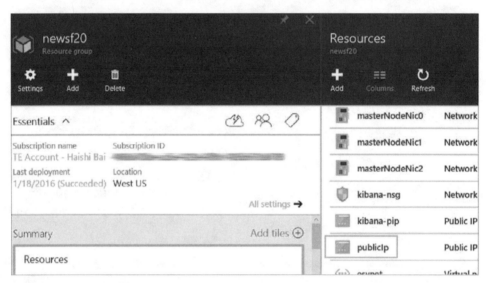

FIGURE 10-3 Public IP resource in the resource group

9. On the public IP blade, note the public IP, as shown in Figure 10-4. You can use this public IP to address the Elasticsearch cluster in the following steps. Optionally, you can create a DNS record for the public IP by clicking the All Settings link and then entering a DNS name label in the Configuration blade. Once the DNS name label is created, you can address the Elasticsearch cluster via *[DNS label].[cluster location]*.cloudapp.azure.com.

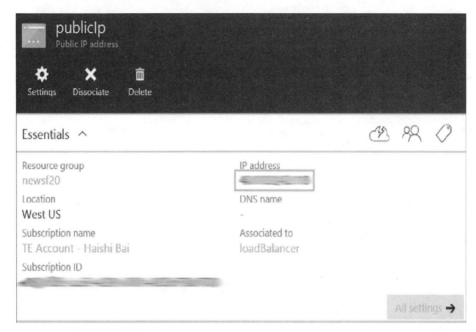

FIGURE 10-4 Public IP blade

10. To verify the cluster is working, send a GET request to http://*[IP address]*:9200/_cat/health?v
with a basic authentication header. There are many tools you can use to generate web requests.
My preference is Postman (*https://www.getpostman.com/*). The tool helps you generate basic
authentication headers, which should be the "Basic *[username]:[password]*" string encoded
with base64 encoding. Figure 10-5 shows a screen shot of Postman. The screen shot shows
that a Basic Auth option is selected for Authorization and the credential of the *es_admin* user is
entered. You can click the Update Request button to generate the correct authorization header.
The bottom of the screen shows the result of the GET request. You can see the cluster is "green"
(healthy), with six nodes total and three data nodes.

FIGURE 10-5 Postman UI

Configuring Kibana

The Marketplace template provisions an Elasticsearch cluster and a single virtual machine Kibana instance. By default, the Kibana is not configured to talk to the Elasticsearch cluster. The following are the steps to modify Kibana settings to link the Kibana instance to the Elasticsearch cluster.

1. Locate the *kibana-vm* virtual machine in the above resource group. The virtual machine is configured with a public IP. Note the IP address.

2. SSH into *kibana-vm* using the user credential (see step 6 in the previous walkthrough) and the public IP:

   ```
   ssh [user]@[public ip of kibana-vm]
   ```

3. Edit the */opt/kibana/config/kibana.yml* file.

   ```
   elasticsearch.url: "http://[Elasticsearch cluster IP]:9200"
   elasticsearch.username: es_admin
   elasticsearch.password: "[es_admin password]"
   ```

4. Save the file and reboot the machine. If you are familiar with Kibana, you can restart the Kibana service without restarting the machine.

   ```
   sudo reboot
   ```

5. Once the machine is restarted, open a browser and navigate to *http://[public ip of kibana -vm]:6501/.* You should see the Kibana home page loaded, as shown in Figure 10-6.

FIGURE 10-6 Kibana UI

Reporting logs to Elasticsearch

Now, let's walk through an example that uses a diagnostics listener to report log data to the Elasticsearch cluster.

In the walkthrough, we'll be using a *Microsoft.Diagnostic.Listeners* library that is part of an open-source sample application named Azure Service Fabric Party Cluster. A hosted version of the application can be found at *http://tryazureservicefabric.eastus.cloudapp.azure.com/.* It provides a number of free, publicly hosted Service Fabric clusters where you can deploy your applications for learning and testing purposes.

1. Create a new Service Fabric application named *ElasticsearchLogApplication* with a stateless service named *StatelessLogTest*.

2. Clone the source code of the party cluster sample from *https://github.com/Azure-Samples /service-fabric-dotnet-management-party-cluster.*

3. Copy both the Microsoft.Diagnostics.EventListeners folder and the Microsoft.Diagnostics. EventListeners.Fabric folder from the party cluster application folder to your application folder.

4. In the *ElasticsearchLogApplication*, add both projects to the solution.

5. Right-click the StatelessLogTest service project and select the Add, Reference menu. Then, in the Reference Manager dialog box, select both projects under the Projects, Solution category and click the OK button, as shown in Figure 10-7.

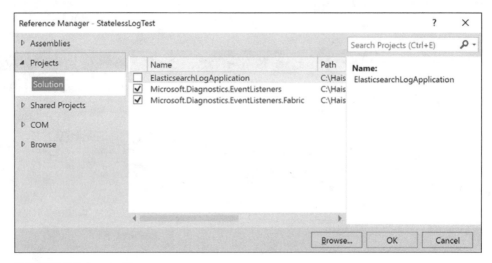

FIGURE 10-7 Reference Manager

6. Right-click the service project again and select the Manage NuGet Packages menu.

   In the NuGet Package Manager, search for "Microsoft.Diagnostics.Tracing" and add a reference to *Microsoft.Diagnostics.Tracing.EventSource*. This step is necessary before .NET Framework 4.6, which supports some event listener APIs required by *Microsoft.Diagnostics.EventListeners*, is supported by Microsoft Azure.

7. Open *ServiceEventSource.cs* and replace

   ```
   using System.Diagnostics.Tracing;
   ```

   with

   ```
   using Microsoft.Diagnostics.Tracing;
   ```

8. Open *Program.cs* and replace the try block in the *Main()* method with the following code (new code is in bold):

   ```
   const string ElasticSearchEventListenerId = "ElasticSearchEventListener";
   FabricConfigurationProvider configProvider =
       new FabricConfigurationProvider(ElasticSearchEventListenerId);
   ElasticSearchListener esListener = null;
   if (configProvider.HasConfiguration)
   {
       esListener = new ElasticSearchListener(configProvider, new FabricHealthReporter(Elas
   ticSearchEventListenerId));
   }
   using (FabricRuntime fabricRuntime = FabricRuntime.Create())
   {
       fabricRuntime.RegisterServiceType("StatelessLogTestType", typeof(StatelessLogTest));
       ServiceEventSource.Current.ServiceTypeRegistered(Process.GetCurrentProcess().Id,
   typeof(StatelessLogTest).Name);
       Thread.Sleep(Timeout.Infinite);
   ```

```
        GC.KeepAlive(esListener);
    }
```

9. Modify the *PackageRoot\Config\Settings.xml* file to include Elasticsearch connection settings:

```xml
<?xml version="1.0" encoding="utf-8" ?>
<Settings xmlns:xsd="http://www.w3.org/2001/XMLSchema" xmlns:xsi="http://www.w3.org/2001/
XMLSchema-instance" xmlns="http://schemas.microsoft.com/2011/01/fabric">
    <Section Name="ElasticSearchEventListener">
        <Parameter Name="serviceUri" Value="http://[Elasticsearch cluster IP]:9200/" />
        <Parameter Name="userName" Value="es_admin" />
        <Parameter Name="password" Value="[es_admin password]" />
        <Parameter Name="indexNamePrefix" Value="myapp" />

    </Section>
</Settings>
```

10. Press F5 to launch the application on your local cluster or deploy the application to your Azure-based Service Fabric cluster. In a moment, you'll see application log entries appearing on Kibana, as shown in Figure 10-8:

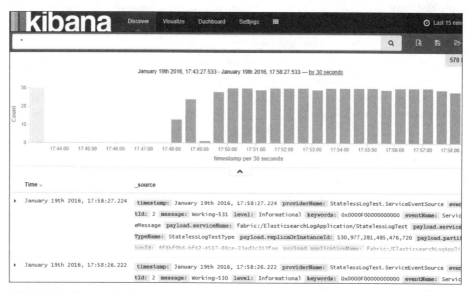

FIGURE 10-8 Kibana with Service Fabric logs

The above walkthrough introduced basic steps of getting Elasticsearch and Kibana up and running. For details on how to manage and use your data indices, refer to documentation on elastic.co (*https://www.elastic.co/guide/index.html*).

Azure Operations Management Suite

Azure Operations Management Suite (OMS) provides a single pane of glass that allows you to visualize, combine, correlate, and analyze log data from your on-premises servers and cloud-based servers. You can connect a server directly to OMS by installing an agent, or you can write log data to a data store where OMS can pick it up.

> ## Azure Operational Insights and OMS
>
> OMS log collection, analysis, and visualization is provided by an Operational Insights component that originally was previewed as an independent service. OMS integrates other Azure features such as Automation, Backup, and Azure Site Recovery. In this book, I only discuss only log-related features.

Provisioning an OMS workspace

To use OMS, you first need to sign up and create a workspace. You can use either the OMS website (*http://www.microsoft.com/OMS*) or the Azure management portal. The following walkthrough assumes you are using the OMS website.

1. Navigate to the OMS website.

2. You can either create the Try For Free link to create a trial workspace or use the Sign In button to link to an existing Azure subscription. Here, I'll take the second route.

3. After you sign in using your Microsoft account, you are taken to a page where you can link to an existing Azure subscription, as shown in Figure 10-9. Choose the Azure subscription to which you want to link and then click the Link button to continue.

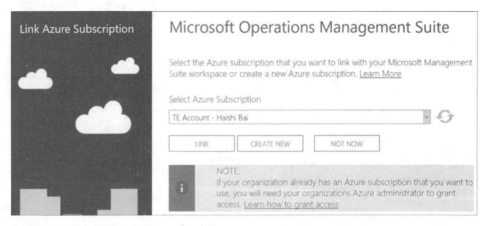

FIGURE 10-9 Link OMS to an Azure subscription

4. On the next page, enter your email address and click the Confirm & Continue button, as shown in Figure 10-10.

FIGURE 10-10 Email confirmation page

5. Once you receive the confirmation email, click the provided link to confirm your email address. The link takes you to the OMS website Overview page, as shown in Figure 10-11.

FIGURE 10-11 OMS website Overview page

Linking OMS to a data source

At the time of this writing, there wasn't a nice UI experience for linking Azure Storage accounts based on Azure Resource Manager to OMS. The following walkthrough links to a storage account using Windows PowerShell.

1. First, you need to find out the name of the OMS workspace. To do this, use the Get-AzureRm OperationalInsightsWorkspace command, which lists all OMS workspaces linked to the Azure

subscription. If you only have one workspace, you can get the name from the Name field. If you have multiple workspaces, you can compare the CustomerId with the guid in your OMS dashboard URL to find out the correct workspace name. Figure 10-12 shows a sample output of the command.

FIGURE 10-12 Sample output of the Get-AzureRmOperationalInsightsWorkspace command

2. Select the workspace using the Get-AzureRmOperationalInsightsWorkspace command with the *Name* parameter and the *ResourceGroup* parameter. You can get the correct value for the two parameters in the output of the previous command (see Figure 10-12).

```
$workspace = Get-AzureRmOperationalInsightsWorkspace -Name [workspace name]
-ResourceGroupName [resource group name]
```

3. Select the storage account using the Get-AzureRmStorageAccount command. The *[storage account name]* should be the account name that holds the diagnostics tables. The *[resource group name]* should be the resource group holding the storage account.

```
$storageAccount = Get-AzureRmStorageAccount -Name [storage account name]
-ResourceGroupName [resource group name]
```

4. Now, create the link using the following code snippet.

```
$key = Get-AzureRmStorageAccountKey -Name [storage account name] -ResourceGroupName
[resource group name]
$validTables = "WADServiceFabric*EventTable", "WADETWEventTable"
$insightsName = $storageAccount.StorageAccountName + $workspace.Name
New-AzureRmOperationalInsightsStorageInsight -Workspace $workspace -Name $insightsName
-StorageAccountResourceId $storageAccount.Id -StorageAccountKey $key -Tables $validTables
```

5. Once the link has been created, you can observe that you have a data source connected on the OMS workspace Overview page, as shown in Figure 10-13:

FIGURE 10-13 Settings tile on the OMS workspace Overview page

6. Click the Log Search tile.

7. Type in a search such as **Type=ServiceFabricReliableServiceEvent** to search for indexed log entries. It can take several minutes for the log entries to be indexed and made available for queries.

The preceding walkthrough is an exercise to get you started with OMS. You can perform complex queries once you learn more about how to use OMS. For example, to find out if exceptions are thrown by a stateful service *fabric:/MyApp/MyStatefulService*, you can use a query similar to this:

```
Type=ServiceFabricReliableServiceEvent AND ServiceName="fabric:/MyApp/MyStatefulService" AND
TaskName=StatefulRunAsyncFailure
```

At the time of this writing, OMS was still in preview. Operation steps, UI layouts, and system capabilities are subject to change. So, instead of focusing on operational details, you should understand the key philosophy of OMS, which is to provide an easy-to-use yet powerful single pane of glass over all connected resources. Many tedious and difficult tasks such as indexing large amounts of log data and correlating data from multiple distributed data sources are shielded from you so you can focus your energy on quickly gaining insights into vast numbers of log files.

Monitoring

For a cloud-based system, reducing mean time to repair (MTTR) is the key to improving system availability. As I've discussed in Chapter 6, cloud systems have to embrace errors because in a complex platform, there are many possibilities for failures, including hardware problems, platform failures, service defects, connectivity issues, or even intentional throttling. So, the faster a software or hardware component can be fixed (the lower the MTTR), the better the system availability will be.

Logs and traces are useful to find out root causes of problems. However, they don't notify you when something bad has happened. To detect problems early, you'll have to employ a monitoring system that actively monitors the health of your clusters and services and generates alerts so you can take immediate actions.

The health of a component can be determined either proactively or passively. On the one hand, a monitoring system can wait passively for health reports from individual components, such as the health reports you've seen in Chapter 6. The reporting can be done directly inside the application code or by a generic agent that reports on common or customized telemetry. Some agents also can instrument application code automatically to insert tracing points around selected methods. On the other hand, a monitoring system can query components proactively for their health info, such as how a load balancer determines if a node is responsive by using probes.

In this section, I'll first introduce how to use Service Fabric Explorer to monitor cluster and application health. Then, I'll introduce how to generate custom health reports in your code. Finally, I'll introduce some other monitoring options using Azure and third-party monitoring solutions.

Service Fabric Explorer

Each Service Fabric cluster, including the local cluster, comes with a web-based Service Fabric Explorer at port 19080. You can access the site by the address http(s)://*[cluster address]*:19080/Explorer. Service Fabric Explorer uses a simple UI layout: to the left is a tree view of the cluster, and to the right is a pane showing details of the currently selected item and an Action button with possible actions you can perform on the item. Figure 10-14 shows a sample screen shot of Service Fabric Explorer with a summary of an application displayed in the right pane.

For entity health, Service Fabric Explorer follows a simple color code system: green means healthy; yellow means warnings; and red means errors. The site periodically refreshes so you can keep it running as a continuous monitoring tool. At the upper-right corner of the screen is a slider that you can use to control how frequently the page refreshes itself.

The site calls a REST API to retrieve updated information. If you turn on the network monitoring, you'll see periodic requests to the API. For example, the following request is to get the status of the nodes on the cluster:

```
http://localhost:19080/Nodes/?api-version=1.0&_rnd=1453271006680
```

The following query gets load information on the cluster (the _rnd_ parameter is a random number to avoid cached responses).

```
http://localhost:19080/$/GetLoadInformation?api-version=1.0&_rnd=1453271006679
```

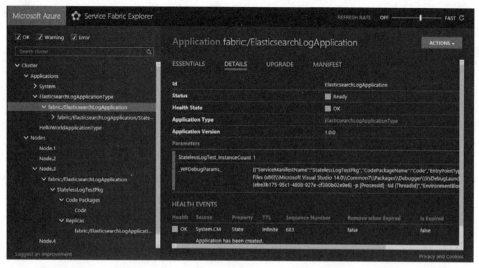

FIGURE 10-14 Service Fabric Explorer

Visual Studio Application Insights

Visual Studio Application Insights is an Azure service that monitors the usage and performance of your mobile applications and web applications hosted on Azure, other cloud platforms, and on-premises servers. With Application Insights, you get immediate alerts on performance and availability issues so that you can respond faster to keep your services available.

You can integrate Service Fabric with Application Insights in a similar way to how you integrate with Elasticsearch: use an event listener to send ETW events from your application to Application Insights. Then, you can use Application Insights features to monitor your applications and respond to errors.

Creating an Application Insights instance

The following walkthrough shows you how to create a new Application Insights instance via Microsoft Azure management portal.

1. Sign in to the Azure management portal.

2. Click the New link at the upper-left corner. Type **application insights** in the search box on the New blade and then press Enter to start the search.

3. In the search results list, click the Application Insights (Preview) entry.

4. On the Application Insights (Preview) blade, click the Create button.

5. On the Application Insights blade, enter a name for the instance. For Application Type, select the Other (preview) type, as shown in Figure 10-15. Then, choose the subscription and the resource group you want to use. The Location option is locked at Central US during preview. You

should be able to pick different locations when the service is released. Finally, click the Create button to create the instance.

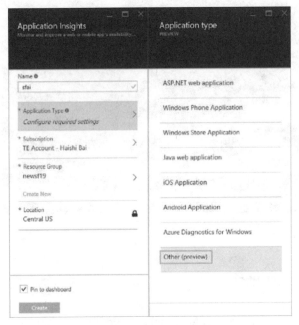

FIGURE 10-15 New Application Insights blade

6. After the Application Insights instance is provisioned, open its Settings And Diagnostics blade by clicking the Settings icon at the top of the instance's blade.

7. Click the Properties link and then copy the Instrumentation Key from the Properties blade. You'll need to provide this key to the Service Fabric code shown in the next section.

Sending events to Application Insights

The preview version of the Service Fabric SDK comes with a *Microsoft.ServiceFabric.Telemetry. ApplicationInsights* NuGet package, which contains an event listener that is designed for Application Insights. In the following walkthrough, you'll go through a simple scenario that uses the NuGet package.

1. Create a new Service Fabric application named *AppInsightsApplication* with a stateless service named *StatelessInsights*.

2. Right-click the *SatelessInsights* project and select the Manage NuGet Packages menu.

3. Search for "servicefabric" to locate and install the *Microsoft.ServiceFabric.Telemetry. ApplicationInsights* package.

4. Open *Program.cs*. Add the following line to the top of the *Main()* method:

```
Microsoft.ApplicationInsights.Extensibility.TelemetryConfiguration.Active.
InstrumentationKey = "[your instrument key]";
Microsoft.ServiceFabric.Telemetry.ApplicationInsights.Listener.Enable(EventLevel.
LogAlways);
```

In this code, the instrument key is inserted directly into the code. You can keep the key in configuration files or in Azure Key Vault if desired.

5. Deploy the application. Your logged events should be transmitted to Application Insights. The events will appear under the Custom Events category.

Using Application Insights alert rules

In addition to the preceding event listener, you can use *Microsoft.ApplicationInsights.TelemetryClient* directly to send application metrics to Application Insights. In the following walkthrough, we'll use the client to send data to Application Insights and practice how to set up monitoring UI and alert rules.

1. Continue with the previous solution. Open the *StatelessInsights.cs* file under the *StatelessInsights* project.

2. Insert the following line at the top of the *RunAsync()* method:

```
Microsoft.ApplicationInsights.TelemetryClient client =
    new Microsoft.ApplicationInsights.TelemetryClient();
```

3. Modify the *while* loop in the *RunAsync()* method (the code in bold in the new code to be inserted):

```
while (!cancelServiceInstance.IsCancellationRequested)
{
    ServiceEventSource.Current.ServiceMessage(this, "Working-{0}", iterations++);
    client.TrackMetric("MyTest", iterations,
    new Dictionary<string,string>
    {{"ServiceName", this.ServiceInitializationParameters.ServiceName.AbsoluteUri} });
        if (iterations > 1000)
            iterations = 0;
        await Task.Delay(TimeSpan.FromSeconds(1), cancelServiceInstance);
}
```

The preceding code sends "MyTest" values to Application Insights along with the current service name as a property. The value is reset whenever it reaches 1,000.

4. Deploy the application to your local cluster.

5. In Microsoft Azure management portal, open the Application Insights instance.

6. Click the Metrics Explorer icon.

7. On the Metrics Explorer blade, click the Add Chart icon.

8. On the Chart Details blade, select Chart Type Is Line. Then, select the MyTest metric under the Custom category. (It can take several minutes for this to show up.) As you make selections, you'll see the chart refreshed with your metric data, as shown in Figure 10-16. Note that you can select a range on the chart and use the zoom in icon to zoom in or use the zoom out icon to zoom out.

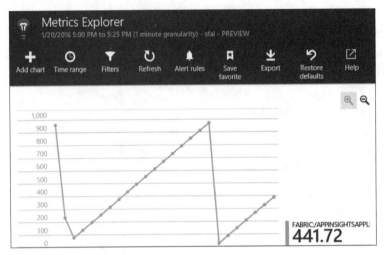

FIGURE 10-16 Metrics Explorer

9. Click the Alert Rules icon.

10. On the Alert Rules blade, click the Add Alert icon.

11. On the Add An Alert Rule blade, set the following values (and leave others at defaults):

   - **Name:** Enter a name for the alert rule.

   - **Metric:** Select *MyTest*.

   - **Condition:** Select "greater than."

   - **Threshold:** Enter **500**.

   - **Period:** Select Over The Last 5 Minutes.

   - **Additional administrator email(s):** Enter an email address.

12. Click the OK button to define the rule.

13. After a few minutes, you'll start to receive email notifications. Figure 10-17 shows a sample of how these emails look. If you don't see the emails in your Inbox, look in your spam, junk, or clutter folder because your mail system might have identified them as spam email.

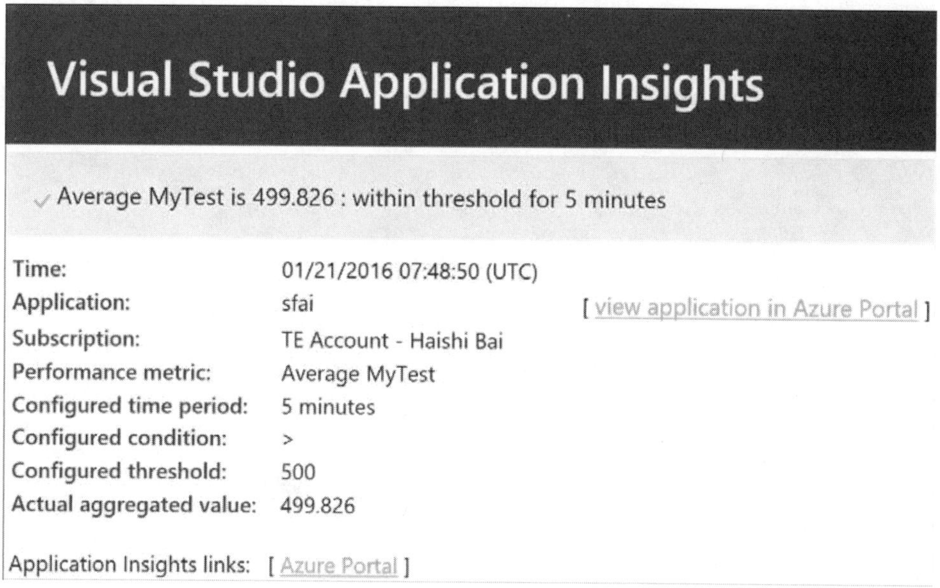

Visual Studio Application Insights

✓ Average MyTest is 499.826 : within threshold for 5 minutes

Time: 01/21/2016 07:48:50 (UTC)
Application: sfai   [view application in Azure Portal]
Subscription: TE Account - Haishi Bai
Performance metric: Average MyTest
Configured time period: 5 minutes
Configured condition: >
Configured threshold: 500
Actual aggregated value: 499.826

Application Insights links: [Azure Portal]

FIGURE 10-17 Sample Application Insights alert email

14. Once you are done with your test, you can go back to the alert rule to disable it or delete it to stop the email notifications.

Additional information

At the time of this writing, all of the above services are still in preview, and integrations between Service Fabric and these services are still being developed. As the services mature, many details may change. However, the overall trend is clear: instead of reinventing the wheel, Service Fabric tries to leverage what Azure has provided to deliver an integrated diagnostics and monitoring experience.

Application Insights is showing a lot of promise to become a universal monitoring system across infrastructure as a service (IaaS), platform as a service (PaaS), and software as a service (SaaS) offerings on Azure. And Azure Operational Management Suites (OMS) is expected to provide a single pane of glass over all of your compute resources, regardless of location. In a complex system, Service Fabric might be only one component. Technologies such as Application Insights and OMS provide you a unified view across all components in your system, including Service Fabric services, database and storage, and other related services.

In this chapter, I presented a couple of samples of in-process monitoring in which tracing events are reported directly from the application process. You also can use out-of-process monitoring agents such as Azure Diagnostics agent and agents from third-party vendors such as New Relic and AppDynamics. Out-of-process monitoring can be reconfigured without modifying application code, and it can monitor events such as process crashes that are hard for in-process monitoring to capture.

CHAPTER 11

Testing

This chapter is about testing. I'll first discuss testability as a generic term and cover how Service Fabric helps you test the functionalities of your components. Then, I'll move the discussion up a level to cover load testing. Finally, I'll move into Service Fabric testability tools to cover more details on how to use the tools to improve the reliability of your system in a production environment.

Software testability

Testability has two meanings in this book. First, testability is used as a generic term that reflects the ease with which a system can be tested. Second, testability refers to the set of tools provided by Service Fabric to inject errors into your system to simulate real-world failures. In Chapter 6, "Availability and reliability," you've seen an example of how the Service Fabric testability tools work.

This section discusses testability as a generic term.

Software testability refers to how well a software system supports testing in different contexts. It can't be measured accurately, but it can be assessed by examining the system architecture and observing how system components interact with one another. Over the past decades, a number of principles, practices, and technologies have been developed to improve testability of software systems. Before we move on to specific discussions, let's review what contributes to a testable system.

To evaluate the testability of a system, you can conduct a simple test that I call a "dizziness test": Imagine you are going to test an arbitrary component in a system you maintain. How much your head spins reflects how difficult it is to test the system. This assessment certainly is subjective. However, it does reflect the level of testability of the system in question. If you want to make more objective assessments, you should examine the following characteristics of the system:

- Controllability

- Observability

- Isolateability

- Clarity

Controllability

Software controllability measures how easy it is to provide input to a system to control its state and behaviors.[1] To test different execution paths, it's a common practice for testers to provide a number of inputs, including normal inputs, boundary inputs, and invalid inputs. The ease of generating and feeding these input combinations to a system heavily affects the testability of the system.

Service Fabric advocates for Microservices architecture. Each service in an application is an independent entity with clear boundaries to the outside world. This allows simulated inputs to be fed to service instances just like user requests are sent.

In software tests, automated tests are much preferable to manual tests because they are not subject to human interpretations and errors. They also provide a reliable test harness for you to verify whether a fix is effective and to keep your application behaving as designed.

Automated test cases also are crucial to continuous integration (CI). They can be executed automatically upon every code check-in to make sure no one on the team is breaking the system unintentionally. Running continuous tests also helps avoid a situation in which multiple updates are accumulated before a regression is found, which could be really cumbersome to resolve.

I'll walk you through the steps of setting up continuous integration later in this chapter.

Observability

A testable system has to be observable, which means a tester should be able to observe how the system behaves during tests. Depending on the test type, different types of telemetries and tracing information need to be collected and analyzed.

A system with low observability is hard to test or diagnose. The following are some typical systems with low observabilities:

- A system that generates too little or too much tracing information. If a system doesn't generate enough traces, it's hard to diagnose what goes wrong when a function doesn't generate expected output. If a system generates too many traces, these trace entries become noises that obscure the actual problems.

- A system that silently fails. Failing silently is one of the worst coding practices and should be avoided by all developers. Not only does failing silently hide problems, it also leaves the system in an unknown state. As the system continues to act on the unknown state and keeps failing silently, the behavior of the system becomes so elusive that it becomes random and unpredictable.

- An over-engineered system with a single responsibility scattered to multiple components. Tracing distributed systems is inheritably difficult, especially in a busy system where many concurrent requests are interleaved with one another. Without a proper correlation mechanism, isolating and correlating trace entries for a specific transaction is hard.

---

1   Paul Ammann, Jeff Offutt. 2008. *Introduction to Software Testing*. Cambridge University Press

Service Fabric uses Azure Diagnostics to collect traces on cluster nodes and to transfer traces off the nodes to reliable storage. Because the diagnostics agent runs as a separate process, it can capture events when Service Fabric services or even Service Fabric runtime crashes.

Isolateability

As we've learned from middle-school science classes, when you conduct a test, you want to keep control variables constant so that you can get accurate measurements of dependent variables as you manipulate independent variables.

Software testing follows the same principle. When you test a component, you want to use mocked components that are scripted precisely to follow the product specification to replace all other components so the component under test has a reliable runtime environment that doesn't vary during the tests.

Using mocked components calls for dynamic dependency resolutions. With techniques such as dependency injection, real components can be replaced by mocked components to create the stable runtime environment for the component under test.

In a distributed application such as a Service Fabric application, mocked reliable services and mocked actors can be used to replace real service and actor implementations. All you need to do is use a different address when you use a service proxy or an actor proxy to connect to a service instance or an actor instance. Furthermore, you can set these addresses as configurable entries so that you can switch between mockups and real implementations by rolling out a new configuration version.

You should be aware that an environment constructed with mockups is different from the real environment in several ways. First, the mocked components usually provide a single execution path to ensure consistency. In contrast, the responses from the real components will have lots of variations. So, with mocked components, you are testing only some of the key scenarios instead of covering a broader range of use cases. Second, the mocked components usually have different performance and scalability characteristics. For example, some mocked components may bypass complex database lookups to provide predefined responses directly. Such components have better performance, and they often mask the possible data access bottlenecks.

So, the main goal of controlled tests is to verify the "correctness" of a component, which is to verify that a component is implemented according to the specification. They are not meant to test performance and scalability characteristics of a component except in cases when the compute complexity or storage complexity of an algorithm is measured.

Isolateability allows components to be tested in isolation. In a well-designed system, a component has a single responsibility, and its interfaces with other components are simple and clear. If you find that a number of components always need to be kept working together to do anything meaningful, component boundaries may have been drawn incorrectly during design.

Service Fabric naturally allows you to test services or actors in isolation. In Service Fabric, there are no special server-to-server communication channels. All communications across component boundaries happen in a client-server pattern. So, to a service instance or an actor instance, there aren't any differences if the request comes from another service, a client, a test script, or an automation tool. You easily can simulate client request and server-to-server communications by sending requests directly to the component under test.

Furthermore, because stateful services and actors keep their states locally, their states are isolated from one another. Manipulating the state of a service instance or an actor has no direct impact on any other services or actors. This is a major benefit over shared state storage, where changing states may have unexpected effects on multiple components.

Clarity

For source code, clarity means the code is easily understandable by someone other than the creator. For test cases, clarity means the test cases have clear and unambiguous assessment criteria for what's being tested.

The value of clear test cases is not just to verify the correctness of the software at a point of time. Instead, these test cases serve as living specifications that can be repeatedly verified against to make sure the software doesn't drift away from the originally designed behaviors. More often than not, software is maintained by developers other than the original creators. And as the ownership of the software gets transferred to different people over time, the original design philosophy and ideas easily can be lost. Clear and precise test cases are far more effective than any specifications on paper.

By examining the clarity of test cases, you can assess how well the system is designed. If you find that lots of test cases are needed to test a single component, it probably means the component takes on too much responsibility. In contrast, if you find lots of test cases making assessments without apparent meanings, it probably means the system has been over-engineered with a single responsibility scattered to multiple components.

Service Fabric gives you clear boundaries around services and actors, which encourage modular design with clear separation of concerns. However, this doesn't stop you from coming up with incorrect system designs. Another way to assess the quality of your architecture is to examine the communication patterns among services and actors: if many services are talking to the same service, the service likely is taking on too much responsibility. And if many services need constant communication among them, the system likely is over-engineered.

Writing basic test cases

In this section, I'll walk you through a simple example to set up a test case against a Service Fabric application using the Visual Studio Unit Test Framework. In this case, I'm using the framework to write a functional test instead of a unit test. Instead of starting with a new project, the following example uses the actor-based Tic-Tac-Toe application in Chapter 4, "Actor pattern." I'll write a couple of test cases to reinforce the following behavior of the Game actor:

- A player can't join the same game session twice.

- A game session has to have two players before it can be started.

The following are the steps to implement these test cases:

1. Load the Tic-Tac-Toe application in Visual Studio.

2. Add a Unit Test Project named TicTacToeTests to the solution.

3. Add references to the Games.Interfaces project and the Player.Interfaces project.

4. Add a reference to the NuGet package *Microsoft.ServiceFabric.Actors*.

5. Change the project platform to x64.

6. Rename the *UnitTest1.cs* file to *GameTests.cs*.

7. Implement the test cases:

```
[TestClass]
public class GameTests
{
    [TestMethod]
    public void APlayerCanOnlyJoinOnce()
    {
        var gameId = ActorId.NewId();
        var game = ActorProxy.Create<IGame>(gameId, "fabric:/ActorTicTacToeApplication");
        var result1 = game.JoinGameAsync(1L, "Player 1").Result;
        var result2 = game.JoinGameAsync(1L, "Player 1").Result;
        Assert.AreEqual(false, result1 & result2);
    }
    [TestMethod]
    public void GameCanBeStartedWith2Players()
    {
        var gameId = ActorId.NewId();
        var game = ActorProxy.Create<IGame>(gameId, "fabric:/ActorTicTacToeApplication");
        game.JoinGameAsync(1L, "Player 1").Wait();
        var result = game.MakeMoveAsync(1L, 0, 0).Result;
        Assert.AreEqual(false, result);
    }
}
```

8. Rebuild the solution.

9. Select the Test, Run, All Tests menu as shown in Figure 11-1. Wait for the test cases to complete.

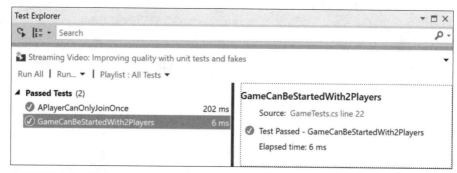

FIGURE 11-1 Test Explorer

Setting up continuous integration

Continuous integration (CI) enables you to build, test, package, and deploy continuously to shorten iteration cycles. In this section of the book, I'll walk you through the steps of setting up continuous integration using Visual Studio Team Services.

> ## Visual Studio Team Services, Visual Studio Online, Team Foundation Service, and Team Foundation Server
>
> In online documentation and literature, you may see all these names: Visual Studio Team Services (VSTS), Visual Studio Online (VSO), Team Foundation Service (TFS), and Team Foundation Server (TFS).
>
> Team Foundation Server is Microsoft's on-premises application life cycle management product that you buy and host yourself. Later, Microsoft launched Team Foundation Service, which essentially is a hosted version of Team Foundation Server. Then, Team Foundation Service was extended and renamed to Visual Studio Online. Recently, Visual Studio Online was renamed to Visual Studio Team Services.
>
> Like many of the services mentioned in this book, Visual Studio Team Services is still in preview at the time of this writing.

Preparing the Visual Studio Team Services project

To set up continuous integration on Visual Studio Team Services (VSTS), first you need to create a VSTS account. Then, you need to create a VSTS project for your work. The project then is linked to a source repository where you check in your source code. Then, a pipeline can be configured to build, test, package, and deploy your application upon events such as code check-ins.

Let's start preparing the VSTS project.

1. Sign in to the VSTS site at *https://www.visualstudio.com/products/visual-studio-team-services -vs.aspx* with your Microsoft account. If you don't have an account, you can sign up for a free trial. If you or your company has a MSDN subscription or a Visual Studio subscription, please check with your subscription administrator to check VSTS benefits with your subscription.

2. Once your subscription is active, navigate to the VSTS home page and click the New link under the Recent Projects & Teams section to create a new project, as shown in Figure 11-2.

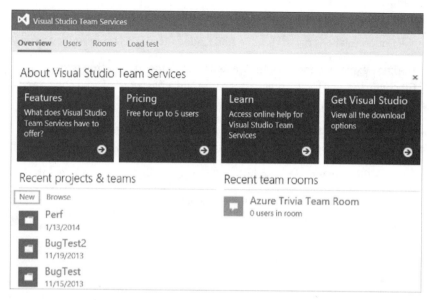

FIGURE 11-2 VSTS home page

3. On the Create New Team Project dialog box, enter a name for your project. You can choose from a number of project templates such as Agile, CMMI, and Scrum. And you can pick which version control system to use, including Git and Team Foundation Version Control. In this walkthrough, I'll use the Agile process template and the Git version control. Click the Create Project button to create the project, as shown in Figure 11-3.

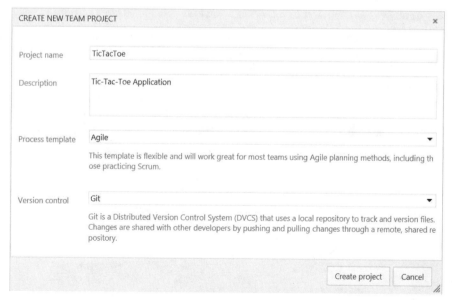

FIGURE 11-3 Create New Team Project dialog box

4. Once the project is created, you can click Navigate To Project to open the project page.

5. On the Congratulations page, click the Add Code button. This takes you to the code explorer.

6. On the code explorer page, click the Generate Git Credentials button to generate a credential for Git command-line tools. Enter a user name and a password of your choice and click the Save Git Credentials button to save the credential.

7. Next, clone the repository. You can use any Git client or use the Clone In Visual Studio button to clone the repository by using Visual Studio. This is the path I'm going to follow in this tutorial.

8. Clicking the Clone In Visual Studio button launches Visual Studio and opens the Team Explorer.

9. Click the Manage Connections icon at the top of the Team Explorer. Then, double-click the project, as shown in Figure 11-4.

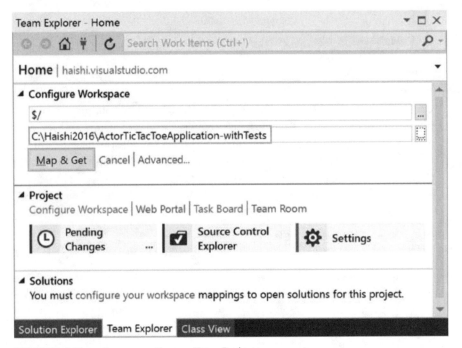

FIGURE 11-4 Managing connections on Team Explorer

10. Click the Clone Repository link (shown in Figure 11-5). Then, choose a local folder to hold your local repository and click the Clone button to clone the repository.

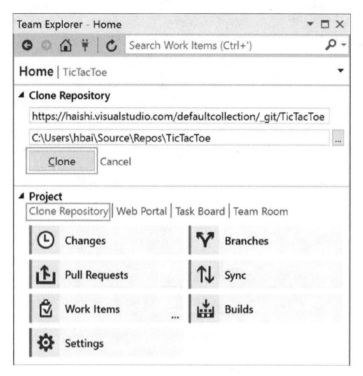

FIGURE 11-5 Clone source in Team Explorer

11. Copy the TicTacToe application folder into your local repository. Then, under the Untracked Files section, click the Add All link to add all files. Then, enter code commit comment and click the Commit button to submit the code to your local repository, as shown in Figure 11-6.

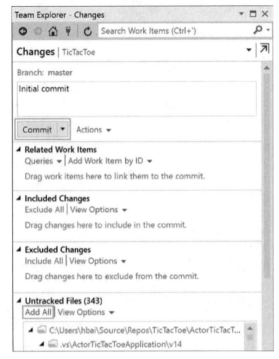

FIGURE 11-6 Committing changes in Team Explorer

12. Once the code is committed, click the Sync link at the top of the page. Then, on the Synchronization page, click the Push link to push the code to the online repository.

13. Click the Manage Account icon (the icon with a cog) on your VSTS home page to open the administrative page.

14. Switch to the Agent Pools tab. Then, click the New Pool link. I'll explain what a build agent is in the next section. Here, we are just creating a new collection so we camanage our experimental agents as a group.

15. In the Create Agent Pool dialog box, enter a name for your new agent pool and click the OK button to create the new pool, as shown in Figure 11-7.

FIGURE 11-7 Create Agent Pool dialog box

Preparing the build machine

With VSTS continuous integration, your application is built on a build server that runs a build agent. VSTS provides a number of default build agents that allow you to build common application types such as Windows applications, Windows Unified Platform applications, and Java-based applications. Building Service Fabric applications requires a build machine with Service Fabric SDK installed, which isn't available out-of-box at the time of this writing. Fortunately, you can set up you own build servers and register them with VSTS to provide build services. Check online VSTS documentation to see if a built-in Service Fabric build agent has become available before you take the following steps to provision a build server manually.

1. Sign in to Microsoft Azure management portal.

2. Click the New icon at the upper-left corner of the dashboard.

3. On the New blade, search for Visual Studio 2015.

4. On the search result page, click Visual Studio Enterprise 2015 With Azure SDK 2.8 On Windows Server 2012 R2. Then, on the newly opened blade, click the Create button.

5. Follow the creation wizard to create the virtual machine.

6. Once the machine is created, connect to the machine using Remote Desktop Connection.

7. Install Service Fabric SDK using Web Platform Installer. You should pick the same SDK version as on your development machine.

8. Next, we'll define a custom NuGet source to obtain the Service Fabric NuGet package. First, create a *%SYSTEMDRIVE%\Windows\ServiceProfiles\LocalService\AppData\Roaming\NuGet* folder if it doesn't exist.

9. Create a *NuGet.config* under this folder with the following content:

```xml
<?xml version="1.0" encoding="utf-8"?>
    <configuration>
  <packageSources>
    <add key="Service Fabric SDK" value="[path to Service Fabric SDK]\packages" />
  </packageSources>
</configuration>
```

   By default, the path to Service Fabric SDK is: C:\Program Files\Microsoft SDKs\Service Fabric.

10. The build process runs under the Local Service account. We need to configure the account's PowerShell module path so it can find Azure PowerShell modules. Open Registry Editor (regedit.exe) and add the following Expandable String Value under HKEY_USERS\.Default\Environment:

   • Name: PSModulePath

   • Value: %PROGAMFILE%\WinodwsPowerShell\Modules

11. Sign in to your VSTS site and navigate to the Agent Pools page (see step 15 in the previous section). Click the Download Agent link to download a preconfigured VSTS build agent package named *Agent.zip*.

12. Unpack the package to a c:\agent folder on the build machine. You also can choose any other folder. However, you should pick a short folder path because sometimes a Visual Studio solution may contain long paths that, when joined with long paths, exceed Windows path length limitations.

13. Open a Command Prompt window and launch **c:\agent\ConfigAgent.cmd**. The script will ask for a number of parameters:

   - **Agent name**   Accept the default value, which is *Agent-[machine name]*.

   - **URL to the Team Foundation Server**   Enter the URL of your VSTS site, such as *https://[your-Team-Services-account-name].visualstudio.com*.

   - **Agent pool name**   Enter the name of the agent pool you just created (see step 15 in the previous section).

   - **Agent working path**   Accept the default value (*c:\agent_work*). This is where the agent builds your application.

   - **Install the agent as a Windows service**   Yes.

   - **User account to run the build service**   Accept the default value (*NT AUTHORITY\LocalService*).

14. You'll be prompted to sign in using your Microsoft account. You should sign in using the Microsoft account that you've used to create your VSTS account. Then, the script will finish configuring the agent. Figure 11-8 shows the output of a sample run of the script.

```
c:\Agent>ConfigureAgent.cmd
Enter the name for this agent (default is Agent-SFBUILD)
Enter the URL for the Team Foundation Server (default is ) https://haishi.visual
studio.com
Configure this agent against which agent pool? (default pool name is 'default')
SFAgentPool
Enter the path of the work folder for this agent (default is 'c:\Agent\_work')
Would you like to install the agent as a Windows Service (Y/N) (default is N) Y
Enter the name of the user account to use for the service (default is NT AUTHORI
TY\LOCAL SERVICE)
Installing service vsoagent.haishi.Agent-SFBUILD...
Service vsoagent.haishi.Agent-SFBUILD has been successfully installed.
Creating EventLog source vsoagent.haishi.Agent-SFBUILD in log Application...
```

FIGURE 11-8 The ConfigureAgent.cmd script

15. To verify that the agent has been registered successfully, return to the Agent Pools page of your VSTS site. Refresh the page and observe if a new agent is added to your agent pool and if the agent is in a healthy state, as shown in Figure 11-9.

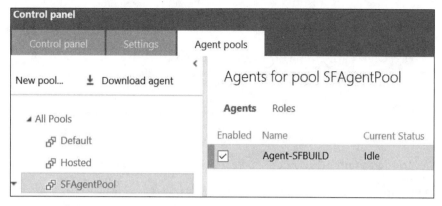

FIGURE 11-9 Agent status in the agent pool

Creating a build definition

Now that the build machine is ready and the build agent is registered, you can create a new build definition that drives the build, package, and deployment process when you check in new code.

1. Return to the project's page on VSTS and click the Build link at the top of the page.

2. On the left pane, click the Plus icon to create a new build definition.

3. In the Create New Build Definition dialog box, select Empty (to start a new build definition from scratch) and then click the Next button.

4. On the next page, select your build agent pool for the Default Agent Queue and select the Continuous Integration check box. Then, click the Create button to create the build definition, as shown in Figure 11-10.

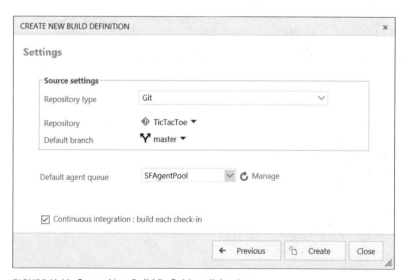

FIGURE 11-10 Create New Build Definition dialog box

5. When the Build Definition page opens, click the Add Build Step link.

6. In the Add Tasks dialog box, click the Add button next to MSBuild under the Build category. Then, click the Close button to close the dialog box.

7. Configure the following settings of the MSBuild build step:

- **Project** Click the [...] icon to select your Tic-Tac-Toe solution file.

- **Platform** ($BuildPlatform)

- **Configuration** ($BuildConfiguration)

- **Restore NuGet Packages** Selected.

Then, click the Save icon to save the build definition, as shown in Figure 11-11.

FIGURE 11-11 MSBuild build step

8. A message box opens prompting you to enter a new name for the build definition. I chose to use the name Build Tic-Tac-Toe in the walkthrough.

9. Click the Add Build Step link again and add another MSBuild step.

10. Click the pencil icon beside the build step and rename the step to "Package."

11. Configure the following settings of the MSBuild build step:

- **Project** Click the [...] icon to select your Tic-Tac-Toe service application project file (the .sfproj file under the ActorTicTacToeApplication folder).

- **Platform** ($BuildPlatform)

- **Configuration** ($BuildConfiguration)

- **MS Build Arguments** /t:Package

- **Clean** Clear the check box.

- **Restore NuGet Packages** Clear the check box.

Then, click the Save icon to save the build definition, as shown in Figure 11-12.

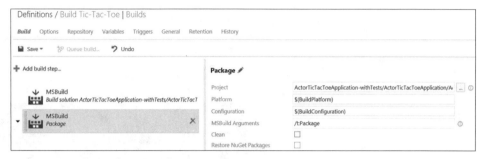

FIGURE 11-12 Package build step

12. Click the Add Build Step link again to add a new build step. Select PowerShell under the Utility category this time. In this build step, we'll use PowerShell to publish the new application to the production Service Fabric cluster.

13. Set the following properties of the build step. Basically, the build step calls the PowerShell script generated by Visual Studio tooling with the cloud deployment profile. For this to work properly, you need to make sure your cluster's connection endpoint has been configured in the cloud deployment profile, and the endpoint has to be unsecured. If you get certificates configured as introduced in Chapter 8, "Managing Service Fabric with Windows PowerShell," you also can set up a secured cluster as deployment destination. I'll leave it to interested readers.

   - **Script filename** ActorTicTacToeApplication/ActorTicTacToeApplication/Scripts/Deploy
     -FabricApplication.ps1

   - **Arguments** ApplicationPackagePath '$(Agent.BuildDirectory)\s
     \ActorTicTacToeApplication\ActorTicTacToeApplication\pkg\$(BuildConfiguration)'
     -PublishProfileFile '$(Agent.BuildDirectory)\s\ActorTicTacToeApplication
     \ActorTicTacToeApplication\PublishProfiles\Cloud.xml' -DeployOnly:$false
     -UnregisterUnusedApplicationVersionsAfterUpgrade $false -ForceUpgrade $false
     -OverwriteBehavior 'SameAppTypeAndVersion' -ErrorAction Stop

14. Save the build definition.

15. On the Build Definition page, click the QueueBuild link to queue a new build.

16. You can observe how the build progresses on the website. Figure 11-13 shows a sample build process; all build steps have been completed successfully.

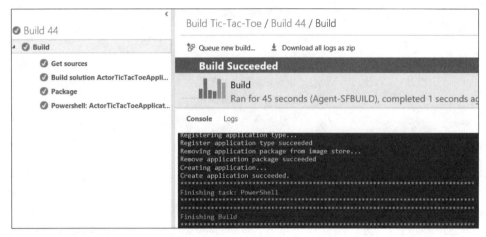

FIGURE 11-13 Build progress

Running tests upon code check-ins

The continuous integration process is triggered every time you check in new code. The new code will be built, packaged, and deployed upon new check-ins. However, before the new code is deployed, you need to make sure it passes all your test cases before it gets pushed to your production environment.

In the next exercise, you'll modify the build definition to deploy the application to a test cluster and test it with all test cases before publishing it to the production cluster.

1. Connect to the build machine using Remote Desktop Connection.

2. Launch PowerShell as an administrator.

3. Run *c:\Program Files\Microsoft SDKs\Service Fabric\ClusterSetup\DevClusterSetup.ps1* to launch a local Service Fabric cluster.

4. On your development machine, add a new *tests.runsettings* file to the TicTacToeTests project with the following content. We need this test run settings file because the Visual Studio test framework runs test cases compiled for x86 architecture by default. We need to use the settings file to force the CPU architecture to be x64.

    ```xml
    <?xml version="1.0" encoding="utf-8" ?>
    <RunSettings>
      <RunConfiguration>
        <ResultsDirectory>.\TestResults</ResultsDirectory>
        <TargetPlatform>x64</TargetPlatform>
        <TargetFrameworkVersion>Framework45</TargetFrameworkVersion>
      </RunConfiguration>
    </RunSettings>
    ```

5. Select the Test, Test Settings, Select Test Settings File menu. Select the run settings file you created in the previous step.

6. Run all the test cases locally to make sure everything is still working.

7. Commit and push the above file to VSTS.

8. On the VSTS site, modify the build definition to add a PowerShell build step. The build step should be identical to the previous PowerShell build step except for the deployment profile, which is *Local.xml* instead of *Cloud.xml*.

9. Add a build step by adding a Visual Studio Test task under the Test category.

10. Modify the build step settings to set the Run Settings File to *ActorTicTacToeApplication/ TicTacToeTests/tests.runsettings*. Also, make sure the Continue On Error check box is clear. Accept all other default values.

11. Rearrange the build steps by drag-and-drop. The order of the build steps should be: build, package, deploy to local cluster, run test cases, and deploy to production (if all tests pass), as shown in Figure 11-14:

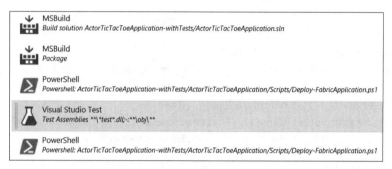

FIGURE 11-14 Build steps

12. Save the build definition.

13. Trigger another build. Observe how test cases are executed. Figure 11-15 shows a sample screen shot of all tests passing. If any of the test cases fail, the build process is stopped to avoid deploying a broken version to the production cluster.

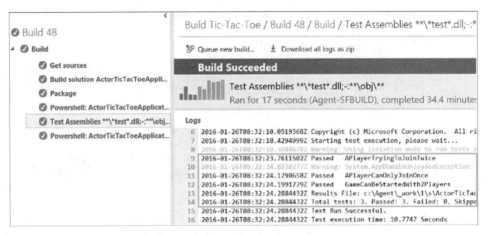

FIGURE 11-15 Running test cases during build

Running load tests with VSTS

Load tests put a system under simulated loads to test if the system performs well under anticipated heavy loads. The most challenging part of load tests is generating and controlling the load. If you use many test agents on a single test machine, resources such as CPU, memory, and especially network bandwidth can be exhausted easily before a reliable load can be generated. It's also impossible to simulate a geographic distribution from a single test machine. If you use many test machines, however, you have to face the complexity of managing a large number of test machines.

VSTS provides built-in load test features that enable you to run load tests easily using VSTS managed test agents. You can simulate traffic patterns from global locations without worrying about managing any of the agents. VSTS load testing features are not specific to Service Fabric. The following walkthrough shows you the basic steps to get started. Please refer to VSTS documentation for details on setting up a proper load test.

1. Go to your VSTS project page.

2. Click the Test link at the top of the page. Then, click the Load Test link below the tabs.

3. Click the New link to create a new Single URL test. In this simplest form of load test, you can provision a number of test agents to hit on a single service URL and collect performance telemetries.

4. On the Test Definition page, pick a URL and click the Run Test button to launch a load test with all default settings, as shown in Figure 11-16. The figure shows that test agents will be located in Virginia and will simulate 25 concurrent users. The test runs for a minute, and a simulated user thinking time of one second is inserted between tests. Of the test users, 60 percent use Internet Explorer, and 40 percent use Chrome. As you can see, even with all default values, you can implement a solid load test with minimum effort.

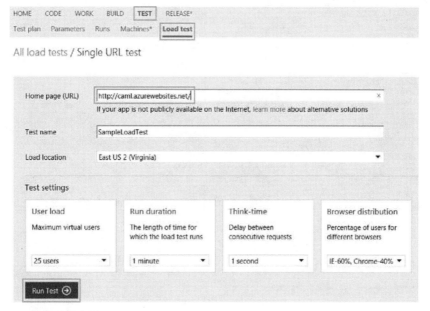

FIGURE 11-16 Defining a load test

5. Wait for the test to complete. Once the test completes, you can access the test results during the retention period. Figure 11-17 shows a sample result. You can see that during the load test, 9,000 requests from 25 simulated users were handled successfully by the web service with an average response time of 77 milliseconds.

All load tests / sampleloadtest.loadtest_96

✅ sampleloadtest.loadtest (Run ID: 96) - Completed ·

Completed 17 minutes ago, 1/26/2016 1:33:00 AM

Requested URL	http://caml.azurewebsites.net/
Load duration	60 seconds
User load	25
Load location	East US 2 (Virginia)
Start time	1/26/2016 1:31:15 AM

Application performance

AVG. RESPONSE TIME	TOTAL REQUESTS	FAILED REQUESTS
0.077 sec	9K	0
👍 Your app's response time looks good		👍 No failed requests

Learn more about the metrics and criteria

— Avg. Response Time — User Load — Requests/Sec — Failed Requests/Sec

FIGURE 11-17 A sample load test result

For more sophisticated load tests, you can use Visual Studio to record a web test that simulates typical user sessions and then load the web test into a load test to simulate concurrent user sessions. Complete coverage of web tests and load tests is out of the scope of this book. Refer to related Visual Studio and VSTS documentation for more details.

Testability subsystem

Earlier in this chapter, I introduced how controllability is an important aspect of a testable system. If a system is viewed as a function that projects the input space to the output space, it's important to test the system with typical, boundary, and invalid inputs from the input space to verify that the system functions correctly for all valid inputs and rejects invalid inputs properly (such as throwing argument exceptions).

When your applications run on a platform as a service (PaaS) platform such as Service Fabric, how the platform behaves has a huge impact on your applications. When part of a cluster fails, Service Fabric makes necessary arrangements to restore the cluster and the hosted services. You need to make sure that your application can cope with such rearrangements. However, these cluster-level activities can't be tested by your application-level test cases. Instead, there must be a mechanism to simulate cluster failures outside your application.

There are two fundamental requirements on these simulated errors. First, the simulated errors must have sufficient fidelity with actual error conditions. Second, the simulated errors must be controllable so that failing scenarios can be simulated, observed, and analyzed systematically. Controlled simulations also condense failing scenarios to a short period of time so that more failing scenarios can be tested and verified efficiently. Service Fabric's built-in testability subsystem meets both requirements by providing high-fidelity, controllable failure simulations for you to test how your applications would react to cluster-level events such as node crashes and quorum loses.

In Chapter 6, I've introduced the basics of using the testability subsystem by writing a test harness using Service Fabric's testability assemblies. Here, I'll provide more details and introduce additional testability concepts and scenarios.

Testability actions

The samples in Chapter 6 use testability scenarios to simulate continuous, interleaved failures on a cluster. Telemetries and traces of your applications are collected during the test session so you can analyze how your applications behave in such a chaotic environment. Although the chaos tests are inspired by the testing-in-production idea, Service Fabric's testability subsystem allows you to perform similar tests on any type of environment in a consistent manner. If you feel performing chaos tests on a production environment is too risky, you can use the same testability subsystem to perform such tests on your testing environments or even development environments.

In addition to chaos tests, Service Fabric supports testability actions that you can use to simulate specific failures such as restart of a node or removal of a replica. You can use these injected failures to test if your application code is ready to deal with these typical failures. Because you have precise control over when and how an error happens, you can establish a well-controlled environment to prepare your code to deal with the error in isolation (Table 11-1).

TABLE 11-1 Summary of testability actions provided by Service Fabric:

Action*	Description	Managed API	PowerShell
CleanTestState	Removes all test states from the cluster in case of a bad shutdown of the test driver.	CleanTestStateAsync	Remove-ServiceFabricTestsState
InvokeDataLoss	Induces data loss into a service partition.	InvokeDataLossAsync	Invoke-ServiceFabricPartitionDataLoss
InvokeQuorumLoss	Puts a given stateful service partition into quorum lost.	InvokeQuromLossAsync	Invoke-ServiceFabricQuorumLoss
Move Primary	Moves the specified primary replica of a stateful service to the specified cluster node.	MovePrimaryAsync	Move-ServiceFabricPrimaryReplica
Move Secondary	Moves the current secondary replica of a stateful service to a different cluster node.	MoveSecondaryAsync	Move-ServiceFabricSecondaryReplica

Action*	Description	Managed API	PowerShell
RemoveReplica	Removes a replica.	RemoveReplicaAsync	Remove-ServiceFabricReplica
RestartDeployedCodePackage	Restarts a code package deployed on a node.	RestartDeployedCodePackageAsync	Restart-ServiceFabricDeployedCodePackage
RestartNode	Restarts a node.	RestartNodeAsync	Restart-ServiceFabricNode
RestartPartition	Restarts some of all replicas of a partition.	RestartPartitionAsync	Restart-ServiceFabricPartition
RestartReplica	Restarts a persisted replica.	RestartReplicaAsync	Restart-ServiceFabricReplica
StartNode	Starts a stopped node.	StartNodeAsync	Start-ServiceFabricNode
StopNode	Stops a node.	StopNodeAsync	Stop-ServiceFabricNode
ValidateApplication	Validates the availability and health of all services within an application.	ValidateApplicationAsync	Test-ServiceFabricApplication
ValidateService	Validates the availability and health of a service.	ValidateServiceAsync	Test-ServiceFabricService`
* Testability actions (data source: *https://azure .microsoft.com /documentation/articles /service-fabric-testability -actions/*)			

Invoking testability actions using PowerShell

You can invoke testability actions easily by using PowerShell. The following exercise walks you through the steps to use the Restart-ServiceFabricNode command to restart a Service Fabric node.

1. Connect to your Service Fabric cluster (see Chapter 8 for details on how to make a connection to a secured cluster) using the following command:

```
Connect-ServiceFabricCluster [cluster endpoint]
```

2. List current node statuses using the Get-ServiceFabricNode command:

```
Get-ServiceFabricNode | Select NodeName, NodeUpTime, HealthState
```

This command generates the following output on my environment. Figure 11-18 shows that my cluster has five nodes that have been running for about five minutes, and they all are healthy.

```
PS C:\Users\hbai> Get-ServiceFabricNode | Select NodeName, NodeUpTime, HealthState

NodeName NodeUpTime HealthState
-------- ---------- -----------
_App2    00:04:44          Ok
_App1    00:04:42          Ok
_App0    00:05:14          Ok
_App3    00:04:47          Ok
_App4    00:04:45          Ok
```

FIGURE 11-18 Get-ServiceFabricNode before node restart

Now, restart a node by using the Restart-ServiceFabricNode command:

```
Restart-ServiceFabricNode -NodeName [node name]
```

3. Run the Get-ServiceFabricNode command again, as shown in Figure 11-19.

```
PS C:\Users\hbai> Get-ServiceFabricNode | Select NodeName, NodeUpTime, HealthState

NodeName  NodeUpTime  HealthState
--------  ----------  -----------
_App2     00:14:02    Ok
_App1     00:14:00    Ok
_App0     00:00:00    Ok
_App3     00:14:05    Ok
_App4     00:14:03    Ok
```

FIGURE 11-19 Get-ServiceFabricNode after node restart

4. Instead of selecting which node to restart by name, you can use a partition locator or a replica locator to choose a node that is holding a specific replica. This allows you to conduct a targeted test against a particular service replica.

   For example, the following command selects the node that is hosting the primary replica of partition with key 30 of service *fabric:/ActorTicTacToeApplication/GameActorService*:

```
Restart-ServiceFabricNode -ReplicaKindPrimary -PartitionKindUniformInt64 -PartitionKey 30
-ServiceName fabric:/ActorTicTacToeApplication/GameActorService
```

   This command generates the output shown in Figure 11-20. You can see that node *_App0* is selected and restarted in this case.

FIGURE 11-20 Select node by replica

5. Next, let's try to move the primary replica of a stateful service. First, use the Get-ServiceFabricPartition command to list partitions of a stateful service, for example:

```
Get-ServiceFabricPartition -ServiceName fabric:/ActorTicTacToeApplication
/GameActorService | select PartitionId
```

6. Then, get replicas of any of the partitions, for example:

```
Get-ServiceFabricReplica -PartitionId deae96e3-05d2-4940-89fb-cd83e1fd22e9 | select
NodeName, ReplicaRole, ReplicaStatus
```

This command generates the following output on my environment:

```
NodeName      ReplicaRole ReplicaStatus
--------      ----------- -------------
_App2     ActiveSecondary      Ready
_App4     ActiveSecondary      Ready
_App0             Primary      Ready
```

7. Now, move the primary replica to a node that is not in the list, for example:

```
Move-ServiceFabricPrimaryReplica -PartitionId deae96e3-05d2-4940-89fb-cd83e1fd22e9
-ServiceName fabric:/ActorTicTacToeApplication/GameActorService -NodeName _App3
```

8. Repeat the Get-ServiceFabricReplica command in step 7. Observe that the primary replica is moved to a new node, for example:

```
NodeName      ReplicaRole ReplicaStatus
--------      ----------- -------------
_App4     ActiveSecondary      Ready
_App3             Primary      Ready
_App0     ActiveSecondary      Ready
```

In this section, I focused on using PowerShell. You also can use testability APIs to compose test cases. Because you can use these APIs against any environment, you can set up automated tests in your CI system to test if your service code is robust enough to deal with key failing scenarios that interest you. I'll leave this as an exercise for interested readers.

Additional information

This chapter can cover only a small segment of application testing. Specifically, the chapter walk-through only the most basic load testing you can do with VSTS. For a more complete walkthrough, please refer to *https://www.visualstudio.com/get-started/test/load-test-your-app-vs*. As you repeat the tests, lots of data will be generated. Please refer to the following article to learn about how to set up data retention policies to trim test data: *https://www.visualstudio.com/get-started/test /how-long-to-keep-test-results*.

If you are interested in the Netflix open-source Chaos Monkey project, please visit the project's GitHub site: *https://github.com/Netflix/SimianArmy/wiki/Chaos-Monkey*.

PART III

Patterns and scenarios

CHAPTER 12

Web applications

Hosting a web application is one of the primary use cases of Service Fabric. As you've seen in earlier chapters, Service Fabric embraces existing web stacks such as ASP.NET and Node.js to deliver web applications. What makes Service Fabric stand out from the many platform as a service (PaaS) platforms that support these web stacks? In this chapter, I'll first review the PaaS ecosystem on Azure. My goal is to provide you enough details so you can make an informed decision as you choose from among hosting options.

Then, I'll move to a couple of web applications to show you several design patterns and reference architectures you can consider when designing your own web applications hosted on Service Fabric.

Azure PaaS ecosystem

At a high level, Azure provides three PaaS offerings for hosting web applications: App Services, Cloud Services, and Service Fabric. They overlap in areas, but they have unique capabilities. So, it might be confusing when you choose which platform to use.

Each of the PaaS platforms is targeted at different scenarios and different developer communities. I hope that once you finish reading the following sections, you have a clear idea of what they are designed for and when you would choose one over the others.

> ### Microsoft Azure Container Services
>
> At the time of this writing, Microsoft Azure Container Services is in limited preview. This Mesos-based container orchestration service has the potential to become another PaaS platform that provides hosting solutions for containerized applications.

App Services

App Services has evolved from Azure Websites, one of the oldest and the most popular services provided by Azure. As the name suggests, Azure Websites is designed for modern web developers to develop and host mission-critical, highly scalable web applications with a global reach.

In 2015, Azure Websites was rolled into a new service named App Services and became the Web Apps component of the new service. App Services also integrates a number of other application types including Mobile Apps, Logic Apps, and API Apps.

Agility and productivity are at the core of the design philosophy of App Services. One of the primary goals of App Services is to provide web developers a familiar, efficient, and powerful environment to build, host, and scale high-quality websites quickly.

App Services provides some powerful features for developing scalable and available web applications, including but not limited to the following:

- **Built-in supports for different runtimes including .NET Framework (v3.5, v4.6), PHP (5.4, 5.5, 5.6), Java (Java 7, Java 8), and Python (2.4, 3.4)**   Service Fabric also can host runtimes other than .NET through its customization mechanisms. However, App Services provides native supports for these runtimes. Cloud Services provides built-in supports for .NET (both Visual C# and Visual Basic), Node.js, PHP, and Python.

- **Built-in continuous deployment**   App Services supports continuous deployments from a number of code sources such as Visual Studio Team Services, OneDrive, Local Git Repository, GitHub, Bitbucket, Dropbox, and any public Git or Mercurial repositories. You also can set up continuous deployment for Cloud Services and Service Fabric using VSTS. However, at this point only App Services provides an integrated portal experience to configure continuous deployments directly from Microsoft Azure management portal. App Services also supports deploying websites via FTP uploads.

- **Built-in hybrid connectivity**   App Services provides native support to connect your web applications to your on-premises resources and services via VPN or BizTalk Hybrid Connections. For example, you can connect your Azure-hosted websites to a SQL Database hosted on your on-premises servers via a VPN connection. Because Service Fabric is built on top of Azure Resource Manager and a typical Service Fabric cluster is provisioned on an Azure Virtual Network, it's also fairly easy to set up VPN connections to connect to your on-premises resources. However, this requires you to configure the resource group underneath the Service Fabric cluster manually. Cloud Services presents a similar situation: you can deploy Cloud Services applications onto an Azure Virtual Network; however, you need to manage your hybrid connections by yourself.

- **Built-in troubleshooting tools to observe, analyze, and mitigate problems**   App Services provides a wide range of tools for you to observe and analyze live HTTP traffics, system events, failed request logs, and various metrics. Figure 12-1 shows a sample screen shot of the App Services site metrics view. These features are not only available, but also automatically configured by default so that you can diagnose issues immediately without making any configuration changes. And if you need to collect more data, you always can change the diagnostics settings to collect more verbose data. In contrast, Cloud Services and Service Fabric rely on Azure Diagnostics and ETW for tracing and logging. In addition, Service Fabric provides a separate Service Fabric Explorer as a monitoring/management UI. All three platforms are integrated with Azure Application Insights.

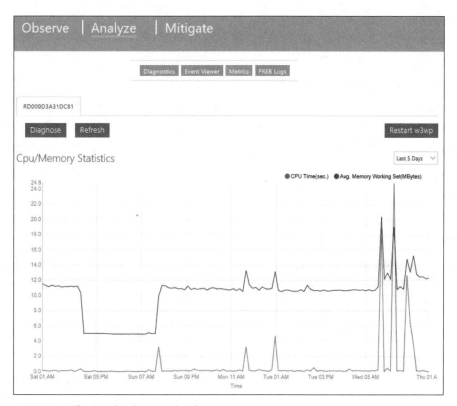

FIGURE 12-1 The App Services metrics view

- **Built-in backup and restore** App Services supports automatic backups of web applications and SQL Databases or MySQL Databases that are linked to these applications. Service Fabric provides API supports to back up and restore service states (see Chapter 6, "Availability and reliability"). Cloud Services doesn't provide built-in backups and restores.

- **Support for multiple deployment slots** You can define deployment slots for different purposes such as production, dev, and test. For instance, you can deploy a new version of your website to a staging slot to test it before swapping it into the production slot. During the swap operation, the traffic rerouting is seamless and no requests are dropped. This allows you to perform zero downtime upgrades. Slot swaps also can be automated so that each code check-in will trigger an automatic slot swap.

- **Scaling with autoscale based on telemetries or scheduled scaling** For instance, you can set up an autoscaling rule that scales out or scales in a deployment based on CPU usage percentage. Or, you can set up scheduled scaling in anticipation of expected traffic spikes during weekends.

- **Support for Web Jobs, which runs background processes** You can run background jobs continuously or on schedule within the context of your web applications.

As you can see, App Services makes every effort to streamline the DevOps processes. All its features aim to provide a painless, intuitive, and agile web application development and hosting environment.

Cloud Services

The history of Cloud Services can be traced back to the beginning of Azure. Microsoft correctly predicted that PaaS would take center stage in the cloud. However, Cloud Services, as one of the first large-scale PaaS offerings, was released ahead of its time. I feel it hasn't been receiving the attention it deserves. And with the release of Service Fabric, Cloud Services seemingly is fading into history. Regardless, at the time of this writing, Cloud Services remains a first-class PaaS offering of Microsoft Azure.

Cloud Services is designed for enterprise-level, multitiered applications. The following list highlights some of its features:

- **Built-in support for web roles and worker roles**　Cloud Services supports the concept of roles that segment applications into front-end tiers and background tiers. The web roles serve as the front-end tiers that interact with end users; the worker roles serve as background processors that handle long-running processes. Cloud Services primarily uses loose coupling. Although roles can communicate with each other using internal endpoints, commonly roles are loosely coupled by Microsoft Azure Service Bus queues.

- **Support for host customization**　Cloud Services supports a number of runtimes including .NET (both Visual C# and Visual Basic), Node.js, PHP, and Python. Cloud Services started with .NET runtime and added supports for other runtimes. Moreover, Cloud Services allows hosting environments to be customized by installing additional components and running custom configuration scripts. Deep customizations such as updating registry entries isn't possible for Web Services. Service Fabric also supports host customizations.

- **Local emulators**　Similar to Service Fabric, Cloud Services provides an emulated environment for you to test and debug web roles and worker roles locally.

- **Staging slot and production slot**　Similar to App Services deployment slots, Cloud Services supports two deployments where you can deploy your applications. As you swap the slots, the staging slot becomes the production slot and the previous production slot becomes the new staging slot.

- **Autoscaling**　You can set up autoscaling rules to adjust the capacity of your deployments. This is more suitable for gradual workload increases or decreases. Cloud Services assumes that all roles are stateless. When a new role instance is created, there's no attempt to sync its states with existing instances. And when an existing instance is destroyed, there's no attempt to preserve its states.

Cloud Services is designed for multitiered applications. However, you certainly can use Cloud Services to implement other architectures. For example, you can implement an application with a single web tier using a web role by itself. Or, you can implement a background batch processing service with a single worker role.

Service Fabric

Service Fabric provides a number of features that are not provided by either App Services or Cloud Services. The following list is a quick summary:

- **Stateful services**   Both App Services and Cloud Services require services to be stateless so that they can create and destroy service instances freely as needed. Service Fabric supports stateful services. As I've explained in earlier chapters, stateful services have some obvious advantages over stateless services. However, stateful services introduce additional complexity. On the one hand, managing stateful services is more complicated. Service Fabric has to deal with problems such as state replication and leader elections. On the other hand, developers are exposed to more concepts before they effectively can develop and manage stateful services.

- **Scaling by partitions**   Both App Services and Cloud Services scale out applications by adding new service instances behind a round-robin load balancer. All user requests are distributed evenly to these instances. Such a routing scheme doesn't work for stateful services. To avoid excessive data movements, it's preferable that replicas remain stable and be relocated only when absolutely necessary. This means traffic can't be routed blindly to any instances. Instead, a more sophisticated routing is needed so that requests will land on correct nodes that form the state quorum. Partitioning allows a large number of such quorums to coexist to share the load of the whole system.

- **Heterogeneous cluster**   Both App Services and Cloud Services support scaling up options. You can pick different plan levels or virtual machine sizes that suit your application requirements. However, all hosting nodes are configured identically. In contrast, Service Fabric allows you to define multiple node types on the same cluster. And you can use placement constraints to place different service instances onto different node types.

- **Flexible communication stacks**   App Services is designed specifically for web applications. Cloud Services provides more flexibility with different endpoint types such as HTTP, HTTPS, and TCP/IP sockets. Service Fabric allows you to customize the entire communication stack. This flexible design enables interesting scenarios. You'll see a web socket example in Chapter 14, "Real-time data streaming."

- **Rolling updates and partial updates**   Both App Services and Cloud Services perform updates by swapping deployment slots. Service Fabric supports rolling updates, in which a new application version gradually is introduced into the cluster by walking through upgrade domains. Service Fabric also supports updating configuration, code, and data separately so that minor changes can be pushed out quickly without rebuilding the whole instance.

- **Actor programming model**   Service Fabric provides the actor programming model that enables you to tackle complex, distributed systems at a higher, more intuitive abstraction level. For example, many complex systems that are comprised of interactive, independent agents can be modeled with the actor programming model. Chapter 18 of this book, "Modeling complex systems," is dedicated to modeling complex systems with the actor programming model.

Choosing PaaS platforms

If you are building a website only, in many cases App Services would be your best choice. However, if you are building a complex system with web front ends and background processors, you can choose between Cloud Services and Service Fabric, with Service Fabric being the preferred choice. If you are building stateful services, Service Fabric is a clear choice over the other two options.

The following are some typical scenarios with recommend choices. Of course, each project is unique. You'll need to evaluate the specific requirements of your project before you make a decision.

- Host a website with global reach

  App Services provides an available and scalable hosting environment for websites. You easily can scale your web applications to meet the demand. For global deployment, you can deploy the site to multiple Azure datacenters and use Traffic Manager to route end users to servers providing the best performance. App Services provides 99.9 percent availability SLA and is compliant with industrial standards such as ISO and PCI.

- Provide a web-based access point to on-premises data

  App Services provides built-in support for hybrid connections that enable your web applications to connect directly to on-premises databases. Furthermore, you can use Azure Active Directory (Azure AD) to project users in your local Active Directory to the cloud so that they can continue to use their corporate credentials to sign in to both the web and the on-premises database.

- Migrate on-premises multitiered applications to the cloud

  Migrating an on-premises system to the cloud is a complex problem. It's hard to make a single recommendation for all these projects. Both Cloud Services and Service Fabric support multicomponent applications. This allows you to manage the multitiered application as a single unit. In contrast, if you use Web Apps to host the web tier, you'll need to manage the other tiers separately.

  In many cases, it's hard to make code changes to legacy systems. So, you might be facing a situation in which none of the PaaS offerings can meet your requirements. In such a case, you may consider using virtual machines directly to lift and shift the application to the cloud first and then seek opportunities to adopt PaaS gradually.

- Host open-source blogs and CMS platforms

  Azure Marketplace provides hundreds of ready-to-use web application templates (*https://azure.microsoft.com/marketplace/web-applications/*) that you can use to quickly create App Services applications, including many popular open-source solutions such as Drupal, Umbraco CMS, WordPress, and Tomcat.

- Develop new cloud-based, distributed applications

  Service Fabric is designed for Microservices applications. If you are starting from scratch to build a cloud-based, distributed application, Service Fabric is a good choice because it allows the application to be separated into individual services that can be developed and evolved independently. With agile application development, an application often needs to go through many revisions. Microservices architecture helps you control the risks by isolating problem domains.

Azure Services for your web applications

Regardless of which PaaS offering you choose, you can use many of the Azure services to provide necessary supports for and enhancements to your web applications. The following is a quick summary of some of the common services that you can use in conjunction with your web applications.

- Data storage

    - SQL Database provides a hosted relational database that is compatible with SQL Server.

    - Azure Storage provides reliable storage for blobs, semi-structured data, files, and disks.

    - DocumentDB is a NoSQL JSON database with automatic indexes and low-latency data reads and writes.

    - SQL Data Warehouse is a cloud-based data warehouse.

- Quality of service

    - Traffic Manager allows you to set up traffic routing profiles for scenarios such as performance-based routing and failovers.

    - Redis Cache provides high-performance in-memory cache for frequently accessed data.

    - Azure CDN offers a content delivery network for serving cached contents directly from CDN's edge nodes instead of from the original servers.

- Security and identity services

    - Azure AD provides claim-based authentication for your applications. You'll see an example of using Azure AD later in this chapter.

    - Key Vault offers a secured repository for your access keys and other secrets.

- Developer services

    - Visual Studio Team Services (VSTS) provides services for a team to manage code, trace work, and manage application life cycles.

    - Visual Studio Application Insights provides application tracing and monitoring.

Scenarios and patterns

In this part of the chapter, I'll go through several typical web application scenarios: e-commerce websites, mass-source websites, and enterprise portals. The goal of these scenarios is not to teach you the exact steps of building these kinds of websites. Instead, the scenarios are used as a vehicle to introduce a number of patterns, including fan-out indexes, Personalization Actor, claim-based authentication, self-service, and message-based integration.

Although this book is about Service Fabric, the following scenarios are not constrained to using Service Fabric. Other Azure Services are included as part of the architectures whenever applicable.

E-commerce websites

An e-commerce website sells merchandise or services to end users. Although the idea sounds simple, e-commerce websites are among the most complex websites you can build. Figure 12-2 shows typical building blocks of a modern e-commerce website. As you can see, a comprehensive e-commerce site is made up of many interacting components. However, a minimum e-commerce site can be constructed by using only a Payment subsystem and a Catalog subsystem (components with bold borders in Figure 12-2). When you design an e-commerce website, these two components form the base of the system, and other components are built around them to provide other essential features. Microservices architecture works well in such situations. Once you get the baseline ready, you can design, build, and evolve other pieces independently to build up a site that best fits your requirements.

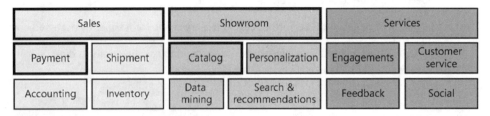

FIGURE 12-2 e-commerce website building blocks

Pattern: Mock-based Service Design

Many people are familiar with the Test-Driven Development (TDD) process and Behavior-Driven Development (BDD) process. Both processes require unit tests to be written before the actual implementation is put in place. The unit tests intentionally fail and then are fixed with minimum code. Finally, the implementation is refined and refactored into final code.

Mock-based Service Design defines service behaviors by using service mocks directly. Instead of writing unit test cases, developers directly model service behaviors by defining a minimum service interface. As additional behaviors are needed, the service interface is extended to provide desired behaviors. As the interface evolves, a mockup implementation is maintained to implement the interface. Unlike TDD or BDD, the mockup implementation doesn't intentionally fail. Instead, it provides a functional implementation as a placeholder for the actual service implementation.

Mock-based Service Design uses client requirements directly to drive the design of the service interface. It allows developers to focus on the service implementation at hand without being distracted by dependent services. In addition, it helps developers refine the dependent service interfaces before the services are implemented.

For example, before a payment system is implemented or selected, an e-commerce site can mock up expected behaviors. The mockups will be replaced when the payment system is ready. The mockups can be kept in automated tests of other components without incurring actual monetary transactions. In contrast, if a payment system is selected in advance, it is easy for the e-commerce site developers to be influenced by how the selected system behaves when designing the interface to the payment system. If the payment system has to be replaced, the interface might be difficult to implement using the new system because of the incompatibility of the two systems.

Pattern: Personalization Actor

Modern e-commerce sites strive to provide a personalized shopping experience by ranked search results, targeted recommendations, and proactive engagements. These recommendations usually are generated by a recommendation engine.

A recommendation engine works on individual user data and collective data from the entire user base. Often, a hybrid recommendation system with multiple engines is used. Integrating these engines into the e-commerce site while keeping a stable and manageable interface could be challenging. The Personalization Actor pattern uses an actor to encapsulate all user behavior data and communications with various recommendation engines.

Figure 12-3 shows a diagram of the Personalization Actor pattern. At the center is the Personalization Actor, which is a stateful Service Fabric Actor representing a user profile. The actor contains the following types of state data:

- **Purchase history**   This state records a history of user purchases. The actor exposes an interface for the sales subsystem to feed in purchase data. Purchase history is an important vector in making recommendations because a user generally has a tendency to buy from similar brands, categories, and price ranges.

- **Search history, ad impression, and feedbacks**   This state records a history of user behaviors such as search queries, explicit feedbacks, and ad impressions from the user. For example, what a user searches shows what the user is interested in. When a user conducts a number of related searches and spends time browsing search results, it's a strong indication that the user is interested in the searched items.

- **Social engagements**   Social networks are great places to collect user feedbacks. Automatically crawling generally is hard, and correlating social data to a particular user is unfeasible in most cases. If your site does collect social data, you can consider setting up one or more abstract Personalization Actor instances representing different social platforms. Although these actor instances don't directly contribute to recommendation generations, they can participate in matching processes that update user profiles based on similar users.

- **User preference** This state represents what a user is interested in, especially what a user is likely to buy. This information is crucial to making effective recommendations to the user. Interfaces built around this state serve as the stable abstraction for the rest of the system to query for recommendations.

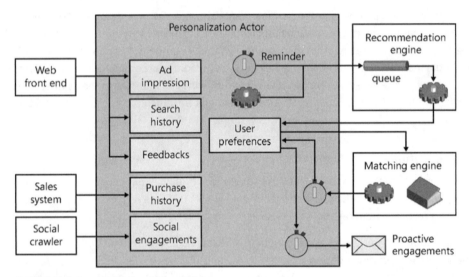

FIGURE 12-3 Personalization Actor pattern

When the state of a Personalization Actor is updated, it queues up a new request to the recommendation engine. The message payload contains the actor state and the actor address for the engine to call back with user preference updates. This design decouples the Personalization Actor and the recommendation engine. The Personalization Actor serves as the center of truth of a user's preference, but it shouldn't have specialized knowledge to make recommendations. With this design, the actor is unaware of how recommendations are generated, and it serves as an abstraction layer that shields recommendation details from the rest of the system.

The Personalization Actor also has a number of associated reminders. These reminders are used to connect to different engines and engagement systems at certain intervals. Figure 12-3 shows three examples of such scheduled invocations—to a recommendation engine, to a matching engine, and to a proactive engagement system:

- **Recommendation engine** This reminder periodically calls to a recommendation engine to refresh recommendations for a user. As a recommendation engine accumulates knowledge, it's likely to make different recommendations over time. For example, when a new product line is released, it should be factored into the recommendation process, probably with heavier weights, to generate more profitable recommendations (because it's all about making profits, after all). These scheduled calls ensure these new recommendations are picked up at reasonable intervals.

- **Matching engine** This reminder calls to a matching engine that assesses similarities among users. In Figure 12-3, the matching engine is wrapped by a stateful service that maintains a local dictionary of users and their profile scores, assuming user similarities can be assessed by the differences among their profile scores.

- **Proactive engagement system** This reminder sends signals to a proactive engagement system. Note that the reminder itself doesn't contain any proactive engagement logics. It merely sends a signal to the service. A benefit of this design is that the proactive engagement system doesn't need to keep a catalog of the Personalization Actors.

The Personalization Actor separates user behavior states and the logic that makes assessments on these states. The recommendation engine is a complex piece that will take time to perfect. Such separation provides a stable programming interface to the rest of the system while allowing the recommendation engine to be developed independently.

The turn-based concurrency ensures consistent updates from multiple data sources. And because each Personalization Actor corresponds to a single user, inter-user locks are avoided. Finally, because user behavior states can be queried directly from the corresponding actor without going through underlying engines, the pattern provides fast performance.

Pattern: Persistent shopping cart

For an e-commerce site, nothing could be worse than losing an opportunity for a sale. A persistent shopping cart survives across multiple user sessions so that if a user disconnects from the site either intentionally or unintentionally because of service or network errors, the shopping cart is kept for the user to continue shopping at a later time.

A persistent shopping cart also allows end users to engage with the sales process from multiple media. For instance, a user can add items to the cart from the link from an email promotion, from a mobile client, or from a sponsored search link. Although these items are added through different user sessions and different devices, the persistent shopping cart collects all requests and allows the user to purchase everything at the same time.

A persistent shopping cart can be implemented easily by a Service Fabric stateful actor. A persistent shopping cart actor should be addressable by a user id or a user account, and its state is a list of merchandise that has been placed in the cart. If Personalization Actors also are used, the shopping cart actor should signal the corresponding Personalization Actor to trigger recommendation refreshes as new items are placed in the cart. This process generates cross-sale and up-sale opportunities to drive up the order value.

Figure 12-4 shows how a persistent shopping cart and Personalization Actor work together to drive cross-sale and up-sale opportunities. As a new item is added to the shopping cart, the cart notifies the corresponding Personalization Actor, which in turn schedules a recommendation refresh request with the recommendation engine. The shopping cart UI queries the persistent shopping cart to display the shopping cart contents. At the same time, it queries the Personalization Actor to display recommendations to drive additional sales opportunities.

Because a Service Fabric actor has an independent lifetime, even if the user session is terminated for any reason, the actor's state is not lost. When the user signs in later, the shopping cart state still can be queried by the user id.

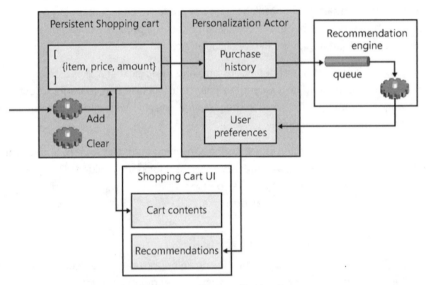

FIGURE 12-4 Persistent Shopping cart and Personalization Actor

Mass-source websites

A mass-source website provides a platform for its members to upload and share user-generated content. This is a broad definition that covers both social websites such as Facebook and content-sharing websites such as Flickr. Such websites have the following characteristics:

- **High scalability**   These websites have to be designed with massive scale in mind. Although only a few mass-source websites can reach a significant user base, it would be unfortunate if the website is constrained by scalability limitations if the site were to go viral.

- **Discoverability**   The user-generated content has to be easily discoverable. The website needs to be able to retrieve and present relevant data quickly to its users to keep them engaged.

- **Performance**   As the site accumulates more user-generated content, the performance of data storage, mining, and query need to be maintained to ensure the overall system performance.

- **Multiple engagement channels**   Modern mass-source websites often use multiple engagement channels to interact with users. These channels include the website itself, mobile applications, and email notifications. Moreover, some large mass-source websites also open APIs for third parties to develop customized applications. These applications are increasingly important for these sites to build and maintain vibrant ecosystems.

Figure 12-5 shows high-level building blocks of a mass-source website. The overall architecture is fairly simple: data is collected from the user base, stored and analyzed, and eventually fed back to the users. However, when you try to do everything at scale, things become more challenging. Designing for massive scale is not an easy task. I hope the following patterns give you some ideas when you design your mass-source websites.

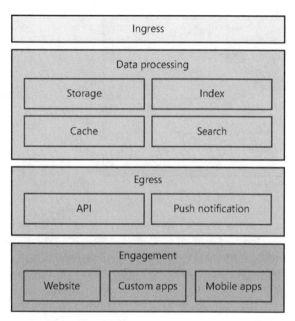

FIGURE 12-5 Building blocks of a mass-source website

Pattern: Fan-out Indexes

Most websites have more reads than writes. Providing a fast and smooth read is the key to providing a good overall user experience. Caching is an effective way to provide fast reads by serving precalculated contents to user queries. However, when lots of customized views for individual users need to be cached, the cost might be too high.

The Fan-out Indexes pattern sacrifices write performance to gain read performance. When a new entry is written, the index of the data is written to all possible views of the data. For example, when a user posts a new picture, the index of the picture immediately is replicated to all photo feeds of his friends so that his friends can get immediate updates. In contrast, if a photo feed is built by querying latest updates from all of a user's friends, the query could take a long time. Fan-out Indexes is not a new idea. In fact, data denormalization has been used for a long time to improve query performance. What's different in this case is that instead of replicating the original data, Fan-out Indexes only replicates indexes of the data. This saves lots of storage space and avoids replication costs of duplicating large amounts of binary data and unstructured data.

Figure 12-6 shows a possible architecture of the Fan-out Indexes pattern. When new content is fed into the ingress system, the system consults a friends graph to figure out the feeds to be updated. Then, write requests are sent to a fan-out writer that replicates the data key to all identified user feeds.

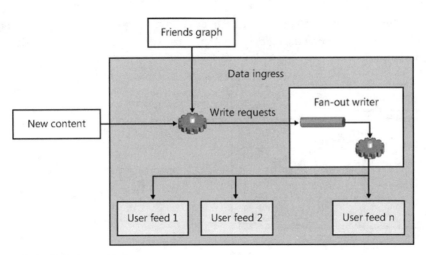

FIGURE 12-6 Fan-out Indexes

The fan-out writer can be implemented as a stateful Service Fabric service. The service uses a local job queue to remember the writes to be completed, and it writes to identified feeds. Each of the user feeds can be a stateful actor. The fan-out writer can use partitions to scale out to massive scales. And because all writes happen asynchronously with the original write requests, the impact on write performance is minimized. Last but not least, the user feed actors should maintain only a certain number of latest updates to keep the overall storage size under control.

Fan-out Indexes may encounter problems when there are many interactions among users. For example, when a user replies to a message posted by a popular user, her reply may arrive at her friends before the original message is propagated to them. The problem can be addressed by using additional sorting by time stamps before the data is presented.

Another potential problem is handling updates from extremely popular users who have huge friend circles. Each write from these users will generate a huge number of write requests that will overload the system. There are several ways to deal with this problem. First, the friends in these circles can be prioritized so that the most active friends will get updates first. Another approach is to skip Fan-out Indexes for these popular users altogether. Instead, their updates can be merged dynamically into other feeds at query time. The latest updates from these users can be kept in high-speed in-memory cache so that they can be retrieved and merged quickly. This approach slows down the query process, but in return you get huge savings by avoiding an excessive number of writes.

Just before the data is served to an end user, lookups are performed to pull in the actual data. The pulling requests can be initiated by the client, and only the browsed contents are pulled down from data storages or CDN nodes.

Pattern: Service API

As mobile devices become an increasing part of everyday life, it's rare to see a popular website without some sort of mobile front end, such as a native smartphone application or a mobile version of the website. And because of the segmentation of the smartphone market, multiple versions of client applications are needed for different platforms such as iOS, Android, and Windows. Furthermore, as cloud-based services become increasingly ubiquitous, even more variations of the client are needed for different devices such as smart TVs, game consoles, and wearable devices.

The Service API pattern reinforces the separation between the functionalities and the presentations of a website. All front ends, including the website itself and various customized client applications, are viewports to the same set of functionalities. The Service API pattern ensures that a user has a consistent experience no matter what clients she uses, and it avoids duplicated efforts to support different types of clients.

You should note that consistent experience doesn't mean identical experiences across all clients. Instead, each client should be customized to take full advantage of the specific platform to provide the best possible user experience. Consistency means coherence across platforms in user preference, user interaction, and graphic design.

A Service API can be implemented easily as a stateless Service Fabric service such as an ASP.NET API service. For large-scale deployments, you can consider deploying a separate service instance for each of the supported platforms. Such topology allows you to monitor traffics from different platforms more easily, and it allows you to adjust capacities for different platforms independently. More importantly, because different types of clients may evolve at different speeds, they may need different versions of the API.

For managing consistent user states, you can use a user state actor. Because Service Actors always exist virtually, you don't need to worry about whether multiple clients are trying to create or update the actor at the same time. Service Fabric ensures that a single actor exists for the user's states. And because the actor has its own life cycle, crashes in one Service API won't affect the state availability for other Service APIs. Figure 12-7 shows a sample deployment topology of Service APIs.

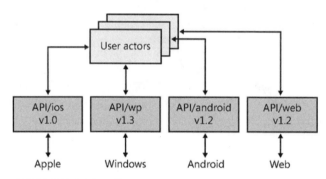

FIGURE 12-7 Service API

Additional Azure services

One of the main benefits of Microservices is that each service is independent. You can choose to develop all required services yourself. Or, you can choose from many of the software as a service (SaaS) offerings from Azure. Using an existing service is a smart choice, especially for services that are complex and consume lots of resources. For mass-source websites, the following Azure services could provide practical help:

- **Notification Hubs**   Notification Hubs provides a multiplatform pushing infrastructure you can use to send push notifications to mobile platforms such as iOS, Android, Windows Phone, and Windows Store. It hides details of different platform notification systems (PNSs) and provides an easy-to-use API for you to reach out proactively to your mobile users.

- **API Management**   API Management provides end-to-end management of your APIs. You can use API Management to monitor your API consumption, to set up throttling and quotas, and to gain analytic insights into your API usage. It also provides a developer portal that helps you build up a developer community that uses your API to develop customized applications.

- **Microsoft CDN**   Azure provides the industry-leading solution for content delivery. By serving static content directly from CDN edge nodes, CDN gives users faster response time. And because requests for static content are offloaded to CDN, your servers are freed up to take on more write requests.

The above list is not exhaustive. I encourage you to go to *azure.microsoft.com*, open the Products tab, and explore many Azure services that you can incorporate into your solutions.

Enterprise portals

There are several driving forces behind enterprise portals. First, the increasing mobility of workforces requires enterprises to enable their employees to carry out normal business functions outside their corporate networks. Second, enterprises need to provide a consistent, manageable, and auditable experience for their employees and partners to consume enterprise applications. Third, many large enterprises seek ways to automate common workflows by enabling self-services. And last but not least, as enterprises try to gain value from deep insights into business data, they need to make data and analysis results easily accessible to their employees.

Figure 12-8 shows a high-level architecture of an enterprise portal. The portal is made up of a number of subsystems, including Customer Relation Management (CRM), subscribed SaaS services, legacy apps, Business Intelligence (BI), and Enterprise Resource Planning (ERP). All these subsystems are connected to services hosted on the cloud or at on-premises datacenters. Your portal may have more or fewer components than shown in the diagram.

To the right of the diagram are three cross-cutting components: authentication and security, tracing and auditing, and analytics. Authentication and security ensures services are accessible only by authenticated users. Tracing, auditing, and analytics are for tracing and analyzing service usage for compliance and optimization purposes.

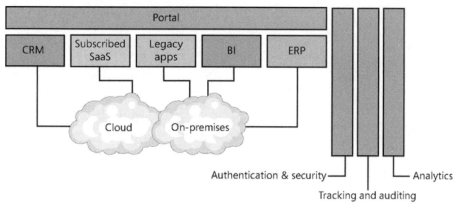

FIGURE 12-8 Enterprise portal

Pattern: Claim-based authentication

One the most important experiences an enterprise portal provides is the Single Sign-On (SSO) experience, which means a user only needs to sign in once to gain access to all required services.

For SSO to work, there must be a trust relationship among the services. Claim-based authentication creates a circle of trust by delegating all authentications to a central identity provider. The identity provider verifies the user's identity and provides the user's information to participating applications, called *relying parties* in this case, through security tokens. A security token is a signed and often encrypted package that contains assertions made by the identity provider on the authenticated user. These assertions, or claims, contain necessary user information such as user id, name, email address, and role for applications to identify a user. Then, the applications make authorization decisions based on the values of these claims. Because all applications in the circle trust the same identity provider, a user only needs to sign in once to generate necessary claims for all participating applications.

Claim-based authentication has become the industry standard of handling authentication. It's carried out by popular protocols such as ws-Federation and oAuth, and it's used by nearly all established websites on the Internet. Chances are, the services you need to integrate into your enterprise already support claim-based authentication. So when it comes to authentication method, there isn't a better choice than claim-based authentication.

Azure Active Directory (Azure AD) acts as an identity provider in claim-based authentication. And the Visual Studio tooling provides an integrated experience to configure ASP.NET applications to use Azure AD as the identity provider.

When you create a new ASP.NET service in your Service Application, the Visual Studio tooling provides you the option to set up claim-based authentication with Azure AD. Because the ASP.NET site is being created, click the Change Authentication button and then select the Work And School Accounts option in the Change Authentication dialog box. Then, enter the domain name of your Azure AD tenant and click the OK button, as shown in Figure 12-9. You'll be prompted to sign in to your Azure AD account, and the Visual Studio tooling will take care of the rest.

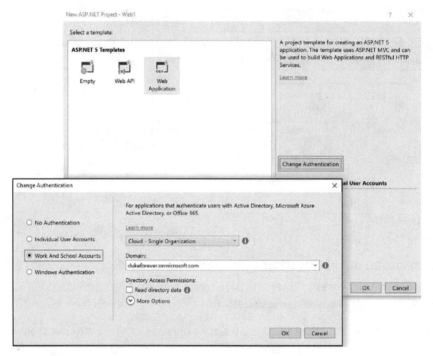

FIGURE 12-9 Setting up authentication for ASP.NET

What happens behind the scenes is that your ASP.NET application is registered as a trusted relying party with your Azure AD tenant, and your application is configured to trust Azure AD as its identity provider. Once this mutual trust relationship is established, all unauthorized requests will be intercepted and redirected to Azure AD for authentication. Later, as other applications establish trusts with the same Azure AD tenant, the circle of trust expands and all applications in the circle can be accessed using the same security token. Figure 12-10 depicts a typical authentication process using claim-based authentication:

1. A user requests access to a service.

2. The service detects the user hasn't been authenticated because the request doesn't contain a security token. So, it redirects the user to its trusted identity provider for authentication.

3. The user authenticates with the identity provider.

4. The identity provider issues a security token to the user.

5. The user submits another request with the security token attached.

6. The service verifies the security token. If the token is valid, the service reads user information from the claims contained in the token.

7. Based on the claim values, the service makes a decision to grant or deny access.

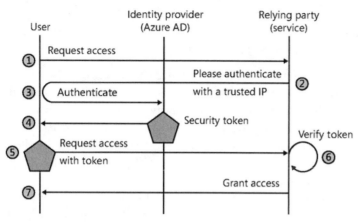

FIGURE 12-10 Claim-based authentication

Notice that an application is identified by its URL. When you use the Visual Studio tooling, the ASP. NET application is registered with Azure AD with a localhost address. The tooling is supposed to update your application configuration to update the URL to the appropriate address on the cloud when you publish the application to Azure.

Visual Studio tooling experience under development

At the time of this writing, the Visual Studio tooling for Service Fabric, especially the integration with Azure AD, still is under development. This is why I'm not including any specific walkthrough in this part. Please consult documentation on azure.com for exact steps.

But what if an application to be integrated already uses another identity provider? Fortunately, Azure AD also is able to act as a broker for authentication. Azure AD allows you to configure SSO with popular identity providers such as Facebook, Twitter, and LinkedIn. And you can project your on-premises Active Directory to Azure AD. Azure AD also extends your circle of trust by providing built-in support for popular SaaS applications such as Office 365, Box, Salesforce, and many others.

Pattern: Message-based integration

Integrating applications can be tough. You may face technical and non-technical constraints: An application may have certain dependencies and can't be migrated to the cloud. The owner of an application may refuse to make any changes. An application may be too slow to process requests received from other applications. An application may be obsolete and need to be replaced. And the list goes on. Besides, as you build your enterprise portals, you often need to manage distributed workflows that span across multiple services. What you need is an integration mechanism that is easy to adopt, cross-platform, and flexible but reliable. You'll also want the applications to be loosely coupled so that changes in one application will have minimum impact on the other applications.

Message-based integration using an Enterprise Service Bus (ESB) is a proven pattern that has been used in many integration scenarios. The pattern uses a highly available and highly scalable message bus for participating services to exchange messages with one another.

The pattern offers several significant benefits. First, the pattern enables loose coupling of services. Because the services don't have hard dependencies on one another, any service can be modified or even replaced without affecting other services. This kind of flexibility is important for dynamic scenarios like enterprise portals. Second, the message bus serves as a moderator that can reconcile performance differences among services. Faster services queue requests to the bus and move on without slowing down, and slower services handle long-running tasks at their own pace. When the job queue is too long, additional service instances can be launched to drain the queue faster (see the competing consumers pattern in Chapter 7, "Scalability and performance"). Third, an enterprise bus also serves as a failover mechanism. For example, a message consumer can place an auto-expiring lock on a job before it processes it. If the job is handled correctly, the message is removed from the queue. If the consumer crashes before it can finish the job, the job reappears on the queue once the lock expires. Then, this job can be picked up by another consumer or be processed when the consumer recovers. Fourth, message-based integration also enables hybrid integration scenarios. Under this pattern, it doesn't matter where the job is originated or where the job is handled. All services can communicate with one another regardless of their locations, as shown in Figure 12-11.

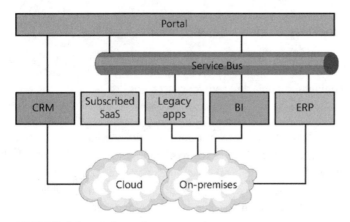

FIGURE 12-11 Integration with a message bus

Service Fabric stateful services support reliable queues out-of-box. For simple integration scenarios, it might be tempting to use a stateful service with a reliable queue as a simple message bus. However, I recommend using existing hosted message queue solutions such as Azure Service Bus because making a highly available, reliable, and scalable message bus isn't an easy task. Instead of wasting time on this task, you should use an existing solution and focus on your core business logics.

Pattern: Finite State Machine Actor

With the message-based integration pattern, services don't invoke each other directly. Instead, each service is self-driven: it monitors the job queue by itself and handles jobs as it sees them. This raises a problem: a distributed workflow may stop silently because of a failing service. For example, a salesperson enters a customer order into a CRM system via the enterprise portal. Then, the CRM system sends a message to the message bus for the ERP system to pick it up. However, the ERP system fails. From the CRM's perspective, the message is sent successfully, so the CRM expects the workflow to continue. From the message bus's perspective, the message is just waiting to be picked up. How can you detect such situations?

Another practical challenge with message-based integration is canceling a distributed workflow. Once a message is sent to the message bus, the message sender loses control over the message. The only way to cancel the request is for the original sender to send another message to revert the original request. Furthermore, because the message no longer is visible to the sender once it is sent, there's no easy way for the sender to track the progress of the workflow. And if the sender is expecting some results to be returned, another return message queue is needed for other services to send the results back to the original requestor. Monitoring workflow progress is even more troublesome because it requires additional intermediate messages to be sent and processed to reflect workflow progress.

Some messaging systems such as Azure Service Bus support automated dead-lettering, which automatically puts a message into a dead letter queue after a time-to-live (TTL) limit. To fix the above problem, the CRM system needs to monitor the dead letter queue and restart the workflow by resubmitting the message.

Now, for each of the services that participate in the integration, it needs to monitor a job queue for incoming messages, a dead letter queue for failed requests, and a return queue for returned messages and progress reports. This sounds complicated. Is there a better way to deal with this situation?

A finite state machine (FSM) is a well-known computation model that has been used broadly in computer programs. A detailed discussion of FSM is out of the scope of this book. The following are some quick facts on FSM:

- A FSM has finite number of states.

- A FSM has only one state at a time.

- A FSM can transit from one state to another when triggered by some events or conditions.

- Intuitively, a FSM can be used to define a workflow.

The Finite State Machine Actor (FSMA) pattern uses a Service Fabric Actor to define a finite state machine workflow. Because a Service Fabric Actor always exists virtually, the corresponding workflow instance exists outside all participating services. Besides, the turn-based concurrency mode ensures no conflicts in state updates. When FSMA is used, a participating service is required to check with the actor instance to see if the workflow is under the required state before it takes any actions. And it's supposed to signal the actor instance to transit to the next state when it's done processing the job. Optionally, a FSMA also can have an associated timer that periodically checks if the workflow has reached a certain state within certain time constrains. If the workflow fails to reach the desired state, the workflow is transited into a failed state.

Figure 12-12 shows an example workflow implemented as a FSMA instance. The diagram shows that Removable Storage Management (RSM) and ERP still use the message-based integration to communicate with each other. However, both of them check workflow state before they take any actions, and they trigger the state machine to transit to next states. The timer in the FSMA instance reinforces time constraints imposed on the workflow by enterprise policies.

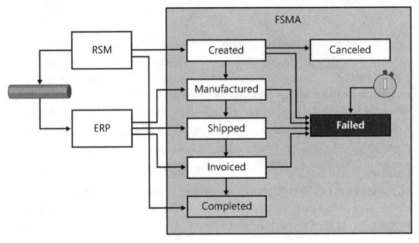

FIGURE 12-12 FSMA Pattern

Now, let's examine how FSMA addresses the earlier challenges:

- **Cancelling an order**   RSM just signals the FSMA instance to transit into the canceled state (while cancelling still is allowed).

- **Detecting failed orders**   The FSMA timer checks if the order reaches desired state within time limit. If not, the FSMA instance transits the workflow state to "failed" and notifies interested parties as necessary.

- **Monitoring order status**   Any services can query the FSMA instance anytime to check the current order state.

Additional information

The following is a list of reference URLs:

- For more details on Notification Hubs, please see *https://azure.microsoft.com/documentation /articles/notification-hubs-overview/*.

- For more details on API Management, please see *https://azure.microsoft.com/services /api-management/*.

- For more details on Azure CDN, please see *https://azure.microsoft.com/services/cdn/*.

- For more details on Azure Service Bus, please see *https://azure.microsoft.com/services /service-bus/*.

CHAPTER 13

Internet of Things

D evices and the cloud are perfect together. As cloud computing becomes ubiquitous, tremendous computing power permeates every aspect of our lives. Cloud computing no longer is limited to PCs and mobile phones—it includes devices such as wearable devices, robots, vehicles, appliances, and buildings. At the same time, these devices continuously feed petabytes of data back to the cloud and refine its models and algorithms to provide better, more intelligent services. It's unavoidable that the physical world represented by devices and the virtual world represented by the cloud will merge into a more intelligent, more convenient, more sustainable, and more creative world.

Internet of Things (IoT) is not just about connecting devices, but also about gaining insight from the collected data and then applying the learning in future improvements and innovations. In this chapter, I'll first review how Service Fabric fits into the overall IoT picture. Then, I'll introduce several patterns that you can consider when you design your own IoT solutions.

Azure IoT solutions

A comprehensive IoT solution is comprised of many interconnected components, as shown in Figure 13-1. Before discussing how Service Fabric fits into the pipeline, I'll briefly go through each of the components in the following pipeline to explain their functions.

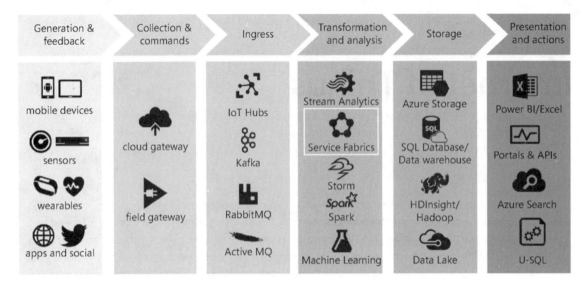

Generation & feedback	Collection & commands	Ingress	Transformation and analysis	Storage	Presentation and actions
mobile devices	cloud gateway	IoT Hubs	Stream Analytics	Azure Storage	Power BI/Excel
sensors	field gateway	Kafka	Service Fabrics	SQL Database/ Data warehouse	Portals & APIs
wearables		RabbitMQ	Storm	HDInsight/ Hadoop	Azure Search
apps and social		Active MQ	Spark	Data Lake	U-SQL
			Machine Learning		

FIGURE 13-1 IoT pipeline

Data generation and feedback

This component represents the vibrant ecosystem of devices. Any devices whose data can be collected remotely are included in this ecosystem, including but not limited to: mobile devices such as smartphones, laptops, and tablets; sensors such as thermometers, speedometers, microphones, and anemometers; and wearable devices such as watches, goggles, and health monitors.

From data's perspective, all these devices are sources of data. They constantly generate large amounts of data to be processed. So, most IoT solutions are designed to ingest, store, and analyze large amounts of data. People soon found out that these solutions can be used to handle massive data sources other than devices, such as social network feeds and system logs. This is why you see "apps and social" in this component.

In addition to generating data, some devices respond to remote commands, making them "smart" devices. For example, a smart drone can follow a predefined path to complete a tour. Often, this apparent smartness comes from a companion compute device or from the cloud. The path is calculated off the drone and is translated into a series of commands that maneuver the aircraft. Then, the commands are sent to the drone to be carried out, creating the illusion that the drone knows how to follow a path.

Command and control

Commonly, it is hard to collect data directly from devices. Devices are made by manufacturers around the world that build on different technical stacks, follow different specifications and standards, and use different communication protocols. Furthermore, just managing the sheer number of connections can be a challenging task.

This is where gateways come in. A field gateway connects to the devices by any means necessary such as by using direct connections, Wi-Fi networks, radio waves, and Bluetooth connections. It collects data from these devices and transmits the data to the cloud over the Internet. A gateway sometimes also serves as a protocol translator at application level that translates between the protocol the devices use and the protocol the cloud uses.

Some TCP/IP-enabled devices can be connected directly to a cloud-hosted gateway instead of a field gateway. A cloud gateway is easier to manage because it's often just a virtual machine or a virtual machine cluster running on the cloud. You don't need to deal with possible hardware and logistical problems managing a physical field gateway.

However, field gateways have a few advantages over cloud gateways. First, connections between field gateways and sensors usually are more stable. Second, field gateways can serve as a temporary data cache when the connection to the Internet is broken. A field gateway can keep collecting sensor data and forwards the accumulated data when the connection to the cloud is restored.

Cloud gateways, in contrast, provide scalable, available, and reliable data collection services. They provide additional features such as failover, throttling, and partitioning.

In addition to collecting and forwarding data, gateways dispatch commands back to the devices.

Data ingress

Before sensor data can be stored and analyzed, it needs to be ingested. In many cases, data is being generated at a much higher rate than it can be consumed. Most data ingress solutions use message queues to mask the speed difference. By using techniques such as the competing consumers pattern (see Chapter 7, "Scalability and performance"), queue partitioning, and dynamic aggregations, message processing can be sped up to keep up with the pace of data generation.

Figure 13-1 lists some of the popular data ingress solutions such as Apache Kafka, RabbitMQ, and ActiveMQ. In the same list, you can find the Azure IoT Hub, which is designed for fast, large-scale data ingress into Azure. IoT Hub is capable of taking in millions of messages per second via a proprietary protocol, HTTP, MQTT, or Advanced Message Queue Protocol (AMQP).

Data transformation and analysis

Once data is ingested into the cloud, interesting things happen. However, first the data packets need to be transformed into a format that the downstream components can understand. Data transformation can be as simple as adapting data formats or as complex as rearranging, splitting, merging, and even repackaging data packets.

The transformed data then is fed into analytics modules. There are two primary types of data analysis: streamed and batched. This is where Figure 13-1 becomes fuzzy. For batched analysis, data often is stored in permanent storages before it is analyzed, so in this case the "Transform and analysis" component and the "Storage" component should have been swapped. However, in the case of streamed analysis, data is analyzed directly off live data streams before it's stored. In fact, in many systems, data is forked and fed to both analytics modules and storage at the same time. So, the IoT pipeline is not necessarily sequential, and the order of the components may be changed as needed.

The streamed analysis also has two types: Event Stream Processing (ESP) and Complex Event Processing (CEP). ESP deals with processing streams of events trying to identify meaningful patterns. CEP is a subset of ESP that focuses on processing more complex events that often span multiple streamed events.

Streamed events usually are analyzed using a distributed compute grid such as Spark, Storm, and custom data processing units. Batched events often are analyzed by using query languages such as SQL or by using full-text indexes.

Storage

Depending on the nature of your data and expected usage patterns, you can choose from the following storage types:

- **Relational databases such as SQL Database**   Although you can save raw device data into a relational database, a relational database often is used to save analysis results for further queries from the presentation module.

- **Distributed file systems such as Hadoop Distributed File System (HDFS)**   Such file systems are optimized for storing large data files across machines in a large cluster and for sequential access, which is a common access pattern for processing streamed device data.

- **Big data databases such as Apache HBase and Azure Data Lake**   These databases are designed to store and recall massive amounts of data efficiently, and they are integrated with analytical components that can run queries and analysis directly on their data. So, they are not storage-only modules, but integrated modules with both storage and analysis capabilities.

- **Key-value storages such as Azure Table Storage and Blob Storage, Redis, and Azure DocumentDB**   These storages are used to save unstructured or semi-structured data. Data stored in these data stores can be retrieved easily by keys or key ranges. Advanced queries can be enabled by full-text search engines such as Azure Search and ElasticSearch. Azure DocumentDB also provides built-in query and ranking capabilities.

- **Cold storages such as Amazon Glacier, Azure Backup, tapes, and optical disks**   Data stored in these storages mostly is for archiving or compliance purposes. The data can't be accessed or queried easily, but the storage cost is low compared to other storage options.

Presentation and actions

In the simplest form, device data is presented on a monitoring portal for real-time monitoring and diagnostics. The monitor portal also displays aggregated data and additional intelligence from the analysis modules.

Analysis results also can be fed into data analysis tools such as Power BI and Excel for additional data mining. These results can be queried via means such as SQL queries, full-text searches, and natural-language queries.

Besides presenting data to end users, the presentation and actions modules generate controlling commands that can be fed back to devices through channels such as Azure IoT Hub. This closes the IoT data loop.

Scenarios and patterns

Service Fabric fits best into the data transformation and analysis module of the IoT data pipeline. This part of the chapter walks through the remote monitoring scenario and introduces a number of related patterns using Service Fabric.

Remote monitoring

Remote monitoring is the most common IoT scenario. In such scenarios, telemetry data from devices is collected, aggregated, and presented. Figure 13-2 shows a possible architecture for a remote monitoring scenario. The diagram shows that sensor data is collected by a field gateway and then forwarded to Azure IoT Hubs. Then, a service written in Service Fabric reads the data from the Event Hubs and writes it to a SQL Database. Finally, the SQL Database table is linked to Power BI for the final presentation.

Next, I'll introduce some patterns that can be applied in this scenario before I walk you through the end-to-end implementation.

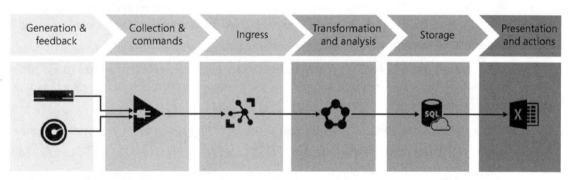

FIGURE 13-2 Remote monitoring

Pattern: Sensor Actor

Service Fabric Actor pattern provides a natural abstraction of sensors: each sensor can be encapsulated as a stateful sensor actor that holds the sensor's state. The Sensor Actor pattern is a simple pattern with some very interesting characteristics:

- **Quick, reliable state updates** Because the state of a sensor actor is saved locally, updating the state doesn't involve remote data storage calls. This means the state of a sensor can be saved quickly and reliably with the actor instance and is sent to permanent storage or analysis module at a lower speed. This helps reduce the workload of downstream services so that the whole system can keep up with sensor updates. For example, when monitoring a thermometer in a smart building, it's not necessary to track every reading from the thermometer. Instead, data can be saved every few seconds, minutes, or at longer intervals without impacting the quality of data.

- **Quick moving average**   A sensor actor can maintain a local history of sensor data and sends only moving averages to downstream services. Not only does moving average reduce the amount of data to be processed by the downstream services, it also refines data in certain scenarios. For example, readings from GPS sensors tend to drift, and moving average is a simple and effective way to alleviate the drifting effect.

- **Short history buffer**   This is another usage of locally cached sensor history in sensor actor states. In the case when a short trail of sensor data needs to be maintained, cached sensor history provides an easier and faster way to retrieve that data. For example, as a drone flies around, a short trail can be read directly from sensor actor state and displayed on a monitoring portal for users to observe sudden deviations from the planned route.

- **Easy recovery**   Because sensor actors virtually exist, if the transformation service crashes, it's not necessary to reinitiate actor instances explicitly. Once recovered, the service just uses these actors as if nothing has happened.

Figure 13-3 shows a possible design of a Sensor Actor. The actor stores last *n* readings of the corresponding sensor. A moving average is calculated as new readings come in. The sensor also contains a timer that periodically pushes sensor state to downstream services. The state also can be pulled by reading the actor state. The actor also contains other attributes that enable several interesting scenarios. Specifically, these attributes allow the actor to simulate some advanced behaviors that are not supported by "dumb" sensors.

- **Baud rate**   By modifying this attribute, downstream services can adjust how often the actor pushes out data. This simulates adjusting the baud rate of the physical sensor. Setting the value to zero disables the sensor feed.

- **Last update**   This attribute saves the time stamp of the last sensor event. This attribute can be used to detect if the physical sensor is still online.

- **Threshold**   This attribute (or a group of related attributes) defines the valid range of sensor readings.

- **Health state**   Health state can be inferred from the last update attribute (to detect if the sensor is still online) and the threshold attribute (to detect if the readings are within expected range).

- **Simulation**   This flag turns on or off a simulation mode, under which the actor sensor generates simulated sensor data for testing purposes.

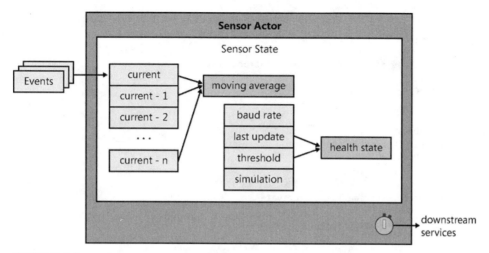

FIGURE 13-3 Sensor Actor

You'll see a sample implementation of Sensor Actor later in this chapter.

Pattern: Aggregators

An aggregator aggregates states from multiple sensor actors. For example, a floor actor aggregates all sensors on the same floor of a smart building. There can be multiple levels of aggregators. Continuing with the smart building example, a floor actor aggregates data from the sensor actors on the same floor, and a building actor aggregates data from all floors.

Sensor states can be aggregated in different ways. For example, sensor states can be pushed to an aggregator. Or, an aggregator can pull states from participating sensors.

Baseline   In the following walkthrough, you'll explore two ways of implementing aggregators. The walkthrough uses two types of actors: sensor actor and floor actor. The sensor actor states are pushed to the floor actor to calculate average values first. Then, you'll switch to pull mode and compare the performance difference.

1. Create a new Service Fabric application named *SensorAggregationApplication* with three stateful actors: *SensorActor*, *FloorActor*, and *GossipSensorActor*.

2. Modify the *ISensorActor* interface in the SensorActor.Interfaces project:

```
public interface ISensorActor : IActor
{
    Task<double> GetTemperatureAsync();
    Task SetTemperatureAsync(double temperature);
    Task<int> GetIndexAsync();
    Task SetIndexAsync(int index);
}
```

3. Modify the *SensorActor* class in the SensorActor project. The following code snippet shows only the updated code:

```
internal class SensorActor : StatefulActor<SensorActor.ActorState>, ISensorActor
{
    [DataContract]
    internal sealed class ActorState
    {
        [DataMember]
        public double Temperature { get; set; }
        [DataMember]
        public int Index { get; set; }
    }
    protected override Task OnActivateAsync()
    {
        if (this.State == null)
        {
            this.State = new ActorState { Temperature = 0 };
        }
        ...
    }
    [Readonly]
    Task<double> ISensorActor.GetTemperatureAsync()
    {
        ActorEventSource.Current.ActorMessage(this, "Getting current temperature value as
{0}", this.State.Temperature);
        return Task.FromResult(this.State.Temperature);
    }
    Task ISensorActor.SetTemperatureAsync(double temperature)
    {
        ActorEventSource.Current.ActorMessage(this, "Setting current temperature of value
to {0}", temperature);
        this.State.Temperature = temperature;   // Update the state
        ...
    }
    [Readonly]
    Task<int> ISensorActor.GetIndexAsync()
    {
        return Task.FromResult(this.State.Index);
    }
    Task ISensorActor.SetIndexAsync(int index)
    {
        this.State.Index = index;
        return Task.FromResult(true);
    }
}
```

4. Add a new console application named *SensorAggregationTest* to the solution. Change the project's target framework to .NET Framework 4.5.1 and its platform target to x64. Add a reference to the *Microsoft.ServiceFabric.Actors* NuGet package.

5. On the same console application, add references to these projects: FloorActor.Interfaces and SensorActor.Interfaces.

6. Modify the *Program* class under the SensorAggregationTest project to define a static *Random* variable:

```
static Random mRand = new Random();
```

7. Add two private methods to the *Program* class:

```
static void SetTemperatures(double average, double variation)
{
    Task[] tasks = new Task[1000];
    Parallel.For(0, 1000, i =>
    {
        var proxy = ActorProxy.Create<ISensorActor>(new ActorId(i),
        "fabric:/SensorAggregationApplication");
            tasks[i] = proxy.SetTemperatureAsync
(average + (mRand.NextDouble() -0.5) * 2 * variation);
    });
    Task.WaitAll(tasks);
}
static void SetIndexes()
{
  Task[] tasks = new Task[1000];
  Parallel.For(0, 1000, i =>
  {
var proxy = ActorProxy.Create<ISensorActor>(new ActorId(i),
    "fabric:/SensorAggregationApplication");
tasks[i] = proxy.SetIndexAsync(i);
  });
  Task.WaitAll(tasks);

}
```

8. Modify the *Main()* method to perform a basic test of setting temperatures on 1,000 sensor actors. There's no aggregation involved at this point, so the measured time will be our performance baseline.

```
SetIndexes();
Stopwatch watch = new Stopwatch();
watch.Start();
SetTemperatures(100, 50);
watch.Stop();
Console.WriteLine("Time to set temperatures: " + watch.ElapsedMilliseconds);
Console.ReadKey();
```

9. Deploy the Service Fabric application and launch the console application. On my laptop, it takes about three seconds to update the 1,000 sensors.

Push aggregation   Now, you'll modify the sensor actor to push its state to a corresponding floor actor for aggregation.

1. Modify the *IFloorActor* interface under the FloorActor.Insterfaces project:

```
public interface IFloorActor : IActor
{
```

```
      Task<double> GetTemperatureAsync();
      Task SetTemperatureAsync(int index, double temperature);
}
```

2. Modify the *FloorActor* class under the FloorActor project. The actor uses an array to store readings from individual sensors, and it calculates the array average on the fly when queried.

```
internal class FloorActor : StatefulActor<FloorActor.ActorState>, IFloorActor
{
  [DataContract]
  internal sealed class ActorState
  {
    [DataMember]
    public double[] Temperature { get; set; }
    ...
  }
  protected override Task OnActivateAsync()
  {
    if (this.State == null)
    {
        this.State = new ActorState { Temperature = new double[1000] };
    }
    ...
  }
  [Readonly]
  Task<double> IFloorActor.GetTemperatureAsync()
  {
    ...
    return Task.FromResult(this.State.Temperature.Average());
  }
  Task IFloorActor.SetTemperatureAsync(int index, double temperature)
  {
    this.State.Temperature[index] = temperature;
    return Task.FromResult(true);
  }
}
```

3. Now, modify the sensor actor to push state updates to the floor actor. Note that in the code, I'm using a fixed floor id (2016), which means all 1,000 sensor actors are connected to the same floor actor instance.

```
private double mTemerature = 0.0;
[DataMember]
public double Temperature
{
    get { return mTemerature; }
    set
    {
        mTemerature = value;
        var proxy = ActorProxy.Create<IFloorActor>
            (new ActorId(2016), "fabric:/SensorAggregationApplication");
        proxy.SetTemperatureAsync(Index, mTemerature);
    }
}
```

4. Finally, modify the *Main()* method of the test client to read back the average value:

```
SetIndexes();
Stopwatch watch = new Stopwatch();
watch.Start();
SetTemperatures(100, 50);
watch.Stop();
Console.WriteLine("Time to set temperatures: " + watch.ElapsedMilliseconds);
watch.Start();
var proxy = ActorProxy.Create<IFloorActor>
    (new ActorId(2016), "fabric:/SensorAggregationApplication");
Console.WriteLine("Average temperature: " + proxy.GetTemperatureAsync().Result);
watch.Stop();
Console.WriteLine("Time to get average temperature: " + watch.ElapsedMilliseconds);
Console.ReadKey();
```

5. Redeploy the Service Fabric application and launch the test client. This time, the client runs much more slowly. On my laptop, the aggregation is returned after 30 to 40 seconds.

This is unacceptable performance. The reason for the performance degradation is the turn-based concurrency of actors. When many sensor actors call into the same floor actor instance, the calls are queued up and handled sequentially. Although when the sensor actor reports the state, it doesn't wait for the asynchronous task to complete, when the aggregation is calculated, the *Array.Average()* call happens only when all previously queued requests have been handled.

Pull aggregation   To avoid the floor actor being called by all the sensor actors, you can have the floor actor pull from sensor actors instead. The main difference between the pull mode and the push mode is that when the floor actor pulls, it can pull all sensor actors in parallel.

1. Change the *SensorActor* implementation to revert the Temperature state to a simple data member:

```
[DataMember]
public double Temperature
{
    get; set;
}
```

2. Modify the *IFloorActor* interface to remove the method for sensor actors to report states because the floor will be pulling:

```
public interface IFloorActor : IActor
{
    Task<double> GetTemperatureAsync();
}
```

3. Now, instead of a double array, the floor actor can use a simple Temperature state:

```
[DataContract]
internal sealed class ActorState
{
    [DataMember]
```

```
                public double Temperature { get; set; }

    }

4.  Last, implement the GetTemperatureAsync() method:

    [Readonly]
    Task<double> IFloorActor.GetTemperatureAsync()
    {
        Task<double>[] tasks = new Task<double>[1000];
        double[] readings = new double[1000];
        Parallel.For(0, 1000, i =>
        {
            var proxy = ActorProxy.Create<ISensorActor>
    (new ActorId(i), "fabric:/SensorAggregationApplication");
            tasks[i] = proxy.GetTemperatureAsync();
        });
        Task.WaitAll(tasks);
        Parallel.For(0, 1000, i =>
        {
            readings[i] = tasks[i].Result;
        });
        return Task.FromResult(readings.Average());
    }
```

5. Publish the application and launch the test client again. The performance should be much better this time. On my laptop, I observed only moderate overhead compared to the no-aggregation baseline.

There also are algorithms that allow self-organized aggregations among actors with a gossip protocol[1]. A detailed description of gossip protocol is out of the scope of this book. Simply put, the protocol works much like the spread of an epidemic. Each node randomly communicates with a few neighboring nodes to gossip and estimates the aggregated value based on the gossips it receives. The estimations converge quickly on the actual aggregations.

End-to-end scenario

As mentioned at the beginning of this chapter, an IoT solution consists of a complete data pipeline. The following walkthrough shows you how to use Service Fabric and related Azure services to build an end-to-end remote monitoring scenario. You'll use a simulated field gateway to generate simulated device data. The data is sent to IoT Hub and then picked up by a Service Fabric service. The service writes the data to an Azure SQL Database. Finally, the database is connected to Power BI for presentation.

Event ingress Azure provides two services for data ingress: Event Hubs and IoT Hubs, with IoT Hubs being the newer and preferred service to use. This part of the walkthrough shows you how to provision a new IoT Hub using Microsoft Azure management portal.

1. Sign in to Microsoft Azure management portal.

---

[1] David Kempe, Alin Dobra, and Johannes Gehrke. 2003. "Gossip-Based Computation of Aggregate Information." *44th Annual IEEE Symposium on Foundations of Computer Science (FOCS).* 482–491.

2. Click the New link at the upper-left corner. Then, in the New blade, type **Azure IoT Hub** in the search box and press Enter to search for the resource type.

3. In the search result, click the Azure IoT Hub link.

4. On the Azure IoT Hub blade, click Create.

5. On the IoT Hub blade, enter a name for the new IoT Hub. Create a new resource group and pick a location. Leave other fields at default values, as shown in Figure 13-4. Then, click Create to create the IoT Hub.

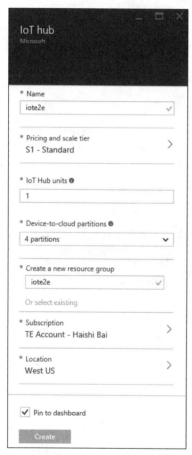

FIGURE 13-4 Creating an IoT Hub

6. Once the Hub is created, its summary blade opens. Note the Hub's host name and then click the Keys link, as shown in Figure 13-5.

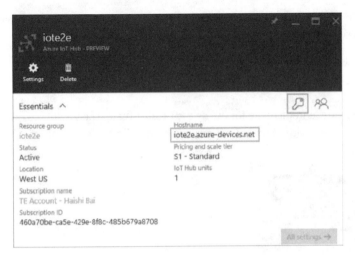

FIGURE 13-5 IoT Hub summary blade

7. On the Shared Access Policies tab, click the Iothubowner policy. This policy has permissions to all operations. Then, on the Iothubowner tab to the right, click the Copy icon to copy the connection string with the primary key, as shown in Figure 13-6. The connection string has the format of HostName=*[IoT Hub Name]*.azure-devices.net;SharedAccessKeyName=iothubowner; SharedAccessKey=*[Key]*.

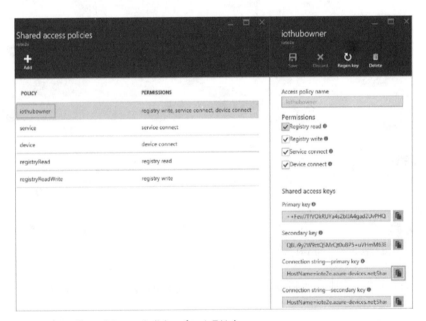

FIGURE 13-6 Shared Access Policies of an IoT Hub

Register a device IoT Hub has a device registry you can use to register devices. Once a device is registered, you gain access to per-device resources such as a message queue and a device endpoint.

At the time of this writing, there is not yet a UI to register a device because in most cases, you want a scriptable way to provision a number of devices. In this part of the walkthrough, you'll create a console application that registers a single device. You can use the code as the base of a registration program that registers multiple devices.

1. Create a new console application named DeviceRegistry. Put the application in an IoTE2E solution, which will hold all projects for this walkthrough.

2. Add a reference to the Microsoft.Azure.Devices NuGet package.

3. Add the following using statement to *Program.cs*:

   ```
   using Microsoft.Azure.Devices;
   ```

4. Modify the *Main()* method to register a device named DemoDevice and get its primary access key. You need to replace the *[connection string]* with the connection string you copied from the previous section. Note that this method can be executed successfully only once. If you try to run the code multiple times, you'll receive a DeviceAlreadyExistsException exception indicating the device already exists. For existing devices, you can use the *GetDeviceAsync* method of *RegisterManager* to get their information.

   ```
   RegistryManager registryManager =
       RegistryManager.CreateFromConnectionString("[connection string]");
   string deviceId = "DemoDevice";
   var device = registryManager.AddDeviceAsync(new Device(deviceId)).Result;
   Console.WriteLine("Device Key: " + device.Authentication.SymmetricKey.PrimaryKey);
   ```

5. Build the solution and launch the console application without debugger. Copy the generated key. It looks something like this: *m9SYbvBW0N+aXAbnhBgB5627vq1ix5NvU8Ri0/RqJ5Q=*.

Simulate device data   Next, you'll create another console application to generate simulated device data. Architecturally, this console application simulates a field gateway that collects and forwards device data to IoT Hub.

1. Add console application named SimulatedGateway to the IoTE2E solution.

2. Add a reference to the Microsoft.Azure.Devices.Client NuGet package, which pulls down Microsoft Azure Devices Client SDK.

3. Add the following using statements to *Program.cs*:

   ```
   using Microsoft.Azure.Devices.Client;
   using Newtonsoft.Json;
   using System.Text;
   using System.Threading;
   ```

4. Modify the *Main()* method to generate simulated sensor data every second. You need to replace *[Iot Hub Name]* with your IoT Hub name and *[your key]* with your device key. The messages you send to IoT Hub are serialized JSON objects with fields of your choice.

   ```
   string iotHostName = "[IoT Hub name].azure-devices.net";
   ```

```
string deviceId = "DemoDevice";
string deviceKey = "[your key]";
Random rand = new Random();
var deviceClient = DeviceClient.Create(iotHostName, new DeviceAuthenticationWithRegistryS
ymmetricKey(deviceId, deviceKey));
while (true)
{
    double temperature = rand.NextDouble() * 100;
    var temperatureData = new
    {
        deviceId = deviceId,
        temperature = temperature
    };
var message = new Message(Encoding.ASCII.GetBytes
(JsonConvert.SerializeObject(temperatureData)));
    deviceClient.SendEventAsync(message).Wait();
    Console.Write(".");
    Thread.Sleep(1000);
}
```

5. Build and launch the program. If everything goes well, you should see a new dot appearing on the console window every second. Press Ctrl+C to stop the program.

Define device data storage   Next, you'll provision an Azure SQL Database for storing sensor data.

1. Sign in to Microsoft Azure management portal.

2. Click the New link at the upper-left corner of the home page and then select SQL Database under the Data + Storage category.

3. On the SQL Database blade, enter a name for the database, such as **iote2e**.

4. Click the Server link and then click the Create A New Server link to create a new SQL Database server. Enter a name, administrator user name, and password for the new server and then click OK to create the new server, as shown in Figure 13-7.

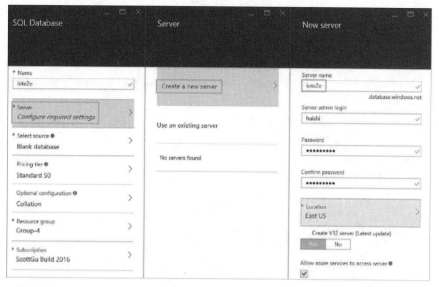

FIGURE 13-7 Create new SQL Database server

5. On the SQL Database blade, choose the resource group you've created in the previous section and click Create to create the database.

6. Once the database is created, click the server name link to open the corresponding SQL Database server.

7. By default, the server firewall disallows any client connections (except for connections made from other Azure services). You have to allow your client IP addresses explicitly before you can connect to the database from your machine. On the SQL Database server blade, click the Show Firewall Settings link. Then, on the Firewall Settings blade, click the Add Client IP icon to add your machine's IP address to the allowed IP ranges. Click the Save icon.

FIGURE 13-8 Set up SQL Server Firewall rules

8. Return to the SQL Database Server blade. Click the Tools icon on its summary blade and then click the Open In Visual Studio link.

9. On the Open In Visual Studio blade, click Open In Visual Studio. This launches Visual Studio.

10. When prompted, sign in using your database credential.

11. In SQL Server Object Explorer, expand the database node. Right-click the Tables node and select the Add New Table menu to create a new table to hold the sensor data, as shown in Figure 13-9.

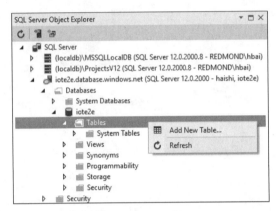

FIGURE 13-9 SQL Server Object Explorer

12. Define four settings: Id (bigint, auto-increment identity), SensorId (nvarchar50), Temperature (float), and Timestamp (datetime). Modify the T-SQL statement to change the table name to **Sensors**. Update the Id column definition to add **IDENTITY(1,1)**. Then, click Update, as shown in Figure 13-10.

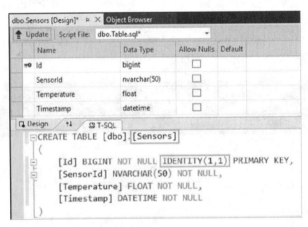

FIGURE 13-10 Table definition

13. On the Preview Database Update dialog box, click the Update Database button.

Save sensor data Next, you'll create a stateful Service Fabric service to read sensor data from IoT Hub and save it to SQL Database.

As a scaling mechanism, IoT Hub supports a concept named device-to-cloud partition (see Figure 13-4), which allows the message pipeline to be split into multiple partitions that can be handled in parallel. Each partition is supposed to have only one active reader. This requires your service partitions to match the IoT Hub configurations. This is problematic because keeping two systems in sync is always troublesome. One way to handle this problem is to use a centralized manager that manages service partitions automatically. In the following exercise, you'll explore a different option that uses a leasing manager actor. When a service partition launches, it first requests a lease on an IoT Hub partition from the leasing manager. If it can't acquire a lease, it will try again later. If it acquires a lease, it periodically will renew the lease with the leasing manager. Otherwise, the lease will be released after a certain time-out.

By using the leasing manager, your Service Fabric service should be configured with enough partitions to cover possible IoT Hub partitions, which can be as many as 32. If the IoT Hub has fewer partitions, some of the Service Fabric service partitions will be mostly idle except for trying to acquire a lease once in a while. Partitions with leases will be processing messages from corresponding IoT Hub partitions. If a partition fails, its lease will expire, and the IoT Hub partition can be picked up by a different Service Fabric partition.

1. Open the IoTE2E solution. Add a new Service Fabric application named SensorDataProcessorApplication with a stateful service named SensorDataProcessor and a stateful actor named IoTHubParitionMap.

2. Modify the *IIoTHubPartitionMap* interface in the IoTHubPartitionMap.Interfaces project. The interface contains two methods: the *LeaseIoTHubPartitionAsync* method is to acquire a lease on an IoT Hub partition, and the *RenewIoTHubPartitionLeaseAsync* method is to renew a lease.

```
public interface IIoTHubPartitionMap : IActor
{
    Task<string> LeaseTHubPartitionAsync();
    Task<string> RenewIoTHubPartitionLeaseAsync(string partition);
}
```

3. In the IoTHubPartitionMap project, add a reference to the WindowsAzure.ServiceBus NuGet package.

4. Modify the *IotHubPartitionMap* class as the following code snippet. When the actor is activated, it uses an EventHubClient to connect to the IoT Hub and reads all the Hub's partitions. The partition names are saved in the actor's state. The actor's state also contains a dictionary of leases. When a lease is acquired, the corresponding IoT Hub partition name is added to the dictionary with a time stamp. The time stamp is renewed when the lease is renewed. The actor has a timer that periodically checks for and removes expired leases.

```
internal class IoTHubParitionMap : StatefulActor<IoTHubParitionMap.ActorState>,
IIoTHubPartitionMap
{
    IActorTimer mTimer;
    [DataContract]
    internal sealed class ActorState
    {
```

```csharp
            [DataMember]
            public List<string> PartitionNames { get; set; }
            [DataMember]
            public Dictionary<string, DateTime> PartitionLeases { get; set; }
        }
        protected override Task OnActivateAsync()
        {
            if (this.State == null)
            {
                this.State = new ActorState { PartitionNames = new List<string>(),
PartitionLeases = new Dictionary<string, DateTime>() };
                ResetPartitionNames();
                mTimer = RegisterTimer(CheckLease, null,
TimeSpan.FromSeconds(30), TimeSpan.FromSeconds(30));
            }
            return Task.FromResult(true);
        }
        private Task CheckLease(Object state)
        {
            List<string> keys = this.State.PartitionLeases.Keys.ToList();
            foreach(string key in keys)
            {
                if (DateTime.Now - this.State.PartitionLeases[key] >= TimeSpan.
FromSeconds(60))
                    this.State.PartitionLeases.Remove(key);
            }
            return Task.FromResult(1);
        }
        protected override Task OnDeactivateAsync()
        {
            if (mTimer != null)
                UnregisterTimer(mTimer);
            return base.OnDeactivateAsync();
        }
        Task<string> IIoTHubPartitionMap.LeaseTHubPartitionAsync()
        {
            string ret = "";
            foreach(string partition in this.State.PartitionNames)
            {
                if (!this.State.PartitionLeases.ContainsKey(partition))
                {
                    this.State.PartitionLeases.Add(partition, DateTime.Now);
                    ret = partition;
                    break;
                }
            }
            return Task.FromResult(ret);
        }
        Task<string> IIoTHubPartitionMap.RenewIoTHubPartitionLeaseAsync(string partition)
        {
            string ret = "";
            if (this.State.PartitionLeases.ContainsKey(partition))
            {
                this.State.PartitionLeases[partition] = DateTime.Now;
                ret = partition;
            }
            return Task.FromResult(ret);
```

```
        }
        void ResetPartitionNames()
        {
            var eventHubClient = EventHubClient.CreateFromConnectionString
    ("[IoT Hub connection string]", "messages/events");
            var partitions = eventHubClient.GetRuntimeInformation().PartitionIds;
            foreach (string partition in partitions)
            {
                this.State.PartitionNames.Add(partition);
            }
        }
    }
```

5. In the SensordataProcess project, add a reference to the Microsoft.ServiceFabric.Actors NuGet package and a reference to the WindowsAzure.ServiceBus NuGet package.

6. In the same project, add a reference to the IoTHubPartitionMap.Interfaces project.

7. Before writing data to SQL Database, implement a version that writes messages to the event data source. Override the *RunAsync* method of the *SensorDataProcessor*. The method tries to acquire a lease first. If a lease is acquired, it starts to read messages from the partition and writes the messages to the event source. It also renews the lease on the IoT Hub every 20 seconds. If a lease can't be acquired, it tries again in 15 seconds.

```
protected override async Task RunAsync(CancellationToken cancelServicePartitionReplica)
{
var proxy = ActorProxy.Create<IIoTHubPartitionMap>(new ActorId(1),
        "fabric:/SensorDataProcessorApplication");
var eventHubClient = EventHubClient.CreateFromConnectionString
("[IoT Hub connection string]", "messages/events");
    DateTime timeStamp = DateTime.Now;
    while (!cancelServicePartitionReplica.IsCancellationRequested)
    {
        string partition = proxy.LeaseTHubPartitionAsync().Result;
        if (partition == "")
            await Task.Delay(TimeSpan.FromSeconds(15), cancelServicePartitionReplica);
        else
        {
            var eventHubReceiver = eventHubClient.GetDefaultConsumerGroup().
CreateReceiver(partition, DateTime.UtcNow);
            while (!cancelServicePartitionReplica.IsCancellationRequested)
            {
                EventData eventData = await eventHubReceiver.ReceiveAsync();
                if (eventData != null)
                {
                    string data = Encoding.UTF8.GetString(eventData.GetBytes());
                    ServiceEventSource.Current.ServiceMessage(this, "Message: {0}",
data);
                }
                if (DateTime.Now - timeStamp > TimeSpan.FromSeconds(20))
                {
                    string lease = proxy.RenewIoTHubPartitionLeaseAsync(partition).
Result;
                    if (lease == "")
                        break;
```

```
            }
          }
        }
      }
    }
```

8. Modify the ApplicationManifest.xml under the SensorDataProcessorApplication project. The following snippet sets up the sensor processor service to use 32 partitions, which is the largest number of partitions supported by a single IoT Hub. You can configure it to use fewer partitions to avoid many idle partitions, but your service will need to be upgraded if you need more partitions later.

```
<Service Name="SensorDataProcessor">
<StatefulService ServiceTypeName="SensorDataProcessorType"
TargetReplicaSetSize="3" MinReplicaSetSize="2">
    <UniformInt64Partition PartitionCount="32" LowKey="0" HighKey="31" />
  </StatefulService>
</Service>
```

9. Deploy the Service Fabric application. Launch the SimulatedGateway again. You should see simulated device messages displayed in the Diagnostic Event Viewer, as shown in Figure 13-11.

```
00:10:11.305  ServiceMessage                    Message: {"deviceId":"DemoDevice","temperature":14.494226739972005}
{
  "Timestamp": "2016-02-14T00:10:11.3058528-08:00",
  "ProviderName": "MyCompany-SensorDataProcessorApplication-SensorDataProcessor",
  "Id": 2,
  "Message": "Message: {\"deviceId\":\"DemoDevice\",\"temperature\":14.494226739972005}",
  "ProcessId": 6784,
  "Level": "Informational",
  "Keywords": "0x0000F00000000000",
  "EventName": "ServiceMessage",
  "Payload": {
    "serviceName": "fabric:/SensorDataProcessorApplication/SensorDataProcessor",
    "serviceTypeName": "SensorDataProcessorType",
    "replicaOrInstanceId": 130999109585249607,
    "partitionId": "c1f1a361-2839-42b6-ad06-654b67592bb0",
    "applicationName": "fabric:/SensorDataProcessorApplication",
    "applicationTypeName": "SensorDataProcessorApplicationType",
    "nodeName": "Node.1",
    "message": "Message: {\"deviceId\":\"DemoDevice\",\"temperature\":14.494226739972005}"
  }
}
```

FIGURE 13-11 Service message in Diagnostics Event Viewer

10. Now, let's write the data to SQL Database. First, get the connection string to the database. To get the connection string, click the Show Database Connection Strings link to reveal connection strings in several popular formats. Copy the ADO.NET connection string, as shown in Figure 13-12.

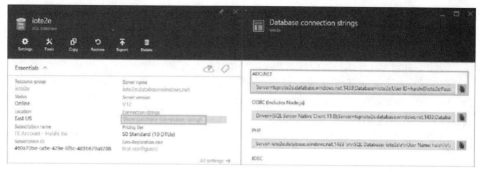

FIGURE 13-12 SQL Database connection string

11. In the SensorDataProcessor project, add a reference to the *System.Data* assembly.

12. Add the following private class to the *SensorDataProcessor* class. This class is used to represent a sensor message.

```
private class SensorPackage
{
    public string DeviceId { get; set; }
    public double Temperature { get; set; }
}
```

13. Define a new private *InsertRecord* method on the *SensorDataProcessor* class. The code directly uses a SQL INSERT statement to add the record and writes the generated record id to the event source.

```
private void InsertRecord(string data)
{
    var obj = JsonConvert.DeserializeObject<SensorPackage>(data);
    using (var conn = new SqlConnection("[SQL connection string]"))
    {
        var cmd = conn.CreateCommand();
        cmd.CommandText = @"
        INSERT dbo.Sensors (SensorId, Temperature, Timestamp)
        OUTPUT INSERTED.Id
        VALUES (@SensorId, @Temperature, @Timestamp)";

        cmd.Parameters.AddWithValue("@SensorId", obj.DeviceId);
        cmd.Parameters.AddWithValue("@Temperature", obj.Temperature);
        cmd.Parameters.AddWithValue("@Timestamp", DateTime.Now);
        conn.Open();
        long insertedId = (long)cmd.ExecuteScalar();
        ServiceEventSource.Current.ServiceMessage
(this, "Records ID {0} inserted.", insertedId);
    }
}
```

14. Redeploy the Service Fabric application. Launch the simulated gateway again. In a moment, you should see records inserted into the SQL Database table. To view table records, right-click the Sensors table in the SQL Server Object Explorer and select the View Data menu.

Other options

As introduced at the beginning of this chapter, Microsoft Azure provides a wide range of options for building an IoT data pipeline. In a simple scenario like this, instead of writing your own data processing unit, you can use a service like Azure Stream Analytics that has built-in integration with IoT Hub and SQL Database (and other services). You want to use Service Fabric to write your processing logic only when a complex scenario can't be implemented using out-of-box features. You'll see a couple of streaming samples in Chapter 14, "Real-time data streaming."

Monitor sensor data   As the last piece of the puzzle, you'll use Power BI to monitor the live sensor data. Power BI is Microsoft's interactive data visualization BI tools. You can access Power BI or get a free trial at *https://powerbi.microsoft.com/*.

1. Sign in to Power BI.

2. On your workspace home page, click the arrow icon at the lower-left corner, as shown in Figure 13-13.

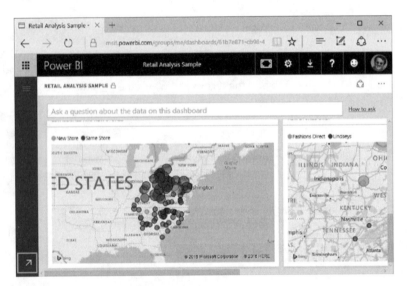

FIGURE 13-13 Power BI workspace page

3. On the Get Data page, click the Get Link On The Databases tile.

4. On the next page, click the Azure SQL Database tile and then click the Connect button.

5. When prompted, follow the connection wizard to connect to your database.

6. Once the connection is established, click the Go To Your Dashboard button to open a new empty dashboard with a single Azure SQL Database tile.

7. Click the Azure SQL Database tile.

8. In the Fields pane, expand the Sensors table and select the Temperature and Timestamp check boxes. Then, in the Visualizations pane, select the Line Chart type. Click Save to save the chart, as shown in Figure 13-14. When prompted, enter a name for the report. This gives you a report with a line chart of the sensor temperature. In this case, you only have one sensor, so this works fine. If you have multiple sensors writing to the same table, you can set up the *SensorId* as a group field to have multiple lines representing different sensors in the same chart.

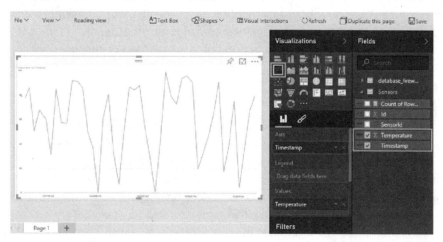

FIGURE 13-14 Power BI chart definition

This concludes the end-to-end scenario. This scenario has included the bare minimum to get some data pumped through the entire IoT pipeline. In an actual implementation, a lot more needs to be considered, such as ensuring data security and communication security, automatically refreshing the Power BI view, using a sensor actor to encapsulate sensor state and behaviors, using data storage options other than SQL Database, and using built-in services such as Azure Stream Analysis. I'll leave these exercises to interested readers.

Other scenarios

The size of this book doesn't allow more detailed discussions on other scenarios. The following are two other typical IoT scenario types for your reference.

Command and Control

In a Command and Control scenario, data flows in both directions. In one direction, data from devices is collected, stored, and analyzed on the cloud. In the opposite direction, commands generated by the cloud are sent back to devices to change device behaviors. For example, in a smart building, room temperatures are collected to the cloud, which analyzes how the values change during the day and sends back appropriate commands to the air conditioning system to adjust temperatures.

In some scenarios, a field gateway receives commands on the device's behalf and ensures the commands are delivered to the device. For example, a field gateway can subscribe to IoT Hub events and then forward the messages to corresponding devices. The gateway also can serve as a safeguard against invalid or dangerous commands. The gateway has the most up-to-date states of the attached devices. In contrast, the state used by the cloud to make decisions might be out of date due to network and application-level delays. So, it's possible that a cloud sends a command that can't be—or shouldn't be—applied. The field gateway can filter out these commands.

Some IoT systems generate notifications to end users or other applications. For example, in a proactive maintenance scenario, an email notification is generated when the sensor reading exceeds a certain threshold. You should distinguish these scenarios from the Command and Control scenarios because the notifications are not sent to devices but to human users or integrated applications and services.

Device orchestration

The collaboration between the cloud and devices is where IoT really shines. By correlating data collected from different sensors, the cloud can gain tremendous insight into the physical environment. For example, by collecting weather station data from different geographic locations, a cloud application can recognize and trace weather systems such as storms and hurricanes. And by accumulating and analyzing historical data, the application can understand how climate changes at the global level. Another example of device collaboration is that some nanostructured devices are not designed to work by themselves. Instead, they are activated by an external energy source, transmit short data packets, and return to hibernation. Their tiny size allows them to be deployed to difficult-to-access places such as deserts, bodies of water, or even under our skins. The individual data points they offer don't mean much when viewed in isolation. However, when they are combined, remarkable insights emerge.

The cloud possesses tremendous compute power, and devices make the power relevant to our physical world by providing real-life contexts to computing. Launching a compute process no longer is an explicit action with computers. Instead, the boundary between the physical world and the abstract compute world is blurred. For example, some of us are used to the real traffic updates on our GPS systems without realizing the continuous data collection, analysis, and sharing behind the scenes. Without any extra effort from us, our GPS systems become more informative, our cars become smarter, and we become more efficient drivers.

Managing a large number of devices could be challenging. The challenges reside not only in the areas of device identification, authentication, and communication, but also in maintaining security and integration of the entire system. For example, by introducing compromised devices into the system, a hacker can pollute the data collected by the cloud and trick the cloud into making inaccurate or even wrong decisions. For example, an artificial traffic jam could be created by injecting faulty traffic data into the system, leading to incorrect route calculations. With many devices deployed, an IoT system has a huge attacking surface that has to be protected. So, security should be an integral part of any IoT solution in production. This includes reliable device authentication, secured communication channels, data encryption over the wire and at rest, abnormality detection, data signature checks, and other protections against malicious attacks.

Additional information

As you can see from this chapter, a complete IoT solution contains many interleaved pieces. To help you manage the entire IoT pipeline, Microsoft provides an Azure IoT Suite service that allows you to bootstrap your IoT projects quickly with prebuilt solutions such as remote monitoring and proactive maintenance. To learn more about Iot Suite, please visit *https://azure.microsoft.com/solutions /iot-suite/.*

There are a number of protocols that standardize IoT communications for different industry verticals. For example, Open Platform Communication (OPC) is an interoperability designed for secured communications in industrial automation spaces and other industry verticals. For more information on OPC, visit *https://opcfoundation.org/.*

CHAPTER 14

Real-time data streaming

Real-time data streaming handles a continuous stream of data and performs real-time analyses. It's required in a wide range of scenarios that need instantaneous responses to data patterns, including trading, monitoring, fraud and abnormality detection, risk management, and fleet management.

Real-time data streaming is one of the most demanding compute scenarios because it needs high throughput, high performance, and usually high scalability at the same time. Although there are many techniques to improve on one of the areas, they often require sacrifices in other areas. A practical real-time data streaming system often is the result of tradeoffs and rebalancing to achieve key performance goals. This chapter provides some guidance and patterns that could help you design your own real-time data streaming solutions.

The chapter is structured in the same way previous patterns and scenarios chapters are organized: First, it reviews the real-time data streaming options on Azure and presents how Service Fabric fits into the big picture. Then, it covers a couple of data streaming scenarios with several reusable patterns.

Real-time data streaming on Azure

Real-time data streaming often is studied in the context of big data. Before digging into real-time data streaming, let's review characteristics of big data and related Azure services.

Five Vs of big data

There are five characteristics, commonly known as Five Vs[1], of big data:

- **Volume** is where the name *big data* comes from. Big data handles a vast amount of data, especially the massive digital footprints generated by many connected devices and services every second. Before big data, studying a universe usually needed careful sampling of data before reliable conclusions could be drawn. Big data takes a different approach. Instead of sampling data, it gulps every possible data point it can find and uses massive parallel compute to gain insights into the data.

---

[1]   Martin Hilbert. 2015. "Digital Technology & Social Change (online course)." *YouTube*. 8 15. Accessed Feb. 15, 2016. *https://www.youtube.com/playlist?list=PLtjBSCvWCU3rNm46D3R85efM0hrzjuAIg*.

- **Velocity** refers to both the speed of data moving across the system and the timeliness of conclusions. This is where real-time data streaming comes into play. Real-time data streaming eliminates all intermediaries and works directly with the input data stream. The goal is to move data across the system as quickly as possible and draw immediate conclusions based on live data. For example, a system that monitors abnormalities in sensor readings has to be able to keep up with data generation so that it can produce prompt notifications when something bad happens. Any significant delays will render the system unusable.

  Real-time data streaming can reduce the amount of data to be processed further by dynamic aggregation, filtering, duplication removal, feature abstraction, and sampling. You'll see several of these techniques later in this chapter.

- **Variety** refers to the different types of data. Modern big data systems can harness a great variety of data types, including structured data, unstructured data, text data, and binary data. This requires a big data system to be able to connect to different types of data sources and to efficiently analyze, store, and transmit all kinds of data objects.

- **Veracity** refers to the authenticity, accuracy, and reliability of data. In modern big data systems, the requirements for data accuracy and reliability often are relaxed. In many cases, the data flowing into a big data system is incomplete or inaccurate. By applying data mining techniques such as clustering and neural networks, accurate conclusions still can be drawn reliably.

  Data authenticity, in contrast, needs to be ensured. Most big data solutions run unattended. If the data source is polluted, the behavior of the system can be manipulated in harmful ways. Such attacks on data sources are hard to detect. First, when the attack happens, the system still runs normally. There are no exceptions to catch and no abnormalities in system traffic to observe. The system just generates invalid results because of the faulty inputs. Second, in a complex system, there isn't an easy way to verify the outputs independently. For example, faulty inputs can be pumped into a Machine Learning module to generate false positives or false negatives. Because a productionized Machine Learning is expected to make correct judgments, such attacks easily can slip through without being noticed.

- **Value** refers to how much value can be derived from the data. This is the ultimate goal of big data. In some big data solutions, great insights are derived from the data but not put to practical use. Insights that generate no return have no value. Gaining such insights is a waste of time and money. So, before you start your big data project, be clear about your end goals. In many cases, a big data project is an exploratory process, which may present unexpected patterns and insights. You'll have to evaluate each of the outcomes, pick the ones that generate actual returns, and focus your efforts on those outcomes.

Azure Stream Analytics

Azure Stream Analytics (ASA) is a hosted real-time processing service with high reliability and scalability. It's capable of handling millions of events per second. And it's able to correlate multiple streams of data to gain additional insights.

Azure Stream Analytics jobs

When you use Azure Stream Analytics, you define an ASA job that takes in a number of input streams and generates a number of outputs. Stream Analytics has built-in support of a large number of input data sources and output sinks, as shown in Figure 14-1. An ASA job can also take in relatively static reference data to enrich live data streams. For example, a postal code reference data source can be used to map geographic locations to corresponding postal codes.

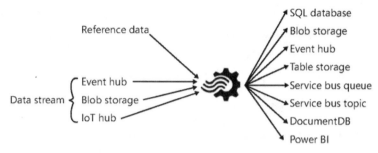

FIGURE 14-1 Stream Analytics job topology

ASA queries

Regardless of the variety of data sources and data sinks, Stream Analytics provides an easy-to-use SQL-like query language that allows you to query across multiple data sources and generate outputs. For example, the following query (from *https://azure.microsoft.com/documentation/articles/stream-analytics-stream-analytics-query-patterns/*) sums up car weights by a tumbling window of 10 seconds.

```
SELECT
    Make,
    SUM(CAST(Weight AS BIGINT)) AS Weight
FROM
    Input TIMESTAMP BY Time
GROUP BY
    Make,
TumblingWindow(second, 10)
```

Service Fabric and Stream Analytics integration

A detailed introduction to Azure Stream Analytics is out of the scope of the book. However, one question must be addressed: If Stream Analytics is designed for real-time data analysis, why do we need Service Fabric? The answer is customization. Stream Analytics supports data analysis and manipulation only via the query language. If you want to run complex business logics on the stream data, you can put the business logics into a Service Fabric service.

Although it's possible that Stream Analytics will support arbitrary web services as input sources and output sinks in the future, such direct integrations don't exist at the time of this writing. However, this doesn't mean you can't use Service Fabric with Azure Stream Analytics. For example, you can use IoT Hub or Event Hub as a message bus to integrate Service Fabric and Stream Analytics into a complete pipeline, as shown in Figure 14-2.

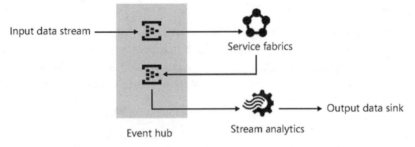

Input data stream

Service fabrics

Event hub

Stream analytics

Output data sink

FIGURE 14-2 Service Fabrics and Stream Analytics integration

The integration path also works in the other direction: the data stream can flow into Stream Analytics before it's forwarded to Service Fabric services.

> ### Extending ASA with Microsoft Azure Functions
>
> Microsoft Azure Functions, which is in preview at the time of this writing, provides an easy and powerful way to extend ASA queries. You can author user-defined functions (UDFs) using Azure Functions and use these UDFs directly in your ASA queries. Furthermore, because hosting of Azure Functions is handled automatically for you, you don't need to worry about managing your service clusters when you use Azure Functions. I recommend using Azure Functions for custom processing when possible and using Service Fabric when you have complex extension services.

Big data storages

When it comes to data storages, Azure provides a number of options. Each storage option is designed for different scenarios and is optimized to manage different types of data. Because all storage options are designed with high performance and high scalability in mind, all of them are viable candidates for short-term or long-term big data storages.

Azure SQL Database

Azure SQL Database is a hosted relational database with high compatibility with Microsoft SQL Server. You can use familiar tools, frameworks, SQL queries, and programming languages to operate SQL Database just like if you were operating a SQL Server database. In other words, you can enjoy the powerful features of SQL Server without the burden of managing database servers.

In 2015, Azure SQL Database introduced the Elastic Database feature that allows you to shard your database for scalability. The feature is useful in continuous data collection scenarios. For example, a new shard can be created for a new date range, and older shards can be decommissioned when data expires.

Azure Data Lake

Azure Data Lake is a distributed storage that stores massive amounts of structured or unstructured data of any kind and size. The data is organized into a Hadoop Distributed File System (HDFS), on top of which runs Apache YARN. YARN supports multiple access engines, such as Spark, Storm, HBase, and Hive, so that you can get up and running quickly using your familiar tools.

Azure Data Lake supports low-latency small writes at massive scale, which are well suited for handling data streams in big data scenarios.

Azure DocumentDB

DocumentDB is a NoSQL database for JSON data. Azure DocumentDB is schema-free. However, it's capable of indexing document contents and fields to support complex queries over the data. So, it combines the flexibility of a NoSQL database and the power of SQL queries.

Azure Tables

Azure Tables is a NoSQL key-value data store. It's suitable for saving large amounts of data such as logs, audit records, and aggregated results. Records in Azure Tables are identified by a combination of a partition key and a row key. How you design your partitions significantly impacts how the storage service behaves. Make sure to check out recommended design strategies (such as *https://msdn.microsoft.com /library/azure/hh508997.aspx*) when designing your partitioning schemes.

Other storage options

In addition to the above options, there are several other storage types from which you can choose. Azure Blob service is designed for storing raw text or binary data. Azure Cache is a highly available in-memory cache cluster built on top of Redis with a data persistence option. Moreover, you can use third-party storage options such as MongoDB, Cassandra, OpenTSDB, and InfluxDB.

Stateful Service Fabric services as storage

Stateful Service Fabric services collocate data with compute. For complex data manipulations, having data close to compute saves many round trips between compute node and storage. And the highly reliable nature of stateful service allows data processing to continue under error conditions such as node crashes.

Scenarios and patterns

In this section, you'll study two scenarios: Service Fabric in a big data solution and a responsive website with live data stream processing. In the first scenario, Service Fabric acts as a data processing unit that coordinates with other services in the big data pipeline. In the second scenario, Service Fabric is used to build an end-to-end solution that directly handles client data streams via Web Socket.

A big data solution

In a big data scenario, data needs to be processed, transmitted, and stored with great speed and efficiency. Services such as Azure Stream Analytics provide powerful capabilities to query and manipulate data streams through a wide range of input and output options. However, in some cases, you still need to host your own data processing units that run complex custom logics. Earlier in this chapter, you've seen how you could integrate Service Fabric and ASA via Event Hub. This is a common pattern that can be used to integrate multiple types of data processing units.

Pattern: Composable data processing units

A big data data-processing pipeline can be constructed using Microservices architecture, with all processing units connected by a scalable message bus such as Azure Event Hub. This design allows these processing units to be composed dynamically into complex pipelines that can include sequences, branches, broadcasts, and iterations. At the same time, these components remain independent and are only loosely coupled. They can be developed, revisioned, hosted, and scaled separately using different languages, frameworks, and platforms. Furthermore, the message bus allows different processing units to operate at different speeds. It serves as a message buffer that balances performance differences among the units.

Figure 14-3 shows some of the composed structures using this pattern.

- **Sequence** A sequence structure can be composed by two Event Hub instances. As shown in the figure, a processing unit reads from one Event Hub instance and writes the processing results to a second Event Hub instance for another processing unit to pick them up.

- **Branches/split** A branch structure can be composed by three Event Hub instances. A processing unit reads from one Event Hub instance, and its internal logic decides where the messages should be forwarded.

- **Broadcast** A broadcast structure can be built using the built-in Consumer Group feature of Event Hub. Each processing unit registers itself as a separate consumer to the same Event Hub instance, and Event Hub sends copies of data to all its consumers.

- **Iteration** An iteration is an extended version of the sequence structure. Instead of writing results to the next Event Hub instance, a processing unit can choose to write the message back to a previous Event Hub instance so the messages can be handled through multiple iterations. Any of the processing units can decide to leave the loop when the results are satisfactory.

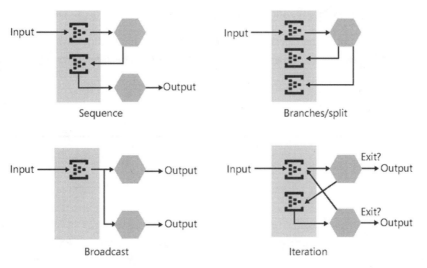

FIGURE 14-3 Composed processing units

Provision Event Hubs   In the following walkthrough, you'll implement a scenario that uses the sequence processing pattern. Your service will read integers from an Event Hub instance, convert them into corresponding English words, and write the transformed data back to another Event Hub instance.

1. Sign in to the Microsoft Azure management portal.

2. Click New in the upper-left corner, search for Event Hub, and then click the Event Hub entry.

3. On the Event Hub blade, click Create, which takes you to the classic Azure portal.

4. Enter a name for the Event Hub, select the region and the subscription you want to use, and then click Create A New Event Hub to create the hub, as shown in Figure 14-4. This action also creates a corresponding namespace. The first hub is for ingesting the raw location data.

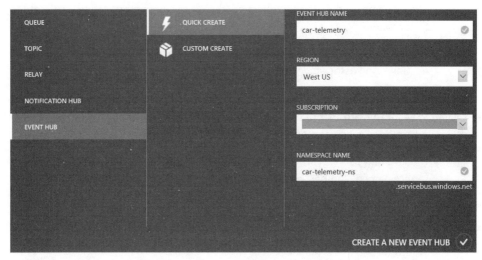

FIGURE 14-4 Creating an Event Hub

5. Create another Event Hub. The second hub is to hold location data augmented with POI data.

6. For each of the Event Hubs, open its corresponding Configure page. Define two shared access policies: Send with Send permission and Listen with Listen permission, as shown in Figure 14-5.

shared access policies

NAME	PERMISSIONS
Send	Send
Listen	Listen
NEW POLICY NAME	⌄

FIGURE 14-5 Shared access policies

7. For each of the Event Hubs, navigate to the Event Hub's Dashboard page. Click View Connection String and copy the corresponding connection strings. For the first Event Hub, you need the connection string for the Listen policy. For the second Event Hub, you need the connection string for the Send policy.

Provision a storage account   For this walkthrough, you also need to provision an Azure Storage account. An Azure Storage account is not mandated by the pattern; it's required by the *EventProcessorHost* class from the Service Bus assembly that you'll use in the service implementation.

1. Sign in to Microsoft Azure management portal.

2. Click New in the upper-left corner.

3. In the New blade, click the Data + Storage category. Then, on the Data + Storage blade, click Storage Account.

4. On the Storage Account blade, click Create.

5. Enter a name for the account, select or create a resource group, and click Create to provision the account.

6. Once the storage account is created, click the Keys icon on its overview blade and note the connection string associated with Key 1.

Create the converter service   Implement the converter service. In the following code, the parts related to Event Hub are adapted from *https://azure.microsoft.com/documentation/articles /event-hubs-csharp-ephcs-getstarted/*.

1. Create a new Service Fabric application named NumberConverterApp with a single stateless service named NumberConverterService.

2. In the NumberConverterService project, add a reference to the Microsoft.Azure.ServiceBus. EventProcessorHost NuGet package.

3. Add a new *NumberConverter* class to the project. The class implements an *IEventProcessor* interface. You need to replace *[Event Hub connection string 2 - send]* and *[Event Hub name 2]* with your Event Hub settings. Note the code in the *ConvertNumberToWords* method is omitted.

```
public class NumberConverter : IEventProcessor
{
    Stopwatch checkpointStopWatch;
EventHubClient eventHubClient = EventHubClient.CreateFromConnectionString
("[Event Hub connection string 2 - send], "[Event Hub name 2]");
    public async Task CloseAsync(PartitionContext context, CloseReason reason)
    {
        if (reason == CloseReason.Shutdown)
        {
            await context.CheckpointAsync();
        }
    }
    public Task OpenAsync(PartitionContext context)
    {
        this.checkpointStopWatch = new Stopwatch();
        this.checkpointStopWatch.Start();
        return Task.FromResult(1);
    }
public async Task ProcessEventsAsync(PartitionContext context,
IEnumerable<EventData> messages)
    {
        foreach (EventData eventData in messages)
        {
            int data = int.Parse(Encoding.UTF8.GetString(eventData.GetBytes()));
            eventHubClient.Send
(new EventData(Encoding.UTF8.GetBytes(ConvertNumberToWords(data))));
        }
        if (this.checkpointStopWatch.Elapsed > TimeSpan.FromMinutes(5))
        {
            await context.CheckpointAsync();
            this.checkpointStopWatch.Restart();
        }
    }
}
private ConvertNumberToWords(int number)
{
    …
}
}
```

4. Modify the *NumberConverterService* class to add a private variable:

```
EventHubClient eventHubClient;
```

5. Modify the *RunAsync* method of the *NumberConverterService* class:

```
protected override async Task RunAsync(CancellationToken cancelServiceInstance)
{
    string eventHubName = "[Event Hub name 1]";
    string eventHubConnectionString = "[Event Hub connection string 1 - listen]";
    string storageConnectionString = "[Storage account connection string]";
eventHubClient = EventHubClient.CreateFromConnectionString
```

```
(eventHubConnectionString, eventHubName);
    string eventProcessorHostName = Guid.NewGuid().ToString();
EventProcessorHost eventProcessorHost = new EventProcessorHost(eventProcessorHostName,
eventHubName, EventHubConsumerGroup.DefaultGroupName, eventHubConnectionString,
storageConnectionString);
    await eventProcessorHost.RegisterEventProcessorAsync<NumberConverter>();
}
```

Create a test client   Next, you'll create a console application as a test client. The application sends integers to the first Event Hub and listens to the second Event Hub for converted strings.

1. Create a new console application.

2. Add a reference to the Microsoft.Azure.ServiceBus.EventProcessorHost NuGet package.

3. Modify the *Program* class to add a *SendMessages* method:

```
static void SendMessages()
{
var eventHubClient = EventHubClient.CreateFromConnectionString
(connectionString1, eventHubName1);
    while (true)
    {
        try
        {
            var message = random.Next(0, int.MaxValue);
            Console.WriteLine("{0} > Sending message: {1}", DateTime.Now, message);
            eventHubClient.Send(new EventData(Encoding.UTF8.GetBytes(message.
ToString())));
        }
        catch (Exception exception)
        {
            Console.ForegroundColor = ConsoleColor.Red;
            Console.WriteLine("{0} > Exception: {1}", DateTime.Now, exception.Message);
            Console.ResetColor();
        }
        Thread.Sleep(200);
    }
}
```

4. Add a *ReceiveMessages* method:

```
static void ReceiveMessages(string partitionId)
{
    var eventHubClient = EventHubClient.CreateFromConnectionString(connectionString2,
eventHubName2);
    var defaultConsumberGroup = eventHubClient.GetDefaultConsumerGroup();
    var receiver = defaultConsumberGroup.CreateReceiver(partitionId);
    while (true)
    {
        var data = receiver.Receive();
        if (data != null)
        {
            Console.ForegroundColor = ConsoleColor.Green;
            Console.WriteLine("{0} - {2} > Data: {1}", DateTime.Now, Encoding.UTF8.
GetString(data.GetBytes()), partitionId);
```

```
                    Console.ResetColor();
                }
            }
        }
    }
```

5. Define local variables:

```
static string eventHubName1 = "[Event Hub name 1]";
static string connectionString1 = "[Event Hub connetion string 1]";
static string eventHubName2 = "[Event Hub name 2]";
static string connectionString2 = "[Event Hub connection string 2]";
static Random random = new Random();
```

6. Finally, modify the *Main()* method to start a thread for sending and four threads for listening. This is because by default an Event Hub is divided into four partitions. You'll launch a listener for each of the partitions. This implementation is different from the service implementation, which uses the Event Hub processor host that manages receivers automatically:

```
static void Main(string[] args)
{
    ThreadPool.QueueUserWorkItem((a) => SendMessages());
    ThreadPool.QueueUserWorkItem((a) => ReceiveMessages("0"));
    ThreadPool.QueueUserWorkItem((a) => ReceiveMessages("1"));
    ThreadPool.QueueUserWorkItem((a) => ReceiveMessages("2"));
    ThreadPool.QueueUserWorkItem((a) => ReceiveMessages("3"));
    Console.ReadKey();
}
```

Test the solution   Deploy the Service Fabric application. Launch the test client. You should see the integers are sent and the corresponding English words are returned. You can also observe that the messages come from different partitions of the Event Hub, as shown in Figure 14-6.

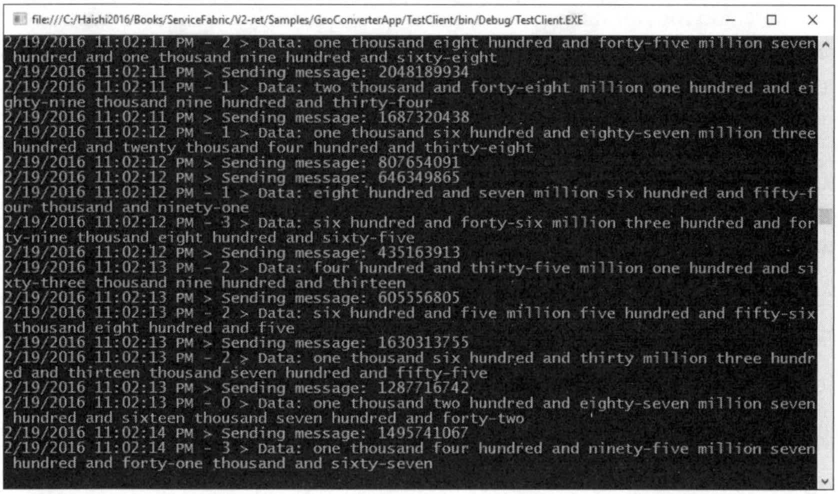

FIGURE 14-6 Test client outputs

Pattern: Processing topologies with actors

Composing data processing pipelines using a message bus is powerful. However, the pattern introduces extra communication steps because all messages need to go through the bus. For example, the sequence pattern in Figure 14-3 requires a message to be passed through the message bus twice. If the two processing units communicate directly with each other, the number of messages flowing through the system is cut in half.

It's easy to compose scalable processing topologies with actors. Next, you'll explore several processing topologies using actors. Each of the topologies starts with a message stream through a message bus. The stream is handled by a partitioned gateway service. The gateway service activates actors that form the corresponding topology. Figure 14-7 shows the general architecture of actor-based processing topologies. The gateway service is implemented as a stateful service that can be partitioned to handle different input stream partitions. This allows the system to be scaled out as needed. In the following examples, the gateway service reads from an Event Hub. The gateway can use other protocols to get the data stream, such as using Web Sockets in the responsive website scenario.

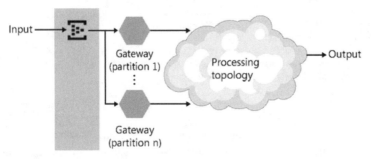

FIGURE 14-7 Actor-based processing topology

Parallel batching   Batching with an actor is easy because an actor easily can accumulate a number of elements in its state. Then, the actor launches another thread to process the accumulated elements. Using a separate thread avoids calls to the actor being blocked when the batched processing happens.

Because actors are virtual, a gateway partition easily can partition the elements again by activating actors following a naming convention. For example, the gateway partition for partition "1" can activate actors with names such as "1-1," "1-2," and "1-n" in a round-robin fashion to distribute elements in the partition to a number of actors. This allows multiple concurrent batches in each partition.

Figure 14-8 shows the architecture of the topology. Elements from the input stream are partitioned into multiple gateway partitions. Each partition is partitioned further into multiple batching actors that accumulate and process elements in batches.

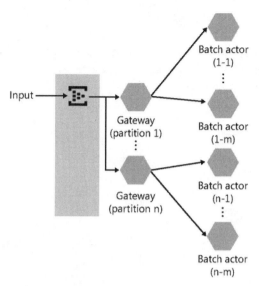

FIGURE 14-8 Parallel batching topology

Streaming top N Finding out top N elements on a stream is a common continuous computation scenario. Intuitively, a single actor can be used as a global filter that keeps track of top N elements. The actor keeps a N-element sorted list and keeps updating the list to keep the top N elements. However, this means the entire stream needs to flow through a single actor, which contains the global state of the system. In the following design, an actor is used for each of the gateway partitions to keep top N elements of the partition. Another aggregator actor is used to find out the global top N elements.

Recalling the aggregator pattern in Chapter 13, "Internet of Things," a push-based aggregation with actors is less effective. So, in the following design, the aggregator actor uses a lazy approach—it pulls partition actors and calculates global top N elements only when it's asked. Figure 14-9 shows the architecture of the topology. Because the global top N actor queries partition top N elements on the fly, it doesn't need to hold state. You can set up multiple global top N actor instances to scale out.

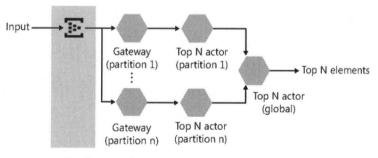

FIGURE 14-9 Top N processing topology

The top N topology can be used to keep top elements based on object attributes. It can also be used to keep the most active elements.

Join by field   Multiple data streams sometimes need to be merged. For example, in a social network analysis system, user-generated contents often need to be correlated based on user names. By using naming conventions, you can aggregate multiple streams into a group of actors that are named after the joint field values. For example, to correlate multiple streams by user names, actors are named after user names, and the gateway services address these actors directly by user names, as shown in Figure 14-10.

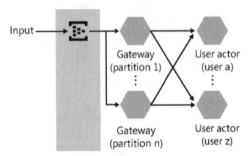

FIGURE 14-10 Join by field topology

Cached lookup grid   Augmenting a data stream by looking up external data sources is another common scenario. However, calling to external services is slow. To keep up with the ingress data stream, a caching solution is needed to cache lookup results. You can use caching services such as Azure Redis Cache for this purpose. Alternatively, you can construct a lookup grid using a group of Service Fabric actors. The actors are named after index names so that other services can find corresponding indexes by addressing directly the corresponding actors. Figure 14-11 shows a lookup grid that is comprised of indexes from A to Z. The diagram also shows scaling out processing actors by using naming conventions, as you've seen in the parallel batching topology.

Note that this topology is more expensive than using a caching service. Furthermore, to provide consistent performance, you don't want to fill in lookup actor states dynamically as requests come in. Instead, the state should be primed before lookup happens. You can consider packing lookup data files as the data package of services.

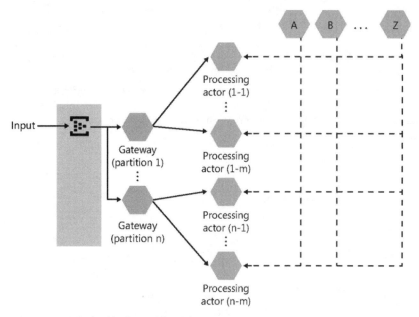

FIGURE 14-11 Cached lookup grid topology

Responsive website with live data stream processing

In the next scenario, you'll build a global e-commerce application that aggregates live sales data from stores around the globe through a Web Socket. The sales data stream is sent to a join by field topology for tracking sales in each of the managed countries. A country/region-wide aggregator aggregates sales data in a country/region, and a global aggregator aggregates sales data around the world to find top-selling products.

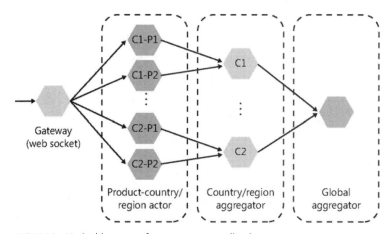

FIGURE 14-12 Architecture of e-commerce application

Sample source

The Web Socket listener implementation in the following walkthrough is based on the implementation here: *https://github.com/Azure-Samples/service-fabric-dotnet-data-streaming-websockets.*

Refer to the preceding link for detailed implementation of Web Socket connections. The following are actor implementations and some key code snippets.

Product Actor

The Product Actor implements a simple interface:

```
public interface IProductActor : IActor
{
    Task<int> GetSalesAsync();

    Task SellAsync();
}
```

A client calls the *SellAsync()* method to sell a product and calls the *GetSalesAsync()* method to read accumulated sales. Product Actors are named as "Country-Product." For example, a product "P1" in country/region "Canada" has a corresponding actor named "Canada-P1." The actor implementation is straightforward:

```
internal class ProductActor : StatefulActor<ProductActor.ActorState>, IProductActor
{
    [DataContract]
    internal sealed class ActorState
    {
        [DataMember]
        public int Sales { get; set; }

        public override string ToString()
        {
            return string.Format(CultureInfo.InvariantCulture, "ProductActor.ActorState[Sales =
{0}]", Sales);
        }
    }
    protected override Task OnActivateAsync()
    {
        if (this.State == null)
        {
            this.State = new ActorState { Sales = 0 };
        }

        ActorEventSource.Current.ActorMessage(this, "State initialized to {0}", this.State);
        return Task.FromResult(true);
    }

    [Readonly]
    Task<int> IProductActor.GetSalesAsync()
    {
```

```
        ActorEventSource.Current.ActorMessage(this, "Getting current sales value as {0}", this.
State.Sales);
        return Task.FromResult(this.State.Sales);
    }

    Task IProductActor.SellAsync()
    {

        this.State.Sales += 1;
        return Task.FromResult(true);
    }
}
```

Country/Region Actor

The Country/Region Actor is a stateless actor with a single method:

```
public interface ICountryActor : IActor
{
    Task<List<Tuple<string,long>>> CountCountrySalesAsync();
}
```

The Country/Region Actor reads from a predefined product list (products that were popular in the 1980s) and tries to find corresponding actors to collect sales counts. It returns a list of product-sales tuples.

```
internal class CountryActor : StatelessActor, ICountryActor
{
    Task<List<Tuple<string, long>>> ICountryActor.CountCountrySalesAsync()
    {
        string[] products = { "VCR", "Fax", "CassettePlayer", "Camcorder", "GameConsole",
                            "CD", "TV", "Radio", "Phone", "Karaoke"};
        List<Tuple<string, long>> ret = new List<Tuple<string, long>>();
        Parallel.ForEach(products, product =>
        {
            string actorId = this.Id.GetStringId() + "-" + product;
            var proxy = ActorProxy.Create<IProductActor>(new ActorId(actorId), "fabric:/
ECommerceApplication");
            ret.Add(new Tuple<string, long>(product, proxy.GetSalesAsync().Result));
        });
        return Task.FromResult(ret);
    }
}
```

Global Actor

The Global Actor implements a method similar to what the Country/Region Actor implements:

```
public interface IGlobalActor : IActor
{
    Task<List<Tuple<string, long>>> CountGlobalSalesAsync();
}
```

The actor implementation is similar to the Country/Region Actor implementation. The Global Actor reads from a list of countries/regions, locates corresponding Country/Region Actors, reads the country/region product lists, and merges the results into a sorted global list.

```
internal class GlobalActor : StatelessActor, IGlobalActor
{
    Task<List<Tuple<string,long>>> IGlobalActor.CountGlobalSalesAsync()
    {
        string[] countries = { "US", "China", "Australia" };
        ConcurrentDictionary<string, long> sales = new ConcurrentDictionary<string, long>();
        Parallel.ForEach(countries, country =>
        {
            var proxy = ActorProxy.Create<ICountryActor>(new ActorId(country), "fabric:/
ECommerceApplication");
            var countrySales = proxy.CountCountrySalesAsync().Result;
            foreach(var tuple in countrySales)
            {
                sales.AddOrUpdate(tuple.Item1, tuple.Item2, (key, oldValue) => oldValue + tuple.
Item2);
            }
        });
        var list = from entry in sales
                    orderby entry.Value descending
                    select new Tuple<string, long>(entry.Key, entry.Value);
        return Task.FromResult(list.ToList());
    }
}
```

Gateway

The gateway is a stateless service that receives client product requests and calls corresponding Product Actors to make a sale.

```
public async Task<byte[]> ProcessWsMessageAsync(byte[] wsrequest, CancellationToken
cancellationToken)
{
    ProtobufWsSerializer mserializer = new ProtobufWsSerializer();
    WsRequestMessage mrequest = await mserializer.DeserializeAsync<WsRequestMessage>(wsrequest);
    switch (mrequest.Operation)
    {
        case "sell":
            {
                IWsSerializer pserializer = SerializerFactory.CreateSerializer();
                PostSalesModel payload = await pserializer.DeserializeAsync<PostSalesModel>(mre
quest.Value);
                //await this.PurchaseProduct(payload.ProductId, payload.Quantity);
                var id = payload.Country + "-" + payload.Product;
                var product = ActorProxy.Create<IProductActor>(new ActorId(id), "fabric:/
ECommerceApplication");
                await product.SellAsync();
            }
            break;
    }
    WsResponseMessage mresponse = new WsResponseMessage
```

```
    {
        Result = WsResult.Success
    };
    return await mserializer.SerializeAsync(mresponse);
}
```

Web Socket listener

For complete implementation, refer to the original sample. The following is the method that binds a Web Socket listener to the gateway service's endpoint:

```
public async Task<string> OpenAsync(CancellationToken cancellationToken)
{
    EndpointResourceDescription endpoint = this.serviceInitializationParameters
        .CodePackageActivationContext.GetEndpoint("ServiceEndpoint");
    int port = endpoint.Port;
    this.listeningAddress = string.Format("http://+:{0}/{1}", port, appRoot);
    this.publishAddress = this.listeningAddress.Replace(
        "+", FabricRuntime.GetNodeContext().IPAddressOrFQDN);
    this.publishAddress = this.publishAddress.Replace("http", "ws");
    this.webSocketApp = new WebSocketApp(this.listeningAddress);
    this.webSocketApp.Init();
    this.mainLoop = this.webSocketApp.StartAsync(this.ProcessConnectionAsync);
    return await Task.FromResult(this.publishAddress);
}
```

You'll need to update the application manifest file to run the gateway service entry point as an administrator:

```
<ServiceManifestImport>
  <ServiceManifestRef ServiceManifestName="GatewayPkg" ServiceManifestVersion="1.0.0" />
  <ConfigOverrides />
  <Policies>
      <RunAsPolicy CodePackageRef="Code" UserRef="SetupAdminUser" />
  </Policies>
</ServiceManifestImport>
...
<Principals>
  <Users>
      <User Name="SetupAdminUser">
        <MemberOf>
            <SystemGroup Name="Administrators" />
        </MemberOf>
      </User>
  </Users>
</Principals>
```

To test the gateway service locally, you'll also need to modify the instance count to 1 to avoid port conflicts:

```
<Parameter Name="Gateway_InstanceCount" DefaultValue="1" />
```

Test client

The test client is a console application that sends sales requests using Web Socket. The client reads global sales results by talking to the country/region actor. If you are interested in generating large loads, refer to the original sample code that includes extensive code to generate large loads using a large thread pool.

```
static void Main(string[] args)
{
            string[] products = { "VCR", "Fax", "CassettePlayer", "Camcorder", "GameConsole",
                           "CD", "TV", "Radio", "Phone", "Karaoke"};
            string[] countries = { "US", "China", "Australia" };
            Random rand = new Random();
    Parallel.For(0, 100, i =>
        {
            SimulateSales(countries[rand.Next(0, countries.Length)], products[rand.Next(0,
products.Length)]);
        });
    var nation = ActorProxy.Create<IGlobalActor>(new ActorId("1"), "fabric:/
ECommerceApplication");
    var list = nation.CountGlobalSalesAsync().Result;
    foreach (var result in list)
    {
        Console.WriteLine(result.Item1.PadLeft(18,' ') + ": " + result.Item2);
    }
}
static void SimulateSales(string country, string product)
{
    using (GatewayWebSocketClient websocketClient = new GatewayWebSocketClient())
    {
        websocketClient.ConnectAsync("ws://localhost:30002/SalesServiceWS/").Wait();
        PostSalesModel postSalesModel = new PostSalesModel
        {
            Product = product,
            Country = country
        };

        IWsSerializer serializer = SerializerFactory.CreateSerializer();
        byte[] payload = serializer.SerializeAsync(postSalesModel).Result;
        WsRequestMessage mreq = new WsRequestMessage
        {
            Operation = "sell",
            Value = payload
        };
        WsResponseMessage mresp = websocketClient.SendReceiveAsync(mreq, CancellationToken.
None).Result;
        if (mresp.Result == WsResult.Error)
            Console.WriteLine("Error: {0}", Encoding.UTF8.GetString(mresp.Value));
    }
}
```

Figure 14-13 shows a sample output of the test client.

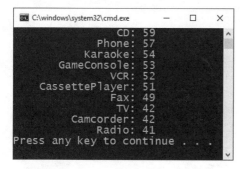

FIGURE 14-13 Test client output

The Web Socket port, 30002, will be different on your system. To get this port, you can use Service Fabric Explorer, as shown in Figure 14-14.

FIGURE 14-14 Service Fabric Explorer

Additional information

For big data scenarios, I recommend using existing Azure services such as Azure Stream Analytics for streamed processing, Data Lake for data storage, and Machine Learning for advanced analysis. For complex custom processing logics, you can use Service Fabric, Azure Container Services, or Azure Functions, a service that is similar to AWS Lamda: https://aws.amazon.com/lambda/. At the time of this writing, Azure Functions is in preview, and the name might change. These custom processing logics can be integrated with the big data pipeline using the composable data processing units pattern.

The responsive website sample code uses Google's Protocol Buffers (*https://developers.google.com /protocol-buffers/*) for serialization. This is not mandatory; you can use other serialization methods.

CHAPTER 15

Multitenancy and hosting

Multitenancy is an architecture in which multiple independent service instances operate in a shared environment. Microsoft Azure is a multitenant system. Azure subscriptions are logically separated from one another. A user from one subscription can see resources only from the subscription she owns. However, these resources are hosted on shared infrastructures in Azure datacenters.

Single tenancy is an architecture in which a single service instance operates in a dedicated environment. This is a typical architecture used in on-premises environments. It can also be used in the cloud, in which case a dedicated environment (such as a virtual machine cluster) is used for each of the supported customers. This deployment topology is also referred to as "single-tenant, multiple deployments."

Authoring a multitenant system is much more complex than authoring a single-tenant system because there are many additional concerns to be addressed, including isolation, dynamic provision and deprovision, resource balancing, and governance and subscription management. However, operating a multitenant system is more efficient than operating single-tenant systems.

Multitenancy on Azure

Microsoft Azure is a multitenant system with many isolated subscriptions sharing an Azure datacenter. So, no matter what architectures you choose, your services will be hosted in a multitenant environment. This is apparent in some cases. For example, when you provision a new Service Fabric cluster, the cluster is hosted on a shared infrastructure (with dedicated virtual machines) provided by Azure. In other cases, it might be hard to realize that your Azure resources are sharing compute and storage resources with other customers. For example, when you run a virtual machine on Azure, the virtual machine could be sharing virtual machine hosts with other customers. The machine is subject to storage IOPS throttling limitations, and it might be migrated to a different host when needed.

In the following discussions, I'll discuss multitenancy and single tenancy as logical architecture choices instead of the hosting environments. When you use single tenancy on Azure, the virtual machines are considered dedicated environments regardless of the fact that they are hosted on shared infrastructure.

Multitenancy vs. single tenancy

Multitenant systems and single-tenant systems differ in many technical aspects and business aspects. Adapting a single-tenant system into a multitenant system is a difficult task that should not be undertaken lightly. Before going into technical details, review some of the major differences between the two architectures.

Dedicated resources vs. shared resources

In a multitenant system, all customers share a pool of compute and storage nodes. In a single-tenant system, each customer has dedicated nodes.

Using shared nodes has a few advantages over using dedicated nodes. First, nodes can be reassigned dynamically as needed. If a customer turns out to use fewer nodes than originally allocated, the unused nodes can easily be repurposed for busier customers. This leads to more efficient resource utilization because more customers are served with fewer nodes. Second, the node pool provides failover opportunities. Because tenants can be redistributed, a tenant can be moved to healthy nodes when its supporting nodes fail. Third, managing a pool of resources is more streamlined than managing distributed deployments at different physical locations.

A Service Fabric cluster provides a shared environment for hosting many applications. However, this doesn't mean a Service Fabric application is multitenant by default. To check if an application is multitenant, review whether your application provides built-in tenant management. If it does, it's likely a multitenant system; otherwise, it's a single-tenant system.

With shared resources, tenants are logically separated instead of physically separated with dedicated resources. This raises both security concerns and resource governance concerns. A multitenant system has to ensure that a tenant doesn't gain access to data from other tenants either intentionally or accidentally. It also needs to make sure that a busy tenant won't exceed the resource consumption quota so that all tenants have fair access to available resources.

Perpetual licensing vs. subscription licensing

Traditionally, boxed software products are sold with perpetual licensing. Once a customer purchases the software, he is the owner of the software copy and is responsible for installing and maintaining the software. For complex enterprise software, installation and maintenance are often carried out by services teams or consulting firms. This implementation process can take weeks or even months.

Subscription licensing is a licensing mode through which a customer leases software instead of owning it. Under this model, the independent software vendor (ISV) owns the software, and the customer gains usage rights with a limited-time subscription. The subscribed service often is available immediately after the subscription is created, so the customer doesn't need to go through a lengthy implementation process to get the system up and running.

Subscription licensing is becoming the mainstream licensing model because it has several characteristics that are attractive to both customers and ISVs.

First, the subscription model helps reduce piracy. Enforcing perpetual licensing is difficult. For example, in many cases it's hard to determine whether a customer is installing another copy of the software for legitimate reasons (such as machine crashes). A hosted service can track usages actively to avoid intentional or unintentional End-User License Agreement (EULA) violations.

Second, a subscription simplifies customer support. With perpetual licensing, an ISV often needs to support a large number of software versions and to maintain software backward compatibility. With a hosted service, customers are kept under the latest versions so there are only a few or even a single version to be maintained. Patching a hosted service is also much easier than patching deployed software with different versions. This means software bugs and vulnerabilities can be fixed more quickly, improving the overall system quality and customer satisfaction.

Third, for customers, subscribing to a service means less upfront investment and lower risk. A customer can start with a low-level subscription to try out the service with minimum investment and roll out to a larger scale only when he's satisfied with the service. In addition, decommissioning a service is much easier than retiring deployed software. This flexibility in the subscription model avoids vendor lock-ins so a customer can shop around to pick the most suitable services with reduced risks and investments. The reduced vendor lock-ins encourage fair competition and faster innovation. Because of the increased mobility of the customer base, ISVs are forced to improve their services continuously to sustain their customers and to grasp opportunities to win over customers from other services.

Last but not least, the subscription model opens up opportunities for new ISVs and new services to reach a large number of customers in a short period of time. In the past decades, we've witnessed many new services reaching tremendous usage scales that were unimaginable with traditional perpetual software. The cloud has played an important role in this phenomenon. Specifically, the elasticity of the cloud allows an ISV to start small and grow rapidly.

Before closing this section, I need to clarify that although the subscription licensing model often is used by multitenant systems, it can be applied to single-tenant systems. For example, you might have a separate Service Fabric instance for each of your customers and offer a subscription model. Architecturally, this is a single-tenant, multiple deployments topology. But you can manage it in a similar fashion as managing a multitenant system.

Azure multitenant support

Azure is a multitenant system. When you host your own multitenant systems, you can leverage native service monitoring and throttling provided by various Azure services to provide certain resource governance. Moreover, Azure provides two services that can provide practical help in operating commercial multitenant systems: Azure Active Directory and Azure Billing API.

Azure Active Directory

When you operate a multitenant application, you need to enable users from different tenants to sign in to your system. You can choose to request all users from all your customer tenants to register with your system. However, this means extra management burden on your system, and users won't get a Single Sign-On (SSO) experience because they have to use accounts registered with your system to sign in.

Azure Active Directory (Azure AD) proposes a different solution: you can register an application as a multitenant application with your Azure AD tenant, and users from all Azure AD tenants will be able to sign in to your application with the user's consent. Once the user signs in, you can read the tenant id claim to detect the user's tenant and make authorization decisions.

Azure Billing API

Azure Billing API is comprised of two APIs: Azure Usage API and Azure RateCard API. Azure Usage API is designed to retrieve aggregated usage information of various Azure resources. The following is an example response snippet from the API. The JSON segment shows that between February 1 and February 2, the storage account in question incurred 1.47 GB of IO traffic. By using the Azure Usage API, you can measure the amount of resources your application consumes to support a particular customer. This information enables you to tailor your service prices precisely to ensure desired margins while maintaining a competitive price.

```
{
    "id": "/subscriptions/…/providers/Microsoft.Commerce/UsageAggregates/…",
    "name": "Daily_BRSDF_20160201_0000",
    "type": "Microsoft.Commerce/UsageAggregate",
    "properties": {
        "subscriptionId": "…",
    "usageStartTime": "2016-03-01T00:00:00+00:00",
    "usageEndTime": "2016-03-02T00:00:00+00:00",
    "meterName": "Standard IO - Page Blob/Disk (GB)",
    "meterCategory": "Storage",
    "meterSubCategory": "Geo Redundant",
    "unit": "GB",
    "meterId": "…",
    "quantity": 1.47
    }
}
```

Azure RateCard API can be used to query available Azure resource offers with corresponding prices. In the "Pattern: Tenant Manager" section later in this chapter, you'll see a pattern of dynamic tenant management in which tenants are provisioned and destroyed dynamically. Before you provision a new tenant, you can use the Azure RateCard API to check if there are sufficient Azure resources to support the tenant. You can also use the API to estimate the cost of each of the new tenants. The following is a sample output of the API extract from *https://msdn.microsoft.com/library/azure/mt219004*. The JSON segment shows that for the Azure US West region, computer hour rate for a Basic D6 VM virtual machine is $.3.136 per hour; the data egress cost is $0.1 per GB; and the computer hour rate for an A6 Cloud Service instance is $0.71 per hour.

```
{
    "OfferTerms": [],
    "Meters": [
        {
            "MeterId": "…",
            "MeterName": "Compute Hours",
            "MeterCategory": "Virtual Machines",
            "MeterSubCategory": "Basic_D6 VM (Non-Windows)",
            "Unit": "Hours",
```

```
    "MeterTags": [],
    "MeterRates": {
        "0": 3.136
    },
    "EffectiveDate": "2015-02-01T00:00:00Z",
    "IncludedQuantity": 0.0
},
{

    "MeterId": "…",
    "MeterName": "Data Transfer Out at 500 Mbps (GB)",
    "MeterCategory": "Networking",
    "MeterSubCategory": "ExpressRoute (IXP)",
    "Unit": "GB",
    "MeterTags": [],
    "MeterRates": {
        "0": 0.1
    },
    "EffectiveDate": "2014-08-01T00:00:00Z",
    "IncludedQuantity": 2048.0
},

{
    "MeterId": "…",
    "MeterName": "Compute Hours",
    "MeterCategory": "Cloud Services",
    "MeterSubCategory": "A6 Cloud Services",
    "Unit": "Hours",
    "MeterTags": [],
    "MeterRates": {
      "0": 0.71
    },
    "EffectiveDate": "2013-12-01T00:00:00Z",
    "IncludedQuantity": 0.0
},
…
]
"Currency": "USD",
"Locale": "en-US",
"IsTaxIncluded": false,
"MeterRegion": "US West",
"Tags": []
}
```

Multitenant data architectures

There are many data storage options on Azure, including relational databases such as SQL Database, NoSQL data storage such as Azure Storage and DocumentDB, big data storage such as Azure Data Lake and SQL Data Warehouse, and archive storage such as Azure Backup. However, when designing data storage for multitenancy, a common pattern applies. Essentially, you need to decide how to segment your customer data based on several criteria:

- **How well the customer data should be isolated** Does the data need to be physically isolated or logically isolated? Will multiple customers share the storage resource, or will they have dedicated resources?

- **How much the customer data will be scaled**   Is a single Azure subscription or storage account sufficient for a single tenant (or multiple tenants), or are multiple accounts needed to support a single tenant?

- **The requirements on cross-tenant aggregations and queries**   When data is shared among multiple storage entities, queries across multiple entities can be tricky. Hosting multiple tenants on a single storage entity facilitates cross-tenant queries but constrains the scalability of the system. For large-scale multitenant systems, a dedicated solution for cross-tenant queries may be necessary.

- **The expected throughput and performance**   Because Azure is a multitenant environment, the storage entities you provision are subject to throttling limits. Although a single storage entity may provide the required storage space, it might be insufficient to satisfy throughput or performance requirements.

Building multitenant systems with Service Fabric

At the beginning of this chapter, I defined multitenancy as multiple independent services running on a shared environment and single tenancy as a single service running on a dedicated environment. These definitions are given from the perspective of service hosting. Multitenancy can also be defined from the perspective of application architecture—if a single service instance serves multiple customers (or tenants), the service is a multitenant system. In contrast, if a single service instance serves only one customer (or tenant), it's a single-tenant system.

The following discussions will use a more relaxed definition of multitenancy. The distinction between multitenancy and single tenancy traditionally resides in how the services are hosted. A single instance per tenant means dedicated hardware for that tenant. To support multiple customers on a single server, the service has to be designed with multitenancy in mind. However, on a modern platform as a service (PaaS) platform such as Service Fabric, multiple instances of the service share the same resource pool. So, even if the service is a single-tenant service, it's hosted in a shared environment, so it fits the first multitenancy definition. The second definition requires a single instance serving multiple tenants. The driving force behind this architecture is efficient resource utilization. If you can achieve higher compute density by packing multiple instances into the same compute node, it doesn't matter if the tenants are served by the same service process.

So, in the following discussions, multitenancy is defined as follows:

> *A multitenant application is a single manageable entity that manages and serves multiple tenants.*

This definition discounts hosting option differences and architectural differences. Instead, it focuses on the functional behavior of the system. As long as an application, as a single manageable entity, serves multiple tenants, it should be considered a multitenant system.

Pattern: Tenant Manager

A Tenant Manager manages lifetimes of tenants on a shared environment. With a Tenant Manager, a single-tenant (or multitenant) application can be hosted as a multitenant application. Tenant Manager dynamically creates and destroys customer tenants as needed, and it can provide additional tenant-level services such as health monitoring, failover, and billing. This is a new component that isn't present in existing PaaS platform and container orchestration engines. Because Service Fabric provides an entire set of management APIs, it isn't difficult to implement a Tenant Manger using Service Fabric.

Figure 15-1 shows an architecture diagram of the Tenant Manager pattern. A Tenant Manager is a hosted service that provides tenant management capabilities, including provisioning new application instances, monitoring application instance health, and upgrading an application instance. The Tenant Manager also hosts cross-tenant logics. Each of the tenants is an application instance. When a new customer joins the system, he talks to the Tenant Manager endpoint to request a new application instance. The Tenant Manager provisions a new application instance and returns the tenant's entry endpoint to the new customer.

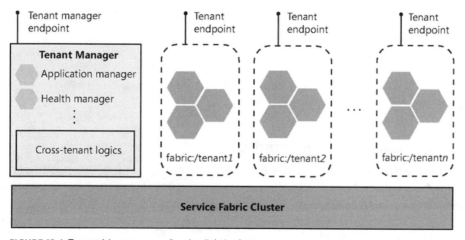

FIGURE 15-1 Tenant Manager on a Service Fabric cluster

Figure 15-1 is a high-level architecture. It doesn't mandate how the Tenant Manager is implemented or define the scope of cross-tenant logics. The cross-tenant logics vary from project to project. In the next pattern, cross-tenant aggregation, you'll learn a pattern that helps you aggregate states from multiple tenants at scale.

The tenant management logics should implement at least the following fundamental capabilities:

- Provision a new tenant by creating a new application instance.

- Retire a tenant by removing an existing application instance.

- Monitor tenant health by monitoring application health. Proactive and reactive actions can be taken to ensure continuous quality service to customers.

- Update one or all of the tenants by performing rolling updates on application instances.

- Adjust tenant capabilities independently to accommodate different loads on different tenants.

Service Fabric SDK provides a *FabricClient* class that you can use to implement the above logics. For example, to provision a new application instance, you can use the class's *ApplicationManager* property, as shown in the following code snippet:

```
FabricClient client = new FabricClient("localhost:19000");
await client.ApplicationManager.CreateApplicationAsync(new ApplicationDescription
{
    ApplicationTypeName = "MyApplicationType",
    ApplicationName = new Uri("fabric:/Tenant1"),
    ApplicationTypeVersion = "1.0.0"
});
```

To retire a tenant, remove the corresponding application instance using the *ApplicationManager DeleteApplicationAsync* method:

```
await client.ApplicationManager.DeleteApplicationAsync(new Uri("fabric:/Tenant1"));
```

To monitor tenant health, you can read application's health report by using FabricClient's *HealthManager*:

```
var health = await client.HealthManager.GetApplicationHealthAsync(new Uri("fabric:/Tenant1"));
var healthState = health.AggregatedHealthState;
```

Pattern: Cross-tenant aggregation

As the scale and the complexity of applications increase, more enterprises and ISVs realize the importance of big data. They want to gain in-depth business insights by mining petabytes of service telemetry, application logs, and user behaviors. The data is collected, transformed, and fed into analysis engines or Machine Learning modules to generate rich insights. The cross-tenant aggregation pattern focuses on the first part—collecting data from multiple tenants.

Intuitively, an easy aggregation design would be either tenants pushing data to the cross-tenant service or the cross-tenant service pulling tenant data. However, this simple design doesn't scale. In many cases, big data is an exploratory process. A user comes in with questions and hypotheses, and she doesn't necessarily know where to look for answers. Therefore, she takes in all the data she can collect, tries different queries, or runs the data through different experiments to discover what data provides the insights she needs. So, to aggregate information from multiple tenants, you need a fast and scalable data pipeline that can ingest a huge amount of data.

What I have been proposing is using prebuilt Azure features instead of rolling out custom solutions whenever possible. Figure 15-2 shows a cross-tenant aggregation implementation using Azure Event Hub, Stream Analytics, Storage, and Machine Learning.

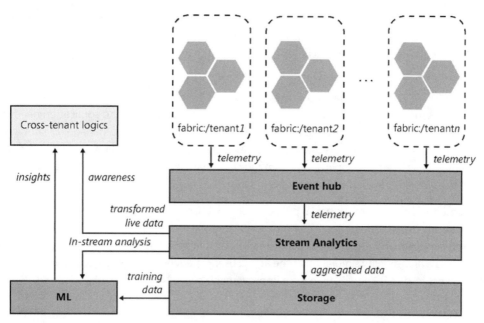

FIGURE 15-2 Cross-tenant aggregation pattern

There are two data paths in the diagram in Figure 15-2: hot path and cold path. The hot path provides real-time monitoring and in-stream analysis. The cold path archives the data for batched data processing later.

In the cold path, application telemetry data flows from tenants into Azure Event Hub, which acts as a scalable message bus. Then, the data is picked up by Azure Stream Analytics. Stream Analytics runs aggregations and transformations before it saves the result data into some sort of storage, such as Azure Storage, Data Lake, or SQL Data Warehouse. The archived data then is fed into a Machine Learning module to train or retrain the module. Finally, the Machine Learning module publishes a REST interface for the cross-tenant logic service to gain business insights.

In the hot path, the transformed live data flows directly from Stream Analytics to the cross-tenant logics to provide real-time monitoring and feedback. Alternatively, Stream Analytics can feed data to the trained Machine Learning module to perform in-stream analysis.

Pattern: Self-service

A key benefit of multitenant system is the ability to onboard a customer quickly. Many modern multitenant systems support self-service onboard, which allows customers to subscribe to the service without the involvement of the ISV's sales or support teams. However, the self-service pattern isn't limited to onboarding. It's applicable to scenarios in which a customer is guided to complete a complex workflow without any assistance.

The Tenant Manager pattern can be used to implement self-service onboarding. And the Finite State Machine Actor pattern in Chapter 12, "Web applications," can be used to implement reliable workflows. Azure Active Directory (Azure AD) can be used to manage authentications from multiple tenants.

When you use Tenant Manager and Azure AD together, however, identifying applications can be a problem. For Azure AD to provide authentication service to an application, the application needs to be registered with Azure AD as a trusted application. However, when the Tenant Manager creates a new application instance, Azure AD isn't aware of this new instance. At the time of this writing, there isn't a programmatic way to add an application to a Azure AD tenant. In this case, some manual operation is required to complete the onboarding process.

Many multitenant systems support a public tenant that has a reduced feature set with a relaxed authentication request; sometimes, a common login credential is provided for any user who wants to try the service to sign in without signing up formally. A public tenant is a great marketing and sales tool that provides a high-fidelity simulation of the actual user experience. It's also a good place to collect user behaviors to identify possible areas for improvements.

Tenant by partitions

In simple cases, you can implement tenants by using service partitions. With this architecture, services are partitioned per customer so that a service partition serves only one customer. This architecture fits into the traditional definition of multitenancy. Figure 15-3 shows a Service Fabric application that consists of a number of services. Each service is partitioned by customers to provide services to a single tenant.

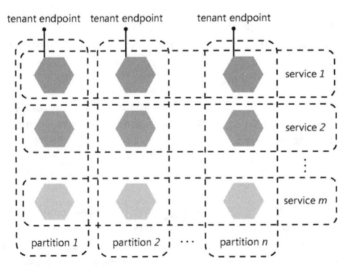

FIGURE 15-3 Tenant by partitions

Figure 15-3 shows that all services are partitioned uniformly. This is not mandatory. For example, the Service Fabric application may have a stateless gateway service as the single entry point for all tenants. The gateway service can be registered with Azure AD as a trusted application for authentication.

Compared to the Tenant Manager pattern, this design has the following constraints:

- Dynamic provisioning is problematic in this design because Service Fabric doesn't allow dynamic service partitioning. As mentioned in Chapter 7, "Scalability and performance," a possible workaround is to preallocate enough partitions to accommodate all possible customers.

- You can't use different versions of the services for different customers. If you want to offer different feature sets to different levels of subscriptions, you'll need to check your service code to ensure only customers with the proper subscription levels can access included features.

- It's hard to adjust per-tenant capacity. With the Tenant Manager pattern, each tenant is a separate application instance. You can scale the services in the application without affecting other tenants. However, if you use partitions for tenants, you can't adjust the capacity of a specific tenant. In addition, with the Tenant Manager pattern, you can deploy different application instances to different node types, providing different service levels to customers with different subscription levels.

- There is weaker isolation. When you share a service instance across multiple tenants (such as the gateway service), requests from multiple tenants are handled in the same service process. This increases the risk of cross-tenant attacks.

Because of these constraints, I recommend you use the Tenant Manager pattern for multitenant systems in general and use tenant by partitions only for simple cases.

If your Service Fabric application uses actors, these actors aren't impacted regardless of which pattern you use. The only difference is how an actor is addressed. For example, an actor representing a user in a tenant might be named after the user name in the Tenant Manager pattern. However, the actor name should have a tenant prefix in the tenant by partitions design to avoid possible conflicts.

Pattern: Metadata-driven system

In the rare case that you need to design and implement a large-scale, extensible multitenant system, it's important to design the system so it can be tailored easily for specific customer needs. If a multitenant system uses the same Service Fabric application instance to serve multiple tenants, all tenants will be using the same code base. If one or a few of the tenants have special needs such as custom workflows, the behavior of the tenant needs to be customizable by something other than changing the code.

The metadata-driven system pattern uses metadata to drive core system behaviors. With this pattern, the system is implemented as a generic metadata processor that reads metadata files and performs actions specified by these files. A metadata-driven system is not a scriptable system, which allows custom code to be uploaded and hosted. Instead, a metadata-driven system defines a finite number of predefined actions for which you can use parameters to control their behaviors. Some metadata-driven systems also allow customized workflows. In this case, a user cannot define an arbitrary workflow but can choose from one of a few predefined workflows.

In a way, a metadata-driven system is a polymorphic Microservices system in which different implementations of a logical operation can be brought in during run time as needed. The following walkthrough demonstrates an implantation of the pattern using Service Fabric actors. The walkthrough assumes that your customers will use a metadata file to drive whether a circle or a rectangle should be painted on the screen.

1. Created a new Service Fabric application named *MetadataDrivenApplication* with a *Shape* stateless service.

2. Modify the *IShape* interface:

```
public interface IShape : IActor
{
    Task<string> DrawAsync();
}
```

3. In the Shape project, modify the *Shape* class as shown in the following code snippet. Note the class is declared as an abstract class because the Shape actor is an abstract actor that isn't supposed to be instantiated.

```
public abstract class Shape : StatelessActor, IShape
{
    public abstract Task<string> DrawAsync();
}
```

4. After you update the class to an abstract class, you need to modify the ServiceManifest.xml file manually to fill in the *ServiceTypes* element and the *Endpoints* element. This is required at the time of this writing, but it might be unnecessary in future versions.

```
<ServiceManifest xmlns:xsd="http://www.w3.org/2001/XMLSchema"
xmlns:xsi="http://www.w3.org/2001/XMLSchema-instance" Name="ShapePkg"
 Version="1.0.0" xmlns="http://schemas.microsoft.com/2011/01/fabric">
    <ServiceTypes>
        <StatelessServiceType ServiceTypeName="ShapeType" />
    </ServiceTypes>
    <CodePackage Name="Code" Version="1.0.0">
        <EntryPoint>
            <ExeHost>
                <Program>Shape.exe</Program>
            </ExeHost>
        </EntryPoint>
    </CodePackage>
    <ConfigPackage Name="Config" Version="1.0.0" />
    <Resources>
        <Endpoints>
            <Endpoint Name="ShapeEndpoint" />
        </Endpoints>
    </Resources>
</ServiceManifest>
```

5. Add a new *Circle* stateless service to the Service Fabric application.

6. In the Circle.Interface project, add a reference to the Shape.Interfaces project.

7. Modify the *ICircle* interface:

```
public interface ICircle : IShape
{
}
```

8. In the Circle project, add a reference to the Shape project and the Shape.Interfaces project.

9. Modify the *Circle* class as shown in the following code snippet. Note the *actor* class is decorated with the *ActorService* attribute. This is because the class implements more than one actor interface. This attribute is used to identify the service type so that a client can connect to the right actor.

```
namespace Circle
{
    [ActorService(Name = "Circle")]
    internal class Circle : Shape.Shape, ICircle
    {
        public override Task<string> DrawAsync()
        {
            return Task.FromResult("Drawing circle");
        }
    }
}
```

10. Add a new *Rectangle* stateless service. The service implementation is similar to the *Circle* service. Note the differences highlighted in bold font.

```
namespace Rectangle
{
    [ActorService(Name = "Rectangle")]
    internal class Rectangle : Shape.Shape, IRectangle
    {
        public override Task<string> DrawAsync()
        {
            return Task.FromResult("Drawing rectangle");
        }
    }
}
```

11. Publish the application. Once the application is published, examine the application instance in Service Fabric Explorer. Note that because the *Shape* class is abstract, there isn't a service created for the Shape actor, as shown in Figure 15-4.

FIGURE 15-4 Metadata-driven application in Service Fabric Explorer

12. Add a new console application to the solution. Change the application's target framework to .NET Framework 4.5.1 and its platform target to x64.

13. Add a reference to the *Microsoft.ServiceFabric.Actors* NuGet package.

14. Add references to the Circle.Interfaces project, Rectangle.Interfaces project, and Shape.Interfaces project.

15. Modify the *Main()* method to simulate a metadata-driven system:

```
static void Main(string[] args)
{
    var metadata = new string[] { "Circle", "Rectangle" };
    string applicationName = "fabric:/MetadataDrivenApplication";
    foreach (var action in metadata)
    {
        IShape proxy = ActorProxy.Create<IShape>(ActorId.NewId(), applicationName,
action);
        Console.WriteLine(proxy.DrawAsync().Result);
    }
}
```

16. Launch the test program and observe that different actors are called as dictated by the metadata file. This is shown in Figure 15-5.

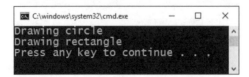

FIGURE 15-5 Test application output

Hosting multitenant systems

A Service Fabric cluster provides a shared environment for hosting multitenant systems. For the rest of the chapter, you'll go through a couple of high-level hosting concerns and patterns.

Hosting service processes

Recall from Chapter 1, "Hello, Service Fabric!," that a Service Fabric node is a service runtime process. In theory, this process can run on any supporting operating system, including the following:

- Physical Windows servers.

- Virtualized Windows servers such as servers running on Hyper-V.

- Containerized Windows Server systems such as Windows containers running on Windows Server 2016.

- With .NET Core Framework on Linux and Apple OS X, Service Fabric process potentially can also run on Linux systems (physical or virtual).

This flexibility allows Service Fabric clusters to be hosted on a variety of environments, including Azure and other cloud platforms, on-premises datacenters, local computers, and container clusters. I'll discuss these hosting options in detail in Chapter 17, "Advanced service hosting."

For service instance placements, you can let Service Fabric decide where the service instances should be placed (see the information on load balancing in Chapter 9, "Managing Service Fabric with management portal"). Or, you can use placement constraints and service affinity (see Chapter 6, "Availability and reliability") to place service instances to specific nodes.

Figure 15-6 shows a tiered deployment scheme. With this policy, a Service Fabric cluster is split into three node types: Gold, Silver, and Bronze. Each node type is used to host tenants with different subscription levels. A number of tenants reside on each type of node. This deployment scheme works well with the Tenant Manager pattern. When the Tenant Manager creates a new application instance, it places the application instance on the corresponding node type based on the customer's subscription level.

Figure 15-7 shows a different deployment scheme. This method works best with a "native" multitenant application that a single application instance serves for multiple tenants. The figure shows that web-tier instances are deployed to a shared Web node type. Then, for different subscription levels, the corresponding business process services are deployed to different node types such as Gold and Silver. Finally, an Actor Host node type is used to host actor instances from all tenants.

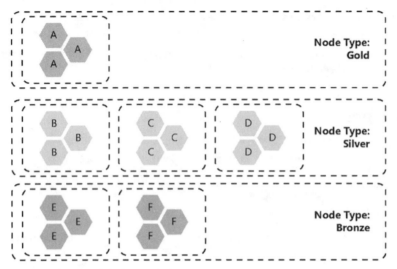

FIGURE 15-6 Tiered deployment scheme

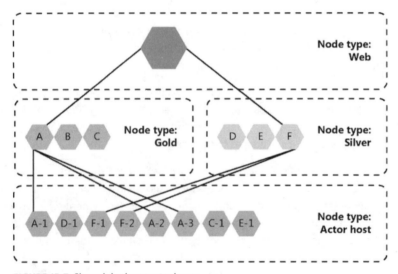

FIGURE 15-7 Shared deployment scheme

Pattern: Throttling Actor

A multitenant system needs to ensure all tenants use a fair share of resources. Each tenant should be constrained to utilizing only a portion of the cluster resources so that all tenants have enough resources to maintain service continuity.

Throttling is an effective way to prevent a busy tenant from consuming all resources. However, it is hard to throttle a service instance at process level. The Throttling Actor pattern uses a high-level throttling that constrains how much workload a tenant can generate. The pattern throttles a tenant in three different ways:

- **Limited request queue length**   The Throttling Actor limits how many requests a tenant can queue during a given period of time. If the tenant attempts to queue more than the allowed number of requests, the request will be rejected.

- **Limited request frequency**   The Throttling Actor limits how frequently a tenant can send requests. This is a stricter throttling that allows only one request per time window.

- **Limited request credits**   Under this throttling pattern, each request costs a number of credit points. The throttling keeps track of how many credits a tenant has spent. If the tenant uses up all its credits, it's not allowed to send new requests.

Figure 15-8 shows the workflow when using a Throttling Actor:

1. A tenant service talks to its Throttling Actor to get a one-time access token.

2. The Throttling Actor checks if the tenant is within the throttling limits. If so, it sends a one-time access token to the service.

3. The tenant service sends a service request to a protected service with the access token attached to the request.

4. Optionally, the protected service calls back to the Throttling Actor to validate the token.

5. If the token checks out, the protected service provides the requested service to the tenant service.

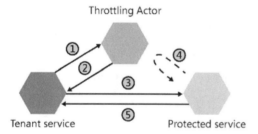

FIGURE 15-8 Throttling Actor pattern

The Throttling Actor pattern doesn't mandate specific access token formats. However, the access token should carry enough information for the protected service to make an authentication decision. In addition, the tokens should be encrypted and signed with embedded time stamps and TTL.

In the following walkthrough, you'll implement a Throttling Actor based on credits. The token generation part is omitted.

1. Create a new Service Fabric application with a stateful actor named *ThrottlingActor*.

2. Modify the *IThrottlingActor* interface:

```
public interface IThrottlingActor : IActor
{
    Task<string> GetAccessTokenAsync(string actionId);
}
```

3. Modify the *ThrottlingActor* class. The actor keeps a local action-to-credit mapping in its state. In a real implementation, this mapping probably is saved in a database whose records can be updated easily.

```
internal class ThrottlingActor : StatefulActor<ThrottlingActor.ActorState>,
IThrottlingActor
{
    [DataContract]
    internal sealed class ActorState
    {
        [DataMember]
        public int Credit { get; set; }
        [DataMember]
        public Dictionary<string, int> ServiceCreditScore { get; set; }
    }

    protected override Task OnActivateAsync()
    {
        if (this.State == null)
        {
            this.State = new ActorState
            {
                Credit = 100,
                ServiceCreditScore = new Dictionary<string, int>
                {
                    {"action1", 50 },
                    {"action2", 25 },
                    {"action3", 10 }
                }
            };
        }
        return Task.FromResult(true);
    }
    Task<string> IThrottlingActor.GetAccessTokenAsync(string actionId)
    {
        if (!this.State.ServiceCreditScore.ContainsKey(actionId))
            return Task.FromResult("Unsupported action.");
        int credit = this.State.ServiceCreditScore[actionId];
        if (this.State.Credit - credit >=0)
        {
            this.State.Credit -= credit;
            string token = "Remaining credit: " + this.State.Credit;
            //1. Generate a symetric/asemetric key
            //2. Generate an access token
            //3. Encrypt and optionally sign the token
            return Task.FromResult(token);
        }
        else
            return Task.FromResult("Insufficient credit");
    }
}
```

4. Add a new console application to the solution. Change the application's target framework to .NET Framework 4.5.1 and its platform target to x64.

5. Add a reference to the Microsoft.ServiceFabric.Actors NuGet package.

6. Add references to the ThrottlingActor.Interfaces project.

7. Modify the *Main()* method to request access tokens for "action1" a couple of times. Because each "action1" requires 50 credits, only the first two calls will succeed.

```
static void Main(string[] args)
{
var proxy = ActorProxy.Create<IThrottlingActor>(new ActorID("tenant1"),
"fabric:/ThrottlingActorApplication");
    for (int i = 0; i < 3; i++)
        Console.WriteLine("Token:" + proxy.GetAccessTokenAsync("action1").Result);
}
```

8. Deploy the Service Fabric application and launch the test program. The program should generate the output shown in Figure 15-9.

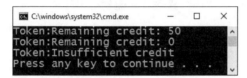

FIGURE 15-9 Test application output

In the preceding implementation, service credits are spent as soon as the *GetAccessTokenAsync* method is called. Alternatively, you can collect service credits when the protected service calls back to validate the access token.

How do you recharge the credits? One way is to keep credit information in an external storage. Alternatively, you can define a separate management interface that you can use to add credits to a tenant. The following walkthrough continues the above example and implements a new management interface on the actor.

1. In the ThrottlingActor.Interfaces project, define a new *IThrottlingActorManagement* interface:

```
public interface IThrottlingActorManagement: IActor
{
    Task<int> AddCreditsAsync(int credits);
}
```

2. Modify the *ThrottlingActor* class to implement both interfaces. Note that because the actor now implements two actor interfaces, you need to add an *ActorService* attribute to name the service explicitly.

```
[ActorService(Name = "ThrottlingActor")]
internal class ThrottlingActor : StatefulActor<ThrottlingActor.ActorState>,
IThrottlingActor, IThrottlingActorManagement
...
```

3. Implement the *IThrottlingActorManagement.AddcreditsAsync* method:

```
Task<int> IThrottlingActorManagement.AddCreditsAsync(int credits)
{
    this.State.Credit += credits;
    return Task.FromResult(this.State.Credit);
}
```

4. Modify the test application to recharge and spend service credits repeatedly:

```
static void Main(string[] args)
{
var proxy = ActorProxy.Create<IThrottlingActor>(new ActorId("tenant1"),
"fabric:/ThrottlingActorApplication", "ThrottlingActor");
var mgtProxy = ActorProxy.Create<IThrottlingActorManagement>(new ActorId("tenant1"),
"fabric:/ThrottlingActorApplication", "ThrottlingActor");
    while (true)
    {
        Console.WriteLine("Credits: " + mgtProxy.AddCreditsAsync(150).Result);
        for (int i = 0; i < 3; i++)
            Console.WriteLine("Token:" + proxy.GetAccessTokenAsync("action1").Result);
        Thread.Sleep(1000);
    }
}
```

5. Redeploy the application and launch the test program again. The test program should be able to run forever because the credits will never run out, as shown in Figure 15-10.

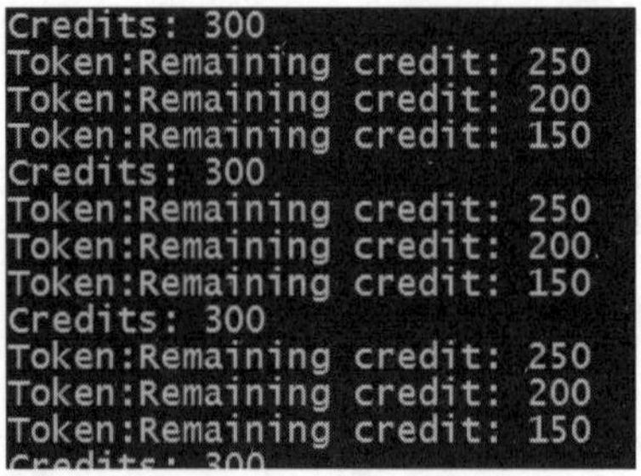

FIGURE 15-10 Test application output

CHAPTER 16

Multiplayer gaming

Like many programmers out there, my lifelong pursuit of programming started with video games. I spent most of my teenage afterhours re-creating games I liked such as Tetris, Pac-Man, and, later, Golden Axe and Wolfenstein 3D. Playing games surely is fun. Creating a virtual game world that provides amusement and adventure to players is something different—the pure creativity, the boundless imagination, and the nifty craftsmanship are almost addictive and very satisfying.

As I took on increasingly complex games, I quickly realized that creating a polished game was far beyond the capacity of a single programmer. Creating games was a dream of mine that was fading away. I have been fortunate enough to work on other interesting projects; however, creating a game has been a lasting idea that I couldn't shake off.

Selfishly, my goal for this chapter is to get the dream back. Although creating a complete game seems out of reach, designing a game engine brings back the joy of creation. In this chapter, I'll present two fictional game titles: Messy Chess and A.I. Quests. The Messy Chess game focuses on basics of implementing an online game using Service Fabric. The A.I. Quests game focuses on designing game engines that support large-scale, multiplayer online games. I hope these two games will inspire you, the creators, to join the wonderful world of gaming with me.

It's impossible to cover all aspects of game programing in one short chapter. Instead, the chapter focuses on a few key areas in scalable game design and presents some usable patterns.

Messy Chess

The first game we are going to create in this chapter is Messy Chess. As the name suggests, the game is a chess game. However, it's not played by two players, but by up to 128 players on the same chessboard. The movements of chess pieces follow the regular chess rules. However, everything else is different from a traditional chess game. This is a small-scale game that allows us to explore some simple patterns before we take on more challenging ones.

Chessboard and game goal

A Messy Chess game can be played on a variety of chessboard layouts. The chessboard has a number of baselines, one for each participating team. Behind each baseline is the team's castle. Any piece that reaches a baseline of a rival team scores points (or does damage to the castle). Once a certain number of points are accumulated, the opponent's castle is taken. The goal of the game is to take all enemy castles while protecting your own castles.

Figure 16-1 shows the "classic" layout of Messy Chess. It has four baselines for four competing teams.

FIGURE 16-1 Messy Chess chessboard

Game rules

The game has the following rules:

- A player can join a game session at any time until all 128 player slots are filled. A player can leave a game session at any time.

- Once he has joined the game, the player is assigned to a team. The system tries to keep balanced numbers of players in each team.

- A player randomly is assigned a piece from the standard chess set. The piece will not be reassigned until it reaches an enemy baseline or is taken by an opponent piece.

- A player can make moves as quickly as possible.

- Taking an opponent's piece scores the number of points associated with the piece.

- Reaching an opponent's baseline does damage to the opponent's castle.

- A castle is taken after accumulating certain damages. The last team that did damage to the castle owns the castle. All pieces and players are merged to the owning team.

- The game finishes when there's only one team standing.

Extended rules

We'll implement the basic rules in this chapter. However, the game can be extended in several ways to make the battle messier.

- **Hazards**   Random hazards such as water, fire, and tornado can be introduced to the board.

- **Props**   Players can exchange their scored points for offensive props or defensive props such as bombs and drawbridges.

- **Ranks**   Players accumulate points to increase their ranks. Players with higher ranks can make moves more frequently, and in a 50-50 chance of piece encounter (when two players move their pieces to the same slot at the same time), the player with higher rank wins.

- **Alternative rules**   Castles can be destroyed instead of taken. Players can choose to join a team instead of being assigned randomly. When the game ends, the team with the highest score wins.

Challenges

Messy Chess is a relatively simple game. However, to deliver a pleasant gaming experience, you have to address two key concerns:

- **Fairness**   There will be as many as 128 players trying to make moves at the same time. The system has to provide fair opportunities for all players to make moves. This is a general concern that is applicable to most multiplayer games. I'll discuss player coordination in the "Players" section.

- **Performance**   The system has to provide real-time, consistent board updates to all players. Performance is a universal requirement of games. Providing global consistency while maintaining performance is a key challenge to address in this and similar games. I'll discuss how to use partitioning and the Observer pattern to provide scalable game board updates in the "Game board" section.

- **Player simulation** For testing purposes, you need a way to deploy simulated players (or bots) to a game session. I'll discuss how to use actors to implement both human players and simulated players in the "Players" section.

Game board

To design the game, a key problem to address is how to handle the concurrent reads and writes of chessboard status. If you use a chessboard actor with an array as its states, updating the chessboard is serialized by the actors' turn-based concurrency, which forbids concurrent reads and writes. If you use a stateful service with an array as its states, updating the chessboard is isolated by transactions, which also disallows concurrent updates. First, let's design a game board service that supports concurrent updates.

Game board service

The game board service is designed as a reliable stateful service. To enable concurrent updates, the service needs to be partitioned. Figure 16-2 shows a possible way to partition the chessboard. The chessboard is partitioned into 20 partitions so that we can have 20 concurrent updates on the chessboard. Note the partition has intermittent partition names. This is to help clients find the correct partition with which to talk. The coordinate of pieces is a 24-by-24 space, and the partition name is calculated using this formula:

$$(y \div 4) \times 6 + (x \div 4) + 1$$

For a small-scale game like this, a single partition will work well. I'm showing this partition scheme as an example of partitioning a large board that needs to support many concurrent updates.

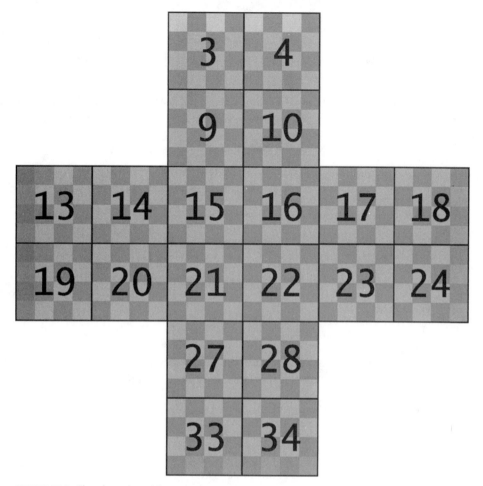

FIGURE 16-2 Chessboard partition

In the application manifest file, the service is partitioned by named partitions:

```
<Service Name="Chessboard">
    <StatefulService ServiceTypeName="ChessboardType" …>
      <NamedPartition>
          <Partition Name="3" />
          <Partition Name="4" />
          <Partition Name="9" />

        …
      </NamedPartition>
    </StatefulService>
</Service>
```

When a client tries to connect to a specific partition, it uses a partition name to indicate the partition with which it intends to work:

```
IChessboard chessClient = ServiceProxy.Create<IChessboard>("9", new Uri("fabric:/MessyChess/
Chessboard"));
```

Updating the board

The game board supports two update methods: to place a piece on the board and to take a piece from the board. Each shard (partition) of the board uses a reliable collection to save its state. Updating the board updates values in the dictionary.

Taking a piece from the board is easy—the method clears the cell identified by a 2D coordinate key to an empty structure. Before the code removes the piece, it checks if the piece is still on the board.

```
public async Task TakeAPieceAsync(ChessPieceInfo piece)
{
var myDictionary = await this.StateManager.GetOrAddAsync
<IReliableDictionary<string, ChessPieceInfo>>(mDictionaryName);
    var key = piece.X + "-" + piece.Y;
    using (var tx = this.StateManager.CreateTransaction())
    {
        var result = await myDictionary.TryGetValueAsync(tx, key);
        if (result.HasValue && result.Value.ActorId == piece.ActorId)
        {
            await myDictionary.SetAsync(tx, key, ChessPieceInfo.Empty);
        }
        await tx.CommitAsync();
    }
}
```

Putting a piece on a board is a more complicated—if the cell is occupied, your piece is taking another piece. I'll discuss how to model chess pieces later. For now, I'll leave this as a to-do item:

```
public async Task PutAPieceAsync(ChessPieceInfo piece)
{
var myDictionary = await this.StateManager.GetOrAddAsync
<IReliableDictionary<string, ChessPieceInfo>>(mDictionaryName);
    var key = piece.X+ "-" + piece.Y;
    using (var tx = this.StateManager.CreateTransaction())
    {
        var result = await myDictionary.TryGetValueAsync(tx, key);
        if (result.HasValue)
        {
            if (result.Value.ActorId == "")
            {
                await myDictionary.SetAsync(tx, key, piece);
            }
            else
            {
                //TODO: Take a piece
            }
        }
        else
        {
            await myDictionary.AddAsync(tx, key, piece);
        }
        await tx.CommitAsync();
    }
}
```

Reading the board: Observer pattern

I chose to shard the board to allow more concurrent updates. The consequence of this choice is that reading the entire board becomes more complex because the entire board needs to be reconstructed from all the shards.

To keep a global view of the entire board, I'll use a common pattern in game programs: the Observer pattern. With this pattern, a subject keeps a list of observers and notifies each of the observers when something interesting happens. Within the context of this project, I'll create a new game board observer service that observes the entire board. Whenever a board shard has a state update, it will broadcast its entire state (a four-by-four grid) to all registered observers.

The observer interface is defined as the following:

```
public interface IChessboardObserver: IService
{
    Task Notify(string partitionName, List<ChessPieceInfo> boardShard);
    Task<KeyValuePair<string, List<ChessPieceInfo>>[]> GetBoard();
}
```

The *Notify* method is used for a subject (board shard) to notify its observers. The *GetBoard()* method is for a client to retrieve the entire board.

The following code snippet is a sample implementation of the observer interface using a stateful service:

```
internal sealed class ChessboardObserver : StatefulService, IChessboardObserver
{
    private const string mDictionaryName = "board";
    protected override IEnumerable<ServiceReplicaListener> CreateServiceReplicaListeners()
    {
        return new[] { new ServiceReplicaListener(parameters =>
new ServiceRemotingListener<ChessboardObserver>(parameters, this)) };
    }
    public async Task Notify(string partitionName, List<ChessPieceInfo> boardShard)
    {
        var myDictionary = await this.StateManager
.GetOrAddAsync<IReliableDictionary<string, List<ChessPieceInfo>>>(mDictionaryName);
        using (var tx = this.StateManager.CreateTransaction())
        {
            await myDictionary.AddOrUpdateAsync(tx, partitionName, boardShard,
(k, v) => boardShard);
            await tx.CommitAsync();
        }
    }
    public async Task<KeyValuePair<string,List<ChessPieceInfo>>[]> GetBoard()
    {
        var myDictionary = await this.StateManager
.GetOrAddAsync<IReliableDictionary<string, List<ChessPieceInfo>>>(mDictionaryName);
        return myDictionary.ToArray();
    }
}
```

The *Chessboard* class needs to be updated. First, it needs to keep a list of observers. Note that under the microservice architecture, observer references are service proxies instead of class references as in a stand-alone program.

```
private List<IChessboardObserver> mObservers = new List<IChessboardObserver>();
protected override Task RunAsync(CancellationToken cancellationToken)
{
    string serviceName = this.ServiceInitializationParameters.ServiceName.ToString();
serviceName = serviceName.Substring(0,
serviceName.LastIndexOf("/"))  + "/ChessboardObserver";
    mObservers.Add(ServiceProxy.Create<IChessboardObserver>(new Uri(serviceName)));
    return Task.FromResult(1);
}
```

In addition, the *Chessboard* class needs to use a *NotifiyObservers()* method that iterates through its observers and sends notifications to them, as shown in the following code snippet.

```
private async Task NotifyObservers()
{
  var myDictionary = await this.StateManager
    .GetOrAddAsync<IReliableDictionary<string, ChessPieceInfo>>(mDictionaryName);
  Parallel.ForEach<IChessboardObserver>(mObservers, observer =>
    observer.Notify(this.ServiceInitializationParameters.PartitionId.ToString("D"),
    (from kv in myDictionary.ToList() select kv.Value).ToList()));
}
```

Last, whenever the board shard needs to notify its observers, it calls the *NotifyObservers()* method:

```
await NotifyObservers();
```

Furthermore, the Observer pattern can be used to extend the game in a couple of ways without impacting the board logic:

- To generate notifications such as achievements

- To generate a thumbnail of the game world map

Game pieces

Game pieces are individual entities that have static properties (such as type and color), dynamic properties (such as location), and behaviors (such as how they move across the board). Intuitively, these pieces can be abstracted as actors.

However, there are not just game pieces that roam around the game board. In future versions of the game, there will be props lying on the board for players to pick up, and there will be hazards that bring new challenges and twists to the game. Although their behaviors are different, they share basic characteristics: they are independent agents that move on the board and interact with one another.

Actor polymorphism

So, instead of a single GamePiece actor type, we have a hierarchy of actor types, as shown in Figure 16-3. At the top of the tree is an abstract Agent actor that encapsulates shared properties such as location and *is-alive* flag. Game pieces, props, and hazards are subclasses of the Agent actor. In Chapter 15, "Multitenancy and hosting," you've seen an example of actor polymorphism. Although the inheritance structure is more complex in this case, the implementation follows the same pattern. In Figure 16-3, each game piece type is defined as a separate subclass of the Piece actor type. Whether you need this is debatable because the only difference among these piece types is their moving rules. Is this difference sufficient to justify a different type? Some people automatically will chose to use subclasses. However, having a single Agent actor is not all bad because you have fewer actor projects in your solution.

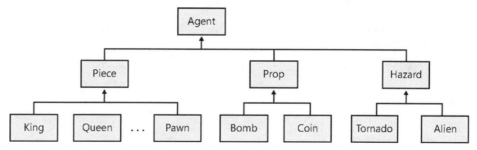

FIGURE 16-3 Game agent inheritance hierarchy

Pattern: Game Piece Dispenser

When a new player joins the game, the game needs to assign a game piece to the player. It has to be sure no game pieces will be assigned to more than one player. And if all pieces are assigned, the player has to wait for a piece to become available. To ensure fairness, we need to build up a wait list of players who wait for a piece. If a player doesn't accept the offer of a piece within a short time window, she forfeits the offer and the piece becomes available for the next player. And if a player becomes inactive (such as becoming offline) for a period of time, the assigned game piece is reclaimed so it can be assigned to a new player.

These are quite complex requirements: you'll need a globally consistent catalog of game pieces, a waiting list, a way to manage the waiting list, and a monitoring mechanism to monitor players and to reclaim pieces from inactive players. A stateful actor can meet these requirements well. First, its state can be used to save the catalog of game pieces and the waiting list. The turn-based concurrency ensures consistency in these data structures. Second, it can implement the waiting list management logic easily. It doesn't need to be concerned about any concurrency or integrity issues because it can manipulate the locally saved waiting list. Monitoring is a bit tricky, but you can use the Observer pattern discussed in the previous section to observe activities of players, which I'll discuss in the next section. It will also monitor the game board so that when a game piece is taken, the piece is put back into the pool to be reassigned.

I name this component a "Game Piece Dispenser" to avoid possible confusions with the Factory pattern. Functionally, the component provides a similar functionality to an object factory. The difference is that instead of instantiating objects, it manages actor proxies that are used to talk to game piece actors.

Now, let's consider consistency and performance. When a piece is taken, the corresponding board shard notifies the dispenser that the piece is available. Because the dispenser is the only entity that dispenses game pieces, the game piece won't be made available accidentally by other channels. In terms of performance, when using actors, you should watch out for concurrent requests to one actor instance. If a large number of players keep pulling for available pieces, the dispenser will be busy handling these requests. Instead, a player should register with the dispenser and wait for notification that a piece is available. This can be achieved by using the Observer pattern.

The dispenser can also be used for generating hazards. A dispenser has a built-in timer that triggers at different intervals depending on game difficulties.

The key logic of the dispenser resides in the game piece catalog itself:

```
[DataContract]
public class ChessPieceCatalog
{
    private static Random mRand = new Random();
    [DataMember]
    public List<Tuple<bool, ChessPieceType>> Pieces { get; set; }
    public ChessPieceCatalog()
    {
        Pieces = new List<Tuple<bool, ChessPieceType>>();
    }
    public  ChessPieceType GetAPiece()
    {
        List<int> candidates = new List<int>();
        for (int i = 0; i < Pieces.Count; i++)
            if (Pieces[i].Item1 == false)
                candidates.Add(i);
        if (candidates.Count == 0)
            return ChessPieceType.Undefined;
        else
        {
            var index = mRand.Next(0, candidates.Count);
            Pieces[candidates[index]] = new Tuple<bool, ChessPieceType>(true,
Pieces[candidates[index]].Item2);
            return Pieces[candidates[index]].Item2;
        }
    }
    public void ReturnAPiece(ChessPieceType piece)
    {
        for (int i = 0; i < Pieces.Count; i++)
        {
            if (Pieces[i].Item2 == piece && Pieces[i].Item1 == true)
            {
                Pieces[i] = new Tuple<bool, ChessPieceType>(false, Pieces[i].Item2);
                return;
            }
```

```
        }
        throw new ArgumentException(string.Format("Piece '{0}' can't be returned.", piece));
    }
    public static ChessPieceCatalog Initialize()
    {
        ChessPieceCatalog catalog = new ChessPieceCatalog();
        catalog.Pieces.Add(new Tuple<bool, ChessPieceType>(false, ChessPieceType.King));
        catalog.Pieces.Add(new Tuple<bool, ChessPieceType>(false, ChessPieceType.Queen));
        catalog.Pieces.Add(new Tuple<bool, ChessPieceType>(false, ChessPieceType.Bishop));
        ...
        return catalog;
    }
}
```

Players

A player is another good candidate for a Service Fabric actor. Because a player actor instance is associated with a single player, there won't be concurrent requests to the actor instance. And multiple player actors can operate in parallel. So, we can enjoy the simplicity of the Actor pattern without worrying about creating bottlenecks.

Players and bots

An automated player, or a bot, operates on the assigned game piece using its artificial intelligence (AI) capabilities. Intuitively, an automated player can simulate button pushes from a human being to control the game piece. Alternatively, the automated player can send commands directly to the game piece. Figure 16-4 shows both design options. To the left, both the Player actor and the Bot actor feed commands into the assigned Piece actor. To the right, the Bot actor generates simulated inputs and feeds those into the Player actor that maps them into commands and forwards them to the assigned Piece actor.

Both designs would work, but option (B) has a few more favorable characteristics. First, the Bot can't perform options that a Player can't do. This increases fidelity of the player simulation. Second, only the Player knows how to map inputs into corresponding commands. This provides a single point of change when operations on a Piece actor need to be changed. Third, both Player and Bot are server-side components. Although logically the Player actor is taking user inputs, the inputs would have been relayed through an actor proxy on the client side. So, architecturally, the inputs also are commands.

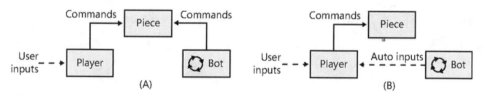

FIGURE 16-4 Automated player design choices

The Command pattern[1] is a common pattern in gaming scenarios.[2] The pattern can be used on the client side to map user inputs to corresponding commands. On the server side, both Player and Bot use a *MoveAsync()* method defined on the *Agent* class to move a chess piece.

```
public interface IAgent : IActor
{
    ...
    Task MoveAsync(int xDirection, int yDirection);
}
```

The Player class also defines a *MoveAsync()* method:

```
public interface IPlayer : IActor
{
    ...
    Task MoveAsync(int xDirection, int yDirection);
}
```

The following code snippet is a simplified implementation of the *MoveAsync()* method on the *Player* class. It also shows how a game piece is assigned to a player.

```
IChessPiece mPieceProxy;
Task IPlayer.SetChessPieceInfoAsync(ChessPieceInfo piece)
{
    this.State.ChessPiece.CopyFrom(piece);
    mPieceProxy = ActorProxy.Create<IChessPiece>(new ActorId(piece.ActorId),
GetActorUri(piece));
    return Task.FromResult(true);
}
async Task IPlayer.MoveAsync(int xDirection, int yDirection)
{
    if (this.State.ChessPiece.PieceType != ChessPieceType.Undefined && this.State.ChessPiece.
ActorId != "")
    {
        await mPieceProxy.MoveAsync(xDirection, yDirection);
    }
}
```

Player coordination

Messy Chess is not a turn-based system, so there's no need to ensure players take turns as in the Tic-Tac-Toe example. However, we need to put some controls on the players. A centralized controller can form a bottleneck easily. To avoid this, this section focuses on a few self-organizing techniques.

- **Self-throttling** In games like Messy Chess, speed is a great advantage. If piece movements are instantaneous, you'll have a board filled with jumping pieces, making the game hard to follow (there's a fine line between amusing mess and complete chaos). To provide a better gaming experience, chess piece movements are animated. This means that at any given time, a piece

---

[1] Gamma, Eric, Richard Helm, Ralph Johnson, John Vlissides, and Grady Booch. *Design Patterns: Elements of Reusable Object-Oriented Software* (Addison-Wesley Professional, 1994).

[2] Nystrom, Robert. *Game Programming Patterns* (Genever Benning, 2014).

might be standing on a board cell or be transiting from one cell to another. While the piece is in motion, the player can't make another move. Chapter 15 presented a throttling actor that can be used to throttle requests from a tenant. A Player actor can use a similar mechanism to be self-throttled. Once the associated piece is in motion, the Player actor will discard all commands until the piece has landed. This mechanism keeps the input queue drained so when the piece can respond to commands again, it will be responding to the latest command instead of commands that have been queued up while it was in motion.

- **Self-expiring**   To detect an inactive player, the Player actor runs a timer and keeps time span since last user activity. If the user has been inactive for an extended time, the Player actor returns the assigned piece to the piece dispenser. When the player becomes active again, she will need to acquire a new piece to rejoin the game.

- **Local decisions**   There's no central component to decide which piece is taking which piece. Instead, a single actor makes the decisions locally. When a piece is about to land, it checks if the cell is occupied by another piece. If the cell is occupied, the occupant is taken. A notification is sent to the taken piece to disable it. It takes a moment for a piece to take off and land. On the one hand, this delay gives a piece a brief window to make a narrow escape. On the other hand, this delay exposes a piece undefended for a moment no matter how quickly a player tries to move the piece.

Game hosting

Messy Chess uses a Client-Server (C/S) architecture in which all game clients are connected to the same server. However, with the Tenant Manager pattern, each game session can be considered a separate tenant, and each tenant has its own dedicated game application instance. Because each of the tenants can be customized independently, players can create highly customized game servers.

In Chapter 17, "Advanced service hosting," you'll learn how to host Service Fabric clusters and applications in various environments including local environments and cloud platforms other than Microsoft Azure.

When you serve players around the world, you can deploy Messy Chess to multiple Azure datacenters and use a simple host election process to select a host for a specific player. When the player tries to join the game, a tenant is selected based on communication latency differences between the client and different game hosts. You can build such an election mechanism yourself. Or, you can use Azure Traffic Manager. By using Azure Traffic Manager, you can register multiple endpoints (such as URLs to your game sites at different geolocations) with Traffic Manager and set up a performance-based policy to direct users to a server that provides the best performance. For more information on Traffic Manager, please see *https://azure.microsoft.com/services/traffic-manager/*.

A.I. Quests

A.I. Quests is a Massive Multiplayer Online Game (MMOG) with an open world for thousands of players to interact simultaneously. The sheer number of concurrent players and the massive scale of the world call for additional techniques and design patterns. It's impossible to cover the entire game in these pages. However, I want to present several of the key patterns and techniques that may help you design game engines for similar games.

Unlike the Messy Chess game, the plot of A.I. Quests is not original. Although I can't recall the exact games, I remember seeing games with similar premises—you, as a robot, roam around an open world trying to find parts to improve yourself while killing monsters and hostiles. You can join clans and build settlements. You can collect various parts that enhance your physical capabilities. But more importantly, you can acquire A.I. modules that enhance your compute powers so that you can perform more difficult tasks.

In this case, the twist is that the game world is the actual world. Your character can freely roam around the world virtually. However, some quests need to be carried out in the real world, and some parts can be picked up only at certain geolocations and only during a certain time.

Game world

Unlike Messy Chess, the game world of A.I. Quests is not described by grids. The massive scale of the world prevents it from being described in a single grid. The first problem we need to solve is how to describe the world.

Describing the world

How do you describe the whole world in a game? A.I. Quests uses sparse geographic shapes to describe the world. Gaming areas are inserted into the world map as geographic polygons. Figure 16-5 shows a number of fictional features inserted into a local map of the real world.

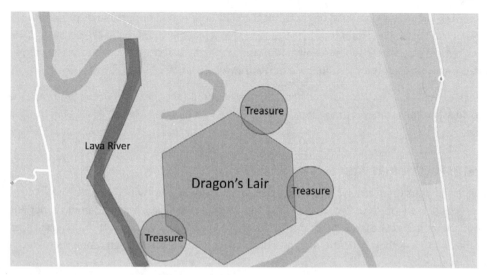

FIGURE 16-5 Fictional features laid out in physical world

Although the above layout looks complex, it can be described by five vector shapes. A circle is easiest to describe because a center point and a radius are enough to describe a circle fully. For example, the three treasure spots can be described by the following data structure:

```
[
  {"lat": 47.53, "long": -122.082, "radius": 30 },
  {"lat": 47.03, "long": -122.084, "radius": 30 },
  {"lat": 47.02, "long": -122.083, "radius": 30 }
]
```

As a robot roams around, the gaming client keeps calling a microservice that serves up shapes within the proximity. At any given time, only a few shapes are pulled down from the server. The user interaction experience is provided by the client. For example, as a robot enters the territory of a dragon's lair, a boss fight with a fierce dragon commences. The fighting experience is provided by the client, and the client reports the result to the server. During the whole boss fighting experience, the server provides only a polygon. This design allows the game to support more concurrent players with fewer resources. Furthermore, the robot's coordinate can be rounded up to fewer decimal places so that repetitive shape queries can be avoided. This also allows query results be cached to reduce the load on the server further.

Although we greatly simplified how the world map is described, building up virtual features across the world still is tedious work. One possible approach is to use mass-source that allows users to upload custom-built features into the game. Another more interesting approach is to leverage map queries provided by popular mapping services. By performing map queries with services such as Bing, you can find points of interest (POIs) near a geolocation. You can use these query results to generate features automatically—a grocery store is mapped to a weapons shop; a restaurant is mapped to a potion station; a sports field is mapped to an arena; and so on.

When the virtual world and the physical world collide, interesting opportunities present themselves. For example, you can tie certain types of virtual store to a real merchant in the physical world. To get certain items, a player needs to make an actual visit to the physical store. Or, to complete a physical quest, you can request a player to follow a trail within a time limit.

When multiple players are near one another, they all should see the same virtual features. One way to provide such consistency is to use the Dynamic Game Room pattern, which I'll cover in the "Players" section.

Pattern: Partitioned world

As millions of users roam around, you'll have a great diversity of users with different levels. Your map features need to adapt to current user levels so that each user will have a good gaming experience—you don't want to throw a level-100 dragon in front of a level-1 user. When multiple players enter the same map feature at the same time, a common approach is to use the median user level to decide the feature level.

One interesting thing to notice is that no one—not even the game server itself—ever knows exactly how the world looks. There is no global world state because there's no need for one; the world is just a collection of quests and battles. This design might be counterintuitive to you because in a typical client/server architecture, the server holds the authoritative state that can be shared with multiple clients. However, this no-global-state design works well in large-scale open-world games. Figure 16-6 shows a world with two battle zones, two quest zones, and a passage between the two battle zones. The whole world is defined by three shapes. Although there are 11 players on this map, they are segmented into different zones. This means only player states within the same zone need to be synced among this group of players. This design partitions a big world into small, manageable segments to provide better performance and scalability.

Furthermore, each of the zones can be partitioned further into multiple parallel sessions. For instance, each of the zones can be configured with a max number of participants. If there are more players trying to join the zone, they will be partitioned into multiple independent sessions, and battles will happen concurrently. The sessions are independent—they happen in parallel universes without interfering with each other.

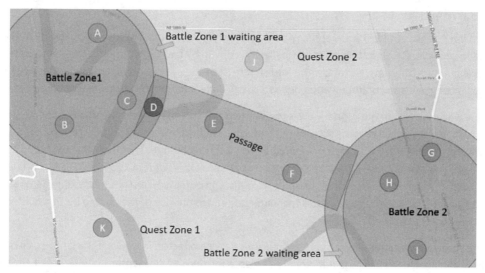

FIGURE 16-6 An abstract world layout

Spatial model

What is described above is a variation of the "aura-nimbus" model.[3] The "aura" means the area that bounds the presence of a player in the world. And the "nimbus" is an area in which a player can perceive other players. In the above examples, each zone is a nimbus that defines a small universe (or parallel universes with partitioned sessions) for players to interact with one another. Players are unaware of any updates outside the nimbus.

Auras can be used to decide random encounters. For example, when a player roams in a quest zone, when its aura intersects with the aura of a monster, a random battle is engaged.

You may have noticed that each battle zone has a waiting area. When a player enters the staging area, she becomes a candidate participant of the next battle. When any of the players in the staging area engages in the battle (such as by stepping in to the battle zone), the battle starts with all candidate participants in the waiting area. This design allows players to self-organize teams without an explicit team-matching stage. This design provides different experiences to players with different playing styles:

- Single players or small groups of players can charge through the waiting zone and enter the battle without waiting.

- Large groups of players can group in the waiting area before launching a large-scale assault.

- Cautious players can enter the waiting area and observe battle states before they decide if they want to join a battle (if the battle is still open).

---

3 Jean-Sébastien Boulanger, Clark Verbrugge, Jörg Kienzle. "Comparing Interest Management Algorithms for Massively Multiplayer Games." *NetGames* (2006): ACM. 1–12.

Global map

If the server doesn't hold a global state, what do you do if you want to present a global view of the world to all players? Generation of this global view is driven by two requirements: the refresh rate and the granularity of the view. Normally, the refresh rate decreases as the granularity increases because of the extra compute and communication needed to calculate and transmit high-resolution global views.

One way to generate this global view is to use the Aggregation pattern. The world is segmented into a grid with each grid cell presenting summary information from the corresponding region. Figure 16-7 shows a low-resolution world map generated by using this technique. The original map[4] (Population Density of the World, 1990–2015, *http://svs.gsfc.nasa.gov/vis/a000000/a002900/a002912/*) is 1,024 × 576 pixels, and the low-resolution map is 14 × 8 pixels. Of course, you are not necessarily generating an image file. The example shows you a technique to reduce the size of the data to be transmitted to clients.

The aggregation can be done by a Service Fabric service or actor. However, for a large-scale deployment, you may want to leverage additional services as introduced in Chapter 13, "Internet of Things," to handle this problem as a big data problem. For example, players report their states to an Event Hub, and a Stream Analytics job picks up the raw data and generates summaries.

The above technique shows aggregated statistics (such as number of players) on the map. If you want to display a map with individual players on it, here are some techniques that can help you improve the speed.

- **Different refresh rates by distance**   Information with close proximity is refreshed at a faster rate, while information farther away from the player is refreshed at a slower rate. This gives a clear, up-to-date view of the player's immediate surroundings while providing a rough view of the global world.

- **Random refresh grid**   Instead of trying to refresh the entire map, the map can be refreshed by randomly selected regions. Although it takes time to refresh the entire map, the randomness creates the illusion that the entire map is being updated.

- **Sampling**   Instead of refreshing every player on the global map, a random subset of players (or players with higher weights) is selected during each iteration of refresh.

---

[4] NASA/Goddard Space Flight Center Scientific Visualization Studio, Gridded Population of the World (GPW), Version 3: 1990, 1995, 2000. Gridded Population of the World: Future Estimates, 2015. Center for International Earth Science Information Network (CIESIN), Columbia University; Food and Agricultural Organization (FAO); and Centro Internacional de Agricultura Tropical (CIAT), 2005. Available at (*http://sedac.ciesin.columbia.edu/gpw*).

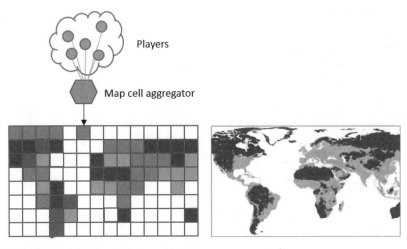

FIGURE 16-7 A low-resolution world map

Player interactions

Once you sort out the world map, you move on to players. As described previously, a player in this game is free to roam around the global map, and he can join and leave any quests or battles at any time. By using the spatial model, you allow a large number of smaller game sessions to occur independently. And for each of the sessions, you'll need some kind of "game room" or "game server" to serve for the session. This is where the Dynamic Game Room pattern comes into play.

Pattern: Dynamic Game Room

In some online games, especially first-person shooter (FPS) games such as Call of Duty, there is a distinct phase of finding matching teams before a game session starts. In some other open-world games such as Destiny, there are specially designed transitioning areas or passages on the map designed as staging areas. Only players at the staging areas at the same time are allowed to join the same battle. A.I. Quests follows the open-world method: while entering a battle zone, a player is not engaged in a battle directly. Instead, the player can choose to hang around in the outer perimeter waiting for more players to join the battle. As more players join, any of the players can initiate the battle by stepping into the battlefield. Once a battle is initiated, it's closed to other players. In your game, you can choose a different strategy; for instance, keeping the battle open at all times. However, when you do this you need to make sure no players can sneak in at the last moment of the battle and steal points and loot.

The Dynamic Game Room pattern dynamically creates game rooms to host game sessions. Each game is a new Service Fabric service instance that is initiated for a specific game session. It's destroyed after the game session completes. Figure 16-8 shows the architecture of the Dynamic Game Room pattern.

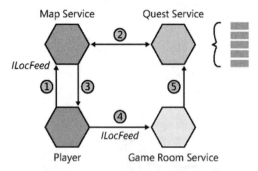

FIGURE 16-8 Dynamic Game Room pattern

The best way to understand the Dynamic Game Room pattern is to follow a series of events leading to a new game session:

1. The Player actor periodically reports its location to a Map Service. The Map Service detects if the player has entered a battle zone.

2. If the player has entered a battle zone, the Map Service contacts a Quest Service to find a game room. The Quest Service keeps a catalog of Game Room Service instances and picks (or creates) a game room.

3. The address of the selected Game Room Service instance is returned to the player.

4. The player starts to report its information to the Game Room Service instance. The player can stay in the waiting area to observe the game or enter the battle zone to initiate or join the battle.

5. It's up to the Game Room Service instance to decide when a battle is closed to new partici-pants. The service instance reports battle states to the Quest Service instance so that the Quest Service can update its catalog. A closed battle doesn't appear in future queries. And once a battle is finished, the Game Room Service instance is destroyed.

Both the Map Service and the Quest Service can be partitioned for scalability. For example, for any geolocation described by a latitude-longitude pair, each can be mapped to an integer id using a simple formula such as:

$[Latitude] \times 360 + [Longitude]$

The above partition scheme has a potential problem, which is common to grid spatial models. Figure 16-9 shows that players A, B, and C are monitored by four different Map Service partitions. Although all players are within the range of the battle zone, only player C is detected correctly because only the partition at the lower-right corner knows about the battle zone.

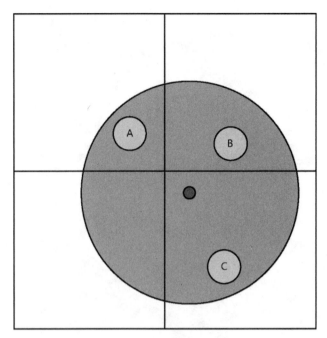

FIGURE 16-9 Map Service boundary problem

A possible alternative is to use a Voronoi diagram. (See *http://mathworld.wolfram.com /VoronoiDiagram.html* to partition the map, as shown in Figure 16-10.) This works well in most cases because by definition a player belongs to a region only when the player's position is closest to the corresponding battle zone center.

The Voronoi diagram looks nice on paper; however, you can't use a simple coordinate mapping to choose a partition. Instead, you'll need to run the geolocation through a detection algorithm to determine the region to which the player currently belongs and then use the region id to select the corresponding partition. Regardless, you will face similar boundary problems in some cases.

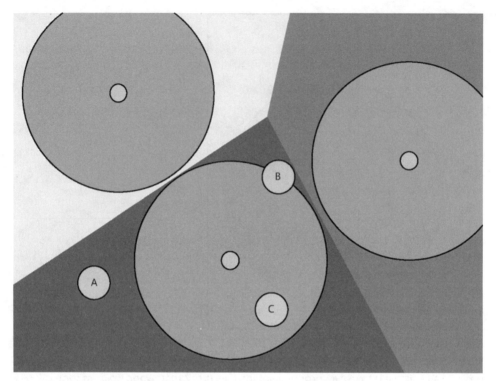

FIGURE 16-10 Service partitions with a Voronoi diagram

> ### Spatial interpolation
>
> A Voronoi diagram is equivalent to the nearest-neighbor interpolation, which is one of the spatial interpolation methods. There are other methods such as natural neighbor, bilinear, and bicubic.

Pattern: Coverage Map

To overcome the constraints of the above spatial interpolation methods, you can use a Coverage Map pattern that utilizes the statefulness of Service Fabric services. The Coverage Map pattern requires that when a battle zone is defined, it needs to register itself with all the coordinate grid cells it touches. Figure 16-11 shows how the pattern works: Each of the map cells maintains a list of battle zones. And two battle zones (zone 1 and zone 2) register with the Map Service all the cells they touch.

Once battle zones are registered, you can use the previous simple grid mapping formula to query for battle zones easily and use appropriate strategies to pick from multiple candidate battle zones. Because the Map Service is stateful, battle zone lookups are preformed locally within the Map Service instance. This method provides better performance than the earlier implementation while maintaining the simplicity and scalability of the Dynamic Game Room pattern.

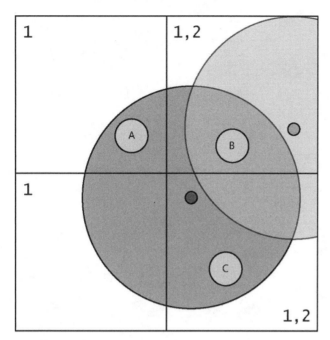

FIGURE 16-11 Coverage map

The Coverage Map can also be used for detecting random encounters among game characters. Each character has an associated "aura" circle that works in the same way as the battle zone range. As a game character moves around, it keeps updating the Map Service with what map cells it touches. In most cases, the character touches only one grid. However, in boundary conditions, a character may cover two or more cells. This pattern makes sure that the encounters at cell edges can also be detected.

Dynamic clustering

Instead of using static partitioning based on coordinates, dynamic game rooms can be created for a cluster of players. For example, in a space shooting game, a group of spaceships engaged in a battle can fly great distances. It would be inefficient to migrate these spaceships around game rooms as they fly into different regions. Instead, they should be kept in a relatively stable game room throughout the game session.

However, as the spaceships fly around, the scope of the game room might become huge, making things like collision detections and state sync more difficult. In this case, a game room can be partitioned dynamically into smaller regions so that collision detections are conducted within small regions (in parallel) to ensure game performance. You also can use data structures such as quadtrees to facilitate the process.

Advanced topics

CHAPTER 17

Advanced service hosting

When you pick a platform as a service (PaaS) platform, it's almost unavoidable that you are locked in with the platform in certain ways. Some PaaS platforms require specific programming languages, some demand certain application architectures, and others reinforce certain development methodologies.

Service Fabric is different. Although there is an emphasis on C# and Microservices in current tooling offerings, Service Fabric is capable of hosting workloads written in various programming languages under different system architectures. Furthermore, Service Fabric can host legacy binaries directly based on either Windows core or Linux kernels. Service Fabric clusters can be hosted on Azure, on-premises, or on other cloud platforms such as Amazon Web Services (AWS). The clusters can be hosted on physical machines, virtual machines, and containers.

In this chapter, you'll learn about the openness and the flexibility of Service Fabric in terms of hosting various workloads on top of different infrastructures.

> **Note** At the time of this writing, many of the areas covered in this chapter are still under active development and are subject to change. So, this chapter intentionally avoids discussing details and focuses on explaining how Service Fabric is designed to support various hosting scenarios.

A canonical PaaS platform

Before digging into specifics, it's worthwhile to study the fundamental components of a modern PaaS platform. Such understanding will help you understand how Service Fabric embraces various workloads and integrates with different underlying infrastructures.

At the highest level, a PaaS platform consists of three areas: development, operation, and community. The development area covers programming models, programming languages, application lifecycle management (ALM), and related tooling supports. The operation area covers resource management, service hosting, and other related services and tools that help independent software vendors (ISVs) and enterprises deliver continuous software as a service (SaaS) solutions. The community area covers service discovery, share and reuse, community engagements and contributions, and interoperability among services.

Figure 17-1 shows a canonical architecture of a PaaS platform. There are many PaaS platforms on the market. However, it's rare for a PaaS platform to be mature in all three areas. Most PaaS platforms are strong in one or two areas, and they are used as a foundation to build up a more complete PaaS solution by incorporating additional open-source or proprietary solutions. When you evaluate PaaS platforms, you should examine each of the three areas and make sure the platform provides sufficient coverage and flexibility in all three areas.

The diagram should be self-explanatory. In the following few sections, I'll pick one component from each area—application package, resource orchestration, and application gallery—to explain how these components enable advanced service hosting scenarios on Service Fabric.

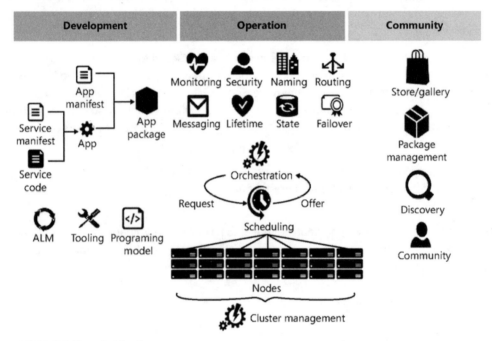

FIGURE 17-1 Canonical PaaS

Application package format

In the development area, the two most important aspects are application package format and ALM. Fundamentally, application package format provides an abstraction layer that allows various applications to be described in a consistent, manageable format. These applications, regardless of underlying programming languages and technologies, are brought into the same ALM system. In addition, some PaaS platforms such as Service Fabric provide higher-level programming models that developers can use to implement common scenarios. Last but not least, everything is tied together by tooling.

The application package format reflects the core design philosophy of a PaaS platform. A simple yet expressive format to a large extent decides the success of a PaaS solution. Simplicity and expressiveness are often contradictory goals. As a PaaS platform evolves, a simple application package may grow into a complicated format, which leads to deeper platform lock-in. For example, if you abstract all services as web services that support only HTTP or HTTPS GET requests, you can abstract any services as URLs. Conceptually, an application can be described by the following JSON snippet:

```
{
  "Name": "MyApp",
  "URL": "https://yarm.azurewebsites.net"
}
```

This is a very simple application format; however, it doesn't support other request methods such as PUT, POST, and DELETE. It is also missing authentication requirements. The application format easily can be extended to support both, as shown in the following code snippet. Although this is a simple extension, the simplicity of the package format starts to degrade.

```
{
  "Name": "MyApp",
  "URL": "http://yarm.azurewebsites.net",
  "Method": "PUT",
  "Authentication": {
    "Service": {
      "Protocol": "ws-Federation",
      "Metadata": "https://someaddress/FederationMetadata.xml"
    },
    "Client": {
      "AuthenticationType": "Certificate",
      "Metadata": {
        "ClientCert": {
          "FindMethod": "ByThumbprint",
          "FindValue": "xxxxxxxxxx"
        }
      }
    }
  }
}
```

Striking a balance between simplicity and expressiveness isn't easy. Maintaining the simplicity while the platform evolves is particularly challenging. As Albert Einstein put it, "Things should be made as simple as possible—but not simpler." As more features are introduced into the platform, often the package format becomes murky trying to accommodate additional features.

Service Fabric uses a simple abstraction model to describe applications and services: a service essentially is a process with any number of endpoints, and an application is a collection of services. This abstraction model allows a great number of workloads to be described; for example, you've seen how a Node.js application can be hosted by Service Fabric in Chapter 5, "Service deployments and upgrades." These workloads have no knowledge of Service Fabric, yet Service Fabric is able to provide important services such as high availability, monitoring, and hosting density. In the "Hosting guest applications" section later in this chapter, you'll see detailed introductions of how this is made possible.

Service Fabric describes an application using a number of metadata files. First, a Service Fabric service is defined as a service manifest file, and a Service Fabric application is defined as an application manifest file. Second, service-level settings are captured by a settings file, and application-level parameters are captured by a parameters file. Finally, application publish settings are captured in publish profiles.

Resource orchestration

When an application is deployed, it needs some compute and storage resources to be allocated to support it. Because an application can be made up of multiple interacting components, resource allocations have to be conducted across cluster nodes in a coordinated manner so that an application can acquire sufficient resources and optimized resource topology for all its services. The situation is complicated further in a multitenant environment where multiple applications are hosted and scaled at the same time on the same physical cluster.

A layered approach works well in dealing with such situations. At the top, an orchestration engine coordinates logical service component deployments. The engine doesn't directly manage underlying compute and storage resources. Instead, it requests desired resources from a scheduling system. The scheduling system maintains a catalog of compute resources on the cluster and offers possible deployment slots to the orchestration engine. The orchestration engine analyzes application requirements, including resource usage, affinity, and constraints, and makes resource requests to allocate the required resources. The process can be carried out in iterations until all resource requests are fulfilled.

There's a clear separation of concerns here. The orchestration engine doesn't know how the underlying nodes are managed. It just asks for resources, such as CPUs, memory, and disks, to host a certain workload. The scheduling system, in contrast, doesn't care about the applications. It's just serving up compute resources to legitimate requestors. This clear separation brings tremendous flexibility into a PaaS platform because it allows the platform to be bound dynamically to different scheduling systems. These systems can be based on physical machines, virtual machines, and containers hosted in local datacenters; on the cloud; or in a hybrid environment that spans multiple datacenters and cloud platforms.

Orchestration engine

In some literatures, the concept of resource orchestration is considered to cover both resource scheduling and cluster management. Here, I treat orchestration engine as an explicit component to illustrate the importance of separation of concerns that enables Service Fabric applications to be deployed on a wide range of environments.

The last piece in resource orchestration is cluster management. Cluster management works closely with the underlying infrastructure and is able to adjust the number of nodes on the cluster as needed. This capability of cluster management brings an additional scaling vector to expand the capacity of a PaaS platform dynamically to adapt to unforeseen workload increases. As introduced in earlier chapters, Service Fabric uses Azure VM Scale Sets to provide cluster management capabilities. Note that this design is another case of separation of concerns. Azure VM Scale Sets has no knowledge of Service Fabric. It just adds machines with specified VM image and extensions. The extensions on these machines bootstrap the machines into the existing Service Fabric cluster.

Application gallery

There are several successful online artifact galleries in the software community, including NuGet for .NET (*https://www.nuget.org/*), npm for JavaScript (*https://www.npmjs.com/*), Python Package Index (*https://pypi.python.org/pypi*), and Docker Hub for Docker images (*https://hub.docker.com/*). Although these galleries serve different communities, they have a few things in common. First, they all provide an easy experience to discover and reuse published packages. Second, they all provide strong publish supports for community members to make contributions. Third, they all are highly reliable to make them trustworthy as an integral part of the development process (without introducing unnecessary runtime dependencies). They already have become reliable partners to developers to address problem domains so that the developers can focus on their tasks at hand.

At the time of this writing, Service Fabric doesn't have a dedicated service gallery. However, a service gallery makes sense. Imagine there's an online payment service you easily can include in your application as if you were including an assembly reference, or there's a natural language translation service you can acquire and scale a tenant as if you were managing a service project in your Service Fabric applications.

The idea of such galleries is not new. There have been several unsuccessful attempts to enable service discovery and reuse, such as UDDI and ebXml. Regardless of the initial adaptions, the developer community has failed to embrace either system for various reasons. In my opinion, the biggest problem is that both systems are trying to provide more features than needed and demand high commitment from developers before they can be adapted. In comparison, the successful package galleries adapt to the development process of particular developer community. They do one thing—deliver required packages to developers—and then they step away.

An active Microservices gallery or store is beneficial to the cloud developer community. Because many of these services would require a large amount of data, intensive computing, specialized algorithms, and customized configurations, their added values to developers are more apparent than static software packages. So, a Microservices gallery or marketplace makes more sense than other types of package galleries. However, because I can't predict if there will be successful galleries or stores emerging in the market, I shall stop speculating further.

Hosting guest applications

Within the context of application hosting on PaaS, a *guest application* refers to an application that is not integrated with PaaS in any way. These applications have no dependencies on any of the features provided by the PaaS platform. They are hosted on the service cluster as generic Windows or Linux processes.

As introduced in the previous section of this chapter, Service Fabric application package format allows arbitrary executables or scripts—guest applications—to be packaged as a service. You can deploy and manage the service along with other services in your application. Guest applications such as Java-based applications are hosted as stateless services on Service Fabric clusters.

Although these services don't leverage any Service Fabric capabilities, Service Fabric can provide essential Quality of Service (QoS) features to these services.

High availability

As you've learned in Chapter 6, "Availability and reliability," Service Fabric provides high availability to hosted applications and services. When you deploy a guest application as a Service Fabric service, you can set up multiple instances to share the workload. These instances also serve as active backups for one another so that when one or several instances fail, the service remains available as long as there is at least one healthy instance.

When a Service Fabric cluster node fails, service instances on the node automatically are migrated to healthy nodes. When a service process crashes, Service Fabric tries to restart it several times until it's recovered or the max number of allowed retries is reached. By default, Service Fabric uses a retry policy that allows 10 retries with increasing intervals over an hour.

Health monitoring

As you've learned in Chapter 5, Service Fabric uses a health model that reports and aggregates health states of various health entities. A guest application is not hooked up into this model by default. If you want Service Fabric to monitor your application more closely than just monitoring the service instance processes, you'll need to integrate the application into the health model.

It's hard to make changes to many legacy applications. In this case, you can create a custom watchdog that watches over the legacy application and reports health events to the health store (see Chapter 5). Moreover, you can continue to use other first-party or third-party monitoring solutions such as Application Insights and Dynatrace (*http://www.dynatrace.com/*).

Application lifecycle management

As you'll see in the following walkthrough, once a guest application is packaged as a Service Fabric service, it can be deployed along with other services in the same Service Fabric application. Moreover, the guest application participates in the same rolling update and rollback processes as other Service Fabric services. So, if you have an application that contains both native Service Fabric services and wrapped legacy applications, all services can be managed as a single logical entity. See Chapter 5 for more details on the rolling upgrade process.

Density

As long as a cluster node can offer sufficient resources, Service Fabric can pack multiple service instances from the same or different applications onto the same Service Fabric cluster node, providing higher hosting densities.

Hosting a simple guest application

In the following walkthrough, you'll host a guest application that is a simple web server implemented as a console application. You'll learn the steps of packaging and deploying the application and conduct several simple tests on QoS services provided by Service Fabric.

Creating a simple console-based web server

1. Create a new console application named *GuestApplication*.

2. Change the application's target framework to .NET 4.5.1 and platform target to x64.

3. Modify the *Main()* method of the application to implement a simple web listener:

```
static int Main(string[] args)
{
    const string commandKey = "COMMAND";
    HttpListener listener = new HttpListener();
    listener.Prefixes.Add("http://+:8088/");
    listener.Start();
    while (true)
    {
        var context = listener.GetContext();
        var request = context.Request;
        if (request.QueryString.AllKeys.Contains(commandKey))
        {
            switch (request.QueryString[commandKey])
            {
                case "kill":
                    return 1;
                case "stop":
                    return 0;
            }
        }
        var response = context.Response;
        string responseString = "Server time now is: " + DateTime.Now.ToLongDateString()
    + " "
    + DateTime.Now.ToLongTimeString();
        byte[] buffer = System.Text.Encoding.UTF8.GetBytes(responseString);
        response.ContentLength64 = buffer.Length;
        using (Stream output = response.OutputStream)
        {
            output.Write(buffer, 0, buffer.Length);
            output.Close();
        }
    }
}
```

4. As you can see, this application has no knowledge of Service Fabric. If you want to try out the application now, you'll need to launch the application as an administrator because port binding requires administrative privileges. Once the application is launched, you can send web requests to the server using a browser and see the current server time.

5. To kill the web server, send a "kill" command to the server, which will cause the program to exist with a non-zero return value:

```
http://localhost:8088/?COMMAND=kill
```

Packaging the application as a service

You've learned how a Service Fabric application package is organized in Chapter 5. You can craft the package manually following the format. Here, I'm going to take a shortcut and use Visual Studio to repackage the application as a Service Fabric service.

1. Add a new Service Fabric application named *TimeServiceApplication* with a single stateless service named *TimeService* to the solution shown previously.

2. In the TimeService project, create a *Code* folder under the PackageRoot folder. We'll be copying our console application executable into this folder.

3. In the console application project, add a post-build event that copies the compiled executable to the TimeService project's *PackageRoot\Code* folder:

```
copy $(TargetPath) $(SolutionDir)\TimeService\PackageRoot\Code
```

4. To make sure we always package the latest console application, change project dependencies so that the Service Fabric application and service are built after the console application.

5. In the TimeService project, create a new *Scripts* folder under the Code folder and then add a Updateacl.cmd file with the following scripts that set up Access Control List (ACL) so the Network Service user can bind to the 8088 port:

```
netsh http add urlacl url=http://+:8088/ user="NT AUTHORITY\NETWORK SERVICE"
exit /b 0
```

6. Modify the ServiceManifest.xml file in the TimeService project. There are several changes worth noticing: First, the service type is declared to use implicit host (*UseImplicitHost=" true"*) to notify Service Fabric that a custom executable is used. Second, a setup entry point is configured to run the configuration script (*scripts\updateacl.cmd*) before the service process launches. Third, the endpoint definition is modified to specify the protocol (*http*) and the required port (*8088*).

```xml
<?xml version="1.0" encoding="utf-8"?>
<ServiceManifest Name="TimeServicePkg" …>
  <ServiceTypes>
    <StatelessServiceType ServiceTypeName="TimeServiceType" UseImplicitHost="true" />
  </ServiceTypes>
  <CodePackage Name="Code" Version="1.0.0">
    <SetupEntryPoint>
      <ExeHost>
```

```
        <Program>scripts\updateacl.cmd</Program>
      </ExeHost>
    </SetupEntryPoint>
    <EntryPoint>
      <ExeHost>
        <Program>GuestApplication.exe</Program>
      </ExeHost>
    </EntryPoint>
  </CodePackage>
  <ConfigPackage Name="Config" Version="1.0.0" />
  <Resources>
    <Endpoints>
      <Endpoint Name="ServiceEndpoint" Protocol="http" Port="8088" Type="Input" />
    </Endpoints>
  </Resources>
</ServiceManifest>
```

7. Next, modify the application manifest. Note that a "run-as" policy is configured to launch the setup script as an administrator because the script needs administrative privileges.

```
<?xml version="1.0" encoding="utf-8"?>
<ApplicationManifest xmlns:xsd="http://www.w3.org/2001/XMLSchema" ...>
    ...
  <ServiceManifestImport>
      <ServiceManifestRef ServiceManifestName="TimeServicePkg"
ServiceManifestVersion="1.0.0" />
      <ConfigOverrides />
      <Policies>
          <RunAsPolicy CodePackageRef="Code" UserRef="SetupAdminUser"
EntryPointType="Setup" />
      </Policies>
  </ServiceManifestImport>
    ...
  <Principals>
      <Users>
          <User Name="SetupAdminUser">
              <MemberOf>
                  <SystemGroup Name="Administrators" />
              </MemberOf>
          </User>
      </Users>
  </Principals>
</ApplicationManifest>
```

8. Deploy the Service Fabric application and test the new time service using a browser. Everything should work as expected, and you should see current server time displayed in your browser view.

Service Fabric feature tests

Next, you'll conduct a couple of simple tests so that you can observe how Service Fabric delivers QoS services.

1. Open Service Fabric Explorer. Identify the node where the time service instance is hosted.

2. Select the node and deactivate it (by using the *Actions*, *Deactivate (restart)* menu).

3. Observe that the service instance is automatically migrated to a healthy node. This test demonstrates how Service Fabric migrates your service instances from the failing node to a healthy node to restore the instances.

4. Once the service instance is migrated, you can use a browser to access the site again. Send a request that simulates an application crash:

```
http://localhost:8088/?COMMAND=kill
```

5. The preceding request will fail because it triggers the console application to exit. After a few seconds, the application will be relaunched and you'll be able to access the site again. This test verifies that Service Fabric is monitoring your service instance process and that it tries to recover a failed process on your behalf.

6. Optionally, you can repeat the test using a "stop" command instead of a "kill" command. The difference is that the stop command causes the application to exit normally (with a return code of 0), but the kill command causes the application to exit with a return code of 1. Regardless, Service Fabric will try to relaunch the process for you.

Implementing a simple watchdog

Next, you'll implement a simple watchdog that monitors the health of a service instance and generates health reports on the guest application. In the following walkthrough, the watchdog is implemented as a stateless service that is affiliated with the *TimeService*. In other words, you'll have a watchdog instance collocated with every *TimeService* instance.

1. Add a new stateless service named *WatchdogService* to the previously described Service Fabric application.

2. Implement the service logic as shown in the following code snippet. The service uses a *WebClient* to access the time service using the localhost address and reports an error if five consecutive requests failed. The watchdog is able to use the local address because it's correlated with the main service using affinity.

```
internal sealed class WatchdogService : StatelessService
{
    private Uri applicationName = new Uri("fabric:/TimeServiceApplication");
    private string serviceManifestName = "TimeServicePkg";
    private string nodeName = FabricRuntime.GetNodeContext().NodeName;
    private FabricClient Client = new FabricClient(new FabricClientSettings() {
HealthReportSendInterval = TimeSpan.FromSeconds(0) });
    protected override async Task RunAsync(CancellationToken cancelServiceInstance)
    {
        int failedCount = 0;
        while (!cancelServiceInstance.IsCancellationRequested)
        {
            using (WebClient client = new WebClient())
            {
                try
                {
                    string payload = client.DownloadString(new Uri("http://
```

```
localhost:8088/"));
                            if (!string.IsNullOrEmpty(payload))
                            {
                                failedCount = 0;
                                var deployedServicePackageHealthReport = new
DeployedServicePackageHealthReport(
                                    applicationName,
                                    serviceManifestName,
                                    nodeName,
                                    new HealthInformation("CustomWatchDog",
"WebServerHealth", HealthState.Ok));
                                Client.HealthManager.ReportHealth(deployedServicePackageHealthRe
port);
                                ServiceEventSource.Current.ServiceMessage(this, "Watchdog is
happy");
                            }
                        }
                        catch (WebException)
                        {
                            failedCount++;
                            ServiceEventSource.Current.ServiceMessage(this, "Watchdog had
detected " + failedCount + " failures.");
                            if (failedCount >= 5)
                            {
                                var deployedServicePackageHealthReport = new
DeployedServicePackageHealthReport(
                                    applicationName,
                                    serviceManifestName,
                                    nodeName,
                                    new HealthInformation("CustomWatchDog", "WebServerHealth",
HealthState.Error));
                                Client.HealthManager.ReportHealth(deployedServicePackageHealthRe
port);
                                ServiceEventSource.Current.ServiceMessage(this, "Watchdog is
sad.");
                            }
                        }
                    }
                    await Task.Delay(TimeSpan.FromSeconds(1), cancelServiceInstance);
                }
            }
        }
```

3. Modify the application manifest to set up affinity between the watchdog and the time service. Note I've also changed the *InstanceCount* on both services to use the same parameter because Service Fabric requires affiliated services to have the same instance count.

```
<DefaultServices>
    <Service Name="WatchdogService">
        <StatelessService ServiceTypeName="WatchdogServiceType" InstanceCount="[Instanc
eCount]">
            <SingletonPartition />
            <ServiceCorrelations>
                <ServiceCorrelation ServiceName="fabric:/TimeServiceApplication/
TimeService" Scheme="Affinity" />
            </ServiceCorrelations>
```

```
                </StatelessService>
        </Service>
        <Service Name="TimeService">
            <StatelessService ServiceTypeName="TimeServiceType" InstanceCount="[InstanceCou
nt]">
                <SingletonPartition />
            </StatelessService>
        </Service>
    </DefaultServices>
```

4. Deploy the application to your local Service Fabric cluster. Open Service Fabric Explorer and observe how the service instances are correlated. As shown in Figure 17-2, the watchdog instance and the time service instance are placed on the same node (Node.2 in this case).

FIGURE 17-2 Service affinity

5. To verify that the watchdog is doing its job, open Cloud Explorer in Visual Studio and expand the Service Fabric node until you see the watchdog service, as shown in Figure 17-3. Right-click the watchdog service and select the View Streaming Traces menu. This brings up the Diagnostic Events view that shows the tracing events generated by the watchdog.

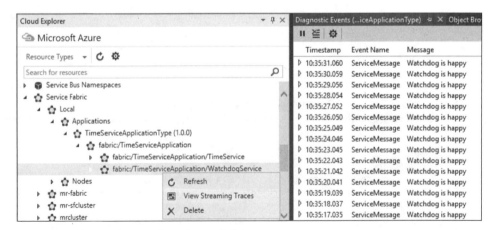

FIGURE 17-3 Diagnostic events from the watchdog

6. Modify the watchdog to make it fail by changing the port number to a different port:

```
string payload = client.DownloadString(new Uri("http://localhost:8089/"));
```

7. Redeploy the application. After a few seconds, you'll see the application is considered unhealthy because of the faulty reports sent by the watchdog. Figure 17-4 shows the unhealthy evaluations generated by the watchdog. Note that application name, service manifest name, and node name are filled with correct values.

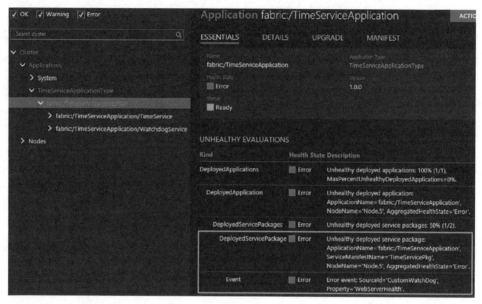

FIGURE 17-4 Failing application on Service Fabric Explorer

Container integration

In recent years, containers have become a hot topic in both service hosting and application distribution. Popularized by companies such as Docker and Mesosphere, container technology is taking the software industry by storm. Many enterprises and ISVs are seeking container-based solutions that provide isolation, mobility, density, and efficiency in application hosting. Before we discuss Service Fabric container integration, let's review how we got here.

History of containers

Computers used to be scarce resources. In the early mainframe systems, compute tasks had to be scheduled in batches because computers could only do one thing at a time. In the 1960s, virtualization technologies such as the IBM CP/CMS operating system emerged that allowed multiple users to share compute resources. In the 1990s, virtualization products such as Virtual PC and VMWare became mainstream offerings to both enterprises and consumers to host multiple guest operations systems on the same hardware. Microsoft released Hyper-V as part of Windows Server 2008. And Hyper-V was then made available to client operating systems such as Microsoft Windows 7 and Windows 8. Virtualization allows multiple users or applications to share hardware as if each of them has exclusive access to compute resources. It provides many benefits such as application isolation and higher compute density that made the technology a popular choice for managing both datacenter servers and personal computers.

In parallel, application virtualization has also been evolving. The idea of application virtualization is to have applications running on an abstraction layer that can be hosted on all kinds of operating systems. Java and .NET Framework are two of the most successful application virtualization frameworks that have been adopted widely in developer communities. Application virtualization provides portability, but it doesn't provide application isolation. To enable multiple applications to coexist peacefully on the same operating systems, resource isolation and governance techniques such as namespaces and cgroups were introduced. These isolation technologies create a virtual environment for the application so that the application feels it has exclusive access to the entire system, although it's sharing the system core with all other applications. In such cases, the application is contained in a virtual environment, which is called a container. The application running in a container is often called a *containerized application*.

Container isolation is not as strong as virtual machine isolation. However, it has several significant advantages. First, containers are more efficient because they share a system core. Because container images don't include system core files, they are lightweight, which allows them to be transferred and shared easily. Second, containers can be launched and destroyed quickly. Hence, failovers and dynamic scaling of containerized applications can be carried out much faster than applications hosted on virtual machines. Third, containers provide higher compute density. Even with powerful servers, only a few virtual machines can be hosted on the same machine. In contrast, hundreds of containers can be packed onto the same physical or virtual machine.

The lightweight nature of containers makes using containers an appealing option for application distribution. A container encapsulates all dependencies of an application with the application binaries into an isolated package. This package can be deployed consistently to any environments that support containers. You don't need to worry about missing dependencies, application compatibility issues, or system configuration differences. System configuration discrepancies in particular have been a major source of friction between development teams and operations teams. The ensured consistency containers provide solves this problem because a containerized application behaves consistently in all environments such as dev, QA, and production.

Many complex applications are made up of multiple components. Managing such applications requires a number of containers to be managed in a coordinated manner. Container orchestration technologies such as Docker Swarm, Mesos, Kubernetes, and Deis are designed to coordinate management of multiple containers.

Container orchestration provides the foundation for hosting Microservices. A Microservices application consists of multiple services, and each service can have multiple instances. Each of the service instances can be encapsulated in a container so that Microservices applications can be hosted, migrated, and scaled easily.

Microsoft provides comprehensive support for Docker containers. Please see Appendix C, "Microsoft and containers," for more details.

Service Fabric and containers

Service Fabric is a PaaS platform that provides a Microservices framework. As a hosted service, Service Fabric provides everything that is needed to deploy and host Microservices, as shown in Figure 17-5. At the same time, Service Fabric is a runtime that can be hosted on physical machines, virtual machines, and containers.

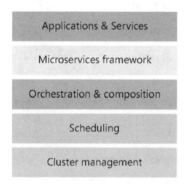

FIGURE 17-5 Service Fabric cluster stack

Service Fabric can be integrated with containers in two ways: to host guest containers and to run inside containers. In the first case, Service Fabric hosts containerized applications as guest applications. In the second case, Service Fabric acts as an application runtime that is hosted in orchestrated containers.

Guest containers

You can host containerized applications as guest applications. Service Fabric is going to support a *ContainerHost* element in the service manifest. The element defines a Docker image and additional parameters. When the service is deployed, Service Fabric pulls down the specified image from Docker Hub (*https://hub.docker.com/*), a Docker Trusted Registry (*https://www.docker.com/products/docker -trusted-registry*), or a private image registry (see Appendix C) and launches the container with provided parameters. The following service manifest snippet shows an example of how the *ContainerHost* element looks in upcoming Service Fabric versions:

```
<ServiceManifest Name="ContosoServiceTypePkg" Version="1.0">
    ...
    <CodePackage Name="CodePkg" Version="1.0">
          <EntryPoint>
                  <ContainerHost>
                          <ImageName>contoso/frontend</ImageName>
                          <Commands></Commands>
                  </ContainerHost>
          </EntryPoint>
    ...
</ServiceManifest>
```

Guest containers are similar to guest applications, but they provide additional resource governance so that an application in a container doesn't consume all compute resources on the host. When a Docker container is launched (via Docker run command, for instance), some options can be specified to constrain the amount of resources the container can consume. Although the exact syntax supported by Service Fabric is unclear at the time of this writing, I assume some (if not all) of the common options will be supported, for example:

- **-m <number><unit>**   Memory limit; for example, "-m 1g" represents an application constrained to consume up to 1 GB memory.

- **--cpu-quota**   Limit the CPU Completely Fair Scheduler (CFS) quota.

- **--cpuset-cpus**   CPUs in which the application is allowed to execute.

- **--device-read-bps <device-path>:<number><unit>**   Maximum read rate from a device.

> **More info**   For a complete list of Docker run options, see *https://docs.docker.com/engine/reference/run/*).

Like guest applications, guest containers are assumed to be stateless. Although the containerized applications can choose to have local states, these states will not be replicated, and consistency problems may arise during failovers.

Service Fabric in containers

To leverage the resource governance capability of containers, Service Fabric is going to support a deeper integration mode in which a Service Fabric run time is packaged inside containers, and it communicates with the Service Fabric run time on the host machine to organize containers into a full-feature Service Fabric cluster. Figure 17-6 shows a high-level view of this integration mode.

The integration mode supports all Service Fabric features, including stateful services. The technical implementation details are unknown at the time of this writing. Theoretically, the state management service is provided by leveraging Docker data volumes. State replications can be carried out at the data volume level with minimum involvement from the containerized applications.

For certain scenarios, the state replication potentially can be completely hidden from the application. The application just accesses data volumes as regular data disk paths, and an independent replication mechanism provided by Service Fabric or a third-party solution will handle state replications automatically. This design allows stateful legacy applications to be containerized and managed by Service Fabric, which brings reliability, availability, and scalability to these legacy applications.

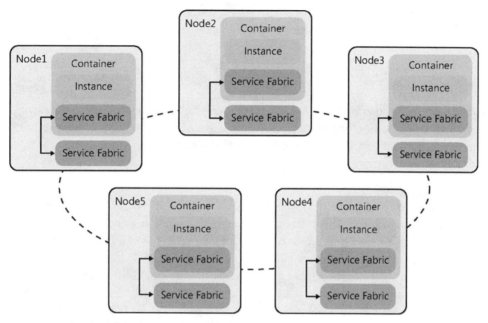

FIGURE 17-6 Service Fabric cluster with containers

The integration model also unifies Azure's Container Service and Service Fabric. Figure 17-7 illustrates the relationships among Service Fabric, Container Service, and VM Scale Sets under this integration model. At the bottom, VM Scale Sets provide scalable cluster management so that the size of the cluster can be adjusted dynamically based on system loads. On top of the VM Scale Sets is Container Service that provides container orchestration and composition. Finally, Service Fabric provides Microservices framework and programming model to application developers.

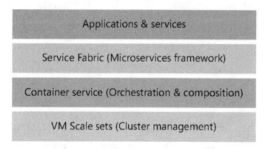

FIGURE 17-7 Service Fabric cluster stack with containers

The integration model allows first-party and third-party container orchestration technologies to be used. A detailed introduction of container orchestration is outside the scope of this book. The following is a quick list of popular container orchestration solutions on the market:

- Docker Swarm (*https://www.docker.com/products/docker-swarm*)

- Mesos (*http://mesos.apache.org/*)

- Kubernetes (*http://kubernetes.io/*)
- Deis (*https://deis.com/*)

Container types

Container integration allows Service Fabric to host containerized applications and to operate on existing container clusters. At the time of this writing, there are three major container types: Docker Containers, Windows Server Containers, and Hyper-V Containers. Service Fabric supports all three types of containers.

Docker Containers

Docker Containers are based on Linux technologies such as namespaces and cgroups, and they share Linux kernels. In other words, Docker containers are Linux-based. Service Fabric is based on C++, so in theory the code can be adapted and compiled for Linux distributions. In fact, some early tests with Service Fabric running on Linux showed promising results. It is clear that Service Fabric is progressing to become a truly cross-platform PaaS solution. Furthermore, with .NET Core (*https://dotnet.github.io/*) coming to Linux and ASP.NET Core 1.0 (*https://get.asp.net/*) coming to .NET Core, .NET developers can implement their services and websites in C# and host these services on both Windows and Linux.

Windows Server Containers

Windows Containers is the Microsoft container implementation based on Windows kernel. Starting with Windows Server 2016, two types of Windows Containers are supported out-of-box on Windows servers: Windows Server Containers and Hyper-V Containers.

Windows Server Containers is Docker Container's counterpart on Windows. Windows Server Containers share Windows kernel, and they use process and namespace isolation technology to provide isolations among containers.

In upcoming versions, Service Fabric will provide native support for both container integration modes on Windows Containers.

Hyper-V Containers

Windows Server Containers and Docker Containers share a system kernel. As container technology progresses, escaping from containers could become increasingly hard. However, there's no guarantee that a malicious application won't escape from its container and damage other applications or even the host. So, containers are ideal for hosting applications in the same trust scope so that the danger of container escapes is minimized.

However, in some cases you need to host applications that are less trusted. For example, on a multitenant PaaS platform, applications from different tenants are hosted in a shared infrastructure. To reinforce strong isolations among tenants, virtual machines need to be used, which means the agility and density benefits of containers can't be enjoyed.

To solve this problem, Microsoft provides Hyper-V Containers. Hyper-V Containers have their own copies of Windows kernel and directly assigned memory. They provide the same isolation level found in virtual machines. They are less efficient than Windows Server Containers, but they provide strong isolations. Hyper-V Containers and Windows Server Containers use the same image format. Thus, tradeoffs between isolation and efficiency are deploy-time decisions.

Deploy anywhere

As introduced earlier in this chapter, Service Fabric is a complete PaaS solution. It's also a runtime that can be deployed on a wide range of environments, including local physical and virtual machines, cloud-based virtual machines, and different types of containers.

At the time of this writing, the exact experiences of deploying Service Fabric in different environments are being defined. At a high level, the following deployment scenarios will be supported.

Deploy stand-alone clusters

Service Fabric provides an install package that you can use to create stand-alone Service Fabric clusters. The cluster can be hosted on a group of on-premises servers (Windows Server 2012 R2, Windows Server 2016, and Linux servers) or on a group of virtual machines on Azure or other cloud platforms such as Amazon Web Services (AWS) .

When using stand-alone clusters, you are responsible for maintaining the health of the underlying infrastructure. Additionally, you won't have access to Azure features such as Microsoft Azure management portal, Azure Diagnostics, Operational Insights, and autoscaling. However, you'll be able to use the Service Fabric Explorer to monitor and manage your clusters.

Stand-alone clusters have several benefits over hosted services. First, you are not locked in with a particular cloud vendor. Second, you can avoid unexpected outages of cloud platforms. Third, you can deploy highly customized applications such as applications that require GPUs or specialized hardware. For example, a 3-D printer farm can be managed by a stand-alone Service Fabric cluster that uses GPU for 3-D model processing and schedules print tasks to the printer grid.

Deploy on Azure Stack

Azure Stack (*https://azure.microsoft.com/overview/azure-stack/*) brings the power of Azure to your local datacenters. With Azure Stack, you can deploy your private copy of Azure and enjoy services such as Virtual Machines and Virtual Networks, Azure Storage, and App Services in an isolated, fully controlled environment.

Azure Stack is a unique hybrid cloud platform product that allows you to use and deliver Azure infrastructure as a service (IaaS), PaaS, and SaaS services from your own datacenters. It enables powerful hybrid scenarios such as bursting to cloud, failover, and mobility between on-premises and the cloud.

For Azure Stack, the long-term goal is to provide parity between on-premises datacenters and cloud environments. Because it is an important PaaS offering, it's expected that Service Fabric will be natively supported by Azure Stack. When Service Fabric is integrated with Azure Stack, provisioning and managing a Service Fabric cluster on Azure Stack will be a similar (if not identical) experience to managing an Azure-based cluster.

Deploy on Amazon Web Services (AWS)

You can deploy stand-alone Service Fabric clusters on other cloud platforms such as Amazon Web Services (AWS) . For example, you want to use Service Fabric, but you have an existing plan with AWS. Instead of provisioning Service Fabric clusters on Azure, you can put the clusters on AWS so that the Service Fabric services are collocated with your other hosted services on AWS. However, when you deploy a stand-alone cluster, you don't get any benefits of hosted services.

Service Fabric standalone package

Microsoft provides a stand-alone Service Fabric package for Windows Server 2012 that you can use in the above deployment scenarios. You can get a copy of the package from *http://go.microsoft.com/fwlink/?LinkId=730690*. The package is a zip file that is named as Microsoft.Azure.ServiceFabric.WindowsServer.*<version>*.zip. The package contains a number of files, among which is a ClusterConfig.JSON file. You'll need to modify this file to configure your cluster and then run a CreateServiceFabricCluster.ps1 script to provision the cluster.

> **Note** This section is based on the article on azure.com. For the complete article, go to: *https://azure.microsoft.com/documentation/articles/service-fabric-cluster-creation-for-windows-server/*

Machine prerequisites

The virtual or physical machines hosting Service Fabric nodes need to satisfy the following prerequisites:

- Minimum of 2 GB memory is recommended.
- Network connectivity. Make sure that the machines are on a secure network or networks.
- Windows Server 2012 R2 or Windows Server 2012 (you need to have KB2858668 installed).
- .NET Framework 4.5.1 or higher, full install.
- Windows PowerShell 3.0.
- The cluster administrator deploying and configuring the cluster must have administrator privileges on each of the computers.

Planning for your cluster

Before you provision your cluster, you need to go through a planning process to decide several things such as: how big your cluster is, what the node types on the cluster are, and how many fault domains and upgrade domains the cluster has. Once you've made these decisions, you can modify the ClusterConfig.JSON file accordingly:

- **properties\nodeTypes** You need at least one node type defined in this array. The package defines three node types by default. You can remove the ones you don't want or define additional ones.

- **nodes** You define each of the cluster nodes and both fault domains and upgrade domains in the nodes array. For each node, you need to specify a name, an IP address or DNS name, a node type reference, and fault domains and upgrade domains. The following code snippet shows a sample node definition on localhost.

```
{
    "nodeName":"vm1",
    "iPAddress":"localhost",
    "nodeTypeRef":"NodeType0",
    "faultDomain":"fd:/dc1/r0",
    "upgradeDomain":"UD0"
}
```

The upgrade domains and fault domains are identified by string names of your choice. In addition, fault domains support hierarchical structure so that you can use fault domains to reflect your infrastructure topologies, for example: "fd:/Site1/Room1/Rack1/Machine1."

To provision a one-box cluster for testing, specify the same IP address for all nodes.

Deploy the cluster

To deploy the cluster, invoke the CreateFabricCluster.ps1 script:

```
.\CreateServiceFabricCluster.ps1 –ClusterConfigFilePath c:\SFPackage\ClusterConfig.json
-MicrosoftServiceFabricCabFilePath c:\SFPackage\MicrosoftAzureServiceFabric.cab
```

Note that if the version of the script isn't signed, you'll need to modify your PowerShell execution policy to unblock the script.

Running Service Fabric on Linux

At the time of this writing, Service Fabric provides a limited preview of Linux support. The preview allows you to run a single-node or multinode cluster on Ubuntu Server 15.10.

CHAPTER 18

Modeling complex systems

It's fascinating to observe how our society functions. Each of us is an independent individual who makes uncoordinated decisions. However, as we interact with one another, some interesting phenomena emerge.

In 2007, a baby boy named Charlie in the United Kingdom bit his brother's finger while they were playing in a chair. This little event should have gone unnoticed in human history—babies bite things coming into their mouths all the time. Yet, a 58-second video was captured and uploaded to YouTube, and the clip became the most-viewed video clips at the end of October 2009 (*https://en.wikipedia.org/wiki/Charlie_Bit_My_Finger*). How can such an insignificant event become a global phenomenon and now part of our history? How did millions of people around the world decide this video clip was worth watching? The study of adaptive complex system tries to understand such phenomena generated by self-motivated, interacting agents.

Service Fabric, especially Service Fabric Actor pattern, provides a powerful tool in the field of complex system study. This chapter introduces some early attempts to apply Service Fabric in complex system study.

Adaptive complex systems

A complex system comprises many interacting agents. Each agent makes independent decisions based on the agent's experiences and sometimes on the agent's anticipation of other agents' reactions. The decisions agents make are not necessarily intelligent. And the decisions are made without central coordination. However, in many cases, there seems to be an invisible hand that orchestrates collective behaviors. For example, standing ovations in theaters are spontaneous. Yet individual viewers somehow decide to stand up and applaud at the same time, and a standing ovation often ripples through the entire audience.

Agents are connected by different levels of connections. Some of the connections are strong and enduring, such as members in a family, while some of the connections are weak and temporary, such as passengers riding in a same subway car. An agent's behavior is often affected heavily by its connections and the environment in which it resides. For example, different groups have conducted a few social conformity experiments in public elevators. In these experiments, a group of researchers rides with strangers facing in the same direction. And at a certain point, they all turn around. This action often triggers the strangers to turn around so everybody is facing the same direction again.

Complex systems and complicated systems

Both complex systems and complicated systems are made up of various elements. A *complicated* system can be studied by examining the properties of individual elements in isolation. A space shuttle is a complicated system. However, it can be decomposed into subsystems and then into individual parts because the behavior and properties of individual parts don't change. A *complex* system, in contrast, can't be studied in small pieces because an agent's behavior will change when it's put into a different environment.

The dynamics among agents are what make complex systems fascinating; however, they also make studying a complex system difficult. We are used to studying a system piece by piece. The properties of the pieces can be measured accurately, and their behaviors can be reasoned and mathematically proofed. When these pieces are put together, their collective behaviors can be predicated reliably; hence, you gain complete insight into the entire system. Decomposing a complex system kills the system because you lose all the interesting interactions that make a complex system what it is. So, how do you study a complex system?

If you can't decompose a system, how about just observing the system as a whole, very carefully? This method may sound puerile. However, it turns out to be effective. In fact, many of you are familiar with or at least have heard of the method: *big data*. A big data solution ingests a tremendous amount of data and tries to find patterns and trends by using systematic analyses or Machine Learning experiments.

Another method, which is the main focus of this chapter, is modeling. The goal of modeling is to simplify the reasoning process while retaining a certain affinity to the reality. A problem can be modeled in different ways depending on the questions you want to answer. In many cases, a good model only emerges after rounds of trials and errors. This is where computer simulation comes into play. Computer simulations help you observe and verify the correctness of your models. Furthermore, computer simulations enable you to run experiments to discover new models.

Emergence

The primary interest of complex system study is to analyze how emergent phenomena form as the result of activities of individual agents. Figure 18-1 shows a portion of the *Mona Lisa* presented in ASCII art. When examined individually, each pixel in the picture is a text character. If you read the text line by line, you won't be able to make out what the text represents. However, if you step back from the picture, you can recognize the world-famous painting.

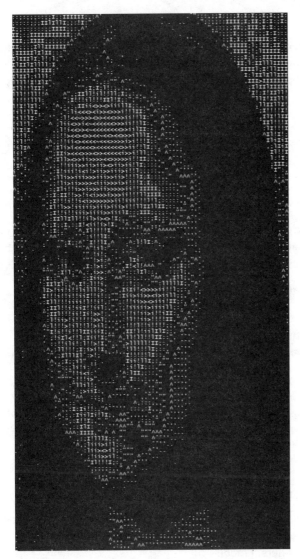

FIGURE 18-1 Mona Lisa in ASCII art

In some cases, the behaviors of agents have clear connections to the collective behavior. For example, a dirt passage across a lawn is the direct result of many people taking the same shortcut. In other cases, it's unclear how the individual activities contribute to the global behavior. In his 1759 book, *The Theory of Moral Sentiments*, Adam Smith described how an "invisible hand" drives unintended social benefits from individual actions. In many rewarding discoveries, the local behaviors of agents seem completely disconnected from the aggregated result. Later in this chapter, you'll see a couple of examples of emergences.

A simple model

To better illustrate how to model a complex system, I'll present you a simple model that simulates how termite piles are formed. Termites are known to collect woodchips and put them in piles. There isn't a "master" termite that dictates where these piles should be placed. Yet somehow the termites choose a few places to put the woodchips.

This simple model uses two basic instincts of a termite: it tends to pick up a woodchip when it finds one, and it tends to pile up woodchips. These two local behaviors are not imaginary—they can be observed. However, we don't have much else to work with. Can you build a meaningful model based on just these two observations? It turns out you can. The model is designed as follows:

1. In an N-by-N 2D grid, a number of woodchips and a number of termites are placed randomly.

2. The termites roam randomly in the grid. When a termite encounters a woodchip, it picks it up and carries it around. When a termite carrying a woodchip bumps into another woodchip, it finds a nearby empty place and puts down its woodchip.

3. The process continues. Eventually, the woodchips end up in a single pile.

This model is simple and easy to understand. It also faithfully simulates the fascinating global behavior: a random place is picked in the grid, and all woodchips are collected into that place. In this case, the termites don't communicate with one another at all, yet an agreement is formed by these simple rules.

Given enough time, the woodchips converging to a single pile can be reasoned perfectly: Let's say we view every woodchip as its own pile to begin with. As time elapses, these piles either expand or contract. Because termites never put woodchips in empty spaces, once a pile disappears it never will reappear. And because the probability of a pile disappearing is not zero, the number of piles will decrease and eventually reach 1.

Modeling and computational modeling

The termite model is one of the few complex system models that can be easily described and clearly reasoned. The model focuses on a single question: Will a single pile be formed? Different questions lead to different levels of abstractions and different models.

Most complex system models are not concerned with static states. Instead, these models study the dynamics of interacting agents. A complex system is both dynamic and adaptive. Some models focus on the dynamic nature of the system. Generically speaking, a dynamic system includes the following components: a *phase space* whose elements represent all possible system states; a continuous or discrete *time* dimension; and an *evolution law* that is used to derive state at time *t* based on the knowledge of all states of previous times.[1]

Some other complex system models focus on the adaptive nature of a complex system. Many complex systems are fragile. However, some complex systems show great robustness regardless of the constant changes of agents. An obvious example is a human society. Generations of people come and go.

---

[1] Nino Boccara. 2010. *Modeling Complex Systems*. New York: Springer.

And with the increasing mobility of modern people, the construct of a society is constantly changing. Yet, the society holds its normal functions regardless of these changes. Although occasional disruptions such as riots occur, a society can find its way back to a stable state unless some devastating events such as wars occur that exceed the society's ability to adapt. This is when a complex system breaks down.

The dynamic and adaptive nature of complex systems makes static reasoning difficult. Systematical reasoning and mathematical proofs still are the key ingredients in complex system study. However, computational models provide powerful tools to verify, simulate, and explore new possibilities with the help of computers. Most interestingly, agent-based computational models naturally demonstrate the dynamic and adaptive nature of complex systems, so they show amazing affinity to real-world problems in many cases. Computational models have been studied extensively in some literatures (Simon A. Levin 2007). This chapter presents a few examples and patterns that help you build agent-based computational models using Service Fabric actors and reliable services.

The termite model

The first complex system model you'll build is the termite model that was introduced earlier in this chapter. In this model, a termite is implemented as a stateful actor. The world in which the termites roam is implemented as a stateful service. In this case, scalability is not a concern, so you'll use a singleton partition for the stateful service. You'll learn about how to scale the model after completing the basic implementations.

Set up the solution

1. Create a new Service Fabric application named *TermiteModel* with a stateful actor service named *Termite*.

2. Add a new stateful service named *Box* to the application.

3. Add a new class library named *Box.Interfaces* to the solution. This assembly defines the service interface of the Box service.

4. In the *Box.Interfaces* project, add a reference to the *Microsoft.ServiceFabric.Services* NuGet package.

5. Add a new console application named *ModelTest* to the solution.

6. Change the target framework for both the *Box.Interfaces* and the console application to .NET Framework 4.5.1 and platform target to x64.

7. In the *Box* project, add a reference to the *Box.Interfaces* project.

8. In the console application project, add a reference to the *Box.Interfaces* project and a reference to the *Termite.Interface* project.

9. Add a reference to the *Microsoft.ServiceFabric.Actors* NuGet package.

Implement the Box service

The Box service provides a 50-by-50 grid. A number of woodchips are scattered on the grid. Termite actors will roam around on the board and try to pick up woodchips or put down woodchips. The service also provides a method for the test client to query and display board states.

1. Modify the *IBox* interface:

```
public interface IBox : IService
{
    Task<bool> TryPickUpWoodChipAsync(int x, int y);
    Task<bool> TryPutDonwWoodChipAsync(int x, int y);
    Task<List<int>> ReadBox();
    Task ResetBox();
}
```

2. Define a number of private variables:

```
private static Random mRand = new Random();
private const string mDictionaryName = "box";
private const int size = 100;
```

3. Implement the *ReadBox()* method, which is for clients to read the box state:

```
public async Task<List<int>> ReadBox()
{
    var myDictionary = await this.StateManager.GetOrAddAsync<IReliableDictionary<string,
int>>(mDictionaryName);
    List<int> ret = new List<int>();
    using (var tx = this.StateManager.CreateTransaction())
    {
        for (int y = 0; y < size; y++)
        {
            for (int x = 0; x < size; x++)
            {
                var value = await myDictionary.TryGetValueAsync(tx, x + "-" + y);
                if (value.HasValue)
                    ret.Add(value.Value);
                else
                    ret.Add(0);
            }
        }
        await tx.CommitAsync();
    }
    return ret;
}
```

4. Implement the *ResetBox()* method that resets the box to initial state with randomly placed woodchips:

```
public async Task ResetBox()
{
    var myDictionary = await this.StateManager.GetOrAddAsync<IReliableDictionary<string,
int>>(mDictionaryName);
    await myDictionary.ClearAsync();
```

```
            using (var tx = this.StateManager.CreateTransaction())
            {
                for (int y = 0; y < size; y++)
                {
                    for (int x = 0; x < size; x++)
                    {
                        await myDictionary.SetAsync(tx, x + "-" + y, 0);
                    }
                }
                for (int i = 0; i < size* size / 4; i++)
                {
                    var x = mRand.Next(0, size);
                    var y = mRand.Next(0, size);
                    await myDictionary.SetAsync(tx, x + "-" + y, 1);
                }
                await tx.CommitAsync();
            }
        }
```

5. When a termite moves around, it keeps trying to pick up a woodchip. The *TryPickUpWoodChipAsync* method checks the current element in the state dictionary that corresponds to the termite's current location. If the element is larger than zero, which means at least one woodchip is at the location, the termite is allowed to pick up one woodchip. Otherwise, the method returns false and the termite has to try somewhere else.

```
public async Task<bool> TryPickUpWoodChipAsync(int x, int y)
{
    var myDictionary = await this.StateManager.GetOrAddAsync<IReliableDictionary<string,
int>>(mDictionaryName);
    var ret = false;
    using (var tx = this.StateManager.CreateTransaction())
    {
                string key = x + "-" + y;
                  var result = await myDictionary.TryGetValueAsync(tx, key);
                  if (result.HasValue && result.Value == 1)
                  {
                      ret = await myDictionary.TryUpdateAsync(tx, key, 0, 1);
                  }
                  await tx.CommitAsync();
    }
    return ret;
}
```

6. Similarly, a terminate carrying a woodchip keeps trying to put down the woodchip. The *TryPutDownWoodChipAsync* method checks if a woodchip is at the current location. If yes, the termite places the woodchip it carries in a nearby location. If all nearby locations are taken, the termite cycles around the location a couple of times trying to find an empty place to put the woodchip. If it can't find an empty space, it keeps the woodchip and continues roaming around.

```
public async Task<bool> TryPutDonwWoodChipAsync(int x, int y)
{
    var myDictionary = await this.StateManager.GetOrAddAsync<IReliableDictionary<string,
int>>(mDictionaryName);
    var ret = false;
```

```
            int lastX = x;
            int lastY = y;
            using (var tx = this.StateManager.CreateTransaction())
            {
                string key = x + "-" + y;
                var result = await myDictionary.TryGetValueAsync(tx, key);
                if (result.HasValue && result.Value == 1)
                {
                    for (int r = 1; r <=2; r++)
                    {
                        double angle = mRand.NextDouble() * Math.PI * 2;
                        for (double a = angle; a < Math.PI * 2 + angle; a +=0.01)
                        {
                            int newX = (int)(x + r * Math.Cos(a));
                            int newY = (int)(y + r * Math.Sin(a));
                            if ((newX != lastX || newY != lastY)
                                && newX >=0 && newY>=0 && newX < size && newY < size)
                            {
                                lastX = newX;
                                lastY = newY;
                                string testKey = newX + "-" + newY;
                                var neighbour = myDictionary.TryGetValueAsync(tx, testKey).
Result;
                                if (neighbour.HasValue && neighbour.Value == 0)
                                {
                                    ret = await myDictionary.TryUpdateAsync(tx, testKey, 1, 0);
                                    if (ret)
                                        break;
                                }
                            }
                        }
                        if (ret)
                            break;
                    }
                }
                await tx.CommitAsync();
            }
            return ret;
        }
```

7. Last, define a replica listener on the Box service:

```
protected override IEnumerable<ServiceReplicaListener> CreateServiceReplicaListeners()
{
        return new[] { new ServiceReplicaListener(parameters =>
            new ServiceRemotingListener<Box>(parameters, this)) };
}
```

Implement the termite actor

1. The termite actor implements a simple interface. The only method on the interface is for read-
    ing the actor state:

```
public interface ITermite : IActor
{
```

```
        Task<TermiteState> GetStateAsync();
}
```

2. The state of a termite is defined as a separate class. The state includes a 2D location and a Boolean flag indicating if the termite is carrying a woodchip.

```
[DataContract]
public sealed class TermiteState
{
    [DataMember]
    public int X { get; set; }
    [DataMember]
    public int Y { get; set; }
    [DataMember]
    public bool HasWoodchip { get; set; }
}
```

3. On the *Termite* class, define a few local variables:

```
private IActorTimer mTimer;
private static Random rand = new Random();
private const int size = 100;
```

4. Implement the *OnActivateAsync()* method, the *OnDeactivateAsync()* method, and the *GetStateAsync()* method. The code is straightforward: when a termite actor is activated, its state is created and a timer is created to drive the termite to move around on its own. The timer is destroyed when the actor is deactivated.

```
protected override Task OnActivateAsync()
{
    if (this.State == null)
    {
        this.State = new TermiteState { X = rand.Next(0,size), Y = rand.Next(0,size),
HasWoodchip = false};
    }
    mTimer = RegisterTimer(Move, this.State, TimeSpan.FromSeconds(1), TimeSpan.
FromMilliseconds(50));
    return Task.FromResult(true);
}
protected override Task OnDeactivateAsync()
{
    if (mTimer != null)
        UnregisterTimer(mTimer);
    return base.OnDeactivateAsync();
}
[Readonly]
Task<TermiteState> ITermite.GetStateAsync()
{
    return Task.FromResult(this.State);
}
```

5. The *Move()* method is simple: if a termite is not carrying a woodchip, it tries to pick up one; if a termite is carrying a woodchip, it tries to put it down. Then, the termite keeps roaming around in random directions.

```
private async Task Move(Object state)
{
    IBox boxClient = ServiceProxy.Create<IBox>(new Uri("fabric:/TermiteModel/Box"));
    if (!this.State.HasWoodchip)
    {
        var result = await boxClient.TryPickUpWoodChipAsync(this.State.X, this.State.Y);
        if (result)
            this.State.HasWoodchip = true;
    } else
    {
        var result = await boxClient.TryPutDownWoodChipAsync(this.State.X, this.State.Y);
        if (result)
            this.State.HasWoodchip = false;
    }
    int action = rand.Next(1, 9);
    //1-left; 2-left-up; 3-up; 4-up-right; 5-right: 6-right-down; 7-down; 8-down-left
    if ((action == 1 || action == 2 || action == 8) && this.State.X > 0)
        this.State.X = this.State.X - 1;
    if ((action == 4 || action == 5 || action == 6) && this.State.X < size-1)
        this.State.X = this.State.X + 1;
    if ((action == 2 || action == 3 || action == 4) && this.State.Y > 0)
        this.State.Y = this.State.Y - 1;
    if ((action == 6 || action == 7 || action == 8) && this.State.Y < size-1)
        this.State.Y = this.State.Y + 1;
}
```

Implement the test client

The test client is a simple console application with a single *Main()* method. The method first resets the box and then places a number of termites in the box. Then, it monitors the box state and refreshes the screen every half second.

```
static void Main(string[] args)
{
    Random rand = new Random();
    Console.ReadLine();
    int size = 100;
    int termites = 75;
    IBox boxClient = ServiceProxy.Create<IBox>(new Uri("fabric:/TermiteModel/Box"));
    boxClient.ResetBox().Wait();

    ITermite[] proxies = new ITermite[termites];
    for (int i = 0; i < proxies.Length; i++)
    {
        proxies[i] = ActorProxy.Create<ITermite>(new ActorId(i), new Uri("fabric:/TermiteModel/
TermiteActorService"));
        proxies[i].GetStateAsync();
    }
    while (true)
    {
        var box = boxClient.ReadBox().Result;
        Console.ForegroundColor = ConsoleColor.DarkBlue;
        for (int y = 0; y < size; y++)
        {
            Console.CursorTop = y;
```

```
            for (int x = 0; x < size; x++)
            {
                Console.CursorLeft = x;
                if (box[y * size + x] == 0)
                    Console.Write(" ");
                else
                    Console.Write("#");
            }
        }
        Console.ForegroundColor = ConsoleColor.DarkRed;
        for (int i = 0; i < proxies.Length; i++)
        {
            var state = proxies[i].GetStateAsync().Result;
            Console.CursorLeft = state.X;
            Console.CursorTop = state.Y;
            Console.Write("T");
        }
        Thread.Sleep(500);
    }
}
```

Test and analysis

Deploy the application and launch the test client. Figure 18-2 shows the result of a sample run on my environment. To the left, 2,500 woodchips and 75 termites are placed randomly on a 100-by-100 grid. At the center, some smaller clusters have formed after some iterations. And to the right, all the woodchips are piled into a single pile.

After running the program several times, I realized that the phenomenon emerges not because the termites are trying to put the woodchips together but because the rule forbids a termite to put a woodchip back into an empty space. Once an empty space forms with sufficient radius (bigger than 1), no woodchips can be put into it. As time passes, the empty spaces grow and link together, pushing the woodchips to a central location.

In the above implementation, the termites are committed to drop a woodchip whenever they see an opportunity. However, if they just try to find empty cells in the immediate eight neighboring cells and give up if all the cells are occupied (which means they'll keep carrying the woodchips they have and keep roaming around waiting for the next opportunity), you'll get similar results. This works because as long as the termites don't erode the empty spaces, eventually all the woodchips will converge into a single pile.

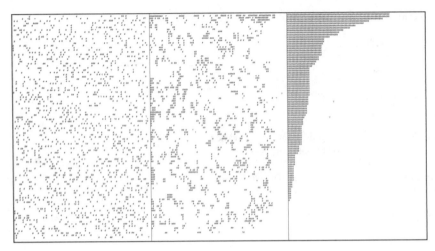

FIGURE 18-2 Termite simulation

Architecturally, there are a couple of problems with this program.

First, it doesn't scale. The Box service is a singleton service instance that holds a global state. All state operations—and there are a lot of them—occur on this single instance. Can you partition the service? It's hard. This is because the termites move around the whole box and there will be constant boundary hits that can't be handled easily by partitioned services. In Chapter 16, "Multiplayer gaming," you could use the Coverage Map pattern because in the map, you only needed low-granularity information (if a battle zone is touching a partition). In this case, every cell is carrying useful information.

Second, it's slow. The simulation can be done using a simple console application with much faster performance. With this design, it takes tens of minutes before a stable state can be reached.

Third, the logics are not separated clearly. The termite actor controls the movement of a termite. However, the logic of picking up a woodchip and putting down a woodchip is implemented in the Box service. The Box service can be "purified" by exposing methods to access individual cells, and all termite logic can be moved back to the termite actor. However, this will generate far more cross-service calls than the above implementation.

Service Fabric for complex systems

If the Service Fabric implementation of the termite simulation is so bad, why would one pursue this route? Service Fabric Actors provide simplicity and scalability. The Actor pattern makes sense because it fits perfectly into the profile of a local agent. More interestingly, multiple actors potentially can be put into the same environment, and interesting interactions among the heterogeneous actors may occur. At the same time, Service Fabric allows great scales. In theory, if you need millions of simulated agents you can scale out your Service Fabric cluster to accommodate the large number of actors.

However, achieving these goals takes work. First, the solution must be designed so the scalability opportunity Service Fabric provides can be leveraged. Second, the solution must be efficient to provide fast compute without consuming an excessive amount of resources. Third, but not least, simplicity must be maintained. This requirement includes the simplicity both in writing new agents and in facilitating interactions among heterogeneous actors.

Distributed data structures

Although simple partitioning is supported out-of-box, it's worthwhile to explore if a simpler syntax can be provided to access a distributed array. In the current Service Fabric version, reliable collections are replicated but not distributed. For example, when you partition a dictionary, each shard of the reliable dictionary associated with a service partition is an independent entity. Each of the partitions needs to be disciplined not to introduce inconsistency in the logical global data structure.

There have been numerous offerings of distributed data structures such as Tango[2] and DDS[3]. Architecturally, they share a structure with an abstraction layer providing a virtual data structure based on a cluster of storage nodes in the back. I can't predict if distributed data structures will be part of the service offering itself. However, it's viable to implement such an architecture with Service Fabric. A distributed data structure is handy in the case of large-scale simulations and multiplayer gaming where large world maps need to be shared.

One of the primary challenges in implementing the distributed data structures is maintaining transactional consistency across multiple storage nodes. Service Fabric provides consistencies across replicas in a same partition, but there are no such guarantees across different partitions. A distributed transaction system such as a log-based system proposed by Tango is needed to provide cross-partition consistencies. However, this is optional because in a simple partition scenario, this extra level of trans-action management brings no additional value.

Figure 18-3 shows a possible implementation of distributed data structures using Service Fabric. In this design, distributed data structures are provided by an extra service layer that sits in front of a number of dynamically managed Service Fabric partitions. The pattern borrows the tenant management concept from the Tenant Manager pattern in Chapter 15, "Multitenancy and hosting." A service manager is responsible for managing service instances that host data structure partitions and providing address lookup services to the distributed data structure service. The actual data operations don't go through the manager. The diagram doesn't illustrate how consistent transactions would be implemented—that belongs to implementation details of the distributed data structure service.

---

[2] Mahesh Balakrishnan, Dahlia Malkhi, Ted Wobber, Ming Wu, Vijayan Prabhakaran, Micheal Wei, John D. Davis, Sriram Rao, Tao Zou, Aviad Zuck. 2013. "Tango: Distributed Data Structures over a Shared Log." *SOSP.*

[3] Steven D. Gribble, Eric A. Brewer, Joseph M. Hellerstein, David Culler. 2000. "Scalable, Distributed Data Structures for Internet Service Construction." *Fourth Symposium on Operating Systems Design and Implementation (OSDI 2000).*

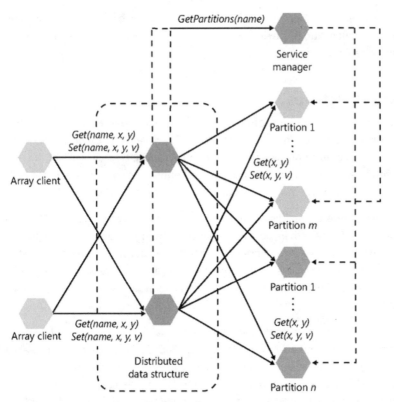

FIGURE 18-3 Distributed data structures

The distributed data structure provides an extra level of abstraction where additional behaviors can be implemented. For example, instead of a full implementation of a distributed transaction system, another approach can be taken for simpler cases where data structures can be partitioned using simple partitions but some reads across partition borders are necessary. The service can implement blurred partition borders that allow the edge of a partition to be copied into its neighboring partitions. The copied edges are read-only to avoid complicated data syncs with multiple data writers. However, these copied edges can participate in bulk read operations on the partition to speed up reads when data processors mostly stay in the same partitions.

The performance of a distributed data structure is decided by several factors. The first factor is whether cross-partition transactions are needed. The service implementation will allow skipping the distributed transaction management if cross-partition transactions are not needed. The second factor is the persistence requirement. If the data structure has to be persisted to disk, the performance will suffer compared to the in-memory-only accesses. The service implementation will allow different state providers to be selected. The third factor is the access pattern. If data is read and written in bulk, additional optimizations such as grouping service requests to reduce the number of cross-service calls are possible.

Actor Swarms

In many cases, an agent participating in a complex system isn't smart, which means the agent implementation carries a minimal amount of code. Although Service Fabric Actors (and Service Fabric reliable services in general) provide high hosting density, it can be pushed further by leveraging a concept I call an *Actor Swarm*.

An Actor Swarm, as the name suggests, is a swarm of actors packed into a single Service Fabric Actor instance. The actor instance, or the swarm host, provides a hosting environment for a large number of virtual actors. It provides the following services to the virtual actors:

- **Lifetime management** The swarm host is responsible for managing lifetimes of virtual actor instances or proxies.

- **State management** The swarm host uses a dictionary of virtual actor state as its own state. For example, if the state of a virtual actor is T, the state of the swarm host is a dictionary of T that is keyed by virtual actor names. This design provides a straightforward mechanism that passes on the state management capabilities such as state replication to virtual actors.

- **Addressing** The swarm host exposes a service contract that inherits the service contract provided by the virtual actors (assuming virtual actors are homogeneous). The new contract adds a *name* field to all the methods so the client calls can be routed to specific virtual actors.

- **Timers and reminders** Actor times and reminders can be used to trigger scheduled events on the virtual actors. The virtual actor actions can be triggered either sequentially or in parallel.

As you can see, an Actor Swarm provides a high-fidelity simulated Service Fabric hosting environment to virtual actors. This means that the logic of an actor can be implemented regardless of whether the actor is hosted as an individual Service Fabric Actor instance or as a virtual actor in an Actor Swarm. This concept is much like the concept of a Docker container (see Chapter 17, "Advanced service hosting") that provides a virtualized operating system based on a shared system core. The difference is that in this case, Actor Swarm provides a virtualized actor host on a shared Service Fabric Actor host.

If timers and reminders are not needed, an Actor Swarm can be implemented with a Service Fabric stateful service. A stateful service can provide all the above services, and timers can be implemented easily. However, reminders and the virtual existence of actors need more work.

Actor Swarms offer actor orchestration capabilities that are useful in many scenarios. For example:

- **Round-based simulations** Some computer algorithms and simulations are round-based, which requires agents perform actions in coordinated steps. An Actor Swarm can coordinate method executions of virtual actors by using a simple loop. The turn-based mechanism on the swarm actor ensures that only one round is triggered at a time. And the swarm actor can invoke corresponding methods on virtual actors in parallel.

- **Gossiping agents** In some simulations, agents need to exchange information frequently. Because all virtual actors reside on the same process, the communication overheads are minimal among virtual actors.

- **Flyweight pattern**   The Flyweight pattern (Gamma, et al. 1994) allows similar objects to share as much data as possible. The pattern is hard to realize with regular Service Fabric Actors. However, it's easy to implement the pattern by using an Actor Swarm. Essentially, the shared data is defined as the state of the swarm host, and agent-specific data is defined as the state of virtual actors.

- **Self-adaptive scaling**   Multiple Actor Swarms can be linked by some naming conventions without needing a central piece. For example, an Actor Swarm with the name "beehive" can spawn additional swarms such as "beehive-1" and "beehive-2" to share its load when needed. Moreover, existing virtual actors hosted on one Actor Swarm easily can be packaged and migrated into a new swarm.

Most interestingly, an Actor Swarm can be generic, or it can be a specialized swarm with additional characteristics. One of the goals of this chapter is to seek a common infrastructure that adapts to different problem types. Specialized Actor Swarms provide such flexibility. Some possible specialized Actor Swarms include the following:

- **Shared-state swarm**   Shared-state swarm provides a shared state for all virtual actors on the swarm. This swarm type covers a number of classic algorithms and simulation scenarios.

- **Spatial swarm**   Spatial swarm provides an *n*-dimensional space for virtual actors. This swarm type is suitable for simulations that require locality factors such as geo-locations.

- **Chaos swarm**   Chaos swarm can randomly block calls from or to the virtual actors to simulate a spotty network environment. This will be helpful to simulate or validate fault-tolerant systems.

The applications of Actor Swarms go beyond the study of complex systems. For instance, they can be used to implement a dynamic computing hosting environment like that provided by Amazon AWS Lamda (Amazon n.d.) or Microsoft Azure Functions. And by leveraging the built-in Service Fabric features, some interesting features such as stateful compute, failover, and scheduled computes can be provided.

Azure Functions

Azure Functions provides similar functionalities to AWS Lambda. At the time of this writing, Azure Functions is still under active development. By the time you read this book, it should have been announced. The exact offering and the availability of the service is unknown at this point.

In the next model, you'll implement a simple Actor Swarm and use the swarm to construct a *socio-physics*[4] model: spatial segregation.

---

[4] Nino Boccara. 2010. *Modeling Complex Systems*. New York: Springer.

The spatial segregation model

In the spatial segregation model, an N-by-N cell is occupied by a number of residents of two different types (such as gender, political opinions, or social classes). Each resident counts how many individuals in his immediate neighborhood have his type. If he has four neighbors of the same type, he will stay where he is. Otherwise, he will try to move to one of the neighboring empty cells. If two residents try to move to the same empty cell, neither of them will move (this kind of conflict resolution is called *timorous walkers*).

Set up the solution

1. Create a new Service Fabric application named *ActorSwarmApplication* with an *ActorSwarm* stateful actor.

2. Add a new console application named *SwarmTest* to the solution.

3. Change the console application's target framework to .NET Framework 4.5.1 and platform target to x64.

4. Add a class library named *Common* to the solution.

5. Change the target framework to .NET Framework 4.5.1 and platform target to x64 for the class library.

6. On the class library projects, add a reference to the *Microsoft.ServiceFabric.Actors* NuGet package.

7. On all projects except the *Common* project and the application project, add a reference to the *Common* project.

Implement shared array with proposal supports

In this scenario, you'll implement a round-based, shared-state, 2D spatial Actor Swarm. The swarm provides a 2D array that all the virtual actors share. And it organizes virtual actors into coordinated rounds. Each round is split into five phases: read, think, proposal, conflict resolution, and commit.

- **Read**   In this phrase, all virtual actors read from the shared state. Because all operations are read-only, there are no locks required for this phase, and all reads can be done in parallel.

- **Think**   In this phase, all virtual actors make independent decisions. This phase is also parallelized with no global state updates.

- **Proposal**   In this phase, virtual actors submit update proposals to the swarm. The swarm records all proposals for the next phase.

- **Conflict resolution**   In this phase, the swarm reviews all proposals and notifies virtual actors if their proposals are accepted or rejected. All decisions are final. Virtual actors don't get to make another proposal until the next round.

- **Commit**   In this phase, all accepted proposals are written to the shared state.

The proposal and conflict resolution phases can be combined in most cases. However, if you want to provide virtual actors opportunities to update their private states based on proposal acceptances or rejections, you should keep the two phases separate.

1. Add an empty *IProposal* interface.

```
public interface IProposal
{
}
```

2. Add a *Proposal2D* class to the *Common* class library:

```
[DataContract]
public class Proposal2D<T>: IProposal  where T : IComparable
{
    [DataMember]
    public int ActorId { get; set; }
    [DataMember]
    public int OldX { get; set; }
    [DataMember]
    public int OldY { get; set; }
    [DataMember]
    public int NewX { get; set; }
    [DataMember]
    public int NewY { get; set; }
    [DataMember]
    public T ProposedValue { get; set; }
    public Proposal2D(int id, int oldX, int oldY, int newX, int newY, T proposal)
    {
        ActorId = id;
        OldX = oldX;
        OldY = oldY;
        NewX = newX;
        NewY = newY;
        ProposedValue = proposal;
    }
}
```

3. Next, implement a *Shared2DArray* class. This class defines a 2D array that provides read-only access to its elements and updates only through proposals. In the following implementation, whenever a conflict is detected, all conflicting proposals are rejected. Other conflict resolution strategies can also be implemented. All proposals are applied sequentially in the following code because all proposals are in a single list. However, the code can be extended to have multiple proposal partitions so multiple proposals can be resolved and applied in parallel. In an extreme case, each cell in the array has its own proposal list so all proposals can be resolved in parallel. The following implementation also uses a simple custom serialization so we can pass the array over the wire.

```csharp
[DataContract]
public class Shared2DArray<T>  where T : IComparable
{
    private int mSize;
    private T[,] mArray;
    private List<Proposal2D<T>> mProposals;
    private object mSyncRoot = new object();
    public Shared2DArray()
    {
    }
    public void Initialize(int size)
    {
        mSize = size;
        mArray = new T[size, size];
        mProposals = new List<Proposal2D<T>>();
    }
    public void Initialize(int size, string[] values)
    {
        Initialize(size);
        int index = 1;
        for (int y = 0; y < size; y++)
        {
            for (int x = 0; x < size; x++)
            {
                mArray[x, y] = (T)Convert.ChangeType(byte.Parse(values[index]),
typeof(T));
                index++;
            }
        }
    }
    public T this[int x, int y]
    {
        get
        {
            return mArray[x, y];
        }
    }
    public void Propose(IProposal proposal)
    {
        if (proposal == null)
            return;
        if (proposal is Proposal2D<T>)
        {
            lock (mSyncRoot)
            {
                mProposals.Add((Proposal2D<T>)proposal);
            }
        }
        else
            throw new ArgumentException("Only Proposal2D<T> is supported.");
    }
    public void ResolveConflictsAndCommit(Action<IProposal> callback)
    {
        foreach (var proposal in mProposals)
        {
            var otherPropoals = from p in mProposals
                                where p.NewX == proposal.NewX && p.NewY == proposal.NewY
```

```
                              && p.OldX != proposal.OldX && p.OldY != proposal.OldY
                              select p;
                if (otherPropoals.Count() == 0)
                {
                    mArray[proposal.OldX, proposal.OldY] = (T)Convert.
ChangeType(0,typeof(T));
                    mArray[proposal.NewX, proposal.NewY] = proposal.ProposedValue;
                    if (callback != null)
                        callback(proposal);
                }
            }
            mProposals.Clear();
        }
        override public string ToString()
        {
            StringBuilder sb = new StringBuilder();
            sb.Append(mSize).Append(",");
            for (int y = 0; y < mSize; y++)
            {
                for (int x = 0; x < mSize; x++)
                    sb.Append(mArray[x, y]).Append(",");
            }
            return sb.ToString().Substring(0, sb.Length - 1);
        }
        public static Shared2DArray<T> FromString(string json)
        {
            Shared2DArray<T> ret = new Shared2DArray<T>();
            string[] parts = json.Split(',');
            int size = int.Parse(parts[0]);
            ret.Initialize(size, parts);
            return ret;
        }
    }
}
```

Implement the virtual actor

In this example, you'll implement a single *Resident* virtual actor. A resident holds a location and a tag
that represents its attribute (1 or 2). At each round of iteration, each resident counts its neighbors. If it
finds it has fewer than four neighbors with the same type, it proposes to the shared array that it would
like to move to an immediate empty cell.

1. In the *Common* project, define an *IVirtualActor* interface. As the interface suggests, a virtual
    actor makes proposals and updates its state if the proposals are accepted.

    ```
    public interface IVirtualActor
    {
        Task<IProposal> ProposeAsync();
        Task ApproveProposalAsync(IProposal proposal);
    }
    ```

2. Define a *ResidentState* class that represents the state of a *Resident*.

    ```
    [DataContract(Name ="ResidentState")]
    public class ResidentState: IComparable
    ```

```
{
    [DataMember]
    public int X { get; set; }
    [DataMember]
    public int Y { get; set; }
    [DataMember]
    public byte Tag { get; set; }
    public int CompareTo(object obj)
    {
        if (obj != null && obj is ResidentState)
        {
            ResidentState that = (ResidentState)obj;
            if (that.X == this.X && that.Y == this.Y && that.Tag == this.Tag)
                return 0;
        }
        return -1;
    }
}
```

3. Define the *Resident* class. The class's logic is straightforward. Note that the class has read-only access to the shared state. It's not allowed to make direct updates to the shared state.

```
[DataContract]
public class Resident: IVirtualActor
{
    ResidentState State;
    Shared2DArray<byte> SharedState;
    int mRange;
    int mId;
    private static Random mRand = new Random();
    private List<Tuple<int, int>> mOffsets = new List<Tuple<int, int>>
    {
            new Tuple<int, int>(-1,0),
            new Tuple<int, int>(-1,-1),
            new Tuple<int, int>(0,-1),
            new Tuple<int, int>(1,-1),
            new Tuple<int, int>(1,0),
            new Tuple<int, int>(1,1),
            new Tuple<int, int>(0,1),
            new Tuple<int, int>(-1,1)
    };
    public Resident(int range, int id, ResidentState state, Shared2DArray<byte>
sharedState)
    {
        mRange = range;
        mId = id;
        State = state;
        SharedState = sharedState;
    }
    public Task ApproveProposalAsync(IProposal proposal)
    {
        if (proposal is Proposal2D<byte>)
        {
            var p = (Proposal2D<byte>)proposal;
            this.State.X = p.NewX;
            this.State.Y = p.NewY;
```

```
        }
        return Task.FromResult(1);
    }
    public Task<IProposal> ProposeAsync()
    {
        int count = 0;
        count += countNeighbour(this.State.X - 1, this.State.Y);
        count += countNeighbour(this.State.X - 1, this.State.Y - 1);
        count += countNeighbour(this.State.X, this.State.Y - 1);
        count += countNeighbour(this.State.X + 1, this.State.Y - 1);
        count += countNeighbour(this.State.X + 1, this.State.Y);
        count += countNeighbour(this.State.X + 1, this.State.Y + 1);
        count += countNeighbour(this.State.X, this.State.Y + 1);
        count += countNeighbour(this.State.X - 1, this.State.Y + 1);
        if (count <= 3)
        {
            var randList = mOffsets.OrderBy(p => mRand.Next());
            foreach (var item in randList)
            {
                if (findEmptyNeighbour(this.State.X + item.Item1, this.State.Y + item.
Item2))
                {
                    return Task.FromResult<IProposal>(new Proposal2D<byte>(mId,
                        this.State.X,
                        this.State.Y,
                        this.State.X + item.Item1,
                        this.State.Y + item.Item2,
                        this.State.Tag));
                }
            }
        }
        return Task.FromResult<IProposal>(null);
    }
    private int countNeighbour(int x, int y)
    {
        if (x >= 0 && x < this.mRange && y >= 0 && y < this.mRange)
            return SharedState[x, y] == this.State.Tag ? 1 : 0;
        else
            return 0;
    }
    private bool findEmptyNeighbour(int x, int y)
    {
        if (x >= 0 && x < this.mRange && y >= 0 && y < this.mRange)
            return SharedState[x, y] == 0;
        else
            return false;
    }
}
```

Implement the Actor Swarm

In this example, you'll implement a simple spatial, turn-based Actor Swarm. The swarm coordinates activities of all its member virtual actors.

1. Modify the *IActorSwarm* interface in the *ActorSwarm.Interfaces* project:

```
public interface IActorSwarm : IActor
{
    Task InitializeAsync(int size, float probability);
    Task EvolveAsync();
    Task<string> ReadStateStringAsync();
}
```

2. In the *ActorSwarm* project, define the actor state as a separate class. Note that the class is decorated with a couple of *KnownType* attributes to make sure the members with related types are serialized correctly.

```
[DataContract]
[KnownType(typeof(Common.ResidentState))]
[KnownType(typeof(Common.Resident))]
public sealed class SwarmState
{
    [DataMember]
    public Shared2DArray<byte> SharedState { get; set; }
    [DataMember]
    public List<ResidentState> VirtualActorStates { get; set; }
    [DataMember]
    public List<IVirtualActor> VirutalActors { get; set; }
}
```

3. Implement the *ActorSwarm* class. In each iteration of swarm evolution, the swarm asks all its member actors to make proposals, reconciles conflicts, and applies changes.

```
[ActorService(Name ="SpatialSwarm")]
internal class ActorSwarm : StatefulActor<SwarmState>, IActorSwarm
{
    int mSize = 100;
    static Random mRand = new Random();
    protected override Task OnActivateAsync()
    {
        if (this.State == null)
        {
            this.State = new SwarmState
            {
                SharedState = new Shared2DArray<byte>(),
                VirtualActorStates = new List< ResidentState>(),
                VirutalActors = new List<IVirtualActor>()
            };
        }

        ActorEventSource.Current.ActorMessage(this, "State initialized to {0}", this.
State);
        return Task.FromResult(true);
    }
    public Task InitializeAsync(int size, float probability)
    {
        this.State.SharedState.Initialize(mSize);
        int count = (int)(size * size * probability);
        for (int i = 0; i < count; i++)
        {
            this.State.VirtualActorStates.Add(new ResidentState { X = mRand.Next(0,
```

```
        size), Y = mRand.Next(0, size), Tag = (byte)mRand.Next(1,3) });
            this.State.VirutalActors.Add(new Resident(size, i, this.State.
VirtualActorStates[i], this.State.SharedState));
        }
        return Task.FromResult(1);
    }
    public Task<string> ReadStateStringAsync()
    {
        return Task.FromResult<string>(this.State.SharedState.ToString());
    }
    public async Task EvolveAsync()
    {
        foreach (var actor in this.State.VirutalActors)
        {
            this.State.SharedState.Propose(await actor.ProposeAsync());
        }
        this.State.SharedState.ResolveConflictsAndCommit((p)=> {
            if (p is Proposal2D<byte>)
            {
                var proposal = (Proposal2D<byte>)p;
                this.State.VirutalActors[proposal.ActorId].
ApproveProposalAsync(proposal);
            }
        });
    }
}
```

Implement the test client

Finally, implement the test client. The code is self-explanatory: it creates an Actor Swarm and drives the swarm through 2,000 iterations of evolutions. It prints out the swarm state every second.

```
static void Main(string[] args)
{
    int size = 50;
    var swarm = ActorProxy.Create<IActorSwarm>(new ActorId("1"), "fabric:/
ActorSwarmApplication", "SpatialSwarm");
    swarm.InitializeAsync(size, 0.65f).Wait();
    int iterations = 2000;
    DateTime refreshTimer = DateTime.Now;
    for (int i = 0; i < iterations; i++)
    {
        swarm.EvolveAsync().Wait();
        if (DateTime.Now - refreshTimer >= TimeSpan.FromSeconds(1))
        {
            Console.Clear();
            var state = Shared2DArray<byte>.FromString(swarm.ReadStateStringAsync().Result);
            for (int y = 0; y < size; y++)
            {
                for (int x = 0; x < size; x++)
                {
                    switch (state[x, y])
                    {
                        case 0:
                            Console.Write(" ");
```

```
                    break;
                case 1:
                    Console.Write("*");
                    break;
                case 2:
                    Console.Write(".");
                    break;
                }
            }
            Console.WriteLine();
        }
        Console.WriteLine("Iteration: " + i);
        refreshTimer = DateTime.Now;
    }
}
Console.WriteLine("Done!");
Console.ReadLine();
}
```

Test the model

Deploy the Service Fabric application and launch the test client. Figure 18-4 shows the result of a test run on my environment. At the beginning, a number of residents with two types (denoted with "*" and "." respectively) are distributed randomly on a 50-by-50 grid. After 2,000 iterations, residents with the same types are clustered together.

Compared to the termite model, the swarm iterates much faster because most of the activities take place in the same process. With Actor Swarms, you can run simulations with larger scales and higher performance using far fewer resources. The *Common* library shows some initial thoughts on what can be generalized to support Actor Swarms. However, the *ActorSwarm* actor itself is not generalized for simplicity.

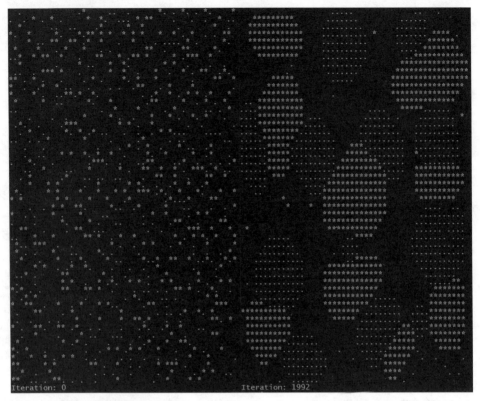

FIGURE 18-4 Spatial segregation model

Future works

This chapter shows some early attempts to use Service Fabric for complex system study. In particular, the Actor Swarm concept allows virtual actors to be packed in fewer Service Fabric Actor instances for more efficient simulations.

If you are interested in the concept of Actor Swarm or want to apply Service Fabric in complex system study, please contact the author (Twitter: @HaishiBai2010) for future developments.

PART V

Appendices

Service Fabric subsystems and system services

Service Fabric has a number of subsystems with a series of system services, which are covered in different chapters throughout this book. This appendix provides a brief summary of these services along with chapter references of where these services are introduced.

Reliability subsystem

The reliability subsystem is responsible for ensuring high availability of Service Fabric services. This subsystem includes Failover Manager, Resource Balancer, and Replicator.

Failover Manager

Failover Manager (fabric:/System/FailoverManagerService) responds to cluster events such as a node being added or removed. When a node is added, it automatically redistributes loads across available nodes. When a node is lost, it reconfigures service replicas to ensure service availability. Failover Manager is covered in Chapter 6, "Availability and reliability."

Resource Balancer

Failover Manager relies on Resource Balancer to provide placement recommendations. Resource Balancer collects load reports from Service Fabric agents running the cluster nodes and makes recommendations based on the loads on the nodes and the placement requirements. Resource Balancer is covered in Chapter 6.

Replicator

Replicator manages replication quorum and ensures primary service replicas automatically are replicated to secondary replicas. Service Fabric uses strong consistency in state management. All state changes are handled in transactions that are committed only when all operations have been applied to a quorum of the replica set. Replicator is covered in Chapter 3, "Stateful services."

Management subsystem

The management subsystem manages application life cycles, including provisioning, patching, upgrading, and deprovisioning. This subsystem includes image store, Health Manager, and Cluster Manager. This is also the main subsystem with which you work via PowerShell cmdlets and APIs.

Image store

Image store is used to store and redistribute application packages. It provides a simple distributed file system from which application packages are uploaded and downloaded. On a local simulated cluster, the image store is a local folder. In a full-scale Service Fabric cluster, the store is a highly available service (fabric:/System/ImageStoreService). Image store is covered in Chapter 5, "Service deployments and upgrades."

Health Manager

Service Fabric defines a complete health model that collects and aggregates health reports from various health entities across the cluster. The health reports are saved in a health store that you can use APIs to query against. Health Manager provides factual data points and triggering events for the management subsystem to make appropriate decisions to ensure application availability. The Service Fabric health model is covered in Chapter 5.

Cluster Manager

Cluster Manager (fabric:/System/ClusterManagerService) works with Failover Manager to place applications on cluster nodes. It's responsible for managing end-to-end life cycles of applications, from provisioning to deprovisioning.

Cluster Manager is not covered explicitly. Application lifecycle management (ALM) is covered in Chapter 8, "Managing Service Fabric with Windows PowerShell." Service placements and advanced rolling updates are covered in Chapter 6.

Hosting subsystem

The hosting subsystem resides on each Service Fabric node and is responsible for managing life cycles of applications on the node. Details on the hosting subsystem are not covered in this book.

Communication subsystem

The communication subsystem provides reliable messaging among cluster nodes. It also provides a Naming Service (fabric:/System/NamingService) that allows clients to discover and communicate with reliable services and reliable actors by their logical Service Fabric addresses (such as fabric:/<application name>/<service name>) instead of IP addresses or DNS names.

Throughout the lifetime of a service replica, it could be placed and migrated on different nodes at different times. The Naming Service abstracts the physical location of the replica from the clients so that the clients don't need to keep track of where the service replicas are deployed.

The Naming Service is covered in Chapter 6.

Testability subsystem

The testability system allows you to inject random or planned errors into a Service Fabric cluster to simulate various possible failures in a cloud datacenter. The testability subsystem enables you to exercise your applications in a condensed timeline that simulates errors during long, continuous service runs. This will help you shake out hidden reliability, scalability, and availability bugs to improve the overall service quality in production operation. The testability subsystem is covered in Chapter 6, "Availability and reliability," and Chapter 11, "Testing."

Transport subsystem

The transport subsystem provides point-to-point datagram exchange channels among Service Fabric nodes. It supports both one-way and request-response communication patterns. This service is secured by x509 certificates or Windows security.

The transport subsystem is a low-level system that isn't directly accessible by applications. It's not covered in this book.

Federation subsystem

The federation subsystem holds a consistent global view of the whole cluster. It provides fundamental services that are required to manage a distributed cluster, including leader election, failure detection, and consistent routing. It's built on top of distributed hash tables (DHTs) with 128-bit token space. DHTs are distributed, fault-tolerant, and scalable information stores from which any nodes on the cluster can efficiently retrieve the value associated with any given key. Cluster nodes are arranged in a ring topology, and each node owns a subset of the token space.

The federation subsystem is not covered explicitly in this book.

System services

You can examine Service Fabric system services in Service Fabric Explorer. Figure A-1 shows system services on a typical Service Fabric cluster. I've covered all the services except the fabric:/System /UpgradeService, which is responsible for updating Service Fabric run time.

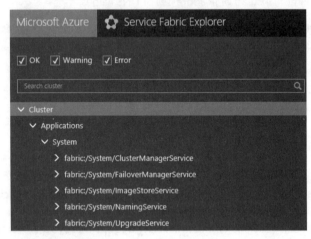

FIGURE A-1 System services on a Service Fabric cluster

Using Microsoft Azure PowerShell commands

This appendix provides instructions to install, configure, and use Azure PowerShell commands.

Installation

Microsoft Azure PowerShell can be installed via Web Platform Installer. Just find "Microsoft Azure PowerShell" and install the software using all default options.

Once Microsoft Azure PowerShell is installed, you can press the Windows key+Q, search for "Microsoft Azure PowerShell," and then click the found entry to launch the command line window. Optionally, you can right-click the found entry and select Pin To Start to pin a tile to the Windows start screen or Pin To Taskbar to pin a launch icon to the Windows taskbar.

Sign in

To sign in, use the following command:

```
Login-AzureRmAccount
```

This opens a browser dialog box where you can enter your Microsoft account credentials to sign in to your Azure subscriptions, as shown in Figure B-1. If your account has two-factor authentication enabled, you might also need to connect to a smart card or use your mobile phone to complete the sign-in process.

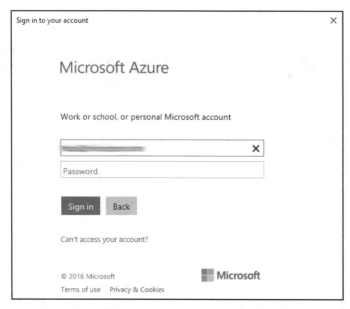

FIGURE B-1 Sign in dialog box

If the sign in is successful, once the dialog box is closed, you'll see a brief summary of your subscription, as shown in Figure B-2.

FIGURE B-2 Subscription summary

If you have multiple Azure subscriptions associated with your Azure account, you also need to choose which subscription to use. To list all subscriptions associated with the current account, use the following command:

```
Get-AzureRmSubscription
```

Copy the subscription ID you want to use and then use one of the following commands to set command context to the selected subscription:

```
Set-AzureRmContext -SubscriptionId [subscription id]
```

Or

```
Set-AzureRmContext -SubscriptionName [subscription name]
```

Discovering commands

Most Azure PowerShell cmdlets follow the same naming conventions, so it's fairly easy to discover commands for CRUD (Create, Read, Update, and Delete) operations following these naming rules:

- New-AzureRm* for creations.

- Get-AzureRm* for reads. A command with no parameters lists all resources of the type in the current subscription. Usually, the combination of a *Name* parameter and a *ResourceGroupName* parameter identifies a unique resource.

- Set-AzureRm* for updates.

- Remove-AzureRm* for deletions.

> ### Azure Resource Manager and Azure Service Management
>
> The letters "RM" in the cmdlets indicate these cmdlets are based on Azure Resource Manager, which uses a newer API than the original Azure Service Management API (Azure Service Management is also known as RDFE). It's expected that all APIs will be unified into Azure Resource Manager in the future. However, if you find you need to access RDFE APIs, you'll need to use corresponding cmdlets without "RM." For example, New-AzureRmVM creates a new virtual machine using Azure Resource Manager, while New-AzureVM creates a "classic" virtual machine using Azure Service Management.

By using the PowerShell auto-complete feature, you likely will be able to guess the exact cmdlets to use by typing the above prefixes with the name of the resource type (such as VM) and using the Tab key to cycle through possible options.

Once you find the cmdlet to use, type a hyphen (-) and use the Tab key to cycle through possible parameters. If you try to invoke a cmdlet without providing all mandatory parameters, you'll be prompted to enter values for the missing parameters.

To get help for a cmdlet, use the Get-Help cmdlet with an optional *–Detailed* switch. For example, the following cmdlet displays brief help info on the New-AzureRMVirtualNetwork cmdlet:

```
Get-Help New-AzureRMVirtualNetwork
```

Managing Azure resource groups

With Azure Resource Manager, everything you provision on Azure is a resource. You can put multiple resources into a resource group. A resource group can be described fully by a JSON document named ARM template. Managing resource groups and using ARM templates to create/update resource groups are the most common operations using Azure Resource Manager.

Basic resource group management

- To create a new resource group, use the New-AzureRmResourceGroup cmdlet. You need to supply a name and a location for the resource group. For example:

```
New-AzureRmResourceGroup -Name sample1 -Location "West US"
```

- To get a list of existing resource groups in your current subscription, use the Get-AzureRmResourceGroup cmdlet. For example:

```
Get-AzureRmResourceGroup | Format-Table -Property ResourceGroupName, Location
```

- To remove a resource group, use the Remove-AzureRmResourceGroup cmdlet. Note that because a resource group defines a management boundary, removing a resource group removes all resources contained in the group. For example, the following cmdlet deletes resource group "sample2" and all resources placed in the group:

```
Remove-AzureRmResourceGroup -Name sample2 -Force
```

Authoring an ARM template

An ARM template is a JSON file that declaratively defines a resource group. A detailed introduction of ARM template syntax is out of the scope of this book. At a high level, an ARM template contains the following top-level elements:

- **Parameters**   Define parameters of the template. Parameters values are supplied in a separate parameters JSON file or through the command line as a collection argument.

- **Variables**   Define template local variables whose value will be used repeatedly at different places in the template.

- **Resources**   Define all resources in the resource group. Each resource, such as a virtual machine, corresponds to a resource element in this array.

- **Outputs**   Define output values from the template. Output values are returned to calling scripts (such as PowerShell scripts) for further processing.

To get started with ARM template editing, you can visit the Azure Quickstart Templates GitHub repository (*https://github.com/Azure/azure-quickstart-templates*). The repository contains hundreds of sample templates for a variety of scenarios. You can use these templates as starting points to author your own templates. In the following exercises, you'll be using a very simple template that provisions an availability set with 3 fault domains and 20 update domains. The template is based on one of the Azure Quickstart Templates: *http://aka.ms/asf/azuredeploy.json*.

```
{
  "$schema": "https://schema.management.azure.com/schemas/2015-01-01/deploymentTemplate.json#",
  "contentVersion": "1.0.0.0",
  "parameters": {
    "location": {
      "type": "string",
```

```
      "metadata": {
        "description": "Location to deploy to"
      }
    }
  },
  "resources": [
    {
      "type": "Microsoft.Compute/availabilitySets",
      "name": "availabilitySet1",
      "apiVersion": "2015-06-15",
      "location": "[parameters('location')]",
      "properties": {
        "platformFaultDomainCount": "3",
        "platformUpdateDomainCount": "20"
      }
    }
  ]
}
```

Deploying a resource group

To deploy a resource group, use the New-AzureRmResourceGroupDeployment cmdlet. For example, the following command deploys the above template to a "sample1" resource group:

```
New-AzureResourceGroupDeployment -ResourceGroupName sample1 -Location "West US"
-Name sample-deployment -TemplateFile .\sample.json
```

Figure B-3 shows the output of the preceding command. Resource group deployments are idempotent. When you deploy resource templates to the same resource group, new resources are added, modified resources are updated, but unchanged resources are not touched. Also, if a resource is removed from a template, deploying the template doesn't remove the resource.

```
PS C:\Users\hbai> New-AzureRmResourceGroupDeployment -ResourceGroupName sample1 -Location "West US
-Name sample-deployment -TemplateFile .\sample.json

DeploymentName    : sample-deployment
ResourceGroupName : sample1
ProvisioningState : Succeeded
Timestamp         : 4/2/2016 9:39:44 PM
Mode              : Incremental
TemplateLink      :
Parameters        :
                    Name                Type                      Value
                    ===============     ====================      ==========
                    location            String                    West US

Outputs           :
```

FIGURE B-3 Deploying an ARM template

When you create a new deployment, it's recommended to use a different deployment name each time so that all changes to clusters are auditable. Figure B-4 shows that you can view deployment history on a cluster's Deployments blade.

FIGURE B-4 Deployment history on Azure portal

Deploying a Service Fabric cluster using an ARM template

The Azure Quickstart Templates gallery provides a couple of sample templates you can use to deploy Service Fabric clusters:

- A five-node cluster: *https://aka.ms/asf/5-node-cluster*

- A five-node secured cluster with WAD enabled: *https://aka.ms/asf/5-node-cluster-with-WAD*

Observing the structure of the template provides some interesting insights. For example, you can see what ports Service Fabric needs for inter-node communications. Similarly, you can examine how Service Fabric run time is installed on a virtual machine as an extension:

```
{
        "name": "[concat('ServiceFabricNodeVmExt','_vmNodeType0Name')]",
        "properties": {
                "type": "ServiceFabricNode",
                "autoUpgradeMinorVersion": false,
                ...
                "publisher": "Microsoft.Azure.ServiceFabric",
                "settings": {
                        "clusterEndpoint": "[reference(parameters('clusterName')).
clusterEndpoint]",
                        "nodeTypeRef": "[variables('vmNodeType0Name')]",
                        "dataPath": "D:\\\\SvcFab",
                        "durabilityLevel": "Bronze",
                        "certificate": {
                                "thumbprint": "[parameters('certificateThumbprint')]",
                                "x509StoreName": "[parameters('certificateStoreValue')]"
```

```
                    }
            },
            "typeHandlerVersion": "1.0"
        }
    }
}
```

Another way to acquire a Service Fabric ARM template is to use Azure management portal. When you create a new Service Fabric cluster, you'll see a Download Template link on the summary page, as shown in Figure B-5. Clicking the link gives you a template that reflects the options you've chosen for your cluster.

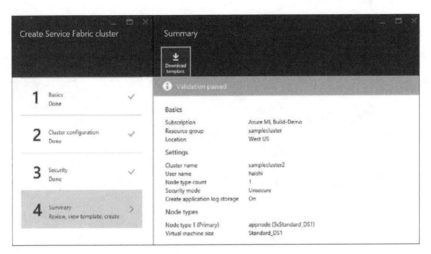

FIGURE B-5 Download ARM template for Service Fabric

Microsoft and containers

In the past few years, Microsoft has been working with companies like Docker and Mesosphere to bring Docker containers into the Windows ecosystem and Microsoft Azure. This appendix summarizes all Docker integration points on Microsoft Azure.

Docker engine on Azure virtual machines

There are four easy ways to deploy Docker engine on an Azure virtual machine: using a pre-built image, using a VM extension, using Azure CLI, and using Docker Machine command-line tool.

Use a pre-built image

Azure provides a pre-built Docker on Ubuntu Server image that deploys an Ubuntu Server 15.10 virtual machine with Docker engine installed. To provision a virtual machine using the image, click the New icon on Azure management portal and type **Docker on ubuntu** in the search box. In the search result list, click the Docker on Ubuntu Server entry and follow the wizard to create the virtual machine, as shown in Figure C-1.

FIGURE C-1 Docker on Ubuntu Server image

Once the virtual machine is created, you can use SSH to connect to the machine and use Docker commands such as docker run to launch containers and docker ps to list running containers.

Use the Docker VM extension

Azure VM extensions are small software packages you can apply to new or existing virtual machines running on Azure. When you use the pre-built image to create a Docker-enabled virtual machine, a Docker extension automatically is installed for you. If you want to apply the extension to another new or existing virtual machine, you can use either Azure PowerShell or Azure CLI.

For example, to get all existing versions of the Docker extensions, use the following Azure PowerShell cmdlet:

```
Get-AzureRmVMExtensionImage -Location westus -PublisherName Microsoft.Azure.Extensions
-Type DockerExtension
```

To check if the Docker extension is installed on a virtual machine, use the following cmdlet:

```
Get-AzureRmVMExtension -ResourceGroupName <resource group name> -VMName <virtual machine name>
-Name <extension name>
```

The preceding command returns a 404 (Not Found) error if the extension with specified name hasn't been installed. At this point, there's no cmdlet (that I know of) that checks extensions by types.

To install the Docker extension, use the following cmdlet:

```
Set-AzureRmVMExtension -ResourceGroupName <resource group name> -VMName <virtual machine name>
-Name MyExtension -Publisher Microsoft.Azure.Extensions -ExtensionType DockerExtension
-TypeHandlerVersion 1.1 -Location westus
```

Once the extension is installed, you can start to use Docker commands against the virtual machine. To check if the extension is installed correctly, you can execute the Get-AzureRmVMExtension cmdlet again. Figure C-2 shows a sample output on my environment:

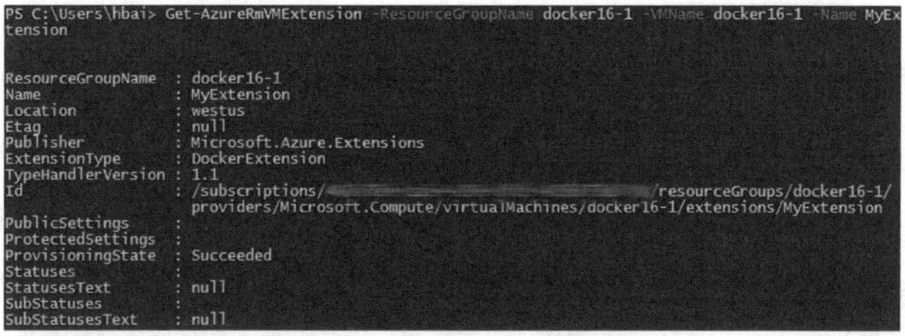

FIGURE C-2 Get-AzureRmVMExtension output

Use Azure CLI

Azure CLI (command-line Interface: *https://azure.microsoft.com/documentation/articles/xplat-cli -install/*) is a cross-platform Azure management tool that runs on Windows, Mac OS, and Linux.

Azure CLI provides an azure vm docker command you can use to create a classic virtual machine with Docker engine. Because the command uses ASM, you first need to switch the command line into the ASM mode. The following script snippet shows an example of creating an Ubuntu 14.04 server with Docker engine:

```
azure config mode asm
azure vm docker create -l "West US" <virtual macine name> b39f27a8b8c64d52b05eac6a62ebad85__
Ubuntu-14_04-LTS-amd64-server-20140724-en-us-30GB <user> <password>
```

The long parameter "b39f27a8b8c…" is the image name of the corresponding Linux OS. To get a list of supported VM images, use the azure vm image list command. The command returns a very long list, so you need to filter the list by using commands such as grep. For example:

```
azure vm image list | grep Ubuntu
```

Use Docker Machine

Docker Machine (*https://docs.docker.com/machine/*) is a Docker command-line tool you can use to install and run Docker on Mac, Windows, and remote Docker hosts. Docker Machine can provision Docker hosts on various cloud platforms such as Digital Ocean, Amazon Web Services (AWS), and

Microsoft Azure. The following walkthrough shows you the steps of using Docker Machine to create a Docker host on Azure.

1. If you haven't done so, create a self-signed certificate. This certificate is going to be uploaded to Azure as a management certificate for authentication:

```
openssl req -x509 -nodes -days 365 -newkey rsa:1024 -keyout mycert.pem -out mycert.pem
```

2. Upload the certificate to Azure via the classic Azure portal (*https://manage.windowsaure.com*).

3. Use Docker Machine to provision a new Docker host:

```
docker-machine create –driver azure –azure-subscription-id <Azure subscription id>
--azure-subscription-cert <management certificate> <virtual machine name>
```

4. Figure C-3 shows a sample execution on my environment. The command creates a new virtual machine named "docker16-3" on my subscription and installs Docker engine on the machine.

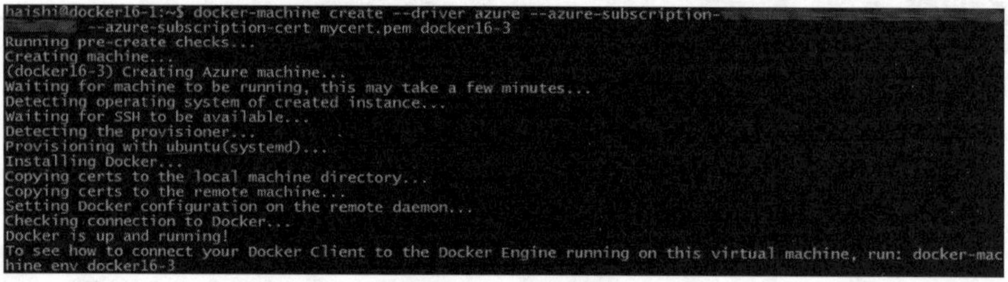

```
haishi@docker16-1:~$ docker-machine create --driver azure --azure-subscription-
          --azure-subscription-cert mycert.pem docker16-3
Running pre-create checks...
Creating machine...
(docker16-3) Creating Azure machine...
Waiting for machine to be running, this may take a few minutes...
Detecting operating system of created instance...
Waiting for SSH to be available...
Detecting the provisioner...
Provisioning with ubuntu(systemd)...
Installing Docker...
Copying certs to the local machine directory...
Copying certs to the remote machine...
Setting Docker configuration on the remote daemon...
Checking connection to Docker...
Docker is up and running!
To see how to connect your Docker Client to the Docker Engine running on this virtual machine, run: docker-mac
hine env docker16-3
```

FIGURE C-3 Docker-machine command

5. After the machine is configured, you can use the following command to configure your Docker client environment:

```
docker-machine env <virtual machine name>
```

Figure C-4 shows a sample output from the preceding command. After the client environment is configured, you can issue Docker commands against the configured host. Figure C-4 shows that a docker ps is issued against the host.

```
haishi@docker16-1:~$ docker-machine env docker16-3
export DOCKER_TLS_VERIFY="1"
export DOCKER_HOST="tcp://docker16-3.cloudapp.net:2376"
export DOCKER_CERT_PATH="/home/haishi/.docker/machine/machines/docker16-3"
export DOCKER_MACHINE_NAME="docker16-3"
# Run this command to configure your shell:
# eval $(docker-machine env docker16-3)
haishi@docker16-1:~$ docker ps
CONTAINER ID        IMAGE               COMMAND             CREATED             STATUS              PORTS
          NAMES
```

FIGURE C-4 Configure Docker client environment

Docker Hub and Docker Trusted Registry

Docker Hub (*https://hub.docker.com/*) is one of the most important contributions made by Docker, Inc., to the community. Docker Hub is a public Docker image repository to which everyone can contribute and use to find and reuse Docker images. It hosts over 100,000 images with billions of downloads.

Docker Trusted Registry (*https://www.docker.com/products/docker-trusted-registry*) is a product that allows you to host and manage a private Docker image repository. Docker Trusted Registry is ideal for enterprises that want to maintain a privately shared image gallery for their applications across different departments.

Accessing images from Docker Hub from Azure management portal

Azure management portal has a selected number of Docker images from Docker Hub integrated into the portal experience. When you create a new resource, you can pick a number of Docker images from the Container Apps category, as shown in Figure C-5. Select any of the images (click See All to browse for more) and then follow the wizard to provision a new Ubuntu server virtual machine with the Docker engine installed and a container created with the selected image.

FIGURE C-5 Container apps on Azure management portal

Provisioning a Docker Trusted Registry

Azure also provides a built-in template you can use to provision a new Docker Trusted Registry. When you create a new resource, search for "Docker" and you'll find a "Docker Trusted Registry" entry. Select the entry and follow the creation wizard to provision your own copy of Docker Trusted Registry on Azure, as shown in Figure C-6.

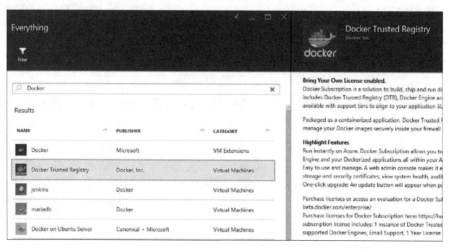

FIGURE C-6 Docker Trusted Registry on Azure

To use Docker Trusted Registry, you need to acquire a Docker subscription (*https://hub-beta.docker .com/enterprise/*), which includes 1 instance of Docker Trusted Registry, 10 commercially supported Docker engines, e-mail support, and 1-year license subscription.

Container orchestration

Container orchestration organizes multiple related containers into a complete application. For instance, you may have an application that is made up of multiple containers: a load-balanced PHP container cluster for web front end, a MySQL container cluster for storage, and a Redis container cluster for caching.

You can run various third-party container orchestration systems on Azure. Or, you can use Azure Container Service to orchestrate your containers. When you use third-party solutions, you are responsible for managing the underlying cluster and the orchestration engine running on top of it. When you use Azure Container Service, the cluster is managed for you.

Third-party container orchestration on Azure

The following is a brief summary of how to run several third-party container orchestration solutions on Azure:

- **Docker Swarm** To use the Azure Quickstart Template, go to *https://github.com/Azure/azure -quickstart-templates/tree/master/docker-swarm-cluster*. This template deploys a cluster with three Swarm managers and a number of Swarm nodes. For more information on Docker Swarm, see *https://docs.docker.com/swarm/*.

- **Deis** To use the Azure Quickstart Template, go to: *https://github.com/Azure/azure-quickstart -templates/tree/master/deis-cluster-coreos*. This template deploys a three-node Deis cluster. For more information on Deis, see *http://deis.io/*.

- **Kubernetes** To use a custom script, go to *http://kubernetes.io/docs/getting-started-guides /coreos/azure/*. This script creates a ring of three dedicated etcd nodes: one Kubernetes master and two kubernetes nodes. For more information on Kubernetes, see *http://kubernetes.io/*.

There are also a couple of templates that are related to Azure Container Service in the Azure Quickstart Template gallery: 101-acs-mesos and 101-acs-swarm. You can use either template to provision a self-managed (not managed by Azure) Azure Container Service cluster.

Azure Container Service

Azure Container Service allows you deploy and manage containers using the tools you choose. You can use Docker Swarm and Compose, or you can use Apache Mesos with a number of frameworks supported by Mesos.

At the time of this writing, Azure Container Service still is in preview. To create a new Azure Container Service, search for "container service" while you create a new Azure resource, select the Container Service (published by Microsoft) entry under the Virtual Machines category, and then follow the creation wizard to create the cluster. During the creation process, you'll be asked to choose either Mesos or Docker Swarm (preview) as the orchestrator.

Windows containers

Windows Server 2016 provides built-in support for containers. Windows Server 2016 Technical Preview version offers several deployment options, including the Server with Desktop Experience, Server Core, and Nano Server. You can run Windows-based containers on top of any of the deployment options.

As introduced earlier, Windows containers are based on Windows kernel. However, they support Docker APIs so you can use Docker tools to manage both Windows and Linux containers. Moreover, you can use Windows PowerShell to manage Windows containers.

The easiest way to get started with Windows containers is to provision a Windows Server 2016 virtual machine on Azure. The following walkthrough is based on the Windows Server 2016 Core with Containers Tech Preview 4 image. Please note the following PowerShell commands are preview commands and are subject to change.

1. Create a new virtual machine using the Windows Server 2016 Core with Containers Tech Preview 4 image.

2. Use Remote Desktop to connect to the instance. The Server Core gives you a command-line prompt. Launch PowerShell by typing the **powershell** command.

3. In PowerShell, list all container images on the machine:

```
Get-ContainerImage
```

4. The above command returns the following outputs on my environment:

```
Name                    Publisher           Version          IsOSImage
----                    ---------           -------          ---------
WindowsServerCore       CN=Microsoft        10.0.10586.0     True
```

5. Create a new container using the above image:

```
New-Container -Name <container name> -ContainerImagename WindowsServerCore
-Switchname <switch name>
```

6. You can get <switch name> by using the Get-VMSwitch cmdlet.

7. Then, you can launch the container by using the Start-Container cmdlet:

```
Start-Container -Name <container name>
```

8. Now, you can enter a new PowerShell session into the container:

```
Enter-PSSession -ContainerName <container name> -RunAsAdministrator
```

Pattern index

A number of design and coding patterns are covered throughout this book. Some of them have dedicated sections. Others are blended in with other discussions without being called out specifically. This index provides you a quick reference of all patterns that are introduced in this book. These are grouped roughly into several categories such as performance and scalability and system architecture. However, each pattern doesn't necessarily belong to a single category.

Distributed computing

- **Competing consumers** (Chapter 7)

  The competing consumers pattern allows multiple job processors to compete for jobs on a common job queue. The numbers of consumers can be adjusted dynamically based on system load.

- **Composable data processing units** (Chapter 14)

  The composable data processing units pattern orchestrates multiple Microservices into a complete, loosely coupled data pipeline.

- **Message-based integration** (Chapter 12)

  The message-based integration pattern allows independent services to be integrated by passing messages to each other.

- **Processing topologies with actors** (Chapter 14)

  Actors can be used to construct various data processing topologies such as parallel batching, streaming top N, join by field, and cached lookup grid.

- **Self-driven workflows** (Chapter 7)

  Self-driven workflows move themselves forward without centralized governance. This design avoids centralized components becoming a bottleneck.

Multitenancy

- **Cross-tenant aggregation** (Chapter 15)

  Cross-tenant aggregation handles aggregation as a big data problem and uses related Azure services such as Azure Machine Learning, Azure Stream Analytics, and Event Hub to provide a scalable aggregation pipeline.

- **Metadata-driven system** (Chapter 15)

  A metadata-driven system describes core system behaviors using metadata files. The system can be customized for each customer by loading different metadata files.

- **Self-service** (Chapter 15)

  Self-service allows customers to perform common tasks without the involvement of sales or support teams.

- **Tenant Manager** (Chapter 15)

  Tenant Manager organizes tenant-specific resources into a managed, multitenant cluster.

- **Throttling Actor** (Chapter 15)

  Throttling Actor controls the number or rate of service requests by issuing service invocation tokens. A service requestor needs to acquire and present valid tokens to the Throttling Actor before it can send service calls.

Gaming and simulations

- **Actor polymorphism** (Chapter 16)

  Actor polymorphism allows actors to inherit from each other to build up an inheritance tree.

- **Coverage Map** (Chapter 16)

  Coverage Map overcomes the boundary problems with a partitioned game world.

- **Dynamic Game Room** (Chapter 16)

  Dynamic Game Room dynamically organizes gamers into different game rooms to provide both performance and scalability for large-scale multiplayer games.

- **Game Piece Dispenser** (Chapter 16)

  Game Piece Dispenser is a factory that creates computer-controlled gaming entities following predefined strategies.

- **Observer pattern** (Chapter 16)

  With Observer pattern, a subject keeps a list of observers and notifies each of the observers when something interesting happens.

- **Self-adapting actors** (Chapter 16)

  Self-adapting actors adjust their behaviors based on environments, including self-throttling actors and self-expiring actors.

- **Shared data structures** (Chapter 18)

  Shared data structures provide read-only access for lockless data reads and a proposal system for coordinated updates.

Performance and scalability

- **Pull-based actor state aggregation** (Chapter 7)

  This pattern uses pulling instead of pushing to aggregate states from multiple actors to ensure parallelism.

- **Batching** (Chapter 7)

  The batching pattern groups multiple related requests together to avoid excessive network round trips between clients and servers or between services.

- **Fan-out indexes** (Chapter 12)

  The fan-out indexes pattern sacrifices write performance in exchange for read performance. When a data entry is written, it's replicated to all possible views for faster queries.

Reliability

- **Finite State Machine Actor** (Chapter 12)

  The Finite State Machine Actor uses a Service Fabric Actor to provide consistent state for a workflow that is carried out collectively by multiple services. It also has a built-in timer to detect abandoned workflows.

- **Persistent shopping cart** (Chapter 12)

  Persistent shopping cart provides reliable storage across multiple sessions via multiple engagement channels.

System architecture

- **Claim-based authentication** (Chapter 12)

  Claim-based authentication uses an external identity provider to handle authentication details. Attributes of the authorized entity are passed as claims.

- **Loose coupling** (Chapter 7)

  Loose coupling encourages components to be designed and implemented in isolation to avoid static dependencies among components.

- **Mock-based Service Design** (Chapter 12)

  Mock-based Service Design uses mocks to drive service design. Instead of writing individual unit test cases, the service is mocked up with the intention that it will evolve into the final service. This practice allows not only the method signatures but also payload schemas to be designed and verified in iterations.

- **Personalization Actor** (Chapter 12)

  A Personalization Actor captures all personalization needs of a user. Because the actor instance exists virtually and can easily be accessed across different services, it provides an easy and consistent state across multiple services.

- **Sensor Actor** (Chapter 13)

  Sensor Actors encapsulate physical sensors. Each Sensor Actor instance represents a physical sensor and provides necessary services such as communication and moving average.

- **Service API** (Chapter 12)

  Service API enforces clear separation between presentation logic and business logic on a web server.

Index

G

S

About the author

HAISHI BAI, senior technical evangelist at Microsoft, focuses on the Microsoft Azure compute platform, including IaaS, PaaS, networking, and scalable computing services.

Ever since he wrote his first program on an Apple II when he was 12, Haishi has been a passionate programmer and he later became a professional software engineer and architect. During his 19 years of professional life, he's faced various technical challenges and a broad range of project types that have given him rich experiences in designing innovative solutions to solve difficult problems.

Haishi is the author of a few cloud computing books. He's the co-host of Microsoft's Cloud Cover show (*https://channel9.msdn.com/shows/Cloud+Cover/*). He also runs a technical blog (*http://blog.haishibai.com*) with millions of viewers. His twitter handle is @HaishiBai2010.

Visit us today at

microsoftpressstore.com

- **Hundreds of titles available** – Books, eBooks, and online resources from industry experts

- **Free U.S. shipping**

- **eBooks in multiple formats** – Read on your computer, tablet, mobile device, or e-reader

- **Print & eBook Best Value Packs**

- **eBook Deal of the Week** – Save up to 60% on featured titles

- **Newsletter and special offers** – Be the first to hear about new releases, specials, and more

- **Register your book** – Get additional benefits